The Case for the Shorter Work Day

Supreme Court of the United States

OCTOBER TERM, 1915.

FRANKLIN O. BUNTING,
Plaintiff in Error,
vs.
THE STATE OF OREGON,
Defendant in Error.

BRIEF FOR DEFENDANT IN ERROR

VOL. II

FELIX FRANKFURTER,
Of Counsel for the State of Oregon.

Assisted by

JOSEPHINE GOLDMARK,
Publication Secretary,
National Consumers' League.

Reprinted by National Consumers' League
289 Fourth Avenue, New York City

TABLE OF CONTENTS.

(VOLUME I.......................Pages 1- 470)

(VOLUME II.......................Pages 471-1021)

PAGE

ARGUMENT ix

PART FIRST—Legislation Limiting the Hours of Labor for Men:.... 1

1. THE AMERICAN LEGISLATION........ 1
2. THE FOREIGN LEGISLATION........ 10a

PART SECOND—The World's Experience upon which the Legislation Limiting the Hours of Labor is Based........ 11

I. MENACES TO NATIONAL VITALITY........ 11

II. THE DANGERS OF LONG HOURS........ 63

A. Bad Effects of Long Hours on Health........ 63

1. Relation of Fatigue to Disease........ 63

a. General Predisposition to Disease........ 63
b. Fatigue and Infectious Diseases........ 79
c. Fatigue and Nervous Diseases........ 88

(1) Nervous Diseases and Statistics of Foreign Sickness Insurance Societies 107
(2) Ages of Incidence........ 121
(3) Nervous Diseases and Heredity........ 123
(4) Nervous Diseases and Overstimulation........ 127

d. General Injuries to Health........ 131
e. Injuries to Eyes and Ears........ 165

(1) Eyes 165
(2) Ears 173

f. Injuries to Other Organs or Parts of the Body........ 185

B. Health-Hazards in Modern Industry........ 193

1. The New Strain of Manufacture........ 193

a. Speed 193
b. Monotony 216
c. Piece-Work 227

2. Injurious Physical Surroundings........ 232

a. Bad Air, Humidity, Extremes of Temperature, Noise, etc. 232
b. Exposure to Dust, Gases, Fumes, Poisons, etc........ 253

PAGE

C. The Nature and Effects of Fatigue 265
1. The Chemical Nature of Fatigue 265
2. The Toxin of Fatigue 285
3. Muscular Fatigue 293
4. The Greater Strain on Fatigued Muscles 310
5. Nervous Fatigue 317
6. The Physiological Function of Rest 339
a. Rest Needed to Repair Expenditure of Energy 339

D. Bad Effect of Long Hours on Safety 360
1. Incidence of Accidents 360
2. Fatigue of Attention 392

E. Bad Effect of Long Hours Upon Morals 404
1. General Loss of Moral Restraints 404
2. Growth of Intemperance 414

F. Bad Effects of Long Hours on General Welfare 428
1. State's Need of Preserving Health 428
2. Injuries to Family Life and the Community 452

III. BENEFITS OF SHORT HOURS 471

A. Good Effect on Morals: Growth of Temperance 471

B. Good Effect on General Welfare 478
1. General Benefit to Society 478
2. Benefit to Leisure and Recreation 499
a. The Experience of Australasia 523

C. Benefit to Citizenship 532
1. Preparedness:
a. Political: The Citizen as Voter 532
b. Social: Americanization of the Foreign-born 550
c. Military: The Citizen as Soldier 572

IV. SHORTER HOURS THE ONLY PROTECTION 605

A. Overlong Hours Make Lightest Work Injurious 605

B. The Remedy: Shorter Hours 614

V. ECONOMIC ASPECT OF REDUCING HOURS 621

A. General Benefit to Commercial Prosperity 621

B. Effect on Production 636
1. Superior Output in Shorter Hours 636
a. Some Recent Instances 636
b. Textile Trades: Cotton, Wool, Linen, Jute 654
c. Metal Trades: Iron and Steel, Tin Plate 669
d. Mines and Quarries: Coal, Slate, etc. 684

PAGE

e. Granite and Stone Cutting 690
f. Glass and Optical Instruments 693
g. Chemicals 701
h. Cigars 715
i. Shoes 717
j. Miscellaneous Instances 720
k. General Comments 725

2. Shorter Hours Increase Efficiency on the Part of the Workers 737
3. Shorter Hours Lead to Improvement in Management 781
4. Relation of Short Hours to Cost of Production 797
5. Long Hours Reduce Efficiency and Result in Inferior Output 819

C. Relation to Wages 847

D. Relation to Regularity of Employment 876

VI. UNIFORMITY OF RESTRICTION NEEDED FOR JUSTICE TO COMPETING EMPLOYERS 893

VII. PROGRESS OF THE SHORTER DAY 902

A. Statistical Evidence 902

B. The Record of 1915 929

VIII. NEED OF LEGISLATION: INSTANCES OF EXCESSIVE HOURS OF LABOR 940

APPENDIX: Hours of Labor and Realism in Constitutional Law 961

APPENDIX II: Index of Authorities Quoted 986

CASES CITED

Holden *v.* Hardy, 169 U. S. 366 .... xi, xiii
Lochner *v.* New York, 198 U. S. 45 .... xii, xiv
Miller *v.* Wilson, 236 U. S. 373 xv
People *v.* Charles Schweinler Press, 214 N. Y. 395 xiv
People *v.* Klinck Packing Co., 214 N. Y. 121 xv
Rast *v.* Van Beman & St. Louis Co., 240 U. S. ix
State *v.* Bunting, 71 Or. 259 .... vii, xv
Tanner *v.* Little, 240 U. S. x

III. BENEFITS OF SHORT HOURS.

A. GOOD EFFECT ON MORALS: GROWTH OF TEMPERANCE.

The good effect of shorter working hours on the uses of leisure is conspicuously shown in the growth of temperance where working hours have been reduced. With better health and a higher moral tone due to the shorter working day, temperance in the use of alcoholic stimulants results automatically.

The Economic and Social Importance of the Eight-hour Movement. GEORGE GUNTON. *New York, American Federation of Labor, 1889.*

It is one of the common charges against reducing the hours of labor that it would only increase the laborer's opportunity for dissipation, and instead of aiding his social refinement, it would only increase his drunkenness and vice. Fortunately, the facts all point the other way. Prof. Levi, in an exhaustive analysis on the consumption of alcoholic drinks and non-alcoholic beverages, has shown* that from 1867 to 1883 the consumption per head of the population of the former steadily diminished, while that of the latter has greatly increased. Prof. Levi's facts show that the quantity of wine and spirits, the beverages of the upper classes, was only reduced during the period 5/100 of a gallon per head, while the consumption of beer, the workingmen's drink, decreased 2 50/100 gallons per head of the population per year. The amount spent upon wine and spirits was reduced 14 cents per head, while that spent upon beer was reduced $1.12 per head, or 11 66/100 per cent., clearly showing that the change is in the habits and character of the laboring classes and not in that of the wine drinking aristocracy.† (Pp. 19-20.)

*Wages and Earnings, 1885.

†Report of the United States Commissioner of Labor, 1886.

United States Congress, House Report No. 1793 (4405). Hours of Laborers on Public Works of the U. S. Report from the Committee on Labor, 57th Congress, 1st Session, 1901-1902.

It is contended by the advocates of the shorter day that the additional leisure given to labor in every instance of the shortening of the work day, as it has been shortened step by step from sixteen hours to fourteen, twelve, eleven, ten, nine, and in many instances eight, has resulted in a decrease of intemperance among laborers, the acquirement of better taste and new and better desires, resulting in better homes, greater domestic felicity, and higher degree of intelligence with an increase of laudable pride as to the clothing of themselves and those dependent upon them. In a word, it has increased their interests in home and better social relations, raising their moral status, and has made them much better consumers of the products of labor, and hence resulted in increased production.

The proposition that without variation the elimination of intemperance, poverty, pauperism, ignorance, crime and their accompanying evils move parallel with and proportionate to the increase of the social opportunities of the laboring class stands without impeachment of its historical accuracy. (P. 8.)

Organized Labor. John Mitchell. *Philadelphia, American Book and Bible House, 1903.*

A reduction in hours means a strengthening of the workman, the growth of a keener intelligence, and an improvement in his home life. The workingman's self-appointed protectors among the employing classes have from the beginning alleged that a reduction in hours means more time spent in drinking and dissipation, since the employee will not know what to do with his newly acquired leisure. This assertion, reiterated incessantly, has been completely contradicted by everyday experience and by the history of the working classes. When the workingman comes from mill or mine, having taxed to the utmost his muscular and nervous energy, depressed by an excessive expenditure of vital force, it is small wonder if he seek a stimulus in alcohol or in other crude pleasures. A man who has labored for ten or twelve hours at exhausting toil is in no fit condition to enjoy books, pictures, music, or the sane pleasures of a well-regulated family life. The unanimous testimony of all competent observers, teachers, ministers, and sociologists, has been to the effect that a reduction in the hours of labor almost invariably means an improvement in the whole moral tone of the community, a raising of the standard of living, a growth of the self-respect of the workingman, and a diminution, not an increase, in drunkenness, violence, and crime. If the American workman can be trusted with the suffrage, it is certainly safe to entrust him with a few hours of leisure. The laborer is worthy not only of his hire, but also of the right to live. (Pp. 124-125.)

The increased wages and shortened hours of labor have in themselves brought about a vast improvement in the mental and moral status of the workers. Workmen who formerly went from their twelve hours of work to the nearest saloon now spend their time with their families, improving their minds, or enjoying a sensible and sane recreation. In most instances increased wages have meant the gratification of the intellectual and artistic sense of the workers; have meant books and pictures; have meant a few extra rooms in the house and more decent surroundings generally; have meant a few years' extra schooling for the children; have meant, finally, a general uplifting of the whole working class. (Pp. 153-154.)

National Civic Federation Review. Vol. I, No. 7. Sept., 1904. Will Labor Make Concessions for a Shorter Work-Day? Answers to Question: Do you believe that a shorter work-day lessens production or increases the labor cost of production?

Thomas M. Nolan, Editor of the Union Label Magazine, Boston:

. . . Another important point is that the general morale of the craft has advanced as the hours have decreased. Temperance, morality, and a general uplifting tendency has been observed to a greater extent among the rank and file of the printing crafts. (P. 7.)

The National Civic Federation Review. Vol. II, No. 8. Jan.-Feb., 1906. The first annual meeting of the New England Civic Federation, Boston, Jan. 11, 1906.

James Duncan, of Quincy, General Secretary of the Granite Cutters' International Union:

You may take any locality in this or any other country where the hours of labor have changed from ten to nine, or nine to eight, and I say that temperance has increased in accordance with that reduction. I had the honor to speak in a meeting in Georgia a short time ago, where the mayor of the town was the presiding officer, and he told me when he first became a municipal officer a great part of the revenue of the town came from fines for drunkenness and disorderly conduct of the working people of the vicinity. The granite industry, with which I am proud to be connected, became busy in that locality, and we began the agitation for the shorter work day. The mayor told me that after we had introduced the eight-hour day—and we were successful, and the other trades working nine hours were afterwards reduced to eight—disorderly conduct and intemperance became so little known in the community that the town had to look for taxation in other directions than the saloons in order to meet its necessary expenses. (P. 9.)

The Case of the Journeymen Bakers. Evils of Night-work and Long Hours of Work. William Augustus Guy, M.D., *Fellow of the Royal College of Physicians, Professor of Forensic Medicine, King's College; Physician to King's College Hospital, etc. London, Renshaw, 1848.*

Health on the other hand, like cleanliness, is an ally of virtue and sobriety. It is favorable to self-control, and to quiet and rational enjoyments. It has the same effect on the mind as it has on the palate; it enables it to relish plain and homely fare, and to dispense with unwholesome stimulants. By abolishing nightwork, and shortening your hours of labor, you would be placed in possession, not merely of new faculties of enjoyment, but of time to use them. (Pp. 12-13.)

A Shorter Working Day. R. A. HADFIELD, *of Hadfield's Steel Foundry Co., Sheffield, and* H. DE B. GIBBINS, M. A. *London, Methuen and Co., 1892.*

Messrs. Brunner, Mond & Co., of Northwich, a firm in a very large way of business, whose extraordinary success in chemical manufactures is so well known, have kindly answered the writer's inquiries as to the effect of the introduction of the eight-hours system into their works. . . . In their case the change was from twelve to eight hours, their men previously working continuously seven days a week for twelve hours per shift, with one shift of twenty-two hours long every fortnight. . . . They reduced it to eight hours, and the managing director says: "We have never had any reason to regret the change. To the men it has been the greatest boon. It has had the most material effect in improving their health and decreasing the amount of drunkenness, which before the adoption of the system was very great indeed.

This is a startling instance of the fact that overwork, now too often existing, produces crime, costing the nation hard cash to look after that crime. Here is positive evidence that the bane of this country, drunkenness, can to some extent be traced to the inhuman hours of labour often imposed. Therefore, if an eight-hour system will encourage the most rational antidote to drunkenness, self-respect, surely a trial would in many ways be found to pay. In face of the above reliable evidence, how much of the enormous drink bill of this country, amounting last year to over 142 millions, might have been reduced? (Pp. 141-142.)

British Sessional Papers. Vol. XXXVI. 1892. Part I. Royal Commission on Labour. Testimony of Mr. Patrick Walls, National Association of Blast-Furnacemen (Cumberland and North Lancashire District.)

14,432. . . . I may say that the men have improved in every way, even from a moral standpoint we find, on taking statistics, that 50 per cent. more men belong to temperance associations at the present time than there did two years ago, and we have got statistics from three friendly societies, and we find that they have paid from 20 to 25 per cent. less sick allowance to the men during 1891 than they did during any of the five years preceding.

14,433. The increase of temperance you would attribute, I suppose, to the diminution of bodily fatigue? Just so.

Eight Hours for Work. John Rae. *London, Macmillan, 1894.*

(West Cumberland blast furnaces, experiment tried.) There seems to be every reason to expect better results next year, because the men were showing decisive signs of both physical and moral improvement. Their temperance societies had increased in membership 50 per cent. during the year, and the provident and trade societies had spent 20 or 25 per cent. less on sick allowances, both results being attributed to the relief from the undue fatigue from which all had suffered before. (P. 92.)

In the first place, generally speaking, we have now been going on shortening hours for half a century and all the time our work-people have been growing in temperance and health and intelligence and efficiency. The British workman used to be notorious beyond all others for his drunken and irregular habits, but though he has received ever and anon more time to indulge those habits if he chose, he has not grown worse but grown better. The testimony of employers at the Labour Commission was uniform and decided on this point. The shortening of the hours has of itself, as I have already shown, suppressed in many trades those habitually irregular habits of working, which had much to do with the other irregularities of his life, and though it has no doubt given to certain individuals increased opportunities of ill-doing which they have used to their hurt, the general effect has been the other way. (Pp. 126-27.)

The Northumberland miners, who work about the shortest hours, are credited with being the most sober and steady class of miners in the whole country. Mr. R. Young and Mr. J. Nixon said they had often been told so by the coal-owners as a body. (Pp. 127-128.)

Messrs. Watts and Manton say, "The habits of the people are changing; there is a greater desire for home life, and greater longing after the means by which it is to be rendered more agreeable." (P. 129.)

I have already mentioned the experience of Messrs. Bushill and Sons, Coventry, that their employés have manifested a striking and increasing dislike to working overtime since their ordinary work hours have been shortened. . . . His firm employs 250 hands, and they have observed no tendency among them to abuse their leisure. "As far as we can tell," says Mr. Bushill, "the extra leisure is well spent." (P. 132.)

B. GOOD EFFECT ON GENERAL WELFARE.

1. General Benefit to Society.

History, which has illustrated the deterioration due to long hours, bears witness no less clearly to the regeneration due to the shorter working day. To the individual and society alike, shorter hours have been a benefit wherever introduced and have raised all the standards of living. Wherever sufficient time has elapsed since the establishment of the shorter working day, the succeeding generation has shown extraordinary improvement in physique, intelligence and morals.

United States Public Health Service. Weekly Public Health Reports. Vol. 29. May 29, 1914. Industrial Conditions. Their Relation to the Public Health. B. S. Warren, *Surgeon, United States Public Health Service and Sanitary Adviser, United States Commission on Industrial Relations.*

Education as to the requirements of hygienic living has been the subject of much discussion, but as yet the business world and the workers have not come to fully realize the importance of the requirements and the results to be obtained. Up to the present time the activities along this line have been mainly confined to a cleaning-up campaign or to what may be called welfare work and placing the physical environment at the place of employment in sanitary condition. There is great need for these improvements; they are the most obvious things to do and will improve labor conditions and demonstrate what may be expected by further improvement. Many lives will be saved in this way, especially in the chemical trades and the dusty trades, but the great mass of workers are to be reached through the improvements in hours and wages.

The great need is to demonstrate to the business world that there is an optimum of hours of labor, speed, and nutrition for the industrial worker, which if adhered to will bring his output up to the maximum of quality and quantity and that at the optimum the worker will have fewer stoppages on account of accident or disease and will last the longest time in a profitable producing state.

In other words, the worker will not have to go to the hospital for frequent disabilities when at the age of best production, and will not be sent to the "scrap heap" when there should be many more years of profitable service if worked in accordance with hygienic standards. If worked at the optimum time, speed, and nutrition, there will be no great loss to the business in the final cost results, because in most cases the increase in quality and quantity of output brought about by the reduced hours of labor will offset to a great degree the increased cost.

It is not well to promise a complete offset as to cost when changed to the optimum, but it is safe to say that the consumer or public will not suffer, because the cost is already borne in the extra charges now made for free hospitals, charity organizations and the like. (Pp. 1353-1354.)

Proceedings of the Government and Citizens of Philadelphia on the Reduction of the Hours of Labor and Increase of Wages. July, 1835.

One of the largest meetings ever convened in the city or county of Philadelphia, assembled on Saturday afternoon, the 6th inst., in the State House yard. . . .

The Committee, through their chairman, reported the following, which were adopted by enthusiastic acclamation.

Whereas the citizens of the city and county of Philadelphia have assembled in town meeting, to express their opinion of the recent movements of the workingmen and mechanics, and whereas this meeting is satisfied that the working classes are the bone and sinew of the land; and whereas, upon their health, virtue and happiness depend the security and perpetuity of our glorious and free institutions; and whereas, it is the duty of every man possessing the ordinary attribute of humanity, to zealously assist in advancing the social comforts and increasing the moral, physical and intellectual enjoyments of man; and whereas, under the former system adopted by employers, it has been found that the demand made upon the system of the employed, is incompatible with either physical comfort, moral improvement or social happiness; and whereas, we are satisfied that ten hours labor out of the twenty-four, is as much as the system can endure, and at the same time preserve health; and whereas, the ten hour system will afford some leisure for the cultivation of the mind, and the pleasures of domestic relationship—therefore be it

Resolved, That we heartily and unanimously respond to the demands of the laboring classes, in favor of ten hours.

Resolved, That ten hours labor is amply sufficient for any reasonable purpose, and that all those who require more time from the laboring men are devoid of the noble principles of humanity, and the mild and charitable virtues of Christianity.

Note.—The committee have not been able to obtain the ordinance of the Government of the city and county of Philadelphia. We state on the authority of the Philadephia Saturday Courier, of June 14, that the Government of that city passed the ordinance reducing the hours of labor on the 6th of June. (Pp. 4-5.)

Massachusetts House Document No. 44. 1867. Report of Commissioners on the Hours of Labor. Minority Report. Edward H. Rogers.

Causes and Connections of the Eight-hour Movement.

The most influential motives of a practical character in the eight-hour movement are to be found in the altered conditions of labor, incidental to the monotony of subdivision, and the intensity of application enforced by the state of society. . . . The prevalence, among thoughtful workingmen, of more definite views respecting manual labor, whether its characteristics should be those of skill and faithfulness, or unreasoning endurance; a clearer recognition of the effect of continuous physical effort on the action of the mind and its capacity, and also on the condition of the workman, as being in an exhausted state during his brief space of leisure; a comparison of the more favored conditions of mercantile and professional life, as affording educational influences during the day, and leaving the body comparatively free from fatigue, to engage with zest and energy in the social privileges or duties of the evening; a conviction that the returns for labor under the present system are not adequate to the reasonable and necessary demands of American citizenship;—these motives, with others, resulting in great unanimity of opinion, that radical reductions of hours are necessary to place labor in its just relations to the other interests of society. (P. 62.)

The most prominent facts, conditions and results of the amelioration in time, may be briefly stated thus:—

Greater relative vigor of the workman, in connection with the imperative obligation to reduce time from the exhausted portion of the day. Less loss of time in consequence of a sensible relief in the daily duration of labor. Greater healthfulness, especially during the summer season. A quicker return to labor, and a more rapid recovery of strength after sickness. The increased respectability of labor, which retains many in production. An approximate equalization of the day's work, which has largely contributed to diffuse employment over the year, and thus diminished distress during the winter season. Multiplied inventions, subdivisions in trades, and, generally, a more intellectual and progressive impetus to production. Openings for the industrial classes in evening exercises of a religious, reformatory, political and miscellaneous character. The noticeably increased influence of woman, closely connected with the fact that the home has gained time formerly devoted to the shop or counting-room. (P. 91.)

I recommend as the result of my investigations, and in view of the expressed wish of the interest of labor in the factories, and, so far as ascertained, on the farms, the enactment of ten hours, as a legal standard for a day's labor—in the absence of contracts—for factory and farm work; and a similar enactment of eight hours as a legal standard—in the absence of contracts—for mechanical labor. (P. 141.)

Report of the Massachusetts Bureau of Statistics of Labor. 1870.

The influence of the ten-hour law in England was to raise the educational condition of the laborers, as was at once shown in their increased attendance on public lectures, public meetings, mechanics' institutes, in the establishment of agricultural and horticultural shows, where were exhibited products raised on grounds hired and worked during the time thus gained. . . . No greater boon was ever given to a people than this ten-hour law, and could a laborer of 20 years before it have come back to England, he would be amazed at the improved condition of the working people. (Pp. 113-114.)

Report of the Massachusetts Bureau of Statistics of Labor. 1872.

The testimony of those who have adopted the shorter time is almost unanimous in its favor. Many reported an improved condition of the employees. No instance is given of decreased wages, though many report an increase, not only in wages, but in production. All of the arguments against reduction made by those working eleven hours and over are answered by those who have adopted the shorter time, and worked under that system for years. The advocates of eleven hours have utterly failed to sustain themselves in their continued adhesion to a system that England outgrew twenty-two years ago, —a system unworthy of our State and nation. (P. 240.)

Report of the Nebraska Bureau of Labor Statistics. 1887-1888.

The reduction of the number of hours required for a week's work has proved to be quite as beneficial to the men and women employed in this establishment as was expected. This change . . . "is worth all the time, expense and labor involved in the controversy." (P. 122.)

Report of the Massachusetts Chief of the District Police. 1889.

The good results of shortening the hours of labor were soon apparent, in the substantial disappearance of discontent among those affected thereby; in the maintenance of the standard of factory productions, both as to quantity and quality; and in placing Massachusetts in the lead, where, by her history and her aspiration, she rightfully belonged.

. . . If experience has shown anything in this matter, it has been the wisdom and statesmanship of the body of laws in our Public Statutes and additions thereto, which are known as industrial legislation. It is sixteen years since the ten-hour law was enacted; and it is entirely safe to say that, if it were stricken from the statutes to-day, not an influential voice would be raised within our borders in favor of the restoration of the order of things which that law changed. The increase of public interest in matters of this kind is a very significant fact. (P. 7.)

The Economic and Social Importance of the Eight-Hour Movement. George Gunton. *New York, American Federation of Labor. 1889.*

The adoption of the eight-hour system would tend to increase wages in two ways: first, by reducing enforced idleness; second, by creating new wants, and raising the standard of living. . . .

The second effect, which would be more gradual, permanent and far-reaching in its nature than the first, would be the result of the increased leisure and social opportunity upon the social character and consumption of the masses. With the removal of enforced idleness, and its degrading influences, over eight million laborers would leave their work each day less exhausted, mentally and physically, and have two hours more leisure. This would mean so much positive opportunity for family life and for general social intercourse, and in a much fresher and more cheerful mood. . . . In short, it means his gradual introduction into a new social environment, the unconscious influence of which would necessarily awaken and develop new tastes and desires for more social comforts. He would naturally begin to desire more wholesome and better appointed homes, more literature, entertainment, and a greater amount of general social intercourse, not to speak of the intellectual, moral and social improvement that would necessarily result from such conditions. The purely economic effect of this would be little short of revolution. In proportion to the frequency and extent with which the new desires were gratified, the development of which no power on earth could prevent, would they crystalize into urgent wants and necessities. The satisfaction of these would soon become an essential part of the standard of living demanded by the social character and habits of the people, and therefore would make a general rise of real wages inevitable. (Pp. 13-14.)

Congressional Record. Vol. XXI. Part X. Pages 9,300-9,301. August 28, 1890. Remarks of Mr. McKinley upon the Eight-hour Bill.

The tendency of the times the world over is for shorter hours for labor; shorter hours in the interest of health, shorter hours in the interest of humanity, shorter hours in the interest of the home and the family. . . . Cardinal Manning in a recent article spoke noble words on the general subject when he said:

"But if the domestic life of the people be vital above all; if the peace, the purity of homes, the education of children, the duties of wives and mothers, the duties of husbands and of fathers, be written in the natural law of mankind, and if these things are sacred far beyond anything that can be sold in the market, then I say if the hours of labor resulting from the unregulated sale of a man's strength and skill shall lead to the destruction of domestic life, to the neglect of children, to turning wives and mothers into living machines, and of fathers and husbands into, what shall I say, creatures of burden? I will not say any other word—who rise up before the sun, and come back when it is set, wearied and able only to take food, and lie down and rest, the domestic life of man exists no longer and we dare not go on in this path." (Pp. 8-9.)

Report of the New York Bureau of Labor Statistics. 1900.

But the good accomplished by each successive factory law was so clearly apparent, that even capitalistic Parliament could not refuse to continue the policy of labor protection. The evidence that this policy wrought a revolutionary change in the amount of crime, pauperism, and misery is superabundant; but it is too familiar to warrant repetition now. (P. 49.)

The best evidence of the overwhelming success of the short-hour law from all points of view is afforded by the complete conversion of its opponents. Thus it came to pass that in 1860, when a bill was introduced to extend the ten-hour law to other branches of the textile industry, J. A. Roebuck, who had originally opposed with bitterness this kind of legislation, made the following recantation:

"I am about to speak on this question under somewhat peculiar circumstances. Very early in my parliamentary career Lord Ashley, now the Earl of Shaftesbury, introduced a bill of this description. I, being an ardent political economist, as I am now, opposed the measure, . . . and was very much influenced in my opposition by what the gentlemen of Lancashire said. They declared that it was the last half-hour of the work performed by their operatives which made all their profits, and that if we took away that last half-hour we should ruin the manufacturers of England. I listened to that statement and trembled for the manufacturers of England [a laugh]; but Lord Ashley persevered. Parliament passed the bill which he brought in. From that time down to the present the factories of this country have been under State control, and I appeal to this House whether the manufacturers of England have suffered by this legislation." (P. 50.)

Sir James Graham, another persistent antagonist of the short-hour laws, followed Mr. Roebuck with a similar recantation:

"I am sorry once more to be involved in a short-time discussion. I have, however, a confession to make to the House. . . . Experience has shown to my satisfaction that many of the predictions formerly made against the factory bill have not been verified by the result. . . . By the vote I shall give tonight, I will endeavor to make some amends for the course I pursued in earlier life in opposing the factory bill." (P. 51.)

Fourteenth and Fifteenth Annual Conventions of the International Association of Factory Inspectors of America. Indianapolis, 1900. Niagara Falls, 1901. (Bound in New York Department of Labor Report, 1901.) Problems of Factory Inspection. The Social Interest of Statistics of Factory Inspection. A. F. Weber, *Chief Statistician, New York State Department of Labor.*

Scarcely any upward movement of the century overshadows in its importance to the moral and material welfare of human society, the progressive shortening of man's working time. If one country be compared with another, it will be found that with hardly an exception the rule holds that the shorter the hours of labor, the higher the civilization. (P. 519.)

United States Congress Senate Document, No. 141. Eight hours for laborers on government work. Hearings before the Committee on Education and Labor of the United States Senate, 1st session, 57th Congress. 1901-1902.

Argument of James O'Connell, President of International Association of Machinists:

The history of the movement in this country where

the hours of labor have been reduced shows a higher standard of manhood and a higher standard of intelligence and of excellency in work and in life, a higher and a better home, a happier and better family life, and a more comfortable and better home. In every trade and industry where the hours of labor have been reduced there has been no reduction of the output. (P. 522.)

Report of the United States Industrial Commission. Vol. XIX. 1902.

Lessening of hours leaves more opportunity and more vigor for the betterment of character, the improvement of the home. . . . For these reasons the short work-day for working people brings an advantage to the entire community. (P. 773.)

Employers and Employees. Full Text of the Addresses before the National Convention of Employers and Employees. Minneapolis, Minn. September 22-25, 1902. The Economic Effects of the Eight-Hours' Day. FRANK L. MCVEY, *Professor of Political Economy in the University of Minnesota.*

The whole tendency of modern industry, even with the shortening of hours, is in the direction of increased exertion. The essential element in the machine organization is the human one, the most precious and the most difficult to replace. The energy of a worker in any industry should always be equal to that of the day before. If the pains of labor are heavy the tone of the workman is lowered and his surplus energy disappears, while he tends to become a mere automaton valuable to society for the net surplus he creates for others. The round of production of energy into goods, goods into utilities, and utilities into energy, is broken down by any such heavy burden. We must therefore hail, certainly from the viewpoint of the community, any movement likely to increase its working power. (P. 194.)

The community desires the highest good and greatest energies of its workers through long periods of time.

This can be accomplished in most industries without any accompanying loss of productive power, by shorter hours of work, as has been proven in the experience of many industries.

. . . In some industries where labor is not employed continuously, but periodically and gathered from any and all sources, the employer finds it to his advantage to push the hours of work to the longest possible limit. Human energies can stand a pace of this kind for a time, and as the employer does not worry about a future supply of workers he expects to win an increased profit by such a policy. These industries have come to be called parasitic. (P. 194.)

Report of the Wisconsin Bureau of Labor Statistics. 1903-1904.

No private individual has any more moral right to exhaust the working energy and working capital of a nation without giving "value received" than he has to take the life of an employee outright. The only difference is that one is a slower criminal process than the other. It is not enough that workmen should obtain barely enough for their labor to enable them to live, but they should receive a competency. They should receive as much energy from their employers in food, clothing, homes, and furnishings amid healthful surroundings as they give to their employers in the articles they produce.

The stronger, healthier and more intelligent a laborer is, the more wealth he represents. The laborers of a nation represent its working capital just as the hands of the farmer, his horse, or his ox, represent his working capital. And the stronger and healthier either may be, the more capital it represents. The more efficient this capital becomes, the more wealth will be produced. Machinery operators represent the working capital of the manufacturer, and he owes it to the nation which protects him in his business to do everything in his power to increase this working capital and keep it in the highest possible state of efficiency. (P. 130.)

General Benefit to Society.—United States

The regulation of factories either by law or by special agreement worked marvellous changes in England. In the course of half a century the "sweated" laborers of this great country whose course of life seemed almost run became energetic, self-reliant, intelligent and efficient workers, owning their own homes, amid wholesome surroundings and working a reasonable number of hours for a day's work.

Not only is factory legislation sound in principle, but wherever put to the test it has been found sound in practice as well. (P. 138.)

The Steel Workers. John A. Fitch. *The Pittsburgh Survey, Russell Sage Foundation Publication. New York. Charities Publication Committee. 1910.*

I visited Sharon and made careful inquiry as to the effect of the eight-hour day. I was much surprised at the unanimity with which the system was endorsed, not only by the mill people, but also by the citizens not directly interested in steel manufacture. The general opinion seemed to be, and it was verified by my own observation, that the eight-hour day had made for better morals and higher intelligence on the part of the working-men. (P. 180.)

United States Congress. Senate Report No. 601. Hours of Daily Service of Laborers and Mechanics upon Government Contracts. Report by Mr. Borah *from the Committee on Education and Labor. Sixty-second Congress, 2nd Session, 1912.*

Much has been said as to the inconvenience which would result to the employers in establishing the eight-hour day. Doubtless in some instances and to some extent this inconvenience, necessitating in some instances rearrangement, will follow: It is perhaps true, that in some instances there may result a greater expense to the Government. But these things we believe are to be considered as of minor importance compared to the general benefit to be derived from an eight-hour day for laborers. We believe it means better work, better citizens, and in the end far better for society. . . .

No doubt some business concerns will suffer a temporary inconvenience or loss. But in the long run the loss will likely not be nearly so great as anticipated, and even if so, when weighed against the general good it ought not to prevail against such legislation. (Pp. 3-7.)

Diseases of Occupation and Vocational Hygiene. Edited by GEORGE M. KOBER, M. D., *Professor of Hygiene, Georgetown University, and* WILLIAM C. HANSON, *M. D., Massachusetts State Board of Health. P. Blakiston's Son & Co., Philadelphia. 1916. Fatigue and Occupation.* FREDERIC S. LEE, *New York.*

In determining the proper length of the working period the factor that should be considered first is not the commercial but the physiological one. No one, except in rare emergencies, should be forced by his employer to labor continuously for such a period that subsequent time allowed for rest is insufficient to enable him to recuperate before the beginning of the next working period. Physiological facts, though exact data are here meager, leave no doubt about the necessity, as a custom for most individuals, of one day's rest or change of occupation in every 7 days if one's body is to be kept in an efficient physiological state. The proper length of the working period of the other 6 days ought to depend, first, upon the degree of fatigue that is induced by the specific labor. Here again exact studies are much needed. . . . Moreover, the sociological question is a legitimate one, namely: What proportion of an individual's working hours ought equitably to be spent in his vocational work? A customary working day of 12 hours can hardly be justified on either physiological or sociological grounds. The limit in most occupations has, therefore, been gradually reduced, and the present goal of most employees is that of an 8-hour day and a 44-hour week, which signifies a half-holiday on Saturday. In those industries, such as the manufacture of certain iron and steel products, where it is claimed that continuous operation of a plant is necessitated by the nature of the processes involved, either a 12-hour or an 8-hour shift would seem, if the claim is true, to be essential. In the steel industry of Great Britain the shorter working period is gradually being introduced. In the United States movement in the direction of an 8-hour day has been hastened by the adoption of such a day with a 44-hour week for all employees of the national government. (P. 263.)

Whether the universal adoption of a rigid 8-hour work day for all industries would ultimately be best for society and the individual is doubtful. In the ideal scheme of labor it would seem that no person ought to be denied the pursuit of his vocation for a longer period than 8 hours in 24, provided the longer labor is not detrimental to him or to society. The leaders in the world's progress have not limited themselves to brief working days; almost invariably they have been persistent hard laborers with whom, impelled by whatever motive, the accomplishment of the task and not the avoidance of fatigue has been the aim. With the masses who follow instead of lead some limitation is necessary for protection, and an 8-hour day is for the present probably the most just, both physiologically and sociologically. (P. 264.)

Speech on the Ten Hours Bill delivered in the House of Commons on the 2nd of May, 1846. Lord Macaulay. Complete Works, Vol. VIII. London. Longmans, Green, and Co., 1866.

If we consider man merely in a commercial point of view, if we consider him merely as a machine for the production of worsted and calico, let us not forget what a piece of mechanism he is, how fearfully and wonderfully made. We do not treat a fine horse or a sagacious dog exactly as we treat a spinning jenny. Nor will any slave-holder who has sense enough to know his own interest, treat his human chattels exactly as he treats his horses and his dogs. And would you treat the free labourer of England like a mere wheel or pulley? Rely on it that intense labour, beginning too early in life, continued too long every day, stunting the growth of the body, stunting the growth of the mind, leaving no time for healthful exercise, leaving no time for intellectual culture, must impair all those high qualities which have made our country great. Your overworked boys will become a feeble and ignoble race of men, the parents of a more feeble and ignoble progeny; nor will it be long before the deterioration of the labourer will injuriously affect those very interests to which his physical and moral energies have been sacrificed. On the other hand, a day of rest recurring in every week, two or three hours of leisure, exercise, innocent amusement or useful study, recurring every day, must improve the whole man, physically, morally, intellectually; and the improvement of the man will improve all that the man produces. (Pp. 372-373.)

Man is the great instrument that produces wealth. . . . Therefore it is that we are not poorer but richer, because we have, through many ages rested from our labour one day in seven. That day is not lost. While industry is suspended, while the plow lies in the furrow, while the exchange is silent, while no smoke ascends from the factory, a process is going on quite as important to the wealth of nations, as any process which is performed on more busy days. Man, the machine of machines, the machine compared with which all the contrivances of the Watts and Arkwrights are worthless, is repairing and winding up, so that he returns to his labours on the Monday with clearer intellect, with livelier spirits, with renewed corporal vigour. Never will I believe that what makes a population stronger, and healthier, and wiser, and better, can ultimately make it poorer. (Pp. 374-375.)

British Sessional Papers. Vol. XV. 1870. Reports of Inspectors of Factories. For Half-year ending 30th April, 1870.

There is a generous feeling springing up on the part of many employers that the act (i. e. 1867) is a proper one; that its enactments are salutary; that though it binds them to certain provisions, they are provisions that are useful both in a social and business point of view; that long hours never produce the best work . . . There is a general improvement in our work people, and their habits of life are changed. There are fewer hours in the factory, and they have more time at home; besides which, when in the factory they are obliged to be clean, quiet and industrious, and these habits tend beneficially on their home life. They are more intelligent, and it is remarkable that while they work fewer hours they earn more money. We have found that longer hours mean listlessness and loss of power. (Pp. 44-45.)

The Eight Hour Day. Sidney Webb and Harold Cox, B. A. London. WALTER SCOTT. *1891.*

We have pointed out that the younger generation of workpeople are eager to educate themselves, and would largely use their new opportunities for this purpose. But this is mainly a question of their individual enjoyment, and only affects the community gradually through its effect upon the race. The point to which we wish now to come is more directly social in its bearings.

The new wants thus arising cannot, as a rule, be satisfied without new expenditure. If people have more opportunities of going out, they will soon begin to want more new clothes. They will be obliged, too, to spend money on omnibus and railway fares. And being out, they must amuse themselves. There will be increased demand for theatres, music halls, and other places of public entertainment. Popular lectures, too, will be in brisk request, and newspapers and magazines will find a wider range of readers. It is needless to extend the list. In every direction the wants of the laboring community will be widened; for men and women who are free to dispose of part of their day as pleases them best will no longer be content with the old narrow life. In this way the working classes will constitute themselves a better market for their own products. (Pp. 148-149.

A Shorter Working Day. R. A. HADFIELD *of Hadfield's Steel Foundry Co., Sheffield, and* H. DE B. GIBBINS, M. A. *Methuen & Co. London. 1892.*

Mr. Chamberlain . . . brushing aside all the usual talk about the interference of the State with adult persons of either sex, declared himself in favor of the principle once laid down by Professor Jevons, that "the State is justified in passing any laws, or even in doing any single act, which, without ulterior consequences, would add to the sum total of happiness." He further argued that an eight hours law would, without any ill effects, add immensely to the happiness of half a million miners in the United Kingdom. His opinion in favor of the bill was based upon the fact that short hours did not mean diminished output. (P. 22.)

As in the past it has been clearly proved that, the longer the hours of work the more the workers become mere machines, surely by a further shortening, which is proved to be absolutely necessary from the altered conditions of their surroundings, and apart from other necessary improvements, the general physique of the citizen will be improved and the nation will correspondingly benefit. (P. 115.)

It is rightly claimed that the shortening of hours would lead to improvements, mental and physical. Any action by which such change or improvement is effected, relating to some 8,000,000 of human beings in this country alone, is not to be lightly put on one side or trifled with. If effected, and if even a partial accomplishment of the end in view can be attained, the raising of such a considerable portion of the community must be of the highest benefit to the nation as a whole. (P. 116.)

British Sessional Papers. Vol. XXI. 1894. Report of the Chief Inspector of Factories and Workshops.

In factory legislation there has been steady progress, and whilst Royal Commissions and Trade Congresses have commended what has been accomplished and the mode of administration of the Factory Acts, they have always pointed to further reforms. Bills have been passed which could not have been introduced had not manufacturers, who were formerly opponents of such legislation, been convinced of its benefits by the results. (P. 5.)

Eight Hours for Work. John Rae, *London and New York, Macmillan. 1894.*

It is not merely the number of the successful eight-hour experiments that is so striking, but also the great variety of the industries in which they have occurred, the frequency with which the old amount of production has been exceeded, and then, over and above all, the positive improvement that has ensued in the physical and even moral condition of the labourers. They have gained alike in health, morals and intelligence, so that we may reasonably expect the next generation of eight-hours workpeople to be not only more efficient while at work, but to have a longer turn of efficient working life. Who shall estimate the value to the nation of an addition of say 10 years more efficient work from the great body of her workpeople? (P. 176.)

Life and Labour of the People in London. Edited by Charles Booth. Vol. IX. Pt. III. Ch. VII. The Hours of Labour. Ernest Aves. *London and New York. Macmillan. 1897.*

A "fair" day's work must stand in a due relation to the other elements that properly make up a man's life. It is not simply as much as he can do. We must look back from the end of the twenty-four hours, as well as forward from the beginning of the working-day, in order to judge fairly the degree of absorption and sacrifice admissible even in the simplest and least exacting forms of employment. Home, rest, and recreation demand recognition, and a not immoderate estimate of their claims leads to the conclusion that even for the least exacting tasks, a ten-hours' working day on regular employment might be taken as a reasonable maximum. Even in the absence of any quantitative expression, the moral force of the idea of a "living day," analogous to that of a "living wage," might with advantage be brought home to the public mind. For the complete absorption of the life, even with the highest pay, is apt to be as injurious to health and character as the most precarious form of livelihood. (P. 286.)

The Case for the Factory Acts. Edited by Mrs. Sidney Webb. *London, Richard, 1901.*

The two great industries which, at the beginning of the nineteenth century, were conspicuous for the worst horrors of sweating were the textile manufactures and coal-mining. Between 1830 and 1850 the parliamentary inquiries into these trades disclosed sickening details of starvation wages, incredibly long hours, and conditions of work degrading to decency and health. The remedy applied was the substitution, for individual bargaining between employer and operative, of a compulsory minimum set forth in common rules prescribing standard conditions of employment. (P. 36.)

. . . What was the result? Fortunately, there is no dispute. Every one who knows these great industries agrees in declaring that the horrors which used to prevail under individual bargaining have been brought to an end. The terms "cotton-operative" and "coal-miner," instead of denoting typically degraded workers, as they did in 1830, are now used to designate the very aristocracy of our labor. (P. 37.)

History of Factory Legislation. B. L. Hutchins *and* Amy Harrison. *Westminster, King, 1903.*

In 1861 the president of the Economic Section of the British Association could say in his address that the results of that bill (ten-hour bill) were "something of which all parties might well be proud. There is in truth a general assent that if there has been one change which more than another has strengthened and consolidated the social fabric in this part of the island, has cleared away a mass of depravity and discontent, has placed the manufacturing enterprise of the country on a safe basis, and has conferred upon us resources against the effects of foreign competitions which can scarcely be overvalued, it is precisely the changes which have been brought about by the sagacious and persevering and successful efforts to establish in manufacturing occupations a sound system of legal interference with the hours of labor." (P. 122.)

Work and Wages: In Continuation of Earl Brassey's 'Work and Wages' and 'Foreign Work and English Wages.' Part III. Social Betterment. By Sydney J. Chapman, M.A. *London and New York, Longmans, Green & Co., 1914.*

The intensification of economic life is in itself all to the good . . . but the community must lose something of culture unless, corresponding with this intensification, there is an expansion of leisure and a specialized use of leisure for the purposes of culture. (P. 255.)

There is some danger lest the growing importance of leisure generally, and of a proper use of leisure, should not be fully realized. Tangible things force themselves upon our attention as the more intangible do not, and some of us who have an economic bent of mind get into the way, in consequence, of thinking too much of the quantity of external wealth produced and too little of the balance between internal and external wealth. In ultimate terms, to those who care to put it that way, all wealth is life, as Ruskin insisted. There hardly appears to be any risk of a general underrating of external goods, but there is some risk of an underrating of the new needs of the life lived outside the hours devoted to production —which should themselves be, not a sacrifice to real living, but a part of it—and of an underrating of the dependence even of productive advance upon the widespread enjoyment and proper use of adequate leisure and an adequate income. (Pp. 255-256.)

Le Premier Mai et la Journée de Huit Heures. [*The First of May and the Eight-Hour Day.*] *With Preface by* JULES GUESDE. J. B. CORIOLAN and J. MORTAIR. *Paris, G. Crépin (1891?).*

Long working days tend to race degeneration through the exhaustion of the working class. We see, in fact, that . . . the relative mortality is higher at all ages, and especially in infancy; and that the length of life is greater among the rich than among the poor.

Only reduction of working hours can at the present crisis check this deterioration of the race. The Birmingham mechanics have moreover clearly proved it: after obtaining 20 years ago the nine-hour day, they saw in 15 years the average length of life among them rise from 33 to 40 years. (P. 19.)

Handbuch der Hygiene. Bd. 8[1]. [*Handbook of Hygiene. Vol. 8*[1].] *Edited by* DR. THEODORE WEYL. *Allgemeine Gewerbehygiene und Fabrikgesetzgebung.* [*General Industrial Hygiene and Factory Legislation.*] DR. EMIL ROTH. *Jena, 1894.*

As the experience of every country daily confirms the fact that the reduction of working hours neither lessens nor deteriorates the working efficiency, nor lowers wages necessarily, there has been in all the civilized countries of Europe during the last ten years a steady tendency to shorten working hours,—a tendency which cannot be too emphatically encouraged in behalf of racial health. (Pp. 26-27.)

. . . We may point out that the social condition of the worker, his home, nutrition, and conduct of life are highly important factors in the rate of sickness, and that, the longer the working hours, the less opportunity is left to him of utilizing these health-preserving forces. (Pp. 27-28.)

2. Benefit of Leisure and Recreation.

After continuous work, a certain amount of leisure and recreation is a physiological necessity. The worker's condition determines in large measure whether or not he takes advantage of opportunities for self-improvement or legitimate enjoyment. The worker who has not exhausted his energies by overexertion turns instinctively to the better uses of leisure.

Of these opportunities the most striking modern instances are the new forms of recreation and education open to wage-earners.

Practically every large city in the United States and many small ones are making increasingly large expenditures for public recreation. The growth of this movement has been phenomenal. It began by providing playgrounds for children. City governments are now more and more assuming as a municipal function the maintenance of neighborhood centers for adults. In 1915, recreation centers and playgrounds were administered entirely or in part by some municipal department in 250 cities. One hundred and thirty-three cities reported that 612 schools or other buildings were used as evening recreation centers. The total average attendance in 73 centers was 54,865 persons.

Side by side with the recreation movement for adults, new opportunities for popular education are developing. Besides regular night schools and public evening lectures within the school system, the extension classes of state and privately endowed universities are growing rapidly. Thus, for instance, 1,600 students were enrolled in the evening extension classes of the University of Minnesota, between September, 1915, and February, 1916. The correspondence department of the University of Chicago had over 3,200 students in the year 1914 to 1915; that of the University of California had nearly 5,000; and that of the University of Wisconsin about 9,000 during 1915 to 1916.

Obviously, all these activities require not only that the workers shall have some leisure after working hours but also that their minds shall be fresh enough to respond to the opportunities offered.

National Civic Federation Monthly Review. Vol. I. October 15, 1904. The Shorter Work Day. F. W. TAUSSIG, *Harvard University.*

Shorter hours of work are a natural and beneficent outcome of the forces of civilization. The great mass of men need not only an increase of income, but an increase of leisure,—leisure for rest, for play, for education, for happier and higher living. No doubt leisure is sometimes abused; but in the main it is a needed means of raising the sum of happiness. Therefore, the short hour movement should have the sympathy of every friend of humanity. (P. 14.)

Evidence Submitted to the Massachusetts Legislature in Favor of the Enactment of a Ten-Hour Law. Lawrence, 1870.

The workpeople of this State as a body have no desire to disturb industrial operations. Their lot is labor; but in toiling for bodily sustenance they desire leisure to feed the *mind.* The evidence of mill-operatives is confirmatory of the truth that, in their case, physical exhaustion renders impossible diligent application to mental improvement. (Pp. 4-5.)

The Economic and Social Importance of the Eight-Hour Movement. George Gunton. *New York, American Federation of Labor. 1889.*

It is one of the characteristic features of modern industrial life that by its division and specialization of labor, it tends to increase the intensity of the strain upon the nervous energies of the laborer. In no country in the world is this fact more prevalent than in America. The persistency with which industrial energies are intensified in this country have come to be almost regarded as a national characteristic. It has become a recognized fact by medical science that the first step toward remedying this condition is more leisure, more physical and mental repose, more and longer periods of relief from the strain which the specialized industrial life imposes. This has become absolutely necessary for both physical and social reasons. For physical reasons, because it makes wholesome living and normal physical health possible, and socially because without it frequent social contact is prevented or the susceptibility to the socializing influence is destroyed. The great mass of laborers are compelled to work all the year round under the same monotonous condition. This is made indispensable by the very nature of modern methods in industry. Under the factory system the laborers become mere wheels in a colossal machine, in which the presence of all is necessary to the efficient labor of any. (Pp. 12-13.)

Discussions in Economics and Statistics. Vol. II. Francis A. Walker, Ph. D., LL. D. *The Eight-Hour Law Agitation. New York, Holt. 1899.*

. . . I have small sympathy with the views so frequently, and it seems to me brutally, expressed, that the working classes have no need for leisure, beyond the bare necessities of physical rest and repose, to get ready for the morrow's work; that they do not know what to do with vacant hours; and that a shortening of the term of labor would, in the great majority of cases, lead to an increase of dissipation and drunkenness. Is it our fellow-beings, our own countrymen, of whom we are speaking? It seems to me this talk . . . is the poorest sort of pessimistic nonsense. It is closely akin to what we used to hear about slavery being a humane and beneficent institution. . . .

. . . We may well desire that somewhat more, and much more, of leisure and of recreation should mingle with the daily life of our fellows than is now known to most of them. It is a pity, it is a great pity, that working men should not see more of their families by daylight; should not have more time for friendly converse or for distinct amusements; should not have larger opportunities for social and public affairs. Doubtless many would always, and still more would at first, put the newly acquired leisure to uses that were lower than the best, . . . were even, in instances, mischievous and injurious.

But the larger part of this would be due to the fact, not that the time now granted was too great, but that the time previously granted had been too small. . . . But such men, who might, it is conceded, become even worse men with more leisure, are not to furnish the rule for the great majority, who are decent, sober, and careful, fearing God, and loving their families. (P. 383-385.)

The Arena. Vol. 24. 1900. New York. Democratic Tendencies. II. The Eight-Hour Day by Legislation. EDWIN MAXEY, *Southern Normal University.*

While the case for an eight-hour day is thus extremely strong from the point of view of physical health, it is even stronger from the standpoint of social health. If you compel men and women to work so long each day that they have little time and energy left for thinking, they will remain unthinking animals. Wider education is, at once, cause and effect of the eight-hour movement. In fact, the real force that gives vitality to the movement is a spontaneous longing for a brighter, fuller life, and a deep conviction that shorter hours of labor will serve this end. Men and women who toil for wages are growing tired of being only working animals. . . . On all sides there is an expansion of life. New possibilities of enjoyment—physical, intellectual, social—are being more and more realized by the masses. Among all classes of laborers the demand for leisure is becoming keener, because leisure means more to them. (P. 239.)

Report of the United States Industrial Commission on the Relations and Conditions of Capital and Labor employed in Manufactures and General Business. Vol. VII. 1900.

Testimony of Mr. Rufus R. Wade, Chief of District Police, Massachusetts:

The question may well be asked, what has been the effect upon those operatives whose hours of labor have been lessened and to the children obliged to work in factories whose school privileges have been secured? The benefit to adults, comprising the laboring classes, by the reduction of the hours of labor has been to lift them up in the level of their manhood to thoughts of better things and to an organized demand for the same. It has given needed time for leisure to the operative, it has encouraged self-culture, it has afforded additional opportunity for recreation, and has given the debating school, lecture room, and library an impetus in every city and manufacturing town in Massachusetts. The large circulation which the daily papers have obtained, in my opinion, is due in part to the fact that the laboring people are considering the questions of public movement.

From an experience which has extended many years, not only through the medium of official duty but from personal observation, I would say, with much confidence, that there has been a gradual yet steady change in the conditions once existing, which has operated to the benefit and well-being of the laboring classes in the opportunities for mental and social culture. (Pp. 79-80).

Fourteenth and Fifteenth Annual Conventions of the International Association of Factory Inspectors of America. Indianapolis, 1900. Niagara Falls, 1901. (Bound in New York Department of Labor Report, 1901.) The Shorter Workday in its Effect upon the Personal Character of the Worker. JOHN HOLBROOK, *Deputy Commissioner of Labor, Michigan.*

. . . Quality of product may be improved by a shorter day, and by this improvement in quality of the product has come to be considered the improvement of the quality of the laborer himself. The greatest capital invested in any enterprise, commercial or industrial, is not of buildings, machinery, and plants, but in the character of the men and women employed, and on this later capital stock there is no return possible of large profits without improvement of personal character.

. . . We reached the second stage of this agitation when the privilege was asked to have opportunities for leisure, for the enlargement of mental grasp, for the cultivation of the home and home life, and for freedom for self-culture. (Pp. 562-563.)

A reduction in the hours of labor means for the handworkers leisure for self-culture and the arts, moralities and the refinements of life. Many causes have contributed toward the elevation of the lot of labor, but one great concurrent cause has been the shortening of the hours. . . .

It has not been shown that the workers' use of leisure has been less wise and moral than the use of leisure by the so-called leisured classes. They have learned to use their leisure hours just as rationally and beneficially as have the wealthier classes, and it would astonish an old-time advocate of constant work for labor, lest Satan should find mischief for idle hands to do, how wisely and well these very classes have used their spare hours; they have come to be constant and intelligent readers of scientific and mechanical journals. They have formed a disposition to read the best books and literature, and as a rule the working people are reading more serious and thoughtful books than any other class of society. (Pp. 563-564.)

United States Congress. House Report. No. 1793 (4405). Hours of Laborers on Public Works of the United States. Report from the Committee on Labor. 57th Congress 1st Session. 1901-1902.

No recognized authority to-day combats the proposition that the condition of the laborer has improved with every reduction in the hours of daily service that has up to this time been made. Nobody is disputing that he has become a better consumer with each reduction. . . . Economists contend with great plausibility that the shorter day results in an increase of wages without an increase of price, as consumption enlarges production, and the larger the scale of production the cheaper the given article is produced; that the laborer, when he has the leisure resulting from the shorter hours, has new aspirations, ambitions, and a greater personal self-respect, and, as before stated, wants a better house, better furniture, better clothes, better food, and becomes a great deal better consumer. (Pp. 8-9.)

United States Congress. Senate Report 2321. The Eight-Hour Law: Report from the Committee on Education and Labor. Fifty-seventh Congress. Second Session. 1902-1903.

Commissioner Carroll D. Wright well says:

The policy of this class of legislation has therefore been settled by Congress, and I need not discuss this phase of the question. All such laws are enacted for the purpose of protecting the laboring man from the injurious consequences of prolonged physical effort, giving him more time for his personal affairs and more time and energy to devote to the cultivation of his moral and mental powers. It has always been expected that they would aid him in the acquisition of knowledge, thus tending to make him a better and more contented citizen. This policy must be admitted by all to be a good one. . . . The Federal government has long been committed to this policy. (P. 2.)

Getting a Living: The Problem of Wealth and Poverty —of Profits, Wages and Trade Unionism. George L. Bolen. *New York and London. The Macmillan Company. 1903.*

Wage workers, and employers too, must have more spare time, and be less spent by their daily tasks, if they are not to shorten their lives, and if they are to make good use of the present abundant means for physical, mental, and moral improvement. The exhausted man must usually be excused for neglecting libraries and lectures. He will do well if he does not want to be excused from church also. Excessive weariness is an inducement to drink. There is a good evidence that shortening the day has everywhere promoted temperance. When the British law of 1847 went into effect, shortening the textile factory day from 11 and 12 hours to 10, there was a decided increase of effort at self-education, fifty night schools being open in Leeds in 1849. As to American miners the testimony is similar. The shortening of the work day, with the increase of hope and energy it evokes, and with the active self-help in unionism necessary to attain it, has doubtless been the main cause of the rise of British and American workmen in efficiency, intelligence, and capable citizenship—the essential elements of strength in a nation. In this way the shorter day has been largely the cause of the unprecedented progress of these two nations in wealth and enlightenment. . . .

In the present speed of activity in America, the welfare of workers in many industries requires a shorter day. Especially is it necessary to give working fathers and mothers more home life, and more pride in their children. Possession of these advantages by parents is most effective in saving children from idleness and crime, and in giving the rising generation the greatest development of body, mind, and character. It is easy to foresee the effect of these qualities on the nation's future, in wealth production, and in well-being of every kind. The buoyancy and efficiency of Australians is believed by many observers to be unequalled, and to be due to their long enjoyment of the eight-hour day. (Pp. 411-12.)

The National Civic Federation Review. Vol. II, No. 8. Jan. Feb., 1906. The first Annual meeting of the New England Civic Federation, Boston, Jan. 11, 1906.

Marcus M. Marks, President, National Association of Clothing Manufacturers:

There is another consideration which prompts the demand on the part of labor for a shorter work-day; it is the greater desire for self-improvement.

This has been encouraged by the advance in the public school of the system which affects our younger workmen in particular; also by the multiplication of popular free lectures, public libraries, cheap books and newspapers, etc., that have awakened in the workmen's minds the ambition to lead a better life, possible only in the enjoyment of a reasonable amount of leisure. (P. 8.)

People v. *Klinck Packing Co., 250 N. Y., 121 (1915).*

We see at the outset that it is applicable to certain classes of employees. But these are they who work in factories and mercantile establishments. We know as a matter of common observation that such labor is generally indoors and imposes that greater burden on health which comes from confinement many times accompanied by crowded conditions and impure air. Thus special conditions are presented which become a reasonable basis for special consideration. (P. 36.)

I suppose that no one would contend that continued and uninterrupted indoor labor would be good even for an adult man. The laws which have been passed and sustained with general approval in almost every jurisdiction limiting the hours of labor for women and children and for those engaged in especially trying employment, such as mining and the operation of railroads, amply evidence the widespread belief that in certain fields the public health and welfare are subserved by generous opportunities for relaxation and recuperation. A constantly increasing study of industrial conditions I believe leads to the conviction that the health, happiness, intelligence and efficiency even of an adult man laboring in such employments as those mentioned in this statute will be increased by a reasonable opportunity for rest, for outdoor life and recreation, for attention to his own affairs, and, if he will, study and education. (Pp. 36-37.)

Principles of Labor Legislation. John R. Commons, *University of Wisconsin, Former Member Wisconsin Industrial Commission, and* John B. Andrews, *Secretary of the American Association for Labor Legislation. New York and London. Harper & Brothers. 1916.*

Though it is the health dangers of long hours which are most often emphasized, the lack of leisure for family life, for recreation, for all the requirements of citizenship, is no less an evil. It should not be forgotten that the time spent in going to and coming from work and the dinner hour often adds two hours to the length of the workday proper, and that an eleven-hour day is likely to mean thirteen hours away from home. The ultimate effects of such hours of labor were thus summed up by the Supreme Court of Georgia in upholding a Sunday rest law: "Without specific leisure the process of forming character can only be begun; it can never advance or be completed; people would be merely machines of labor—nothing more." (P. 202.)

Hennington v. *The State, 90 Ga., 396 (1892).*

There can be no well founded doubt of its (Sunday law) being a police regulation . . . for the frequent and total suspension of the toils, cares and strain of mind or muscle incident to pursuing an occupation or common employment, is beneficial to every individual, and incidentally to the community at large, the general public. Leisure is no less essential than labor to the well-being of man.

Benefit of Leisure and Recreation.—United States

Short intervals of leisure at stated periods reduce wear and tear, promote health, favor cleanliness, encourage social intercourse, afford opportunity for introspection and retrospection, and tend in a high degree to expand the thoughts and sympathies of people, enlarge their information and elevate their morals, . . . Without frequent leisure, the process of forming character could only be begun; it could never advance or be completed, people would be mere machines of labor or business—nothing more.

If a law which, in essential respects, betters for all the people the conditions, sanitary, social and individual, under which their daily life is carried on and which contributes to insure for each, even against his own will, his minimum allowance of leisure, can not be rightfully classed as a police regulation, it would be difficult to imagine any law that could. (P. 397.)

Work and Wealth: A Human Valuation. J. A. Hobson. *New York. The Macmillan Company, 1914.*

The first use of leisure, then, is that it supplies a counterpoise to specialization by the opportunity it gives for the exercise of the neglected faculties, the cultivation of neglected tastes. As the specialization grows closer, this urgency increases. More leisure is required for the routine worker to keep him human.

In the first place, it must afford him relaxation or recreation by occupations in which the spontaneity, the liberty, the elements of novelty, increasingly precluded from his work-day, shall find expression. It must liberate him from automatism, and afford him opportunity for the creative and interesting work required to preserve in him humanity.

An eight-hours day would mean that thousands of men, who at present leave the factory or furnace, the office or the shop, in a state of physical and mental lassitude, would take a turn at gardening, or home carpentry, would read some serious and stimulating book, or take part in some invigorating game.

Thus each man would not merely get more out of each item of his economic consumption, but he would add to the net sum of his humanity, and incidentally of his economic utility, by cultivating those neglected faculties of production which yield him a positive fund of interest and human benefit. (Pp. 237-238.)

British Sessional Papers. Vol. XXII. 1849. Reports of Inspectors of Factories for Half-year ending 31st October, 1848.

When their day's work is over at an early hour in the evening, and they have 3 hours at their disposal before it is time to go to bed, the factory workers then feel the full value of the shortened hours of labour; they can then take advantage of evening schools or other places of instruction, and turn their leisure to good account in many ways, both for moral improvement and for social and domestic comfort. (P. 7.)

Opinions of the Factory Operatives respecting the Ten Hours' Act:

It must be remembered, too, that there has been more than two years of great suffering among the factory operatives, from many mills having worked short time, and many being altogether closed. A considerable number of the operatives must therefore be in very narrow circumstances, many, it is to be feared, in debt; so that it might fairly have been presumed that at the present time they would prefer working the longer time, in order to make up for past losses. . . . I have been very much surprised to find so large a proportion of those receiving very moderate wages, and still more of those receiving very scanty wages, preferring to work 10 hours. The reason for their preference assigned by so many young persons and even adults, that it enabled them to attend evening schools, is a gratifying circumstance, as affording a good sign of the character of the factory population. (Pp. 16-17.)

Under the present mode of working the 10 hours, according to which the working day of young persons and women, and of the greater portion of adults also, is brought to a close at half-past 5 in the afternoon, the employed may derive the greatest benefit from the curtailment of their labour in the evening; for they are then enabled not only to cultivate the domestic affections, to learn domestic habits and so to elevate the character of the working classes, but to avail themselves of those opportunities of mental culture. (P. 99.)

Ibid. Appendix. Evidence of the Opinions of Persons Employed in Factories Respecting the Ten Hours' Act, Collected in September, October, and November, 1848.

Letter from Messrs. Sidgwick, Mill-owners: We consider the plan most conducive to the comfort and advantage of the people employed in factories, is such an arrangement of the working time, in which they have to earn a livelihood, as will leave to them the longest possible space of disengaged time, between ceasing work in an evening and resuming it in a morning, for recreation, improvement, or their private business. (P. 14.)

British Sessional Papers. Vol. XXIII. 1850. Reports of Inspectors of Factories for the Half-year ending 31st of October, 1849.

It is an early stopping in the evening that the work people chiefly value; and if the free evening hours from 6 to 9 be secured the great object sought for by the Ten Hours' Act will be attained; for then the factory workers will be in what may be called the normal state of the operatives in the generality of trades, and will, like them, have leisure for domestic arrangements, for improving themselves by attending evening schools, with opportunities for healthful and reasonable recreations. . . . Where the law is fully carried out, according to its true intention, the work people appear to value the limitation more and more in proportion as they have longer experience of its effects; and the masters appear to be getting daily better reconciled to it; partly by finding that, by the increased alertness of their work people, by the closer application they are now enabled to give, together with some additional speeding of the machinery not before tried, the produce is much nearer to that of 12 hours than it was conceived possible it could be brought to, but partly also by the marked change for the better which they see in the health, appearance, and contentment of their work people. (P. 5.)

Among those who have carefully watched the operation of each successive restriction, the number, I am satisfied, is now large, who would declare themselves content to work only 10 hours a day, . . . and this I believe to be especially the case among mill-occupiers and managers who can from their own experience compare the state and condition of the operative class under the present factory system with their state and condition under the hours of work during which they laboured 20 years ago.

I am assured, that the attendance of young persons at night-schools, and the demand for garden allotments, bear powerful testimony to the advantages of a reduction in the number of working hours, and to the readiness with which the best disposed are willing to make a beneficial use of the additional hours the present restriction leaves them for recreation and improvement. (P. 41.)

In one of the letters sent to me the following interesting statement was given, representing, as I believe correctly, a picture of domestic life almost unknown in the manufacturing district, especially of a large town like Bradford, until the hours of labor were reduced and regulated by the Legislature. The comfort and feelings here described, though naturally of slow growth, are, I hope, daily extending their influence, and may be either much encouraged or much retarded, according as the Government and Legislature of the Country exercise a patèrnal care for the different classes who look up to them for protection:

. . . "I called in to see an old factory weaver; it was very interesting and delightful to behold the old man sitting with his youngest son; they had a basket of potatoes for sets, and both seemed at a loss, being new gardeners, but were very glad to have an opportunity of learning; he had 3 daughters, and 2 young women lodgers, very busy sewing and knitting, and all teaching each other. . . . I asked the old mother how she liked the Ten Hour Bill. She said very well, she did not know how she must do if the girls worked any longer, they assisted her all they could, and were learning to do household work, and could sew and knit better than she could, and could read very nicely too; they could not do with any more than ten hours. The old father said it was a grand thing, the Ten Hours Bill; he was learning to be a gardener, and would not like to give it up, which he would have to do if they worked any more hours." (Pp. 48-49.)

British Sessional Papers. Vol. XIV. 1868-1869. Reports of Inspectors of Factories for the Half-year ending 30th April, 1868.

Assuredly the usefulness of the first hours of rational freedom from late employment has not been overrated. The power which the working classes now possess of making arrangements for out-door enjoyments in the summer, and for intellectual advancement of every kind during the winter months, is fully appreciated, and would be most reluctantly parted with. It is indeed spoken of as a boon which they longed to possess years ago, and is most thankfully acknowledged. (P. 277.)

The Eight-Hours' Movement. Tom Mann. *London, William Reeves, 1889.*

Clearly, then, what is required is to develop the mental powers of the workers, and to give them leisure and capacity to assimilate knowledge. Stupidly slaving away like cattle will not give our country any chance in the competition with others. In that struggle, as long as it lasts, the victory will be with the nation that has the most energetic, intelligent, and capable workers—those, in fact, who work the shortest hours and have the highest standard of comfort. (P. 12.)

The Case for an Eight-Hours' Bill. London: Published for the Fabian Society by JOHN HEYWOOD, *1891. (Fabian Tracts, No. 23).*

The one demand of the laboring masses which to-day forces itself on the attention alike of the willing and the unwilling, is the rapidly growing international movement in favor of an Eight-Hours' Day. . . .

This has come about, not so much from the conviction that the present hours are injurious to health—though that in many cases is the fact—not so much from the theory that shorter hours mean higher wages—though that theory is in the main sound,—but from the strongly-felt desire for additional opportunities for self-cultivation and the enjoyment of life.

Men and women who toil for wages are everywhere growing tired of being only working animals. They wish to enjoy, as well as to labor; to pluck the fruits, as well as dig the soil; to wear as well as to weave. They are eager for opportunity to see more of the great world in which they live—a world of which many of them now for the first time hear from books. On all sides there is an expansion of life. New possibilities of enjoyment, physical, emotional, intellectual, are daily opening for the masses. New aspirations are daily surging up. We need not wonder then that this generation is no longer content to live as its fathers and mothers lived. Hence in all classes the demand for leisure grows keener and keener. (Pp. 3-4.)

The Eight Hours Day. Sidney Webb and Harold Cox. London, Walter Scott, 1891.

We need therefore have no fear that a working population set free will not know what to do with its freedom. The existing facilities for amusement, for study, and for physical recreation will be at once drawn upon, and a demand will arise for further facilities of the same nature. Already indeed we have evidence how a diminution of the hours of labour stimulates the desire for study, even in the most apparently unpromising quarters. Nowhere have University Extension lectures, even on abstruse scientific subjects, been so successful as among the miners of Durham and Northumberland. These men —as explained elsewhere—work on the average less than eight hours a day; and sometimes a miner, after his day's work is done, has been known to walk as much as eight miles every week to attend a course of lectures on astronomy. (Pp. 147-148.)

Ibid. Appendix II. Letters, etc. received from Firms which have already adopted an Eight-Hours' Day. From Burroughs, Wellcome & Co., Importers, Exporters and Manufacturing Chemists, Snow Hill Buildings, London, 16th December, 1890.

6th. . . . We believe that increased intelligence and efficiency follow upon limiting the hours of labour to eight, because opportunities are thus afforded for intellectual and physical development and recreation. We believe that the proper employment of such opportunities tends to elevate the general tone of life, to improve the health, and to cultivate a taste for good society, and precludes that excessive fatigue which demands unnatural stimulant and vicious pleasures. It is therefore our opinion that the general adoption of the Eight-Hours' System would powerfully tend (1) to increase the amount of work produced in a given time, by reason of the improved physical and mental conditions; (2) to decrease the cost of production for the same reason, and also, on account of the improved mental elasticity, lead to inventions in labour-saving machinery; (3) to improve relations between employers and employed, brought about by the disposition evinced by the former to give the employé opportunities for recreation and social advancement. (Pp. 255-256.)

The Problem of the Unemployed. JOHN A. HOBSON. *London, Methuen, 1896.*

The indirect effects of a shorter working-day are not less important. Provided the increased leisure is not purchased by an injurious overstrain in the shorter working-day the increased opportunities it will afford for the cultivation of unused faculties and the satisfaction of new tastes, will furnish an ever growing stimulus towards an elevation of the standard of life. By yielding a continuous demand for the satisfaction of new, strong desires it will supply the moral force which, allied with improved intelligence and the more effective means of organization which modern conditions of industry and of life afford, makes powerfully and persistently for enforcing the claims of the working classes to a larger share of the aggregate consuming power of the community. (Pp. 109-110.)

Life and Labour of the People in London. Edited by CHARLES BOOTH, *Vol. IX. Pt. III. Ch. VII. The Hours of Labour.* ERNEST AVES, *London and New York. Macmillan. 1897.*

In connection with both overtime and the hours of labour, however, there is another and deeper consideration in their effects on the larger question of sustained life-efficiency.

But this consideration is frequently lost sight of by the actual parties to a contract for the employment of labour. . . . It is the more necessary, therefore, to keep steadily in view the main industrial object of securing that desirable combination of hours and work which, without sacrificing private life, secures the most capable, willing, and effective service. From the limited points of view of the individual operative or employer, excessive toil may seem to be consistent with, and even necessary to, their more immediate objects, but since excess implies some subsequent form of deterioration, it can rarely be compatible with the interests of the community at large. (Pp. 294-5.)

With regard to the more personal effect of a reduction of hours that does not impair the chances of employment, the whole question of hours derives its importance from the assumption that greater leisure will be advantageous to the individual worker. . . .

In spite . . . of the waste of leisure that is witnessed on every hand, the common claim for a greater share of it is justified by the great balance of advantages that it tends to secure. An increasingly urgent demand has therefore arisen for a greater margin of leisure available for the home, and for all that rounds life off, and makes it a completer thing—a demand urged not only on behalf of the artisan and mechanic, who in many trades are well situated in this respect, but for all whose industrial position unduly narrows life and makes it run too completely in the grooves of their daily work. (P. 287.)

Diseases of Occupation from the Legislative, Social, and Medical Points of View. THOMAS OLIVER, M. A., M. D., F. R. C. P., *Medical Expert on the White Lead, Dangerous Trades, Pottery, and Lucifer Match Committees of the British Home Office. New York, Dutton, 1908.*

. . . It is held that no employer has the right to utilize the whole of the working part of a man's day, and thus deprive him of the leisure to which he as a human being is entitled. Since his whole nature has to be developed, it is claimed that the intellectual, moral, and physical powers of man cannot be developed if the hours of employment are too long, the work too hard and of a grinding nature. (P. xi.)

Conditions in British Iron and Steel Works. I. A Speech Delivered to the Special Commission on Hours of Labour, International Association for Labour Legislation, June 11, 1912. JOHN HODGE, M. P.

I remember on one occasion, when discussing this question of an eight-hour day at a conference with the employers of the North at Newcastle, pointing out—and I spoke from personal experience—that, working a long day, when a man got home, he was tired out, not only because of the laborious toil, but the exhausting nature of the atmosphere in which work was carried on; the body was tired, the brain was tired—he could not think or read; the mind was not in a condition for it. But, if we had an eight-hour day, it would give the man an opportunity of even attending technical classes on metallurgy, combustion, and chemistry, so that he might fit himself with the theory of his trade instead of working by rule-of-thumb. He would know exactly the chemical action of either the mine with which his furnace was fed or the limestone, and the results would be beneficial to the employer—less waste would occur and better results would be obtained. . . .

My own observations have been that the change to the eight hours has improved the physique and the morale of the men. It has not been in existence for a long enough period to enable us to tell as to the change in the length of life of the worker; but I do know that there are some men working on the eight-hour shift to-day who would, except for the change, have been compelled to give up their trade for a lighter occupation. (P. 7.)

National Conference on the Prevention of Destitution. 1912. Papers and Proceedings. London, P. S. King & Son, 1912. The Limitation of the Hours of Work. George N. Barnes, M. P.

I advocate reduction of hours because I want for the worker more time to think. The solution of industrial problems is becoming more urgent because discontent increases day by day, and the community lives more from hand to mouth, and is therefore more vulnerable to attack on the part of a section. Poverty at the bottom of the social scale is being left to breed disease and disorder quicker than legislation is being introduced to deal with them, and improvements in conditon of the better-off worker only whets the appetite for still further improvement. Education has brought new wants into view, and they will have to be satisfied somehow. People are no longer content to live in small, badly-constructed houses, to be shut out from the beauties of the field or the treasures of literature. The average workman is rightly and instinctively conscious of wrong, and he is searching for the means of rectifying it. He will find those means sooner or later, and there will be changes and improvements. But a great deal depends on time and temper. Industrial organization hitherto has been his main mode of seeking betterment. But political power is a weapon in his hands for good or ill. It will be used for the good of the community in proportion to the time the average man has to give to the discharge of social duties. That, to my mind, is the strongest argument in favor of an eight hours' day. (P. 446.)

Jahresberichte der Gewerbe-Aufsichtsbeamten im Königreich Württemberg für das Jahr 1902. [Reports of the Factory Inspectors in the Kingdom of Württemberg for 1902.] Stuttgart, Lindemann, 1903.

A reduction of working hours appears to be also needed on moral and spiritual grounds. A widespread craving for improved education has in recent years developed in the masses of workers and demands satisfaction. Likewise the desire for family life has become stronger. (P. 209.)

The Relation of Labor to the Law of To-day. Translated from the German by Porter Sherman. Lujo Brentano. *New York, Putnam, 1891.*

Why then does an increase in wages and a decrease in the time of work in general lead to a greater capability for work? Because higher wages and a shorter day's work make it possible for laborers to increase and satisfy their physical and spiritual needs; because better food, more careful fostering, greater and more moral recreation increase the power to work, and because they increase the pleasure in labor. . . . In other words, an increase in wages and a decrease in the time of work lead to a greater performance, because they elevate the standard of living of the laborer, a higher standard of living necessarily spurs to greater intensity of labor, and at the same time makes the same possible. (Pp. 233-234.)

Handbuch der Arbeiterwohlfahrt. Bd. II. [Handbook of the General Welfare of the Working Classes, Vol. II.] Edited by Dr. OTTO DAMMER. *Arbeiterschutz. [The Protection of Working People.]* Dr. ASCHER. *Stuttgart, Enke, 1903.*

It is natural that a workman, in the broad sense of the word, who has only a short rest period at his command, should chiefly use that in sleep, to restore his exhausted physical energy; also natural, that, if he has a little free time to spare, as on Sunday, holidays, he should spend it in coarse pleasures. Thus results the weariness of Monday, physical and brain fatigue. . . . If the workman had, instead, enough free time in the week to be able to come home to his family without being tired out—to read, to hear lectures, work in a garden, and so rebuild and restore bodily energy, he would not so misuse the leisure of Sunday. (P. 69.)

Handwörterbuch der Staatswissenschaft. Bd. I. [Compendium of Political Science. Vol. I.] Edited by DRS. J. CONRAD, *Professor of Political Science in Halle;* L. ELSTER, *Ober Reg. Rath in Berlin;* W. LEXIS, *Professor of Political Science in Göttingen; and* EDG. LOENING, *Professor of Law in Halle. Arbeitszeit. [Hours of Work.].* Dr. H. HERKNER, *Berlin. Jena, Fischer, 1909.*

3. The workman perceives that high wages can bring him real family life, a greater share in the gifts of civilization only when reduced working hours shall have en-

abled him to command some leisure and to retain a certain amount of mental buoyancy. (P. 1204.)

5. The shorter the hours of work, the more time there is for other opportunities, such as participation in public life, general or technical educational courses, and such opportunities are of the greatest value in the social position of the worker. (P. 1204.)

Jahresberichte der Gewerbeaufsichtsbeamten im Königreich Württemberg für 1911. [Annual Report of the Factory Inspectors of Württemberg for 1911.] Stuttgart, Lindemann, 1912.

Fourth District: . . . In Heilbronn a strong movement arose for the introduction of early closing on Saturday. Since the workingman has almost no leisure on weekdays, an entire free afternoon is of all the more value to him. The privilege in itself, of being able to dispose freely of an afternoon he feels as an improvement in his whole position. In addition to this, there are other great advantages of early closing. It offers the possibility of longer physical and mental relaxation, and moreover of outdoor exercise, be it in walks or sport and games. It gives the married workman more time for his family, and a chance to take some part in the up-bringing of his children. It enables the workman with a little plot of land to work in his field or garden, thus keeping him in touch with agricultural life, and making him feel "settled." Far from opposing these interests of the workingmen, the Employers' Association of Heilbronn and thereabouts may rather be said to have shown from the start a sympathetic interest in early closing. In discussing the situation with this Association, as well as with individual firms which desired to introduce the early closing system, the Factory Inspector consistently upheld the view that the fixing of one o'clock (at latest) as a closing hour on Saturday should be the aim, as making possible on the one hand a free afternoon, which could be made full use of; on the other, as involving the least deviation from the regular dinner hour of the workman. . . .

In almost all cases, the introduction of the early closing system means a restriction of the number of working hours per week. (P. 7.)

In Heilbronn, Sontheim, and Böckingen, 11 factories, with 2390 men and 1820 women operatives close at one o'clock on Saturdays; two factories with 570 men and 70 women workers close at halfpast one o'clock; one factory with 200 men closes at a quarter of two; and six factories with 320 men and 50 women close at two. Altogether 20 factories with 4330 operatives have the early closing system. (P. 8.)

a. THE EXPERIENCE OF AUSTRALASIA.

The best examples of the benefits to society and to the workers arising from the short workday are found in Australasia. The movement for the eight hour day began in Victoria over fifty years ago. In New Zealand the eight hour day was established by law in 1901. In most of the other Australasian states, the wages boards or arbitration courts are empowered by law to fix maximum hours of labor. According to Mr. Justice Higgins, President of the High Court of Australia, the "general Australian standard" is the 48 hours' week.

In these colonies the short day has been in operation long enough to show its effects. The testimony of factory inspectors and other observers tends to prove that the workers have gained greatly in force and efficiency and that the social welfare of the entire community has been well served through the operation of the short working day.

A Shorter Working Day. R. A. HADFIELD, *of Hadfield's Steel Foundry Co., Sheffield, and* H. DE B. GIBBINS, M.A. *Methuen & Co., London, 1892.*

What concerns us to observe more especially in this chapter is the general effect of the reductions in the working day upon the working-classes of Australia, in order that we may form thereby some idea of what would be the probable effect of a similar measure in England. . . . It is a remarkable fact that in spite of high wages and short hours, the consumption of spirits has greatly decreased in all the Colonies. Indeed, the active agitation of the publicans against the eight-hours day proves that they did not anticipate any increase in their profits through an increase in the comforts of the labourer's life. (Pp. 66-67.)

It is the general opinion in Victoria that the habits of the working-man have been improved rather than deteriorated by the reduction of hours. . . . Intellectual as well as physical development is a necessary consequence of shortening the working day. A man cannot, unless he be a besotted idiot, spend *all* his spare time in the pot-house (as some among us do vainly talk), but feels, as he acquires time for educating his mind and strengthening his body, that there are other pleasures than those of intoxication, and higher ideals than those of the tap-room. This has been the case, at any rate, in Victoria. (Pp. 74-75.)

Eight Hours for Work. John Rae. London, Macmillan, 1894.

It is almost a universal opinion in the colony (Victoria) that the men work harder now while they are at their work, and that they turn out work of a better quality than they did under the long-hour system. Mr. Hodgkinson, a public man of Victoria, said in his speech at the eight-hours' demonstration of 1873, that he had often watched men working in the Public Gardens, and that though left to themselves very much they worked as well as when under contractors, that the Government stroke was unknown among them, and that he was convinced they did more work now in the eight-hours day than they did before in the ten. A very recent writer, Mr. Charles Fairfield, speaks of the "go" which is conspicuous in some of the out-door trades of Victoria. "The leisure enjoyed by colonial workmen, their brisk, cheerful, and robust appearance, and the activity and 'go' displayed by one or two of the out-door trades (such as masons and house carpenters) who work under the eight-hour system are pleasant to behold." An English business man, who has written an account of his visit to Victoria, says he saw men in Melbourne getting as much work to do in a day as would have been allotted to two men in this country, and that the lifts they took were more suitable for steam power than for human beings. Lord Brassey, in a paper read in 1888 to the Royal Colonial Institute on "Recent Impressions of Australia," speaks of the "remarkable physique" of the Australian navvy, and in the discussion on his lordship's paper Rear-Admiral Sir George Tryon said he had on behalf of the Admiralty spent many thousands of pounds in wages in Australia during the previous few years, and that "though the wages were high, the work done was good, and the cost not so great as might be supposed. The men," he continued, "give a good day's work. It is true that they put down their tools the very instant the dinner-bell rings, but they do not dawdle and prepare for that event half an hour before." Captain W. H. Henderson, R. N., for many years in command of H. M. S. *Nelson* in Australian waters, gave even stronger testimony to the same effect. "During the time I was out there I was brought into communication with every class of society, from statesmen to the shipping population. I have often had much to do with the lumpers—that is, the men who discharge cargoes, coal especially, and I have no hesitation in saying that they do their work better than in the old country, and will coal a ship three times as fast. (Pp. 295-297.)

What use does the working man of Victoria make of the leisure he has obtained through the eight-hours day? The "go" and energy he is said by so many observers to put into his work is itself good evidence that he does not spend his time in vicious dissipation. If a shorter day in the workshop meant only a longer evening in the tavern he could not possibly show such signs of invigoration, and his day's work and his day's wages would soon have hopelessly declined. The general opinion in Victoria is that the habits of working men have improved and not deteriorated through the short hours. By leaving work early in the afternoon they are enabled to live out in the suburbs in neat cottages with little gardens behind them, which are almost invariably owned by their occupiers, and they spend much of their leisure tending their little gardens or in some out-door sport or with their families. The first two effects of the Ten Hours Act in this country were the multiplication of mechanics' institutes, night schools, and popular lectures on the one hand, and the multiplication of garden allotments on the other. Workpeople had neither time nor energy for such pursuits before—the only resource of the languid is the tavern. But with a longer evening at their disposal, it became worth while devising other ways of enjoying it, and the favorite among the English factory hands seemed to be the mechanics' institute in winter and the garden allotment in summer. (Pp. 302-303.)

Report of the New York Bureau of Labor Statistics. 1900.

All travellers unite in testifying to the wonderful energy displayed in their work by the wage-earners of Australia. Such energy is a product not so much of the stimulating climate as the high standard of comfort made possible by the short working-day. Considerable evidence might be adduced in support of the following enthusiastic opinion of John Rae ("Eight Hours for Work," p. 312.)

"The more we examine the subject the more irresistibly is the impression borne in from all sides that there is growing up in Australia, and very largely in consequence of the eight-hour day, a working class who for general morale, intelligence, and industrial efficiency is probably already superior to that of any other branch of our Anglo-Saxon race, and for happiness, cheerfulness, and all-around comfort of life has never had its equal in the world before." (P. 59.)

New Zealand in Evolution. Guy H. Scholefield. *With an Introduction by the Hon. W. Pember Reeves, Director of the London School of Economics. London, T. Fisher Unwin, 1909.*

. . . The colonial worker, both in Australia and New Zealand, is not only more intelligent than his English brother, but he is out of comparison a more willing and energetic worker. The eight-hour day in the Antipodes is eight hours of strenuous labour. It is very rare to find works overmanned. Adequate wages are paid to a sufficient number of men to meet the requirements of the business by working energetically and at full power during the statutory day. There is no encouragement to work overtime. For the employers it means payment at increased rates: for the men a loss of that leisure for recreation and rest which is essential to continued efficiency. As a consequence the work in a colonial factory or engineering shop, while it lasts, is energetic, thorough, and efficient. The everyday complaint of artisans from the Old Country emigrating to the colonies is that the work is too hard: that they require all the residue from an eight-hours labour day to recuperate for the morrow. The colonial worker, too, is eminently sober. (P. 218.)

Report of the New Zealand Department of Labour. 1893.

The numerous mechanical inventions of our century have abolished the necessity for long hours of labour, while the growth of education among the labouring-classes intensifies their desire for hours of relaxation and culture, such as the illiterate workers of past generations could not have put to profitable use. (P. 4.)

Ibid. 1895.

The wages paid to factory-workers in the Australasian Colonies are justified by the economic result. The class of factory-hand on this side of the world is so much stronger and better in every way—in physique, intelligence and education—that the principle of high wages for superior work is established. I have been informed by an employer having large establishments in Great Britain and some in this colony, that the average rates paid by him to women workers in England is from 10s. to 15s. a week. The New Zealand branch of his firm pays its girls from £1 to £1 10s. a week, and can well afford to do so, because the superior strength and ability of the colonial hand allows a class of material to be committed to their charge which is never allowed to be touched by the employés in the Old Country. The manager of Messrs. Bell and Black's match factory tells the same story—that it pays to give colonial girls more in response to the more effective output of the individual. (P. 4.)

Ibid. 1900.

I beg to make the following suggestions as to alterations necessary for rendering the Factories Act more effective. . . .

(11) That no person of either sex should be allowed to work in factories or shops beyond stated hours without a minimum overtime wage. Men at present have the economic advantage of being able to work any hours they like. . . . The advantage, however, is only an apparent one to the male worker, for the employer's "request" for him to stay several hours in the evening has to be acceded to at cost of all hours of rest and recreation to the employe. If business is so pressing and so profitable (for it would not be undertaken without profit) that the assistants or work people have to give a day and a half's work instead of a day's, then it is profitable enough to pay for. If it is not, then there will be little overtime-work done, and the hands will get at least some time for themselves. (Pp. ii-iii.)

Some limit to the hours that men are allowed to work in shops should be fixed. Both for the sake of health and of social needs the time of a shop-assistant should not be wholly absorbed by work. . . . (P. iv.)

Ibid. 1903.

The general prosperity of New Zealand, steadily augmenting year by year, has reached a point in 1903 when even the most pessimistic and morbid of critics is compelled to acknowledge the progressive character of the colony's industrial and commercial enterprises. (P. i.)

The improved Factories Act of 1901 has quite justified the hopes formed concerning it when it first took its place on the statute-book. . . . (P. ii.)

I may add that in my opinion there is no reason for the long hours allowed in the present act as the weekly time of a shop-assistant. The better class of shops does not work its assistants more than an eight-hour day, except for one day in the week; and there is no good reason for a working week of fifty-two hours being considered the equivalent for forty-five hours in a factory. (P. iii.)

Ibid. 1904.

There is no diminution or retardation in the steadiness of New Zealand's economic advance. The year has been exceedingly prosperous for a very large majority of the workers. (P. i.)

Ibid. 1905.

Reviewing the position of the whole body of labour in the colony during the year just closed, it appears to be a highly satisfactory one. New Zealand has continued to expand its internal energies and augment its possessions. . . . An analysis of the imports would show a general purchasing-power not only of the necessaries of life, but of its luxuries, which betokens a very flourishing condition for the average colonist if compared with his expenditure of a few years ago. (P. i.)

Unskilled labour was in excellent demand throughout the period under review. In Christchurch the construction of electric tramways absorbed surplus labour, but the completion of similar tramways in Wellington set free a great many persons for whom work had to be provided. I may mention, in passing, that Mr. Kerwin, the constructing engineer of the Wellington electric tramways, when leaving for Europe, paid a high compliment to the Colonial working-men. He said on a public occasion that "before he came to New Zealand he had been made somewhat nervous by talk about advanced labour laws, and by warnings that he would find he was not driving niggers in the Southern States of the United States of America; but having constructed tramways in the Northern and Southern States, and in Glasgow and in England, he was never better pleased in his life. A great deal of this result had to do with the dignity and pride the working men in New Zealand possessed. Coming to this colony two months late, he finished the work six months ahead of contract time, and he could not have done this without good men, so he gave credit to New Zealand workers." (P. ii.)

Ibid. 1908.

The Industrial Conciliation and Arbitration Act. . . . Expectations were too highly raised at first as to what the result of the Act would be. It has performed everything which could be expected from a single legislative measure. It has raised wages generally to a small extent, but in some cases very considerably. It has shortened hours, given payment for overtime for holidays and for travelling, granted preference to unionists in a restricted way, and many other similar privileges and benefits. It steadied trade and business for many years till it brought prosperity to the employer and reflected prosperity to the employee through the continuity and permanence of work. (P. IX.)

Ibid. 1911.

As to the conditions of work—the pay, hours, and surroundings—they must be described as very satisfactory. The factory legislation of New Zealand is looked upon as safeguarding the interests of the workers to a greater extent than in any other part of the world. (P. VI.)

Ibid. 1912.

This year marks the attainment of the Department's majority. For exactly twenty-one years the Department has conducted its work, and it is fitting that at this juncture a short historical review of its organization and growth should be given. . . . Its chief work on establishment was to try to meet the unemployed difficulty. . . . Today this work is an important branch; but the duty of administering what are generally known as the "labour" laws has formed the chief responsibility of the Department. It is a matter of common knowledge that these laws have been added to or amended from year to year during the twenty-one years under review, and Acts thought to be merely experimental in the early years have been amended and improved, as experience appeared to warrant, until they are now mostly looked upon by the large majority of our citizens as essential for the smooth, effective, and peaceful working of our growing industries. Some of the laws have served as models for other countries to copy, and it is probable that in some respects our legislation is more humane and far-reaching than any yet adopted elsewhere. The Factories Act still stands as one of the best-appreciated measures by all classes, whilst the Workers' Compensation Act has been of benefit to hundreds of workers at a time when assistance is most urgently needed. The Shops and Offices Act, too, is also working smoothly, and, given some amendments, it should prove one of the most humane and beneficial Acts administered by the Department. (P. iii.)

In surveying the twenty-one years' history of the Department I look back upon a record of great and lasting work accomplished by the operation of the humanitarian laws administered by the Department, and the outstanding feature of all is the total abolition of "sweating" of the workers, and a recognition, hard-won perhaps, from both employers and workers that each has gained some mutual benefit by the operation of the labour laws of New Zealand. (P. iii.)

C. BENEFIT TO CITIZENSHIP.

1. Preparedness.

a. POLITICAL: THE CITIZEN AS VOTER.

The welfare and safety of democracy rests upon the character and intelligence of its citizens. For the exercise of the elective franchise is determined by the mental and moral equipment of the voters. Under the conditions of modern industry, for the development of morals and intelligence, leisure is needed. Hence leisure is a prime requisite for good citizenship.

If a democracy is to flourish, the education of the citizen must not end at the 14th birthday, when wage-earning ordinarily begins. It must be a continuous process, to enable men to understand great issues as they arise, to discuss them and reach decisions upon them.

In the interest of the state, therefore, industrial labor must be limited: first, so that leisure may be provided outside of working hours; second, so that the worker shall not be too much exhausted to make use of his leisure.

Massachusetts House Document, No. 44, 1867. Report of Commissioners on the Hours of Labor.

It is certain that men may labor so severely and incessantly, as in the long run to impair the vital energies, and thus reduce the powers of production; and it may be further true, that too great an amount of toil may not only injure the physical powers, but depress or impair the mental faculties, so that in this way the productive capacity of a people may be greatly lessened. And still further, not only the physical and mental, but the moral nature of man may be imbruted by severe and unreasonably protracted toil. All this being apparent, the question of the hours that should constitute a day's labor, is one deserving of a careful and candid examination. The great point to be aimed at in the culture of a people, is to secure the highest production of wealth, consistent with preserving intact all the natural powers of the laborer, and advancing his best and highest interests, his full and complete manhood. (Pp. 22-23.) . . .

The desirableness and even the necessity for leisure, however, increases with the increase of the responsibilities of the citizen. A laborer in the United States needs more leisure, or relief from toil, than one in the same position in Europe, because he has the elective franchise, and is a part of the government. If he is deficient in intellectual training and moral culture, the State will suffer. The American laborer must not only take care of himself, but discharge his civil duties and fulfill his obligations to the interests of religion and morality. This responsibility involves the necessity of intelligence and culture, and these require leisure and opportunity. It is not enough that the laborer have education in childhood; he must have the means of constant improvement and progress in manhood. He must not only know something of the past, but be familiar with the events of the present. New ideas, new discoveries, new issues are made from day to day, and the laborer must have the means of knowing what these are. All this requires time, and not only time, but rest from toil in such a condition that the mind can engage with its full strength in intellectual pursuits. Hence it follows that the hours devoted to labor should not be so extended as not to leave sufficient time and strength to engage in those pursuits which will qualify the laborer for the discharge of his duties to himself, his family, and his government. Great social movements are in continual progress—these, the American laborer ought not only to be cognizant of, but take a part in; yet whether he shall do so efficiently and intelligently or not, must clearly depend upon two conditions: first, that he has the necessary leisure; and secondly, that he improves that leisure for the desired purpose. The mechanics of Massachusetts, as an almost universal fact, work ten hours per day. If we allow two hours for the three meals of the day, and eight hours for sleep, we have still four hours left. Are these sufficient? and if so, is the laborer after ten hours of continuous toil, in a condition of mind and body adapted to the profitable improvement of these hours? (Pp. 23-24.)

Report of the Committee of Stockholders of the United States Steel Corporation. April 15, 1912.

To ascertain the number of employees of the Steel Corporation working on a twelve-hour schedule (exclusive of officers, managers and clerical forces), we have examined the records of 175,715 men. Of this number we find 45,248, or 25¾ per cent., are at present working twelve hours per day. . . . The actual physical labor involved in many of the positions is, to-day, much less than in former years, this being especially true of the open hearth and blast furnaces, where the intermittent character of the work is such that there is less call for actual expenditure of physical energy than in many of the eight and ten hour positions.

Notwithstanding this fact, we are of the opinion that a twelve-hour day of labor, followed continuously by any group of men for any considerable number of years, means a decreasing of the efficiency and lessening of the vigor and virility of such men.

The question should be considered from a social as well as a physical point of view. When it is remembered that the twelve hours a day to the man in the mills means approximately thirteen hours away from his home and family—not for one day, but for all working days—it leaves but scant time for self-improvement, for companionship with his family, for recreation and leisure. It is important that any industry be considered in its relation to the home life of those engaged in it, as to whether it tends to weaken or strengthen the normalness and stability of family life. By a reasonable conserving of the strength of the working population of to-day may we be best assured of a healthy, intelligent productive citizenship in the future. (Survey. Vol. 28. Pp. 252-253.)

Benefit to Citizenship.—United States

From "The Pennsylvanian." At time of Ten-Hour Law passed by City of Philadelphia. Quoted from Proceedings of the Government and Citizens of Philadelphia on the Reduction of the Hours of Labor and Increase of Wages. July, 1835.

Politically, it is of immense importance that a change should be effected. Our institutions place all power in the hands of the very men who are now in a great measure debarred from mental improvement, and shut out from that cultivation which alone can render them capable of wielding their tremendous strength to the advantage of our common country. (P. 7.)

A Documentary History of American Industrial Society. Edited by John R. Commons, Ulrich B. Phillips, Eugene A. Gilmore, Helen L. Summer *and* John B. Andrews. *Vol. VIII. Labor Movement. Cleveland, The Arthur H. Clark Company, 1910. "New York Weekly Tribune," Oct. 16, 1847.*

It concerns us all that our laboring people, the young especially, have opportunity for improving their minds, making themselves acquainted with the events and the ideas of our time, so as to be qualified for discharging faithfully their duties as freemen, citizens, electors, or the mothers of such. Excessive toil, especially in youth, unfits us for some of the most important duties and relations of life. If, therefore, a whole community grossly ignorant of the laws of life and health could be tempted by high wages or driven by want into working fifteen to eighteen hours per day, it would be wrong in the State to allow and right to forbid so destructive a course. (P. 198.)

The Normal Workday of Eight Hours. Memorial of the Central Committee of the Furniture Workers' Union of North America. New York, 1879. Letter of forty-six Furniture Manufacturers of Chicago to the Manufacturers of Furniture of the United States.

The American nation can glory of many achievements, but look at the steady decline of the integrity and honor of our officials, high and low! See how our free institutions are fast running to destruction! How the marrow of our nation's life is eaten up by the cancer of corruption! Should we not lend our helping hand to better this? It certainly is our plain duty, our duty as citizens of this Republic!

But how? By introducing "eight hours as a day's labor!" Thereby our workingmen will find time to keep and read their daily papers; they will learn to form their own ideas concerning the questions of the day, and no demagogue will then so easily mislead them in the movements of a political or social nature by appealing to their passions. They also would gain time to educate their children more properly, and thereby do their share in the great problem of popular education. Verily! little could be expected in this respect of a workingman who was or is compelled to leave his home with the dawn of early morning to return only after nightfall! . . .

In the name of humanity, and as our small contribution to the political and moral regeneration of our American nation, let us then offer to our workingmen what belongs to them by right, and what will, at the same time, prove to be beneficial to ourselves. (P. 7.)

The Economic and Social Importance of the Eight-Hour Movement. George Gunton. *New York, American Federation of Labor, 1889.*

The fact that the general reduction of the hours of labor would, as experience and reason show, be an economic advantage to all classes, to say nothing of its educational and moral effects upon the masses, is amply sufficient to warrant the demand for its immediate adoption. But the social and political necessity for it is more imperative than its more sanguine friends have hitherto realized, or its opponents have yet been able to understand. It is a universal law in society that all social and political institutions are finally based upon the character of the people. Restrictive laws are never made to govern the most moral and orderly, but always the most immoral and disorderly elements in society. The cultured classes are thus compelled to endure the legal restrictions that are necessary to control the uncultured; therefore, the social safety, prosperity and freedom of the rich can only be permanently secured as the poverty, ignorance and barbarism of the masses are diminished and the opportunities for their social culture are increased. It is a universal fact in civilization that all forms of despotism move inversely with wages, increasing as wages fall, and decreasing as wages rise. Since the use of improved machinery and specialization of labor tend to increase the physical and nervous exhaustion of the laborer, unless the working time is correspondingly reduced, the laborer's susceptibility to the refining and elevating influences of his social environment is lessened, and his leisure moments find him dull and indifferent to all moral and political influences.

The inevitable tendency of these conditions is to cause the laborer to gravitate toward the saloon rather than toward the reading room, lecture hall, museum and theatre for his instruction and entertainment. Persons who have to be subject to long hours of continued toil from childhood, amid the foul air of mines, and the sweltering heat and stifling atmosphere of the mills and factories for a bare existence cannot be expected to develop the ambition and force of character necessary to inspire and elevate their domestic and social relations. . . .

The tendency of the modern industrial policy to thus limit the social opportunity of the masses is necessarily inimical to progress; but in no country is its evil influence so dangerous as in this. (1) Because the social character of a large proportion of our laboring population is mainly determined by a lower civilization. (2) Because the political machinery of the government is more directly in the hands of the masses than in any other country. (Pp. 21 and 22.)

Report of the New York Bureau of Labor Statistics, 1900.

A little reflection upon these statements will convince an unprejudiced mind of the real advantages possessed in the long run by the shorter working day. Health and vigor are of primary importance to any body of workers, and whatever policy will promote the health of the community will in the long run prove the best policy, even if its adoption may temporarily cut down profits. The Massachusetts cotton industry affords an excellent example of the wisdom of this policy, notwithstanding the dissatisfaction of a part of the employing classes. For as a result of Massachusetts labor legislation and the competition of Southern factories, Massachusetts factory owners have been obliged to seek the latest inventions and improved processes, to produce finer and more attractive goods. . . . This has of course called for more and more skill on the part of Massachusetts operatives and has led to the establishment of textile schools. The grand result is that Massachusetts has a body of workmen who have leisure to appreciate the public libraries scattered throughout the State; to perfect their technical training as well as to acquire that degree of culture and knowledge which makes an intelligent citizenship and to discharge the duties imposed by that citizenship. (Pp. 67-68.)

Industrial Conference under the Auspices of the National Civic Federation. New York, 1902. The Eight Hour Day. Professor George Gunton, *Institute of Social Economics. Lecture Bulletin. Vol. VI. No. 7.*

The laborer's importance now is, I repeat, as a consumer. That means as a social factor, not as a physical force. This fact recognized, the important question that presents itself is how to expand the laborer as a consumer.

In another phase of the matter, it has now become true that our societary institutions depend on the laborer's growth as a citizen. Civilization is practically in the laborer's hands. Whether we shall have this form of government or that, whether we shall have democracy or despotism, whether we shall have intelligent and honest government or corruption and jobbery; whether we shall have political cleanliness or merely party demagogy as the moving force in our public policy, depends upon the intelligence and social character of the masses. It does not depend any longer upon the opinions of the well-to-do. It depends upon convincing the masses of the wisdom of this or that policy. Now, their capacity for intelligent conceptions and convictions, the understanding of the influence of this or that public policy, depends upon social development. It depends upon the growth of character, the capacity for forming and having intelligent opinions upon public affairs.

This requires, just as any other development requires, opportunity; . . . In this country the opportunity for growth in these two lines, as consumers and citizens, requires first of all release from the excessive pressure upon the nervous and physical energies that the factory system has developed. Opportunity now means leisure, more time for touch with the educational, socializing and civilizing elements in society. (P. 128.)

The Social Unrest. John Graham Brooks. *New York and London, The Macmillan Company, 1903.*

Whenever machinery cannot be used except in conditions that brutalize life, we call it an evil, even if a necessary one. If the speed is so great that the average man or woman cannot stand the strain beyond a half of one's natural life, it is an evil, and an evil far beyond its effect on the individual, for it strikes at parenthood, producing a devitalized offspring that constitutes the chief horror of many industrial centres. (P. 186.)

We are half enslaved by a great deal of our own mechanism. It means that we honestly care more for the machine's output in wealth than we care for manhood, womanhood, and wholesome family life. It means that we do not first and profoundly care for citizenship and a reputable society. If these workers can keep their animal strength and tend the machine, is it not enough? The absolute requisitions of culture of any kind—a minimum of unexhausted leisure, of real freshness of body and mind—would take at least two hours off every working day. It affronts our intelligence to say that the average man can do that kind of work more than eight hours daily, and have left over the leisure, the moral and intellectual surplus of energy, for humanizing objects. The loss to good citizenship, to social peace and safety, is an abiding threat to social peace. If we were not the easy victims of wont and usage, accepting the actual as natural, we should one and all revolt against this awful waste of human values. That the future will class it as a form of slavery, seems to me assured. (Pp. 187-188.)

American Journal of Sociology. Vol. 8. 1903. The Social Effects of the Eight-Hour Day. Frank L. McVey. *University of Minnesota.*

The wear and tear upon human life steadily increases under modern methods of production. This is the third reason urged for the adoption of the eight-hour day. If men are to stand as heads of families, as electors, and even as operators of machines, they must have time for rest, for education, and for family life. The responsibility of government increasingly falls upon the working classes in a democracy. Shorter hours of labor alone can give the worker the leisure for careful study of the present-day problems thrust more and more upon the electorate for decision. (P. 523.)

Not, then, as a means of employing the "reserve army of industry" as the unemployed are sometimes called, is the eight-hour day to be advocated, but rather as a means of giving to men a wider interest in life, the possibility of greater culture and the surety of education commensurate with the problems now forced upon our democracy for solution. It is not, then, as a private measure that this movement is acceptable, but as a public necessity. (P. 526.)

Some Ethical Gains Through Legislation. FLORENCE KELLEY, *General Secretary of the National Consumers' League. New York and London, Macmillan, 1905.*

Obviously the characteristic feature of the industrial life of the nineteenth century was the unprecedented increase in the output of all branches of production. . . . The fundamental ethical question of the century was, in essence, the equitable distribution of these newly acquired possessions of the human race.

More precious, perhaps, than any of those enumerated is the immaterial, imponderable human by-product—leisure. . . .

Assured daily leisure is an essential element of healthy living. Without it childhood is blighted, perverted, deformed; manhood becomes ignoble and unworthy of citizenship in the Republic. Self-help and self-education among the wage-earners are as dependent upon daily leisure as upon daily work. Excessive fatigue precludes the possibility of well-conducted meetings of classes, lodges, co-operative societies and all other forms of organized effort for self-improvement. No experience of residents in settlements in the congested districts of the great cities is sadder than the disorganization which befalls their evening clubs and classes when Christmas approaches and the ablest young people are detained for overtime work, the study and effort of the other members is disorganized, and failure of the whole undertaking often follows. . . .

As machinery becomes increasingly automatic, and the work of the machine-tender reduces itself more completely to watching intently the wholly monotonous performance of the one part confided to his care, leisure becomes indispensable for him in order to counteract the deadening effect upon his mind exercised by his daily work. Instead of educating the worker, the breadwinning task of to-day too often stupefies and deforms the mind; and leisure is required to undo the damage wrought in the working-hours, if the worker is to remain fit for citizenship in the Republic. Without regular, organized leisure, there can be no sustained intelligence in the voting constituency. . . .

In those occupations in which long hours of work prevail, the employees are obliged to live near their place of work, and that congestion is thus intensified, which is one of the more unfortunate features of life in large manufacturing cities. Shortening the hours of labor gives to working people a wider range of selection in the location of their homes, thus benefiting wives and children as well as the operatives themselves. (Pp. 107-109.)

It may be fairly claimed, then, that the establishment of regular daily leisure contributes to the health, intelligence, morality, lengthened trade life, freer choice of home surroundings, thrift, self-help and family life of working people. Granted that not all workers make equally valuable use of free time, just as members of the leisure class vary in the uses to which they apply their leisure, it remains true that, without free time, these benefits are impossible. To be deprived of leisure is to be deprived of those things which make life worth living. (P. 111.)

The Survey. Jan. 21, 1910. Hours in the Continuous Industries. THOMAS SCHLYTTER. (*Match Manufacturer, Norwegian Association for Labor Legislation.*)

Human beings are not intended to be mere machines to work, and eat, and sleep.

Reform in this direction is important not only for the sake of the happiness of the men involved, but so that it may be possible for everybody to reach a certain standard of intelligent citizenship for the sake of his country, the destiny of which everyone influences for good or for ill. (P. 680.)

United States Congress. Senate Report No. 601. Hours of Daily Service of Laborers and Mechanics Upon Government Contracts. Report by Mr. Borah *from the Committee on Education and Labor. Sixty-second Congress, Second Session, 1912.*

According to the dividends paid, as shown by the reports of the United States Steel Co., there was certainly little reason for this exacting service. Every right-thinking American citizen must take pride in the prosperity and the success of our business concerns, as their prosperity is indispensable to the success and the prosperity of the people generally. But when such enormous wealth is amassed, partly, at least, through such a cruel and brutal system of industrial slavery this government is bound in its own defense, for its citizenship is its life, to interpose between the strong and the weak and exert its influence both moral and legal to rescue its citizenship from such conditions. No man can meet the obligations and discharge the duties of citizenship in a free government who is broken in spirit and racked in body through such industrial peonage. Even in the strength of his early manhood he has not the opportunity or time to prepare himself for the duties of citizenship, and before he has reached the prime of life under such conditions, sodden in mind and broken in health, he is cast off as a useless hulk—a burden and a curse to society and a menace to the Government. It is just as much the duty of the Government, when it can do so, to protect its citizens from such outrageous treatment as it is to protect a citizen from the burglar or the highwayman. Everyone knows and everyone is willing to discuss what the duty and obligations of the citizens are toward the Government. But one of the propositions which can no longer be postponed in this country is: What is the duty of the Government toward the citizen? If these laws regulating the hours of labor come, therefore, they come not simply because laboring men ask for them; they come because conditions in the industrial world make it impossible to ignore that request. (P. 7.)

The Survey. Oct. 7, 1911. The Human Side of Large Outputs. Steel and Steel Workers in Six American Cities. I. Lackawanna—Swamp, Mill and Town. JOHN A. FITCH.

Another Lackawanna man, summed up what many steel workers, all over the country have told me when he said, "I don't take any pleasure in my work, nor the other men don't either. If we had eight hours it would be a great job, with lots of excitement, one that I'd want to get back to. But the way it is now, twelve hours a day and sometimes seven days a week, I don't get any pleasure out of the job or out of life."

It is the effect of this working schedule upon everyday life that is most important. The twelve-hour day and seven-day week are . . . effectual barriers against healthy social growth and good citizenship. (Pp. 939-940.)

Constitutional Amendments Relating to Labor Legislation and Brief in Their Defense. Submitted to the Constitutional Convention of New York State by a Committee Organized by the American Association for Labor Legislation. June 9, 1915.

The Effect on Society of Unregulated Conditions.

Excessive hours of labor, such as a 12-hour day even if for six days in the week instead of seven, can have no other effect ultimately than a breakdown of physical and moral qualities, and consequently a destruction of healthy citizenship. (P. 18.)

The Eight Hours Day. SIDNEY WEBB *and* HAROLD COX, B. A. *London, Walter Scott, 1891.*

The case of an eight hours day on account of physical health is thus extremely strong. Even stronger is the case for rest from work for the sake of mental health. . . . If the workers were actually chattel slaves these things would be of little consequence. Make your helots drunk and they will be less likely to rebel. But our helots are citizens and voters. On them, ultimately, if they choose to exert the power, rests the determination of the whole policy of the community. It is surely not wise that a large percentage of those potential despots should be incapable of forming an opinion on the questions committed to their decision.

Nor is it wise that a large proportion of the fathers and mothers in the country should not have leisure properly to discharge the responsibilities of fatherhood and motherhood. Anti-Socialists are for ever denouncing the growing interference of the State between child and parent. But that interference is necessitated because many parents literally have not time to look after their children with proper care. (Pp. 145-146.)

The governing influence in the nation has virtually asked every man in the kingdom to share in the work of government. Whether wise or foolish, the step has been taken, and cannot be recalled. But are the men who have thus been called to rule capable of understanding the task set before them? Undoubtedly a very large number are not capable, and under present industrial conditions cannot possibly become so. Their whole lives are spent in an unending round of work, broken only by a few intervals for feeding and sleeping, and an occasional outburst of drinking. Such men cannot be competent judges of any of the complicated questions that Parliament has to decide. And yet at an election the vote of a man who rolls from the beer-shop to ballot-box counts as much as that of the elector who has taken every pains to form a conscientious opinion on the point at issue. The remedy is not to restrict the suffrage, but to increase the intelligence of the electorate. That can only be done by giving more daily leisure to the bulk of the voters. An Eight Hours Day will for the first time put into the hands of thousands of working men an opportunity of becoming competent for the duties of citizenship. (P. 151.)

National Conference on the Prevention of Destitution. 1912. Papers and Proceedings, London, King, 1912. The Limitation of Hours from the International Point of View. SOPHY SANGER.

It would appear only reasonable that Governments, of whatever party, should be anxiously desirous of giving the great mass of working-class electors the necessary leisure for understanding the very complicated political and social problems on which they are expected indirectly to vote. Each party believing itself right, must necessarily desire greater intelligence on the part of the working man, so that he may be able to see the falsity of the doctrines of other parties. Humane people, too, of whatever party politically, are concerned for the happiness of overworked industrial toilers. But in spite of this, and in spite of the fact that experience has shown how greatly the behavior, as regards sobriety, punctuality, regularity, etc., of the men improves when hours are reduced to reasonable limits, we find the economic objections of the employing class outweighing all others. (P. 459.)

National Conference on the Prevention of Destitution. 1912. Papers and Proceedings. London, King, 1912. The Reduction of the Hours of Work and the Limitation of Overtime. Discussion. MR. H. BARRASS. (*Edmonton Urban District Council.*)

The Eight-hours' system had given him the opportunity of taking an interest in public life, and had enabled him to sit on the Urban District Council of his district. He would not have been able to do that if he had continued working under the nine-hours system. It had also enabled him to become a member of the Middlesex County Council. The officials and the Government had come to realize that it was necessary for workmen, even if they had to lose time, to become members of those bodies. At one time they were not allowed to lose time in the day to attend those bodies, but owing to different men becoming members of the Urban District Council an order was issued that if any man was sitting on any Local Authority he would be allowed time to attend their meetings provided that he was prepared to lose that time. After he had served on the Urban District Council, the workmen had thought that he ought to go a step further, and they elected him on to the Middlesex County Council, and he applied for four and a half hours in each week to attend to the duties. That application was granted, although, of course, at his own loss of time. Therefore, the eight-hours' system, if it could be brought about,—not that he believed it would solve the problem of the unemployed, because they knew it would not—would brighten the lives of the workers, and would give them more opportunity for studying and working for the emancipation of themselves and to bring about better conditions and brighter lives. (P. 463.)

Conditions in British Iron and Steel Works. A Speech delivered to the Special Commission on Hours of Labour, International Association for Labour Legislation, June 11th, 1912. Alderman P. Walls, J. P.

When the question of eight hours was first raised, it was argued that, if a man got shorter hours, it would only mean more time for drinking, but the effect has been exactly the opposite. We have had the eight-hour shift over twenty-one years in one district in the North of England, and over fourteen years in another, and the moral effect is marvelous. The men take an interest in social and economic problems, and are now citizens in every sense of the term. They are in their allotment gardens, out with the wives and children for a walk, or out on their bicycles.

Rational Hours of Work. I. The Case for Reduction. Shorter Hours and Greater Efficiency. A. H. CROSFIELD. *Reprinted from the "Manchester Guardian," June 27th, 1913.*

From the mental point of view, what interest can a man exhausted by these long hours and this excessive strain be expected to take in study, culture, public life, and so forth? It is to be noticed that the conversation of men who become in this way mere working machines tends to turn with weary repetition entirely upon the monotonous details of daily routine. As for morality, can anyone doubt the inevitably brutalising effects of such conditions? Many men no doubt succeed, even under these harsh and trying circumstances, in maintaining the dignity and credit of British citizens. But is it any wonder that others too often prove unable to resist such demoralising influences, sinking back into sensuality and drunkenness as the only kind of change and respite from a life of toil which they are capable of enjoying? (P. 6.)

The Case for the National Minimum. With Preface by MRS. SIDNEY WEBB. *London, National Committee for the Prevention of Destitution, 1913.*

Lowering the Standard of Citizenship.—But the evil results of excessively long hours of labour do not cease with their depredations on the national health and the national purse. The members of a modern state require a constantly rising standard of mental efficiency to perform the duties of citizenship. At the National Conference on the Prevention of Destitution in June, 1912, the workers' representatives repeatedly emphasized this point. Vast numbers of citizens are disfranchised by their long hours of labour preventing the record of their votes. The value of the votes actually given is diminished by the absence of leisure to take an interest in the measures whose fortunes they decide. In such matters as Trade Unionism, Co-operation, and Friendly Societies, active participation is difficult or impossible to masses of workers owing to the length of their working hours. In the important sphere of local government, where representative workers are in such demand, the path is closed to all who are still actively working at their trades, save where shorter hours have afforded the necessary opportunity. (P. 18.)

Work and Wealth: A Human Valuation. J. A. Hobson. *New York, The Macmillan Company, 1914.*

More leisure is a prime essential of democratic government. There can be no really operative system of popular self-government so long as the bulk of the people do not possess the spare time and energy to equip themselves for effective participation in politics and to take a regular part in deliberative and administrative work. This is equally applicable to other modes of corporate activity, the life of the churches, friendly societies, trade unions, co-operative societies, clubs, musical and educational associations, which go to make up the social life and institutions of a country. Leisure, demanded primarily in the interests of the individual for his personal enjoyment, will thus yield rich nutriment to the organic life of society, because the individual will find himself drawn by the social needs and desires embedded in his personality to devote portions of his leisure to social activities which contribute to the commonwealth as surely as do the economic tasks imposed upon him in his daily industry. (Pp. 248-249.)

b. SOCIAL: AMERICANIZATION OF THE FOREIGN-BORN.

In 1910 thirteen million Americans over 10 years of age were foreign-born. Almost three millions, or one in every four, could not speak English. There were between six and seven million foreign-born white males over 21 years of age, of whom more than half (55%) were not naturalized.

Between 1911 and 1914 the additional immigration aggregated about three millions. A large proportion of these millions are employed in industry, especially in the great manufacturing establishments, such as the iron and steel mills, munition plants, textile factories, etc.

Throughout the country there is increasing recognition that the prime necessity for the immigrant is Americanization, that is, opportunity for acquiring the ability to speak and read the English language, and to become acquainted with American institutions.

Americanization is the paramount need not alone for the immigrant but for the very existence of the Republic. Unless the millions of immigrants present and future are made an integral part of the population, understanding our institutions, sharing the standards and ideals of the democracy, the nation itself is imperilled.

No man can become a naturalized citizen unless he can speak English. Learning English is therefore the key to citizenship. It is indispensable for the adoption of American standards of living; for a participation in the life of the community. Ignorance of the English language is the greatest obstacle to industrial advancement. It prevents the distribution of congested immigrant populations. It increases the dangers of industrial accidents, injuries and occupational diseases, owing to the immigrants' inability to understand orders or hygienic regulations printed or orally given in industrial establishments.

The growing recognition of the need of Americanization has resulted in a country-wide movement to provide evening schools to teach English and give special instruction on American institutions. Federal, state and city authorities are urging increased appropriations for these special facilities.

Obviously this whole program of Americanization is impossible unless sufficient leisure is provided *after working hours* to enable the workers to take advantage of the opportunities offered.

The task of teaching adult foreigners a new language is rendered almost hopeless unless they can come to be taught with some freshness of mind. The project of Americanization is defeated when working hours are so long that no evening leisure is left or the immigrant workers are too much exhausted to make use of it.

New York State Department of Labor. Report of the Commissioner of Labor. Third Annual Report of the Bureau of Industries and Immigration. 1913.

General Problems.—The importance of providing for the welfare of our alien residents, for their own protection and health and for their intelligent and normal assimilation cannot be overestimated. Over 2,700,000 persons, or nearly 30 per cent. of our total population, are foreign born whites. Over 700,000 of the male residents of voting age are unnaturalized. In the last decade nearly 840,000 *new* immigrants have settled in this State. The dormant power for future good or evil of this addition to our population is enormous. Only in so far as these prospective citizens receive protection in the early stages of assimilation, will they respect our laws and form of government when later the duties, powers and obligations of citizenship are conferred upon them. Credulous, simple-minded and impressionistic, their open, plastic minds are permanently affected by their early trials and tribulations. Their regard for our laws, their understanding of the keynote of our nation that "all men are created free and equal" and their desire to live according to their own standards of living, will depend, to a large degree, on the helping hand the State can give them on the rough road they must first travel. To this vast internal problem of adjustment should be added the fact that in 1912 over 750,000 aliens passed through the Port of New York in going to or coming from other States. (P. 4.)

Education of the Immigrant.—The educational needs of the immigrant require special study and attention. Only through his early familiarity with the English language and a knowledge of our ideals of government can he be properly assimilated. In a survey of educational work bearing on the assimilation of adult aliens, the North American Civic League, with the co-operation of the Bureau, found that night schools where English was taught to foreigners were maintained last year in thirty-one cities and towns. The attendance at such English to Foreigners' classes for New York City was 14,334 and for the rest of the State 6,660, making a total of 25,000 for the entire State. Approximately 300,000 adult immigrants entered the State during the same period of time, so that only one in every twelve was entered in these English night classes. Nineteen cities in the State . . . with a population ranging from 10,000 to 30,000 and with a foreign born population varying from 1,000 to 7,000 are without any public night classes where immigrants can acquire the ability to speak the English language. Seventeen other cities and towns with populations varying from 2,500 to 10,000 and foreign born populations in excess of 1,000 also lack any night school facilities. . . .

In the thirty-one cities and towns throughout the State where the local school authorities maintain evening classes in English to foreigners, the average length of the session is 60 nights for the year. . . . Evening schools are generally maintained from October to March, which is the period of lightest immigration and the busiest months for general factory work. During the spring and summer, when the hours of work in cities and towns are shortest and immigration is usually heaviest, the evening schools are generally closed. As a result, the sessions do not approximate the heaviest periods of immigration. . . .

The immigrant should receive special instruction to meet his peculiar needs and limitations. Through the study of English and civics his interest in our form of government will be developed and he will be prepared for thorough assimilation. The Bureau can aid by keeping him in constant touch with all the State's sources of information, education, enlightenment and healthy enjoyment. (Pp. 68-69.)

Massachusetts Senate Documents. No. 1. 1874. Address of Governor William B. Washburn to the Two Branches of the Legislature, January 2, 1874.

Furthermore, the large majority of operatives in many of our mills are of foreign birth. What is to be done with them? How are we to protect ourselves from the ignorance that is generally their misfortune rather than their fault? How are we to educate them into unity of aspiration and purpose with native-born citizens? Shall we work them so many hours a day that they will have neither strength, interest, nor time, for becoming acquainted with our institutions or our aims as a people? Or shall we, by shortening their hours of labor, and the establishment of evening schools, if need be, educate them, fit them for the duties of citizenship, and make them a part of ourselves? Unless something of this sort is done, while the census returns may show accumulation and enlargement, there can be no increase of living power. If we are to have in the future a healthful growth of the body politic, all these different elements of population must be blended into one harmonious whole. This will be a work of time and patience, I very well know, but we cannot go on indefinitely without some broader and deeper consideration than we have yet given, as a community, to the well-being of those among us from foreign parts. (Pp. 34-35.)

Massachusetts House Documents. No. 2300. 1914. Report of the Commission on Immigration on the Problem of Immigration in Massachusetts.

The problem of immigration presents two fundamental considerations—the welfare of the State and the welfare of the immigrant. While that of the State is unquestionably paramount, the welfare and destiny of both are linked inseparably. Throughout its investigations and its report the attention of this commission has necessarily been focussed on the immigrant, but the nature of its investigations as well as its recommendations have been determined primarily by the interest of the State.

The State being made up of individual units, it is the moral, intellectual and physical stamina of these units that determine its character and stability. Therefore the healthful development of these units is of supreme importance to the preservation of the Commonwealth. The State must, at whatever cost, prevent the lowering of its moral, mental and physical standards,—the inevitable result of overwork, underpay, unregulated housing in overcrowded tenements. By provision and enforcement of an adequate plan of education it must dispel the ignorance which begets prejudice, makes the uninformed the victims of reckless agitation, and substitutes violence for constitutional methods of securing redress. If the State is unwilling to meet the cost of thus safeguarding its own interests by promoting the welfare of its immigrant population, then it is not difficult to forecast the overthrow of those democratic institutions which are the result of patient, persistent struggle, century after century, by countless thousands, who have devoted life and fortune to the achievement of liberty under the law. (Pp. 13-14.)

Education.

Education is and must always be a most important factor in the solution of the many difficulties and misunderstandings that come with a highly complex population. . . . For the most part, only through special instruction in the evening schools can the adult immigrant be given the opportunity to learn English, to supplement his inadequate training and to prepare for naturalization.

Knowledge of English a First Requisite.

To speak English and to understand it is the vital need of the immigrant. Self-protection requires this; social safety demands it; without it assimilation is impossible; upon it depends the realization of the obligations, privileges and rights of American citizenship. . . . To the diffusion of this knowledge the Commonwealth should address itself with promptness and energy. The arrival of from 70,000 to 100,000 newcomers each year, most of whom are unable to speak English, and consequently—if neglected or ignored—are subject to the abuses, the misdirection, the prejudices of exploiters and irresponsible agitators—cannot but strain the social fabric to the breaking point. (P. 114.)

The following table, compiled from the United States Census reports, shows the number unable to read and write in any language. These figures are based not on tests given by the census enumerations, but on the statement of the people themselves as to whether they were able to read and write. It may therefore be assumed that the census figures understate rather than overstate the numbers.

Table 15.—Number and Per Cent. of Persons in Massachusetts Fifteen Years of Age and Over Unable to Read and Write in Any Language in 1910, 1900 and 1890.

	Number of Persons Fifteen Years of Age and Over Unable to Read and Write.			Per Cent. Unable to Read and Write of Total Population Fifteen Years of Age and Over.		
	1910	1900	1890	1910	1900	1890
All classes	140,844	132,501	112,877	5.7	6.5	6.9
Native white of native parentage	3,302	3,759	4,052	.4	.5	.5
Native white of foreign or mixed parentage	5,523	6,523	5,107	.9	1.3	1.6
Foreign-born white	129,064	118,527	100,733	13.0	15.1	16.9

According to these figures the per cent. of those unable to read and write has decreased among both the native and the foreign-born, but there has been an absolute increase from 132,501 unable to read and write in 1900 to 140,844 in 1910, for which the foreign-born are entirely responsible. Ignorance of English on the part of an increasingly large proportion of the foreign-born has made this whole problem of illiteracy a much more serious one, so that the fact that the number of foreign-born whites in Massachusetts unable to speak the English language increased from 24 per 1,000 population in 1890 to 27 per 1,000 in 1900, and 51 per 1,000 in 1910, is of special significance.

How many have been added to this non-English speaking group since 1910 can be estimated from the annual reports of the United States Commissioner of Immigration. Of the immigrants who arrived during the year ending June 30, 1911, and gave Massachusetts as their destination, 53,635 belonged to the non-English speaking races; during the next year the number was slightly larger,—54,964—while in the year ending June 30, 1913, 85,347 who belonged to the non-English speaking races came to Massachusetts. According to these figures, 193,946 immigrants of non-English speaking races have come to the State since 1910, when there were, according to the census, 171,014 foreign-born white persons ten years of age and over unable to speak English. How rapidly this number of people, very few of whom knew English on their arrival, will acquire the language cannot be predicted. The investigations of the commission showed that of 1,224 immigrants from whom personal history schedules were secured, 504, or 41 per cent., had learned to speak English, while of those who had been here less than three years only 14.8 per cent. were able to do this. . . .

During the school year 1910-1911, when the report of the United States Census and the report of the Commissioner-General of Immigration showed more than 224,000 non-English speaking persons in Massachusetts, the annual per capita expenditure for their education was less than $1. With this wholly inadequate expenditure, 60,785 were enrolled in the evening schools, and the actual average attendance was 25,483. Of this pitifully inadequate enrolment about one-third were in the evening high school and industrial classes, so that, when approximately 224,000 represented the number of non-English speaking persons in Massachusetts, the total enrolment in the elementary evening classes was less than 45,000, and the average attendance about 17,000.

During the year 1912-1913, of the 85,317 additional non-English speaking immigrants who came to Massachusetts, approximately 64,456 were over fourteen years of age. During that year the increase in the evening school enrolment was only 1,454, and the utterly inadequate expenditure of the previous year was decreased. (Pp. 118-121.)

Report of the Commission of Immigration of the State of New Jersey, 1914.

Of the States receiving the largest number of newly-arrived immigrants each year, New Jersey ranks fifth; those receiving larger numbers being New York, Pennsylvania, Massachusetts and Illinois. About five per cent. of the total immigration is destined to this State, although New Jersey in point of area ranks among the smaller States. . . .

New Jersey also ranks fifth in the number of foreign-born whites at present residing in the State, New York, Pennsylvania, Massachusetts and Illinois having respectively a larger foreign-born population. Rhode Island leads the list of those States having the largest percentage of foreign-born residents, its foreign-born population being 32.8 per cent. of its total population, while New Jersey is fifth in rank with a foreign population of 26 per cent. . . . (P. 12.)

Passaic with 28,467 foreign-born whites, representing 52 per cent. of its total population, has the largest proportion of foreign-born whites of all the principal cities of the United States. Lawrence, Massachusetts, has the second largest proportion with 48.1 per cent.; Perth Amboy is third with 44.5 per cent. Throughout the entire United States there are only twelve cities in which the foreign-born whites constitute more than 40 per cent. of the total population; two of these, holding first and third place in rank are in New Jersey.* (P. 13.)

The relation of the alien to the industrial, political and social interests of the State can no longer be ignored. He has become more and more a force in our economic life and an important element in our increasing industrial activities. As soon as he arrives in the State, he becomes a producer as well as a consumer.

His labor is needed on the farm, in the factory, in construction of railroads, on public works and in mines. The majority of aliens enter the country in the prime of life and make their way with remarkable courage and self-reliance.

One of the greatest needs in connection with present immigration is intelligent and comprehensive systems of distribution. While a large majority of immigrants coming to this country are from rural districts, and are therefore unfitted for working or living under existing conditions in our large industrial centers, nevertheless the agricultural interests have great difficulty in securing labor, and the industrial centers are overcrowded. For this condition the State is largely to blame. . . .

* Federal Census of 1910.

With little or no knowledge of the English language, the alien remains unacquainted with the legal and social institutions of the State and is in constant danger of breaking laws of which he is ignorant, and of being exploited by the many individuals and agencies ready to prey upon his ignorance.

With the prospect of a large number of immigrants becoming citizens, the State should take a more active and intelligent interest in their protection and preparation for citizenship. (Pp. 14-15.)

The ideal of the nation is to produce through free and universal education a fairly homogeneous people having a uniform standard of social customs and political institutions. Unfortunately aliens coming to our State, and especially those taking residence in cities, are practically compelled to settle in colonies in congested quarters, where they tend to perpetuate alien groups which speak their native language, and which are frequently uninfluenced by American customs and traditions. The process of assimilation is retarded in these groups, and they are a hindrance to the full application of democratic principles of government. As long as the conditions exist which lead to this racial segregation, it is of the utmost importance that opportunities for acquiring a knowledge of the English language be placed in the reach of all these aliens, to remove as quickly as possible the inclination for continued segregation, and at the same time to make assimilation possible through contact with American thought and public opinion. (P. 111.)

As far as can be ascertained, only a very few public evening schools offer regular courses in civics looking toward citizenship. In some classes text-books in history or civics are used, but generally whatever information the alien adult receives with regard to our federal and municipal government or the requirements necessary in order to become a citizen is obtained in a more or less haphazard and superficial manner incidental to his lessons in English. In addition to learning the English language, the alien should have instruction in matters which more or less affect his daily life. The sooner he becomes familiar with the customs and the institutions which bear an intimate relation to his needs, the sooner he will be placed in an independent position and become an asset rather than a liability to the community in which he is living.

It is of a primary importance for him to understand the educational opportunities and the laws governing compulsory education and child labor; the opportunities for work in various parts of the State; municipal ordinances and the functions of the minor courts. It is also of great importance that he know where he can best keep his money or how it can be transmitted safely. No better place than the schoolroom can be found to bring this information to the ignorant foreigner. Before being admitted to citizenship he should be fairly familiar with the fundamental facts concerning the State and National government. (Pp. 124-125.)

First Annual Report of the Commission of Immigration and Housing of California. January 2, 1915.

This investigation showed great neglect in California of the opportunity to acquire citizenship, and little appreciation of its true value when acquired. The blame for this situation rests not so much on the aliens as on the State, for, while a few political and fraternal clubs and certain evening schools maintain naturalization classes, most of the instruction in citizenship comes from private and doubtful sources. Certain alleged "lawyers" seem to have no other business than that of taking up cases of enterprising aliens seeking citizenship. One Italian, himself barely literate, operated a private class for immigrants, charging a tuition fee of $25 and gave a guarantee that citizenship would be obtained. The survey proved that California continues the same careless methods of citizen making which obtain in most of the big immigrant centers in the East. (P. 12.)

The Immigrant. An Asset and a Liability. FREDERIC J. HASKIN. *New York, Fleming H. Revell Company, 1913.*

No more important or far-reaching question confronts the American people to-day than the problem of our present immigration. Each year approximately a million aliens swarm to our shores. . . . (Pp. 20-21.)

But, although the immigrant constitutes the great American problem, he is also a great American asset. The inquiries of the Immigration Commission show what a tremendous factor he is and has been in our industrial life. In the iron and steel industries he and his children contribute seven-tenths of the labour. In the slaughtering and meat packing industry they give three-fourths of the labour required. They do seventy per cent. of the work in the bituminous coal mines, and nearly three-fifths of that of the glass factories. Seven-eighths of the labour in woollen and worsted manufacturing is contributed by the immigrant and his children, and they produce nearly nine-tenths of the cotton goods, and nearly nineteen-twentieths of the men's and women's clothing of the country. They make more than half of America's shoes, nearly four-fifths of its furniture. Half of the labour in making our collars, cuffs and shirts is contributed by them, and five-sixths of the work in the leather industry is placed to their credit. They make half of our gloves, refine nearly nine-tenths of our oil, and nearly nineteen-twentieths of our sugar. Also they manufacture nearly half of our tobacco and cigars. (Pp. 22-23.)

The Immigration Problem. JEREMIAH W. JENKS and W. JETT LAUCK. *New York and London, Funk & Wagnalls, 1913.*

Inability to speak English, as a matter of fact, is the greatest obstacle to the proper distribution of the recent immigration population. It causes segregation of the immigrant races in industrial towns and large cities, and prevents proper contact with American life and institutions. Moreover, the recent immigrant until he has acquired a knowledge of English must remain in the ranks of unskilled labor, even if he has been a farmer or has had technical training abroad. As soon as a knowledge of English is obtained, not only standards of living change, but there also occurs a distribution and proper adjustment upon an industrial basis. This condition of affairs is quite plainly seen among members of races of southern and eastern Europe who have had a long period of residence in this country. (Pp. 314-15.)

Progress and assimilation along all lines is conditioned more upon knowledge of our language than upon any other factor. Congestion in large cities and industrial localities, as well as the establishment of immigrant colonies, arises largely from the inability of the southern and eastern European to use English readily. . . . The exploitation of the immigrant has its foundation upon the same lack of English-speaking ability. On the other hand, with a larger proportion of immigrants who can speak the language, a much greater dissemination of the foreign-born population may be expected, together with its more rapid absorption and assimilation. Progress in industry, in business, in the trades and professions and in the accumulation of property are all primarily dependent upon the development in the recent immigration population of an English-speaking ability. (P. 316.)

The Education of the Immigrant. Frances A. Kellor. *The Educational Review, New York, 1914.*

"It is not alone the question of the school education of children," says Commissioner Claxton, "the millions of adult men and women, and of children older than the upper limit of the compulsory school attendance age must be looked after; they must be prepared for American citizenship and for participation in our democratic, industrial, social and religious life. The proper education of these people is a duty which the nation owes to itself and to them. It can neglect this duty only to their hurt and its own peril." (Pp. 24-25.)

But, in themselves, as well as in their relation to their children, adult immigrants have well justified the efforts made to educate them. The Federal Immigration Commission found that as soon as English is acquired, not only do the immigrant's standards of living change, but distribution and proper adjustment in industrial ranks occur. (P. 30.)

The night school men, like the children, are keenly interested in geography. . . .Perhaps a night school student would profit little by the task of learning the capital of every State in the Union, but a knowledge of its physical geography, of what are the industries of various towns and cities, of what is raised in California and what in New Jersey may concern him very directly indeed. It has been proposed, in order to relieve the congestion in our cities and to keep peasants and land-lovers out of the sweat-shops, that the Division of Distribution in the Federal Department of Labor shall furnish to the immigrant information about the various agricultural districts and the demand in them for workmen. Although the logical time to do this is at landing, there is at least a possibility that immigrants dissatisfied with their beginning in the new country might, through a study of the country in school, be able to make elsewhere a start in a kind of life for which they are better fitted. (P. 33.)

In this matter of helping the immigrant to find himself industrially, practically nothing has been done. Of his need for instruction in civics, in the study of American law and political conditions, there has been a readier conception. The graded courses in civics that have been outlined cover the general scheme and purpose of government in its city, State and federal functions, and a study of American history conveyed chiefly through its dramatic personalities and struggles. (P. 33.)

Americanizing a City. The Campaign for the Detroit Night Schools Conducted in August-September, 1915, by The Detroit Board of Commerce and Board of Education, under the auspices of the National Americanization Committee and the Committee for Immigrants in America.

If every city and town in the country to-day were to provide night classes in which its non-English speaking adult population could learn English and the first principles of American citizenship, we should have the *machinery* for Americanization. For while Americanization means much more than the English language and civics, English is the indispensable key. A general provision for teaching it would be a tremendous achievement, for we have never had this before. We now have facilities for perhaps one immigrant in ten in the best equipped States, and for none at all in some States. We have requirements for naturalization and—no facilities for meeting them. We tell every immigrant that to be a citizen and a competent resident of the United States he must be able to use the English language and show that he is "attached to the principles of the Constitution." But we have not thought it our responsibility to provide the ways and means. And therefore if night schools and classes on an adequate scale were now provided for in every community with a considerable foreign-born population, we should have at least an Americanization policy and program; and we should be infinitely further along on the road to national unity than we now are.

We must have the night schools and classes as speedily as possible. But behind every one that is established we must have the social force of the particular community, all its agencies, all its resources, all its civic sympathies, if the future of American citizenship is really to be assured. No educational department can carry the work through alone. These are some of the reasons why it cannot:

(1) The immigrant population has not been invited to go to school before; it will be distrustful now.

(2) A good many immigrants will never even know about the night schools—where they are located, when they are open, for whom they are intended, what they will teach—unless special effort is made to carry the news to them.

(3) Some of them work ten or twelve hours a

day. Some of them change their shifts every week or every two weeks. They are not likely to think that a night school from seven to nine for four nights every week has much to do with them. If they finish work at six o'clock, even those who know about the schools and are interested are not likely to feel that they could go home, get supper, wash and change their clothes, and get to night school in time.

(4) Those in the lowest grade of American labor —working for from $1.50 to $1.70 daily—perhaps have long come to feel themselves cut off from the ascending current of American industry. They are not likely to feel that any civic opportunities are intended for them, or that indeed there is any point in trying to reach such opportunities.

The conclusion is this: As a result of our long-continued policy or lack of policy, getting immigrants into night schools on a scale that covers the needs of any community, has become a civic experiment taxing every community resource.

It is the purpose of this sketch to show how this can be done by outlining such an experiment recently conducted in Detroit.

The end attained in this case was not only an increase of 153% in the actual registration in the night schools, but the awakening of the city of Detroit to its vast immigration problem, the assumption of definite responsibilities by many employers and others, the socializing of very varied community forces in co-operating to this one end—the Americanization of a peculiarly heterogeneous and unassimilated city.

What was done in Detroit can be done in every city or town that has an unassimilated foreign population and a night school. (P. 4.)

Detroit is a typical immigration laboratory of the country. . . .

In 1910, 33% of the population was foreign born, and 74% was either foreign born or of foreign-born parentage. It is safe to assume that the 300,000 increase in population since 1910 has not lessened these percentages.

The Detroit factories are placing the city high in production, high in importance in America. They are working out the type of American industry. But thousands of them are not working out the type of American citizenship or American workmen at all.

That, says the practical observer, *is not the business of industry.* And this is true. It is not the business of industry alone; nor of the public educational system alone; nor of municipal government alone; nor of private social organizations alone. It is the business of all of these and it will require them all. . . .

That "English first" is the rational first step in Americanization is well illustrated by Detroit. Many thousands of the foreign born of Detroit do not speak English. In 1910 the non-English speaking numbered 38,038. In 1915, with a population increased by 300,000, the number of those unable to read, write, speak or understand English must have been extraordinarily increased. Last year 2,838 were enrolled in the public night schools. Allowing for those learning English in parochial schools or private classes, it is still evident that although a very considerable percentage of Detroit's population was unable to manage its affairs through the English language and to secure the approach to American institutions which only a knowledge of English can guarantee, *only a very small percentage of these was on the road to learning English and preparing for American citizenship.* (Pp. 5-6.)

Many employers *at once* made it clear to their men that from this time on the firm would prefer those men that were attending night school and making a definite effort to learn English.

But a considerable number of firms went much farther than this. The Saxon Company made night school attendance *compulsory* for its non-English speaking workmen.

The Solvay Company proposed a wage increase of two cents an hour to its employees who learned the English language.

"I am convinced," said the efficiency engineer of the Semet-Solvay plant, "that only through employers offering a material inducement to the foreign laborer to learn English will the public night schools for non-English-speaking operatives be made a success. . . . The foreigner must be shown that it will be of material advantage to him in his job to learn the English tongue. This the employer can well afford to do, for the non-English speaking laborer is a source of danger to himself and everybody else about the plant. I should be afraid to estimate the aggregate amount of waste each year to this company through a non-English-speaking operative's failing to understand an order, with a resultant costly blunder. I have known a single blunder to cost as much as $2,000. Then there are thousands paid out for injuries, many of which may be traced directly to the inability of the employee to understand English."

The Superintendent of the Board of Education met every situation presented to him by industry. A number of firms whose men changed from night to day shifts every week or two weeks consulted him. He assured them that special classes for such men would be arranged wherever numbers made it at all possible. The Morgan and Wright Company, employing hundreds of non-English speaking men have particularly late daily hours, owing to the nature of their work. It would be impossible for their men to reach the night school session in time. The Board of Education guaranteed to furnish ten regular teachers for classes to be held at night in the Morgan and Wright plant, if they would equip ten classrooms. By this arrangement between 700 and 800 men who must otherwise have been denied the night school advantages could be included in its benefits. The Board of Commerce in making the arrangement recommended that part of the time thus spent in the classroom be company time, that the men be able to get supper in the factory, and that adequate facilities for recreation be included. (Pp. 10-12.)

New York State Department of Education. 1916. Citizenship Syllabus. Prepared by Research Department of the Committee for Immigrants in America. New York.

Introductory Note.

The Federal government sets forth in its naturalization laws two main educational requirements for citizenship; first, a knowledge of the English language, and, second, a familiarity with the fundamental principles of American government. It is largely the responsibility of evening schools for immigrants to furnish instruction in these two lines.

The need for educational work in civics, and instruction in naturalization proceedings is obvious. More than 25 per cent. (6,646,817) of all the males of voting age in the United States are foreign-born, and only 45 per cent. are naturalized; the remaining 55 per cent. (3,612,700) give us concretely the "Naturalization Problem" of our country. Most of the three million who have become citizens through the regular naturalization procedure have had little or no training for such citizenship and the other three and a half million are an unassimilated element which gives a great opportunity for the promotion of civic training. Whenever there is in a democracy a large male population of voting age who have not a voice in the government, there is not pure democracy, but often fertile soil for the seeds of anarchy and violent socialism. These facts measure the problem but do not indicate the extent of its human and personal influence upon every American citizen.

The Immigrants in America Review. January, 1916.

Our only reliable statistics are five years old and are very incomplete on many important points, but they indicate the magnitude of the task before us. More than one-fourth of our population is of foreign-born parentage or foreign born. . . . There were, in 1910, 6,500,000 foreign-born white males over 21 years of age, of whom only 3,034,117 were naturalized, leaving 3,500,000 un-Americanized. Out of a foreign-born population of about 13,000,000 over 10 years of age, about 3,000,000 were unable to speak English. That means that about one in four cannot speak English. There were 1,500,000 illiterates, and there are undoubtedly more now, as the 3,000,000 immigrants who have come since 1910, not included in these figures, will more than counterbalance the progress made since 1910 by those already here.

Our task thus becomes clear. We must put America first in the hearts of every resident in America, . . . and make English the common language of all peoples in America, because it is the key to American life. (P. 6.)

United States Bureau of Labor Statistics. Monthly Review. Vol. II. No. 3. March, 1916.

Training of Immigrants for Citizenship.

Recent reports furnished by the Bureau of Naturalization show a very rapid development of its work for the better education of candidates for citizenship, in the principles of American life and government. The need for such work is evident. Each year approximately 100,000 certificates of citizenship are issued. Many of the candidates have only a minimum understanding of the rights and duties attaching to their new status, and, in any case, the great majority would vastly benefit by a more thorough training in these matters.

To some extent the need for such training had been met through the establishment of citizenship classes by public schools, associations, and individuals. These activities, however, covered only a small portion of the field, and, in addition, it developed that a number of them were not in good faith, being simply means for the exploitation of the immigrant.

About a year ago the Bureau of Naturalization, after consultation with various school authorities, worked out a comprehensive plan for the education of candidates for citizenship. Under this plan the bureau arranges to send to the public-school authorities of his community a statement showing the name, address, and nationality of each resident alien who has declared his intention to become a citizen or of each petitioner to be naturalized. At the same time it advises the declarant or petitioner of its action and of the public-school advantages. It then rests with the school authorities to encourage the prospective citizens to enroll in the schools and, if necessary, to establish special courses for their accommodation.

During the fiscal year 1915 the Bureau of Naturalization received approximately 350,000 applications for citizenship. This number includes both declarations of intention and petitions for naturalization, a declarant having to wait two years before petitioning for naturalization. It is estimated that not less than 150,000 of the above applicants had wives, thus making a total of a half million adult alien residents coming within the province of the bureau as prospective citizens of this country.

Out of this number the bureau sent the names of approximately 122,000 to the public schools of the communities where the various applicants resided. The accompanying statement shows the distribution of this number among the States.

The public schools have shown an earnest spirit of co-operation. With the opening of the present scholastic year 50 cities and towns were co-operating. At the end of December this number had grown to 450 and by the end of January, 1916, to 566 cities and towns, representing 44 States. Hundreds of other localities have expressed their interest but have been deterred from co-operation by local conditions which render such work impracticable.

In addition to the class training indicated, the outline also suggests a laboratory method of teaching civics. This method calls for lectures by city officials upon the functions of their respective offices and for the organization of the students into mock governments, with nominations, elections, officers' meetings, etc., for the practical demonstration of governmental organization and purposes. It is also urged that graduates of the schools form alumni classes for continued association and discussion.

The primary purpose of the plan outlined above is to reach those resident aliens who are contemplating becoming citizens. In addition, however, the effort is also being made to reach all foreign-born residents, many of whom have no immediate intention of becoming citizens, but who are living in this country in various degrees of ignorance as to its institutions and political organizations. Also, it has been found that there is a demand and need for such training on the part of many native-born persons.

The bureau has planned to hold a convention next July in Washington, D. C., for the discussion of the various questions in regard to citizenship schools and for exhibiting the result of the work of various schools of this character. (Pp. 9-11.)

C. MILITARY: THE CITIZEN AS SOLDIER.

The State is dependent upon the quality of its citizens not only for its development in times of peace, but in the last resort, for military defense. Industrial conditions which result in physical degeneration of the population are thus a menace to the very existence of the State. In communities where excessive working hours have long prevailed, progressive decline in stature, strength, and efficiency becomes markedly evident. This is conspicuously shown by the large percentage of recruits necessarily rejected from military service for physical unfitness.

Recruiting statistics from Germany are of most value because they cover the entire male population and show the results of the medical examination of all young men of military age. They prove the physical superiority of recruits from non-industrial regions. Between 1902 and 1907 the number of young men fit for service born in the country and engaged in agriculture sank from 61 per cent. to 58.7 while during the same period among those city-born and engaged in industry the percentage sank from 54.7 to 49.9.

In spite of thirty years of social legislation in Germany, it is apparent that industrial labor, together with the strain of city life, have resulted in the highest percentage of rejections for physical unfitness among the recruits.

58 *Kongress der Deutschen Naturforscher und Arzte. Strassburg, 1886. Die Überbürdung der Arbeiterinnen und Kinder in Fabriken. [The Over-work of Women and Children in Factories.]* DR. SCHULER, *Factory Inspector, Switzerland. Reprinted in Vierteljahrsschrift für öffentliche Gesundheitpflege. Vol. XVIII. 1886.*

General attention was directed to the factory work of children in Switzerland by the shock received from the statistics of the recruiting office.

Districts where there were few mills showed that only 14.3% to 18.9% of the recruits were temporarily refused on account of imperfect physical development, while factory districts had from 19.7% to 23.3% of such temporary rejections (rejected for 2 years).

Absolutely rejected as unsuitable for military service there were, in rural districts 23.9-39.2%; while in industrial districts there were from 27.8-31.3% absolutely rejected.

It was then assumed that factory work delayed but did not ruin the development of youth and it was also believed that the better food resulting from the higher wages of factory workers made up for disadvantages to growing youth. But with later investigation it was found that in the Canton of Zug, for example:

Cotton wool operatives had only 37% fit for service.

Handworkers (artisans) had 47 to 83%.

Farmworkers (agricultural) had 49%.

Further it was shown that the figures of the physically unfit were:

Factory hands (all kinds) 32 to 43%; other occupations 7 to 30%.

In another Canton the proportion was 34-39% for the factory as against 12-23% for non-factory hands (P. 134.)

All these unfavorable results could hardly be explained otherwise than by the generally injurious effect of factory life in the young growing person. It appeared that special injuries were not so much in question, but that the general conditions of life were not good for children and young people. (P. 135.)

Verhandlungen des Deutschen Reichstags. 103. Sitzung, 18. April. 1891. [Proceedings of the German Reichstag. 103rd Session. April 18th, 1891.]

Representative Bebel: The one fact alone, that the military recruiting offices all over Germany have found that from decade to decade the number of physically fit recruits in factory and manufacturing districts is diminishing to an appalling extent, so that it is necessary to draw more and more heavily upon the country regions—shows clear and plainly what kind of process is at work upon the development of the national physique, and the more extensive our industry becomes, and the more it invades the country regions, the more and more certainly will it exhaust those sources of strength which are now the only sources to look to for military defence.

For these reasons it is absolutely essential that the laws should promptly provide ample means for overcoming this tendency to deterioration of race in every way. (Pp. 2419-2420.)

Die Sociale Reform als Gebot des Wirthschaftlichen Fortschrittes. [Social Reform as a Condition of Socio-Political Progress.] Dr. Heinrich Herkner. *Leipzig, Duncker, 1891.*

The results of excessive work, insufficient wages and deficient nutrition appear with a distinctness that cannot be ignored in the reports of the recruiting statistics. A military examining physician of the empire (German) reported from a factory region: "In the factory villages, where everyone works from youth up in the factories, almost all recruits were unfit for service, and I believe that, if this goes on, it will be useless to send recruiting commissions to these communities." (Page 4.) (Quoted from Archiv für öffentliche Gesundheitspflege in Elsass-Lothringen, VII, 107.)

Handbuch der Arbeiterwohlfahrt. [*Handbook of Reports on the Welfare of Workmen.*] *Edited by Dr. Otto Dammer. Stuttgart, Enke, 1902. Beschädigungen der Arbeiter bei der Arbeit.* [*Injuries incurred by Workmen at their Work.*] DR. ASCHER, *in Königsberg.*

The extent of injuries incurred through excessive exertions, particularly by young people, seems to be most clearly indicated in the course of recruiting for the army. Whereas in the German Empire at large some 50% (53-56%) are fit for military service, only 26% were found fit during seven years in a hamlet in the district of Schmalkalden, in which forging nails has been the principal industry for a long time, and only 21%, during seven years, in another hamlet where buckles are made, in the homes of the workers—statistics which I owe to the friendly co-operation of a local official who has been interested in the situation for years. The causes of unfitness in men otherwise strong and healthy were: diseased blood-vessels, flat-foot, rupture, one-sidedness. The statistics compiled by Dr. Schultes of Jena, covering 1,255 examinations, corroborate these statements. Dr. Schultes arrived at the following result, dividing his subjects into four classes:

Type of Occupation.	Number of men examined.	Number of men with varicose veins.	Per Cent.
Class I (standing)	315	40	12.7
Class II (standing and moving about)	887	38	4.0
Class III (seated most of the time)	44	1	2.2
Class IV (seated all the time)	111	0	0
	1255	79	

The singularly unfavorable report from the district of Schmalkalden is explained by the fact that the main industry there is forging, and hence the opportunities for over-fatigue are exceptionally favorable; furthermore, the narrow scope of the work (only nails or buckles are made) tends to enforce a mechanical posture on the part of the workman, riveted as it were to the same spot, whereas in larger smithies, the more youthful workers, particularly the apprentices, are compelled, by their activity, to move about frequently, and thereby to exercise their lower extremities.

The prevention of those injuries which constitute a serious menace to the army and navy, lies in the shortening of working hours, and in the employment of free time for gymnastics—a proceeding which aims at a more even development of all the muscles of the lower extremities, but which will also benefit the lungs and heart.

Just what effect is produced by serving at machines, involving as it does the incessant shaking of the pelvis and the over-exertion of the muscular system of the lower extremities as well, is not yet entirely clear. (P. 494.)

Handwörterbuch der Staatswissenschaften. Bd. I. Jena, Fischer, 1909. [*Compendium of Political Science, Vol. I.*] *Edited by* Drs. J. Conrad, *Professor of Political Science in Halle;* L. Elster, *Ober Reg. Rath in Berlin;* W. Lexis, *Professor of Political Science in Göttingen, and* Edg. Loening, *Professor of Law in Halle. Arbeitszeit.* [*Hours of Work.*] Dr. H. Herkner, *Berlin.*

The state approaches the question of working time from another standpoint than does the church. The state is above all the organ of perception of national interests. The bedrock of national strength is an able, loyal, intelligent people. It is therefore important for the state to see that this foundation is not shattered by the prolongation of working hours. First of all, the fatal influence of excessive hours of work came to light in the inferior military fitness of the factory population. . . . According as the proportion of the industrial classes to the whole community is larger, so much more urgently necessary does it become to lessen the serious dangers to health which inhere in industrial as opposed to agricultural occupations, by a wise limitation of the hours of work.

The state needs not only soldiers, but citizens capable and ready to share in public life. Wage-earning must leave some time free for such duties. (P. 1206.)

Rapports Présentés à M. le Ministre du Commerce de l'Industrie des Postes et des Télégraphes. Paris, Imprimerie Nationale, 1900. Par les Inspecteurs Divisionnaires du Travail dans l'Industrie, sur La Question de l'Interdiction du Travail de Nuit. [Reports by Division Inspectors on the question of night work.] Report of M. LAGARD, *Division-Inspector of the Tenth District of Marseilles.*

We may state also, and rightly, that night work makes a very large number of young workmen unfit for military service, and therefore, for the defense of our country. In certain localities where the more important industries are carried on (notably the manufacture of textiles) the number of recruits dismissed has actually grown to 50 out of every hundred, when as in agricultural districts the proportion of the unfit has never exceeded 25 per hundred. (Pp. 72-73.)

La Réduction de la Durée du Travail de l'Employé. [The Reduction of Working Hours for Employees.] VALENTIN VIARD. *Paris, Arthur Rousseau, 1910.*

The existing length of the working-day exhausts the employees, makes them physically enfeebled members of society, often incapable of fulfilling their military duties, and capable if they marry of producing only sickly children who will be a burden and not a help to the community. (P. 46.)

The reduction of working hours would be of great benefit to the employee's health. In the first place, from the mere fact of his working shorter hours he would be less long exposed to the possible contagions of the shop and office. In the second place, he would be less fatigued, less worn out, and consequently less susceptible to disease about him, for it is not work but overwork that lowers vitality, and he would no longer be overworked. (Pp. 47-48.)

Eighth International Congress of Hygiene and Demography, Budapest, 1894. Der physische Rückgang der Bevölkerung in den modernen Culturstaaten mit besonderer Rücksicht auf Oesterreich-Ungarn. [*The Physical Degeneration of the Population in Modern Civilized Countries with Particular Reference to Austria-Hungary.*] DR. JULIUS DONATH, *University of Budapest. Budapest, 1896.*

The purpose of this discussion is to prove the physical degeneration within our own time of the people in several of the modern civilized nations. The historical period for which this assertion holds good, confirms the belief that none of the above-named factors arising from racial differences affect the situation; and the speed with which this process of degeneration is going on indicates with certainty that its cause is not an old cause which has operated steadily throughout the ages, but rather that it is of newer origin, and of very definite nature. And this cause—I will state here and now—lies in modern economic conditions. (P. 605.)

The fact should be noted that according to the law of 1889 governing military service, the annual contingent of recruits was raised from 95,474 men (for Hungary 39,552) to 103,100 men (for Hungary 42, 711). But particular notice is to be taken of the clause of this law which raises the age of liability for military service from 20 to 21. This was done to avoid calling out the fourth class of recruits, which had become necessary through the increasing deterioration of the general physical condition. Although this raising of the contingent required an increased number of recruits, and though the age for service was thus advanced, yet in Austria as well as in Hungary, the percentage of those temporarily rejected because of unfitness increased steadily and with extraordinary rapidity between 1867 and 1892.

THE PERCENTAGE OF THOSE TEMPORARILY REJECTED BECAUSE OF UNFITNESS IN THE FIRST 3 CLASSES. (EQUIVALENT IN NUMBER TO 4 CLASSES.)

	Temporarily rejected in the first 3 classes.			Temporarily rejected in the first 3 classes.	
Year.	Hungary Per Cent.	Austria Per Cent.	Year.	Hungary Per Cent.	Austria Per Cent.
1867	21.56	40.33	1880	60.64	69.25
1868	22.01	29.26	1881	61.65	70.93
1869	32.79	43.76	1882	62.74	69.80
1870	33.64	47.04	1883	60.75	68.94
1871	37.95	49.55	1884	64.19	71.03
1872	38.27	50.51	1885	66.41	73.40
1873	42.94	56.34	1886	65.20	66.65
1874	50.67	50.09	1887	72.35	72.06
1875	52.35	61.62	1888	75.49	76.36
1876	55.59	63.40	1889	68.77	69.87
1877	57.63	65.53	1890	69.05	66.60
1878	58.75	67.82	1891	64.88	70.06
1879	59.61	68.72			

Therefore the percentage of those temporarily rejected on account of unfitness between 1867 and 1888 increased in Hungary from 21.56 to 75.49%, and in Austria from 40.33 to 76.36%. From that time on a moderate decline is apparent. How little consolation this affords is indicated by the official Yearbook of Military Statistics (Militär-Statistisches Jahrbuch) for the year 1892 which says: (page 12) "As is the case in general, the military territorial districts of Vienna, Zara, Prague, Josefstadt, Krakau, Lemberg and Pressburg also report increasingly unfavorable conditions from year to year between 1890 and 1892. The opposite condition is observable only in the military territorial districts of Innsbrück and Hermannstadt during this period. As a matter of fact, only 22.3% in Hungary and in Austria only 19.4% of the men liable for service and examined by a physician, were found fit. (Pp. 608-609.)

In France, as the following table shows, the number of the unfit rises, with fluctuations, from 26.3% in the year 1872 to 31.3% in the year 1885, and then drops again. I also calculated the percentage of the temporarily rejected in addition to those enrolled as auxiliaries; in the light of this set of figures the physical degeneration is seen yet more clearly; for the percentage rises from 16.2 in the year 1872 to 19.5 in the year 1888, despite the enormous increase in the French army, the full strength of which was reckoned in the year 1891 at 5,564,000 men. . . . The case appears in a still more unfavorable light if we examine the "temporarily rejected" men separately. For their number amounted in 1872 to 21,022 out of 303,810 recruits of the first class according to age,—or 6.9%—and climbed steadily to 39,231 out of 295,707 recruits, or 13.3% in 1888. The number of those temporarily rejected is seen nearly to have doubled in the course of 16 years!

Date of Enlistment of Class I.	Unfit. Per cent.	Temporarily Rejected or Enrolled as Auxiliaries.	Temporarily Rejected Per cent.
1872	26.3	16.2	6.9
1873	25.1	16.5	7.2
1874	24.9	14.3	6.9
1875	25.4	13.8	7.6
1876	24.8	14.1	8.0
1877	26.7	14.9	9.2
1878	26.1	14.7	9.4
1879	26.1	15.1	9.7
1880	26.2	14.9	10.1
1881	30.2	17.2	12.2
1882	29.7	17.3	12.3
1883	29.7	17.6	12.5
1884	30.0	17.8	12.4
1885	31.3	18.4	12.9
1886	31.0	19.5	13.6
1887	29.8	18.9	13.0
1888	29.9	19.5	13.3

(Pp. 611-612.)

The Citizen as Soldier.—Italy

In Italy the minimum height was reduced by a law passed July 8, 1883, from 1.56 meters to 1.55; and according to a law of June 29, 1882, the "weak" and those afflicted with curable defects, as well as those who have not attained the minimum height, may be temporarily rejected for one or two years. In spite of all this, the number of the unfit, after dropping from 49.4% to 36.7% between 1871 and 1877, rises again to 47.5 in 1888 and then drops somewhat again. The physical degeneration is still more obvious if we examine the "temporarily rejected"* separately from the altogether unfit,† as we did in the case of Austria, Hungary and France. I have myself computed the two series of percentages on the basis of the absolute figures.‡

Year of Enlistment of Class I.	Temporarily Rejected and Altogether Unfit. Per Cent.	Temporarily Rejected. Per Cent.	Year of Enlistment of Class I.	Temporarily Rejected and Altogether Unfit. Per Cent.	Temporarily Rejected. Per Cent.
1871	49.4	7.7	1882	39.6	21.9
1872	47.6	8.7	1883	40.6	20.3
1873	47.0	8.5	1884	42.3	21.1
1874	42.9	11.0	1885	43.4	22.1
1875	37.5	11.0	1886	43.4	21.8
1876	37.1	10.7	1887	43.3	22.5
1877	36.7	11.0	1888	47.5	26.3
1878	38.2	13.2	1889	42.2	23.2
1879	38.3	13.6	1890	42.9	24.1
1880	41.1	13.5	1891	41.8	23.2
1881	46.0	13.1			

In this table then we see the number of temporary rejections rising steadily from 7.7 per cent. to 23.2 per cent. between 1871 and 1891, and indeed, in the year 1888 reaching 26.3 per cent. (Pp. 612-613.)

I have cited in the foregoing pages a series of proofs which I think, sufficiently established the fact that in modern civilized countries—and this may be shown particu-

* Rivedibili e Rimandati. † Riformati. ‡ (Annuario Statistico Italiano, 1892.)

larly of the important military powers—the physical condition of the population is deteriorating. Furthermore, it can no longer be doubted that, in view of the rapidity of this deterioration, the cause must be of comparatively recent origin. Even though the agricultural occupations may be considered in general less injurious to the health than the industrial, yet the recruiting statistics of Austria-Hungary teach us that conditions in Austria, where industries predominate, and in Hungary, which is mainly agricultural, are equally unfavorable and that generally speaking, the two countries offer in this respect a striking parallel. Even if we give due consideration to another series of injuries, such as wrong principles in the education of the young and the degenerating influences of luxury and the pursuit of pleasure in the higher classes, yet the decisive factor in the physical condition of the population is seen to be the standard of living, and in general, the satisfaction of the wants of the lower and numerically preponderant classes in society. In a word, the physical condition of the population is in the last analysis determined by economic conditions. (P. 615.)

Professor V. Babes understood correctly that this deep-seated evil of the physical degeneracy of the population is not accessible to insignificant little bureaucratic remedies, and in his profound address delivered in Rome at the Eleventh International Medical Congress, he voices these demands: Before all, a radical transformation of the state in the sense of an international and social reform on a definite hygienic basis, with the view first of establishing the principle that individual health is inseparable from public health; that the health of one class is essential to the health of the others; and finally, that it is the health of the lower classes that is of the highest economic value. . . .

The first and most important step to be taken by the government under present conditions of production to check the deterioration of the nation's vigor, is the shortening of working hours. . . . Unduly protracted working hours mean an intensive drain on human energies and their rapid exhaustion. . . .

Not only is the reduction of working hours urgently needed from the hygienic standpoint both for the present generation and for posterity; it is also, thanks to our great and incessant technical advances, feasible here and now; and it is certain that in the course of time, working hours will admit of still further reduction. (P. 616.)

The Pioneer of Progress. JOHN DENNIS. *London, Hamilton Adams, 1860.*

There is a period in the history of a state when the bodily strength of its members becomes a matter of highest moment, when not only dauntless courage, but muscular force may any day be called into requisition, when its political status must be upheld by downright strength of arm, and when physical degeneracy is the invariable forerunner of national decline. (P. 56.)

. . . There can be no question that the health of the country, and especially of the young men and women of the next generation is assuredly a national interest. If the national strength degenerate, it follows that the kingdom will decline. (P. 60.)

Eight-Hour Movement. Verbatim Report of a Debate Between H. M. HYNDMAN *and* C. BRADLAUGH. *London, Freethought Publishing Co. 1890.*

If you take the condition of the workmen and workwomen, their physical strength is being deteriorated by the present system. The height and the chest measurement of recruits have fallen markedly since the Queen came to the throne fifty years ago. Anyone who is acquainted with the manufacturing districts, as I have been since I was a boy, must see not only in the reports of certifying surgeons and sanitary inspectors, but from his own experience and under his own eye he can see perfectly clearly that deterioration continually going on. . . . I say that from any point of view whatsoever a system which not only destroys the present generation, but lays the foundation of weakness and debility for the next, cannot be profitable in any sense of the word, but must be ruinous to the community at large. (Pp. 8-9.)

British Sessional Papers. Vol. XXXII, 1904. Report of the Inter-Departmental Committee on Physical Deterioration. Vol. I, Appendix I. Original Memorandum Prepared by Surgeon-General Sir William Taylor, K. C. B., *Director-General, Army Medical Service.*

1. A deep interest has been aroused, both in the lay and medical press, by the writings of Sir Frederick Maurice and others, who have brought into prominence certain observations pointing to the fact that there is an alarming proportion of the young men of the country, more especially among the urban population, who are unfit for military service on account of defective physique.

The questions naturally arise as to whether this impeachment of the national health has a solid foundation in fact, and as to whether the condition is true of the population as a whole, or only of a certain section of it. The teaching of public health statistics would appear to show that progressive improvement of the national health has steadily followed the improved conditions of life which have been brought about by the advance of sanitary knowledge and its practical application. It has also been pointed out that athletic records are constantly being broken for all sorts of feats of strength, agility, and endurance, facts which would seem to indicate that the physique of the well-to-do classes, at least, is improving rather than deteriorating. It is nevertheless true, and the fact is a disturbing and disquieting one, that a very large proportion of the men who offer themselves for enlistment in the Army are found to be physically unfit for military service.

2. In an article on the National Health, which appeared in a recent number of the *Contemporary Review*, Sir Frederick Maurice states that, according to the best estimate he had been able to arrive at, it has been for many years the case that out of every five men who

wished to enlist, primarily offer themselves for enlistment, you would find that at the end of two years' service there are only two men remaining in the Army as effective soldiers. Of the men who offer themselves, some are rejected by the recruiting sergeant or recruiting officer, some by the examining medical officers, and some, though enlisted, are found after three months to be unlikely to develop into effective soldiers and are summarily discharged. According to General Maurice's experience, at the end of two years not more than forty per cent. of the men who wished to become soldiers will be found serving; or, in other words, sixty per cent. of the men offering themselves are physically unfit to serve as soldiers. He points out that it is no good talking of conscription or of any form of compulsory service if we already have five men offering themselves for every two men who are fit for the work; no one has suggested that we should increase our Army in the proportion of two to five, i. e., make it two and a half times as large as it is now. He then goes on to say that no nation was ever yet for any long time great and free, when the army it put in the field no longer represented its own virility and manhood.

3. But the want of physique, thus shown to exist with regard to a large section of the community, is not only serious from its military aspect, it is serious also from its civil standpoint, for if these men are unfit for military service, what are they good for? As Sir Lauder Burnton says: "Poor in physique as they all are, and poor in mental capacity and power of application as many of them must be, what becomes of them? Many of them probably marry girls as weak as themselves, and have children, some of whom go to swell the lists of infant mortality, some to join the criminal classes, while others grow up more weak and incompetent than their parents." Inquiry is wanted, and it is vital for us to know the truth. Whether part of the physical deterioration is the result of unskilled labor flocking to the towns and there failing to find means for properly rearing a family, or whether it be on account of causes which are attackable, such as early marriages and ignorance of mothers, the result is

that the rising generation of all below the artizan class includes a vast number of men of a very low standard of health and physique. (P. 95.)

* * * * * * * * *

5. Every year a table is published in the Army Medical Department Report, which classifies the recruits examined according to their previous occupations. . . . (P. 95.)

6. Examination of a series of these annual tables shows that the proportion of the different classes remains remarkably constant from year to year, and the figures indicate that the bulk of our soldiers are drawn from the unskilled labor class and consequently from the stratum of the population living in actual poverty or close to the poverty line. As might be expected the highest ratio of rejection is shown for men who have been following indoor occupations.

* * * * * * * * *

8. In his annual report for 1902, just issued, the Inspector-General for Recruiting remarks that the one subject which causes anxiety in the future as regards recruiting is the gradual deterioration of the physique of the working classes from whom the bulk of the recruits must always be drawn, and, when it is remembered, that recruiters are instructed not to submit for medical examination candidates for enlistment unless they are reasonably expected to be passed as fit, we cannot but be struck by the percentage considered by the medical officers as unfit for the service. In the reports from all the manufacturing districts, stress is invariably laid upon the number of men medically rejected for bad teeth, flat feet, and inferior physique. . . .

9. The following table has been compiled from information given in the Army Medical Department Reports, supplemented in some particulars by data obtained from the reports of the Inspector-General of Recruiting. A period of ten years (1893-1902) has been selected, as of course, the greater the number of observations dealt with, the nearer will be our approximation to the truth.

Year.	1. Number of recruits inspected (A. M. D. Report.)	2. Number rejected on inspection (A. M. D. Report.)	3. Number rejected within 3 months after enlistment (A. M. D. Report.)	4. Invalids discharged during the year under 2 years' service (I. G. R. Report.)	5. Ratio per cent. column 2	6. Ratio per cent. column 3	7. Ratio per cent. column 4
1893	64,110	25,999	342	962	40.6	0.5	1.5
1894	61,985	24,705	369	770	39.9	0.6	1.2
1895	55,698	22,548	368	952	40.5	0.7	1.7
1896	54,574	22,698	413	999	41.6	0.8	1.8
1897	59,986	22,370	575	997	37.3	1.0	1.7
1898	66,502	22,983*	387	983	34.6	0.6	1.5
1899	68,087	22,071	433	1,003	32.4	0.6	1.5
1900	84,402	23,105	640	1,514	27.4	0.8	1.8
1901	76,750	21,52[illegible]	1,014	3,825	28.0	1.3	4.9
1902	87,609	26,913*	1,308	2,254	30.7	1.5	2.5
1893–1902	679,703	234,914	5,849	14,259	34.6	0.9	2.1

* Does not include men enlisted in 1902 and discharged under three months' service in 1903.

10. It will be observed that during this decennial period the number of men medically examined for enlistment was 679,703, and of those 234,914 were rejected as medically unfit for service, giving a rejection ratio of 34.6 per cent; of the men passed fit, 5,849 broke down within three months after enlistment, being at the rate of 9 per cent. for this class; while 14,259, or 2.1 per cent. more, were discharged as invalids under two years' service. The smallness of the rate of the rejections within three months of enlistment varying as will be observed, between .5 and 1.5 per cent. speaks well, I think for the thoroughness of the primary medical examination of recruits. But the rejection of one out of every three men examined by the recruiting medical officer points clearly to the poorness of the human material available for army purposes, as a writer in the *Lancet* puts it. Adding together the rates for the three classes of rejections referred to in the table, we find that 37.6 per cent. of the

679,703 men examined during the decennial period proved to be unfit for military service. The Inspector-General of Recruiting states in his report for 1902, that it must be borne in mind, when examining these totals, that they do not represent anything like the total number of rejections of candidates for enlistment into the Army. A large number of men are rejected by recruiting sergeants and recruiting officers and such men in consequence are never medically inspected and do not appear in any returns. In the decennial period under consideration we have only been able to account for 37.6 per cent. of rejections from official statistics; but according to Sir Frederick Maurice's estimate 60 per cent. of the men who offer themselves are unfit for service. This indicates that the number of men turned away by the recruiters themselves as unlikely to have any reasonable chance of passing the medical examination is an appallingly large one. (P. 96.)

12. It has already been stated that a large proportion of the population live in towns, and this has been estimated at 77 per cent., or 25,000,000. Of this town population about 25 per cent. (probably at least 6,000,000), appear from trustworthy investigations, to be not only poor, but living in actual poverty, so as to be unable to rear their children under conditions favorable to health and physical fitness. The bulk of the men who seek enlistment belong to this section of the population, and a very large proportion (but probably not quite three out of five as stated by General Maurice) of the men who wish to join the Army prove physically unfit for military service. (P. 97.)

Note.

To this impressive evidence and that of the witnesses who follow, in regard to the declining physical efficiency of urban laborers the Parliamentary Committee failed to give much weight. This evidence subsequent events have amply corroborated.

Ibid. Vol. 1. Report.

25. Both the Director-General and the late Inspector-General of Recruiting were fain to admit, on being pressed, that the real lesson of the recruiting figures was the failure of the Army, under present conditions, to attract a good type of recruits. Indeed, General Borrett gives up the case for wide-spread deterioration when he says "It is a pity that the physique of the recruit-giving class is as poor as it is, so as to cause such a large percentage of rejections for the Army"; and again when in answer to a question whether "the men who want to be soldiers" were not those people who have no opening in life, or have no occupation, and who drift to the recruiter in the vague hope that they may be passed, he replies, "There are a great many of that kind, no doubt; I must confess a great many are that way." In another part of his evidence he describes them as very largely "Rubbish." (P. 5.)

33. The evidence of Sir Frederick Maurice did not modify the impression produced by that of the two preceding witnesses, nor could the Committee accept the basis of the alarmist statement for which he is responsible, that of those who wish to be soldiers only two out of five are to be found in the ranks at the end of two years. Sir Frederick obtains this result by taking the 34.6 percentage rejections by medical examiners, and 2.1 percentage of those cast before the completion of two years, and adding thereto a purely conjectural percentage as to those previously rejected by the recruiters. (P. 6.)

Testimony of Rt. Hon. Charles Booth, F.R.S.

970. Did your investigations produce the impression that conditions unfavourable to the health of the community were growing in intensity?—I think I should not use the word "intensity." They are growing in amount in connection with the increase of the urban conditions of life. I could not say that the conditions have been more intense, but they are more widespread.

1151. . . . The evidence that I have in the matter is the far greater physical force of those who come into the city from the country. The country, whatever those who are left may be, does send the finest men to the towns, and from that one assumes that the country conditions, which produce these men, are better than the conditions of the towns, which cannot produce them.

Testimony of Mr. Harry James Wilson, Inspector of Factories and Workshops in Newcastle-on-Tyne.

1913. How does the town-bred artisan compare with the type you have taken?—Very unfavourably.

1914. Will you explain how?—Contrasted with this class the town-bred artisans are, more especially in large industrial centers, distinctly less both in height and weight, and their general development inferior. Even shop assistants and clerks drawn from the families of the lower middle classes compare very unfavourably with these men, and their equal is only reached among the upper middle classes where the individuals have been trained to an outdoor life, or allowed sufficient exercise and sleep during the period between leaving school and attaining full growth.

1915. Where do you find most marked degeneracy?—The most marked degeneracy, in my opinion, is found where the greatest number of adverse circumstances are actively at work from birth to maturity, as for instance, among the very poor in our old industrial centers, and is especially noticeable in the case of poorly paid and unskilled indoor workers, the women suffering about equally with the men. This degeneracy can be best studied in certain textile industries, or wherever the remuneration is so small as to attract the lowest in the social scale.

Testimony of Mr. J. Gray, Secretary of the Anthropometric Committee of the British Association for the Investigation into the Physique of the Population.

3272-3. I mention the effect of the Franco-German War in reducing the physique of the generation born during the war. It was found that a much larger percentage of the conscripts who came up twenty-one years after the war had to be rejected. That was explained by the assumption that the most vigorous men had gone to the front and that the parents of the degenerate conscripts of 1891 were the men who were rejected in 1870 for defective physical deterioration.

3343. Progressive?—There are no statistics which would enable anyone to prove that there is a progressive deterioration of the whole population; one can only guess. What statistics we have seem to show some slight improvement in the professional classes and a deterioration in the lower classes. I strongly believe that there is a great deterioration amongst the manufacturing classes in large towns and amongst the poorer population in slum districts in towns.

3344. Do you think that there is any evidence of deterioration amongst the country-bred people?—No, I do not think there is.

3345. Do you think when country people migrate to the towns that they deteriorate because of that migration?—I think so.

Testimony of Mr. Ralph K. Neville, K.C.

4728. Can you tell us what aspect of physical degeneration first attracted your attention to the subject?—I practised what they call locally in Liverpool for eight years, and when I went down I saw a great contrast between the operatives from manufacturing districts and men and women coming from agricultural districts; it was very marked. I was startled by the appearance of the former, and it was some time before I came across the true Lancashire race. The agricultural parts of the county of Lancashire certainly produce as fine a lot of men as any county in England, and the contrast between them and the men of the manufacturing districts was most startling.

4730. What do you take then to be the principal causes of the great physical difference that you have observed?—I should think that the main cause was the difference in the life. In the one case the people spend the most of their time in the mills in a damp atmosphere and under conditions probably not very healthy, although they are quite as healthy as they possibly can be made, and they come to those mills from cottages which are situated in overcrowded districts where the streets are too close together. . . .

4737. What, from the physical point of view, is the most desirable condition for the great bulk of the people? —The most desirable condition is what we cannot get for them, and that is open air to work in, but if we cannot do that, we ought to try to get them open air when they are not at work as long as possible.

Testimony of Mr. T. C. Horsfall.

5574. . . . Speaking of the old township of Manchester Dr. Tatham said, and his words apply to the district today as fully as they did in 1893, "Here is a population of nearly 150,000 persons paying a tax which must be reckoned, not in pounds, shillings and pence, but in years, months, and days—a tax amounting on the average to fully 30 per cent. of the lifetime of every member of the community. Here are men and women entering the period of decline at an age when they ought scarcely to have passed the prime of life. And what is particularly distressing in this regard is the thought that although in some respects the local conditions of life have improved within the last half century, in other respects bad has become even worse. . . .

"The task which lies before us and our successors is nothing less than that of restoring to every infant in the Manchester township the twelve years of life-expectation of which it has been defrauded by the evil surroundings of its birth." The extreme seriousness of the danger caused to the Empire by the unhealthy condition of Manchester and our other large towns cannot be realized, unless we remember that the difference between their death rates and the death rates of the rural districts, by which we chiefly judge of the unhealthiness of the towns, is made much less than it would otherwise be, by the constant movement into the unwholesome towns, and from the wholesome country, of vast numbers of men and women of the ages at which deaths are least numerous, whose removal, therefore, leaves the country with a much larger proportion than towns contain, of persons, very young and old, of the ages at which deaths are most numerous, and gives the towns a much larger proportion than the country contains of persons of the ages at which deaths are least numerous. Moreover, each of these young, vigorous immigrants into the towns for a time raises the average strength and the health of the mass of the urban population, and for the moment increases its power to resist the causes of disease. Now that our urban population forms more than 77%, and our rural population less than 23%, of the whole population, the country can no longer invigorate the town so largely as it has done hitherto, and, unless towns are made much more wholesome, they must have a much more marked effect on causing physical degeneration in the near future even than they have had in the near past. In spite of the invigoration and "juvenation" of the urban population at the cost of the rural population, the death rate in 1901 for England and Wales, excluding the 76 largest towns, was only 15.03 per thousand, while that of the 76 towns, including large areas of low mortality, was 17.7, that of Manchester, in 1902, was 20, and that of Ancoats 25.28. Those are the only figures on that point. The death rate for Manchester in 1902 was 20 per thousand. That was lower than in any previous year, of which we have a record, except 1894. In England and Wales, excluding 76 great towns, it was only 15.31 in 1901. But we must remember that this 20 per thousand is most misleading; the terribly high death rates of many small districts are swamped by the rate of the large district, which includes areas with comparatively low death rates. Whilst the death rate in Manchester was 20 per thousand, in Ancoats it was 25.26 for the central part of the town.

5642. The type has deteriorated in Manchester and its surroundings, do you think?—I have not the least doubt that the children of immigrants into Manchester deteriorate. There is no doubt about it at all that the population in Manchester is inferior in physique to the inhabitants of smaller towns and of the country. I should not like to be understood to say that the people in the worst parts of Manchester are as poor as the people fifty years ago were there. I do not think that is the case. The sanitary arrangements have been improved.

Ibid. Vol. II. Minutes of Evidence.

Testimony of Dr. Arthur Shadwell, M. A., M. D., M. R. C. P.

12259. . . . The only thing which I thought might be of use to you which you have not got (and it is positive evidence as far as it goes) is the statistical evidence from Germany. There the same process of urbanization has been going on. . . .

12261. . . . This process has been going on for a number of years; it has not gone on so far anything like as it has here, but it has attracted attention; I mean the probable effect of the urbanization upon the physique of the people, and it has been much discussed. With them it is a vital question because of its bearing on military strength.

12262. I take it their towns are much healthier than ours?—They are in many respects. The excess of births over deaths is very much greater there than it is here.

12263. Their towns are laid out with greater regard to the conditions of health, open spaces, and so on?—I do not know whether you can say that on the whole; they are better in some respects but not in others. . . . They discuss everything which arises in Germany very thoroughly, and they have proved that rural districts are more healthy, and they have the recruiting returns. Of course their recruiting returns are of the greatest value, because they cover the whole population; the whole male population is medically examined on reaching the age of twenty, year by year, and there is no doubt that from the recruiting returns the physique of the rural population is greatly superior to that of the urban. That is both in general and in detail. Then there is a certain amount of evidence of deterioration since the urbanization began. It does not amount to much. But the proportion of the unfit has risen, and the proportion of the fit has fallen slightly. It does not amount to much, but it is positive evidence as far as it goes.

Ibid. Vol. III. Appendix XIV.

Table of Recruiting Returns in Germany, 1901.

Predominantly Agricultural Districts.	Percentage of Recruits Examined. Fit.	Prospectively Fit.	Less Fit.	Unfit.	Unworthy.
East Prussia	68.6	11.3	13.3	6.6	0.2
Elsass	67.6	14.1	11.7	6.5	0.1
West Prussia	65.1	13.7	14.0	6.9	0.3
Pomerania	60.1	19.3	13.5	6.8	0.3
Posen	59.9	15.9	15.6	8.4	0.2
Predominantly Industrial Districts.					
Rhineland	52.8	20.3	17.4	9.4	0.1
Saxony	54.9 and 50.7	13.5 and 13.6	24.5 and 28.4	6.8 and 7.0	0.3 and 0.3
Hannover	53.7	17.6	18.2	10.3	0.2
Silesia	49.2	15.6	24.7	10.1	0.4
Brand'nbrg	47.6	11.4	33.7	7.0	0.3
German Empire	55.2	16.7	19.7	8.1	0.4

Comparative Table of Recruiting Returns for the German Empire in Years 1894 and 1901.

Year.	Fit.	Prospectively Fit.	Less Fit.	Unfit.	Unworthy.
1894	56.2	16.7	20.0	6.8	0.3
1901	55.2	16.7	19.7	8.1	0.3

The "Fit" have fallen 1 per cent. and the "Unfit" have risen 1.3 per cent.

The Case for the National Minimum. With Preface by Mrs. Sidney Webb. *London, National Committee for the Prevention of Destitution, 1913.*

Deterioration in Health and Efficiency.—The deterioration of the national physique owing to overwork has been a commonplace with the workers for over a century. nation as a whole. In 1900, a year of unparalleled military enthusiasm, when every grade of the industrial population was contributing its quota to the army, 60 per cent. of the persons offering themselves were unfit for military service. The Committee of Inquiry which ensued confirmed the impression as to the effect of over-fatigue on physical deterioration. . . . Its suggestion of further inquiry in this direction was not followed. Indeed, it was hardly necessary. Numerous employers of labour, including Lord Brassey, Sir John Brunner, Sir Alfred Mond, Sir William Mather, and Mr. A. Crossfield, had testified strongly to the detrimental effect of long hours on the health of the workers. An even more authoritative pronouncement has recently been made by a Commit-
But it needed the Boer War to impress this fact on the
tee of the United States Steel Corporation, the largest employer of labour in the world. Its report, dated April, 1912, bears strong testimony to the decrease in vigour and efficiency produced by continuous over-work. (Pp. 16-17.)

Fatigue. A. Mosso, *Professor of Physiology in the University of Turin. Translated by Margaret Drummond, M. A., and W. B. Drummond, M. B., C. M., F. R. C. P. E., Extra Physician, Royal Hospital for Sick Children, Edinburg. London. Swan Sonnenschein & Co., Ltd. New York, G. P. Putnam's Sons. 2nd Edition, 1906.*

The ruin which the exhaustion of fatigue brings about in man appears clearly in the degeneration of our race in some parts of Italy. In the Province of Caltanisetta, for example, in the four years between 1881 and 1884, out of 3,672 sulphur workers who presented themselves for examination, only 203 were declared fit for military service; 1,634 were rejected; 1,835 remanded for another examination; 1,249 were rejected as under the regulation height; 69 for deficiency of chest measurement; 64 for constitutional weakness; 25 for malformation of the chest; 43 for hernia; 48 for spinal curvature; 20 for other physical deformities; 7 for varicocele; 18 for malarial cachexia; 18 for blindness; and 73 for various causes. Here then is a province under the lovely sky of Italy, with a fruitful soil and in a land rich in natural talent, which out of 3,672 youths of twenty years of age, counts only 203 able to bear arms. And when we think of our country, it is with great sorrow and uneasiness that we read these figures.

In the other provinces of Sicily at the same time, about twelve per cent. were rejected for deficiency in height. Out of 3,672 conscripts there would therefore be about 440 rejected on this account, whereas in Caltanissetta there were 1,249, that is to say, about three times as many.

The first time I went to Sicily I was sent thither in the capacity of army surgeon, and the conduct of the levy in the interior of the island was entrusted to me. I still remember as if it had been today, a tiny church in which close to the altar stood the inspectors, the lieutenant of the carabineers, and the noisy crowd beyond the balustrade. I went to see the conscripts behind the high altar in the choir, and found there a line of youths, thin, naked and blackened, and mingled with these, others who were fat, plump and fair, as though they belonged to a different race. These were the poor and the rich. Sometimes there passed before me all the conscripts of entire communes, among whom not one could be found fit to bear arms, so much had toil and fatigue deformed and weakened the population.

The inspectors were humiliated by so much degradation. "They are *carusi,*" they told me; that is to say, men who from childhood have worked as sulphur carriers. (Pp. 158-159-160.)

Die Naturwissenschaften. [*The Natural Sciences*]. *August 13, 1915. The Biological Influence of City Life.* H. Fehlinger.

The greater frequency of mental maladies in cities is in part ascribed to the fact that people suffering from them, even if they come from the country, are for the most part placed in city institutions. Whether these diseases occur more frequently among people born or grown up in the city or in the country population has not yet to my knowledge been proved. It is possible, however, and even probable, for in the strain of the city frail mental constitutions must naturally break down more easily than in the quiet of country life. This does not mean, however, that city life is responsible for their low power of resistance; rather it has made this apparent, while in the country it would have remained concealed. Moreover, it would have probably been transmitted to a larger number of descendants, while the breakdown which happens in the city usually occurs in the midst of the active period of life and puts an end to further transmission of the constitutional weakness. This is true also not only of lower mental resistance, but quite as much in regard to the inclination to other infirmities or diseases which depend on defective heredity. . . . (Pp. 429-430.)

The causes of the excess of mortality in cities are probably primarily of a social nature. It is known that the mortality among the urban laboring classes is by far the greatest, and that they suffer the most adverse conditions. Moreover, it should be specially noted that it is just among these that there are to be found a large number from the country who are not bred to city life, and therefore more subject to selective urban influences than natives. It is very striking, too, how industrial laborers coming from the country to the city deteriorate in the new surroundings. One involuntarily receives the impression that the strong and healthy aspect of these people is rather deceptive. The city man may look less strong and blooming to begin with, yet may evince greater powers of resistance.

It is questionable whether country children come into the world any stronger than city children. This is commonly said, but far from being proved. . . .

According to recruiting statistics, the country population shows a stronger general physique at maturity than that of the city—assuming, that is, that there is no tendency to enlist the rural rather than the city people. Dr. W. Claasen shows that the number of young men fit for service born in the country and engaged in agriculture sank from 61 per cent. in 1902 to 58.7 per cent. in 1907. Among those country-born, but employed industrially, the percentage fell at the same time from 60.2 to 57.5. Among those city-born and engaged in agriculture the decrease was from 60.1 per cent. to 56.8 per cent; and among those city-born and engaged in industry it was from 54.7 per cent. to 49.9 per cent. In considering these figures it must be remembered that the strength of the army remained unchanged while the number of recruits called on for service was increased. . . . (P. 430.)

But even if the rural population is distinguished by greater corporeal strength, this is no evidence of greater biological resistance. Modern city *Kultur* is still very recent, and from the biological standpoint it is not to be regarded as possible that in the short time in which it has been an influential factor it could have caused the degeneration of the masses ascribed to it. Even if it be admitted that through external conditions affecting the nutrition of the germ-plasm an indirect influence is exerted on inheritance, whose consequence might be that in the offspring certain qualities are less developed than are desirable for the welfare of the race, even then it is quite improbable that the economic changes of the last few decades could have occasioned a noticeable constitutional impairment of the people.

The standard of living of the masses has especially in the cities been decidedly improved; danger from trade poisons is increasingly avoided; the consumption of alcohol is diminishing; and the war on disease, especially on the social diseases has made great progress. . . . Whoever assumes an injury to the germ plasm from such causes must admit that the dangers have been decreased.

But the fact remains that in cities the struggle for existence is as a rule keener than in the country, and that therefore congenital defects sooner come to light. . . . This would also explain the lower percentage of military fitness in cities. (P. 431.)

Archiv für Rassen-und Gesellschaftsbiologie. Jahrgang 6, Heft 1, 1909. Die abnehmende Kriegstüchtigkeit im Deutschen Reich in Stadt und Land von 1902 bis 1907. [*The Decrease of Fitness for Military Service in the German Empire in City and Country from 1902 to 1907.*] Dr. W. Claasen.

Since 1902, in connection with the national effort to heighten our military efficiency, the fitness of the recruits for military service has been established with special reference to those from the city and from the country and those engaged in industry and in agriculture. . . .

General View of the German Empire.

Recruits	Examined	Fit for Service in line	Percentage of Fitness among those Examined 1902	1903	1904	1905	1906	1907
I. Country-born.								
a. engaged in agriculture	129,571	76,100	61.0	60.0	59.1	60.2	60.2	58.7
b. engaged in industry	185,772	106,783	60.2	59.2	58.2	58.5	58.3	57.5
II. City-born.								
a. engaged in agriculture	15,624	8,874	60.1	57.9	58.0	57.8	58.6	56.8
b. engaged in industry	199,367	99,420	54.7	53.0	52.6	51.3	50.5	49.9
Summary for Germany	530,334	291,197	58.5	57.1	56.4	56.3	55.9	54.9
Difference between I-a and II-b.....			6.3	7.0	6.5	8.9	9.7	8.8

According to these figures the fitness for military service has markedly decreased in the last five years. . . . We must then assume that the physical efficiency of the German population is still declining.

This decline involves both city and country populations, but the latter to only about one-half the same degree. The main mass of the country population is naturally country-born. There is no return movement from city to country worth mentioning. The city-born agricultural workers for the most part are born in small towns with a considerable agricultural population. Recruiting statistics define as cities all places with more than 2,000 inhabitants. As we further see, country birth acts steadily as a factor in the maintenance of strength. In general we may see by the table, the percentage of fitness declines with the degree of urbanisation. . . .

The city-born industrial population averaging the years 1903-1907 is 8.1% less fit for service than the country-born agricultural population. If we consider specific parts of the country we see that this difference is the more marked in proportion to the density of population. . . .

The decline in military fitness which on many sides is still contested, may be proved since 1893. The earlier figures of the recruiting statistics are not comparable with those since 1893. The percentage of men fit for service in the line, not counting those who were fit but excused from service on account of personal affairs (1903-1907: 1.7 of all recruits), averaged by five years were as follows:

1893-1897	55.8%
1898-1902	55.2%
1903-1907	54.4%.

The decline then is slow but incontestable; apparently, however, it is growing steadily faster. (Pp. 73-76.)

Archiv für Rassen-und Gesellschaftsbiologie. Jahrgang 6, Heft V. 1909. Stadt und Land als biologische Umwelt. [*City and Country as biological Environment.*] J. H. F. KOHLBRUGGE.

It is true to be sure that to-day the city mortality is in general higher than that in the country; but we must take into account that the mortality in almost all cities is falling; and we must give the cities time to adapt themselves to the increase of inhabitants before we pronounce judgment on them. And judgment must primarily be pronounced to-day not against city life as such but against still defective sanitary or hygienic regulations.

Let us remark moreover that no one knows how the mortality figures would stand for the country if all the factories in the cities were in the country. (P. 640.)

On the other hand we have to note, however, that many investigations bear witness to the fact that life in cities weakens the physique, that in cities for example are found a large majority of men unfit for military service, that rachitis, bad teeth, and narrow chests are noticeable there much more often than in the country. (P. 642.)

I will admit besides that the city-bred are in general less healthy and strong than country people; that moreover the expectation of life for men is less by four years in cities than in the country, and it would be perhaps still less, if there were not the constant drift from the country. (P. 642.)

People v. *Havnor, 149 N. Y., 195. (1896.)*

It is to the interest of the State to have strong, robust, healthy citizens, capable of self-support, of bearing arms and of adding to the resources of the country. Laws to effect this purpose by protecting the citizen from overwork, and requiring a general day of rest to restore his strength and preserve his health have an obvious connection with the public welfare. Independent of any question relating to morals or religion, the physical welfare of the citizen is a subject of such primary importance to the State, and has such a direct relation to the common good, as to make laws tending to promote that object proper under the police power, and hence valid under the constitution. . . . (P. 392.)

Increasing Organic Disease. The New Public Health Problem. Address delivered before The American Public Health Association, Rochester, September 9, 1915. E. E. Rittenhouse, *President Life Extension Institute, Inc.*

To sum up, the best available evidence shows that American life waste from the degenerative diseases is excessive; that it is increasing rapidly, both in city and in rural population, and among the native and foreign-born elements; that it is increasing in the younger age groups, but in greater ratio in middle life and old age; that this increased mortality has caused an increase in the general death rate commencing with age group 40-50, and that these increases do not occur in kindred nations in Europe. In short, American vitality appears to be declining. In view of this evidence may we not well consider these questions:

Warships, guns, forts and munitions for national defense are now subjects of serious public concern, and properly so. But is it not time to give thought to the physical efficiency of the men who are to handle these defensive weapons now and in the future?

How much longer may we hope successfully to meet the struggles of peace and war with the proportion of inactive, flabby-muscled, low-powered Americans constantly increasing?

How long can the nation endure with the physical fitness of its producers and defenders steadily declining?

This adverse trend is not only very marked but the death rate from organic disease is very high. The life waste from this cause is excessive. (Pp. 6-7.)

Our National Defense. The Patriotism of Peace. George H. Maxwell. *Rural Settlement Association. Washington and New Orleans, 1915, University Press, Cambridge.*

If we are going to have a citizen soldiery in the country, the first thing we had better set about is to produce a soldierly citizenry. (P. 20.)

Industry will destroy humanity unless a national system of life is universally adopted that will prevent racial deterioration. (P. 123.)

Employers of labor are most directly responsible for these evil conditions. They cannot shirk that responsibility. They cannot evade the fact that the menace against which we most need national defense arises from the degeneracy that we are breeding in our midst. If we cannot do both, we had far better spend our national energies and revenues in fighting the evils that are rotting our citizenship, than in building forts and fortifications, or maintaining a navy and an army for defense against the remote possibility of attacks by other nations. (P. 124.)

Soldiers alone are not all that a nation needs for defense, no matter how well they may be trained and equipped, or drilled and officered, or supplemented by naval strength or fortifications. The foundations on which national defense must be built are social, economic and human. The question involves every element of the problem of preserving and perpetuating even-handed justice to all, social stability, economic strength, independence, a patriotic citizenship and a rugged, stalwart and virile race. (P. 133.)

The Citizen as Soldier.—United States.

The Atlantic Monthly. April, 1916. Preparedness and Democratic Discipline. George W. Alger.

I have given . . . some statistics on the unfitness of the English worker for service in the army. What are the American statistics on the same subject? I have before me as I write the statistics compiled by the United States Marine Corps for the year 1915, showing the number of applicants examined, those accepted for enlistment, and the percentage accepted. For the whole United States, the applicants were 41,168 in number. Of these 3,833, or 9.31 per cent. were found physically fit for the service; in other words, one man out of every eleven examined. Eleven thousand and twelve men applied in New York City, and of these 316 were found fit for service, or 2.869 per cent. Those who find themselves now suddenly interested in physical fitness as a great element in military preparedness may profitably consider these statistics. Industrial anarchy in peace does not make for physical preparedness in war. (P. 483.)

The notion that preparedness is a mere military thing, to be had by superimposing upon the most wasteful, extravagant, and inefficient army and navy establishment in the world a new mass of similar expenditures, is a delusion. If we are so insistent upon preparation for war, and if we are, as we say, still unprepared after spending on such preparations over three billion dollars in the last twenty years, exclusive of pensions, let us at least in our preparation recognize an essential part of its true basis. The power behind military Germany is industrial Germany. The organization of German life is doubtless extreme, but the current preparedness doctrines, however much they may differ on military or naval estimates, agree at least in this: they ignore absolutely every necessity for improving the industrial organization, the economic basis for national unity. Sweatshops, child-labor, industrial anarchy held in check by martial law, the exploitation of the worker, lack of an intelligent policy in handling the immigrant, industrial accidents crippling and burdening the worker, industrial diseases unregulated and unprevented, the almost total absence of effective labor legislation on the side of inspection and regulation . . . all these and a hundred others are true problems of preparedness which are today ignored. . . . True preparedness calls, not merely for an external, but for an internal and industrial programme. (Pp. 485-486.)

IV. SHORTER HOURS THE ONLY POSSIBLE PROTECTION.

A. OVERLONG HOURS MAKE LIGHTEST WORK INJURIOUS.

The length of working hours, irrespective of the nature of occupation, is in itself, a menace to health. Industries not intrinsically dangerous and conducted under good sanitary conditions may become harmful through sheer lengthening of the working hours. Even the lightest work becomes totally exhausting when carried on for an excessive length of time.

Moreover, the man who is employed 12 hours a day is not allowed to leave the plant, except in rare instances, even when the work is not continuous. He is thus on duty and subject to orders more than three-quarters of his waking hours.

United States Congress. Senate Document, No. 110. Report on conditions of employment in the Iron and Steel Industry in the United States. Vol. I. Wages and Hours of Labor. Sixty-second Congress. 1st Session, 1911. Washington, 1911.

During the investigation those in charge of the plants have in their discussions with representatives of the Bureau frequently emphasized the fact that the men working these very long hours are not kept busy all the time. To a considerable extent this is perfectly true; but the employees in question are on duty and subject to orders during the entire period, and they are not, except in rare instances, allowed to leave the plant. It should not be overlooked that it is not simply the character or the continuity of the work, but the fact that in the case of the 12-hour-a-day man one-half of each 24 hours—more than three-fourths of his waking hours—is spent on duty in the mills, which is of significance to the worker and his family. (P. 15.)

Hours of Labor in the Steel Industry. A Communication to 15,000 Stockholders of the United States Steel Corporation. Written after full investigation by John A. Fitch, *for Charles M. Cabot, 95 Milk Street, Boston, a stockholder of the Steel Corporation, Boston, 1912.*

But all these things are more or less beside the point. Supposing it were true that the twelve-hour work is easy and that there were no physical indications of overstrain. The big fact, the only really vital and significant fact, remains that a twelve-hour schedule denies a man all true leisure. It isn't leisure for a man to sit on a bench in a steel mill waiting for his turn any more than it is for a motorman at a street crossing, waiting for the signal to proceed, or a machinist at his lathe, between times of increasing the tension. . . .

It is the workman's right to spend his leisure hours outside the mill yard, and that is something that the twelve-hour day denies him. (Pp. 11-12.)

Buckeye Cotton Oil Co. v. *State, 60 Southern Rep., 775. (1913.)*

The statute protects all employees in a designated class without reference to the sanitary or unsanitary condition of the establishment in which their work is performed. The injurious consequences from which they are protected are such as result from overwork of a certain character, and not such as result from unsanitary surroundings. That it appears from the agreed statement of facts "that the work in which these employees were engaged in no manner impairs their health, physical condition or moral nature, or that of the public," is also immaterial, for the experience of mankind has demonstrated that the contrary is the fact, when it is performed daily for many consecutive hours.

Report of the Illinois Factory Inspectors. 1893.

The lightest occupations are rendered injurious by long hours of labor. (P. 8.)

Overlong Hours Make Work Injurious.—Great Britain

Charities and the Commons, March 6, 1909. Vol. XXI. No. 23. New York. Factory Inspection in Pittsburgh. FLORENCE KELLEY, *Secretary National Consumers' League; Former Chief Factory Inspector, Illinois.*

Injurious Conditions of Work.

Industries may be injurious by reason of the nature of the machinery or of the material used (lead, sulphur, acid, etc.) or of dust produced in the process (steel, brass, cork, etc.) or of strain due to heat, cold, glare, darkness, or speed. Finally, an industry not intrinsically injurious may become so in a high degree by sheer lengthening of working hours, particularly when the workers are required to stand. (P. 1112.)

Even where the . . . work was as simple as wrapping caramels or packing crackers, the long hours combined with enforced standing made a harmless process highly injurious. (P. 1115.)

Evils of the Factory System. Demonstrated by Parliamentary Evidence. CHARLES WING. *London, Saunders and Otley, 1837.*

We must judge of the nature of an employment by its effects. Many employments require considerable exertion of strength, and yet, from being less monotonous, from requiring less of continued attentiveness, and from being carried on in daylight and in the open air, may be much less injurious than factory labour. But, however light, however easy, however healthy an employment may be it may be so protracted as to become neither light, nor easy, nor healthy, and that this has been the case with the factory labour no one who reads the evidence brought before the several committees that have from time to time been appointed can for a moment doubt. (Pp. xxix-xxx.)

Overlong Hours Make Work Injurious.—Great Britain

The Eight Hours Day. SIDNEY WEBB *and* HAROLD COX. *London, Walter Scott, 1891.*

The human body needs frequent change of surroundings, change of exercise, to keep it in perfect condition. A man, and still more a woman, will suffer from protracted occupation at one particular task, even if that task in itself is healthy enough. And of all the manual work done in an advanced industrial community to-day, how much is healthy in its nature or done under healthy conditions? (Pp. 6-7.)

The arguments and facts which we have above brought forward with regard to railway servants apply, with only slight differences of detail, to the employés of tramway and omnibus companies. The conditions of labour of these most useful servants of the public are about as bad as possible. The hours range from thirteen to seventeen a day on tramcars, and about the same on omnibuses. In order not to overstate the case, however, it may be admitted that anything beyond fourteen hours a day is exceptional in the case of omnibuses. On tramways it is to be feared that this limit is often overpassed, and we have been informed, on the best authority, of cases where a man is *regularly* kept at work seventeen hours a day. Of course, too, it must be borne in mind that trams and omnibuses run on Sundays as well as week-days, and on many lines drivers and conductors only get an occasional Sunday off. In one case reported to us while collecting information on this subject, a tramcar conductor had not had a single Sunday off for two years.

It is impossible to speak too strongly about the barbarity of such a system as this. That the work of driving or conducting a tramcar is not in itself exhausting, is no defense for such cruel prolongation. For however light the work itself may be, it involves the loss of liberty during the whole period over which it is continued. A man who is tied fourteen or fifteen hours a day to a moving car or 'bus has no liberty left him for reasonable recreation, no liberty to see his wife and children and his friends; no liberty ever for proper rest over his meals.

He has only just enough spare time to get to his house at night, stow his supper inside him, and tumble into bed.

Moreover, the actual work involved in a driver's or conductor's occupation, though light enough for the first half-hour or hour, or two hours, becomes a serious strain towards the end of a long day. . . . (Pp. 81-82.)

About the unhealthiness of such conditions of life it is hardly necessary to argue.

British Sessional Papers. Vol. XII. 1895. Report from the Select Committee on Shops (Early Closing) Bill.

Witness, Dr. Percy Kidd, M. D., [illegible] University of Oxford, Fellow of College of Physicians and Member of the College of Surgeons. Attached to London Hospital and Brompton [illegible]spital.

5352. [illegible]d this be a fair way of putting it: it is not th[illegible] work of people in shops, but having to be there [illegible]d standing about and sitting about in bad air; it is th[illegible] long hours which is the injurious part of it?—Quite so, the prolonged tension. (P. 218.)

British Sessional Papers. Vol. VI. 1901. Report from the Select Committee of the House of Lords on Early Closing of Shops.

Witness, Sir William S. Church, President of the Royal College of Physicians:

2306. . . . The evils which arise, I think, in these cases are those which arise rather from the long hours of attendance than from the severity of the labour. (P. 108.)

Revue Internationale de Sociologie, Nov.-Dec., 1895. Le Travail Humain et ses Lois. [The Laws of Human Work.] FRANCESCO S. NITTI, *University of Naples. Paris, Giard et Brière, 1895.*

But, says Lagrange, it is not solely the occupation demanding great muscular exertion that produces exhaustion, but it is often, and, in industrial life, almost always, the occupation requiring a great number of hours of work. In such cases, combustion is not very active and its wastes have time to be eliminated; the products of disassimilation do not necessarily accumulate in the organism and there is no auto-intoxication, but what does happen is that much organic material is used up and the organism suffers extensive losses. (P. 1034.)

Soziale Pathologie. DR. ALFRED GROTJAHN. *Berlin, August Hirschwald, 1915.*

Monotonous work is especially unhealthy. Modern industry, unfortunately, with its division of labor to the smallest detail, tends to replace the variety of hand work with the monotony of the shop and factory. The result is a more rapid fatigue of the worker, even in connection with easy work.

Finally unduly prolonged working hours may in themselves be injurious to health even if the work in itself is easy and healthful. We may say without exaggeration that there is no work which hours prolonged to the limit of the worker's strength may not make a torment and a serious menace to health. On the other hand many kinds of heavy and disagreeable work may be disassociated from many of their unhealthful features if performed for a short time only or in alternation with other kinds of work.

From these considerations it is clear that the regulation of working hours is a matter of the highest concern for the student of social hygiene as well as for the student of political science. (P. 467.)

Jahresberichte der Gewerbe-Aufsichtsbeamten und Bergbehörden für das Jahr 1907. Bd. III. [*Reports of the (German) Factory and Mine Inspectors for 1907. Vol. III.*] *Berlin, Decker, 1908.*

Bremen.

While it is quite true that in most cases their work is, by itself, not unreasonable in its demands upon their strength, yet when even easy tasks are performed in connection with highly perfected, rapidly speeded machinery, and are continued for hours and repeated thousands of times, they then constitute work that makes very great demands not only upon the physical endurance, but also upon the nervous system. (P. 24, [4-5].)

Proceedings of the Fifth Meeting of the International Association for Labor Legislation. Lucerne, 1908. Jena, Fischer, 1909.

Factory Inspector Furst:

A celebrated hygienist of Germany, Prof. Sommerfeld, says: "Overstrain may be either the result of unreasonably hard work, or of hours of work that are too long even though the processes of work do not make special demands upon muscular strength. In both cases the same results appear in course of time, sooner, in proportion as other dangers are involved in the occupation, or the organism of the worker is younger and less resistant, or the social conditions of the workers more wretched. (Pp. 124-125.)

Die Krankheiten der Arbeiter. Bd. 2. [The Diseases of Working People. Vol. 2.] Dr. LUDWIG HIRT. *Leipzig, 1878.*

In the second place the working time must be considered, because in this factor of work lies the greatest possibility of exhausting the strength by forced exertion. (P. 266.)

No attitude of the body is harmful in itself; only in prolonging it until it produces harmful results; all the well-known disturbances, such as varicose veins, etc., etc., arise, not through sitting or standing, but through excessively prolonged sitting or standing. (P. 268.)

Verhandlungen des Reichstags, 101. Sitzung, 16. April, 1891. [Proceedings of the (German) Reichstag, 101st Session, April 16, 1891.]

Representative Grillenberger:

If I am told that the laws already protect men from

over-long hours in dangerous employments or those which injure the health of the employee, I reply that therein is a proof of our correctness in demanding a general legal working day. The health of the worker is bound to be injured by over-long hours in any line of work, no matter what it is, and if the Bundesrath wishes to be logical, then it must take the position that the principle already acknowledged in that section of the law must be extended uniformly. It will be more rational to regulate conditions with foresight, by the law, than to leave them to work themselves out by slower methods. (P. 2364.)

Handbuch der Hygiene. Bd. 8[1]. [*Handbook of Hygiene. Vol. 8*[1].] *Edited by* Dr. THEODORE WEYL. *Allgemeine Gewerbehygiene und Fabrikgesetzgebung.* [*General Industrial Hygiene and Factory Legislation.*]. Dr. EMIL ROTH. *Jena, 1894.*

When we take up the question of the effect of special trades upon morbidity and mortality, it must be premised that the idea of industrial diseases or occupational diseases in the ordinary sense of the term is inaccurate, for the specific so-called dangers of trades *as such are not inseparably* bound up with those trades, as the special hygiene of the factory proves daily. Only in so far as the length of working time, and severity of physical or mental labor are concerned in the various trades, or the necessarily close crowding in closed rooms in one or another occupation, can we speak of the different effects of different kinds of occupation upon the organism. (P. 8.)

Jahresberichte des Gewerbe-Aufsichtsbeamten im Königreich Württemberg für das Jahr 1902. [*Reports of the Factory Inspectors in the Kingdom of Württemberg for 1902.*] *Stuttgart, Lindemann, 1903.*

. . . Reduction of hours does not keep pace with advances in technique . . . where there is an obvious tendency to make use of human power to the fullest possible extent. This is especially true in the textile mills, where certain older processes are modified by new contrivances. The result now is that, while the wages of skilled spinners (women) have risen about 12 or 13 per cent., the number of spindles on which they must concentrate attention for 11 hours has been raised from 500 to 750, an increase of 50 per cent. This is not quite the same as saying that the strain upon the spinners is 50 per cent. greater, since a certain number of helpers are provided. Nevertheless the attention and skill demanded are much greater than was formerly the case. Such examples make it plain that, with this increasing intensity of strain in work, the hours of work must be correspondingly shortened if the people are to be protected from ruin of their health. (Pp. 74-5.)

Handbuch der Arbeiterwohlfahrt. Bd. II. [Handbook of the General Welfare of the Working Classes. Vol. II.] Edited by DR. OTTO DAMMER. *Arbeiterschutz. [Protection of Working People.]* DR. ASCHER. *Stuttgart, Enke, 1902.*

The long working hours also explain the well-known fact that waiters and waitresses are "used up" at a comparatively early age. . . . The effect of work carried on during long hours in badly ventilated places is also important. . . . It is clear that many of these evils can be remedied only by shortening the working hours. (P. 70.)

Jahresberichte der Gewerbe-Aufsichtsbeamten im Königreich Württemberg für das Jahr 1903. [Reports of the Factory Inspectors in the Kingdom of Württemberg, 1903.] Stuttgart, Lindemann, 1904.

This uncontested fact of rising claims upon the physical and mental capacity of the workman, which is more or less strikingly evident in every department of labor, has in recent years brought the question of shorter hours to the front. The necessity of compensation through shorter hours is not only recognized by the inspectors, but by many employers as well. (P. 96.)

B. THE REMEDY: SHORTER HOURS.

A decrease of the intensity of exertion in industry is not feasible. The needed protection, therefore, can be afforded only through shortening the hours of labor.

Wealth and Progress. GEORGE GUNTON. *New York, Appleton, 1887.*

In proportion as the use of improved machinery is extended, and the specialization of labor is increased, does this labor become physically and nervously more exhausting; and in proportion as this pressure increases, unless the working time is correspondingly reduced, the laborer's susceptibility to the refining and elevating influences of his social environment is lessened and his leisure moments find him dull and indifferent to all moral and political influences. (P. 359.)

Report of the United States Industrial Commission. Final Report. Vol. XIX. 1902.

It is certain that any programme for reducing this intensity of exertion must fail. The entire tendency of industry is in the direction of an increased exertion. Any restrictions on output must work to the disadvantage of American industry, and the employers are often right in their demand, usually successful, that such restrictions be abandoned. This being true, there is but one alternative if the working population is to be protected in its health and trade longevity, namely, a reduction of the hours of labor. (P. 764.)

So far as restriction of product is designed to avoid excessive strain and to preserve the health and strength of the workers, the object is legitimate, and the method might be sanctioned if there were no better; but the same end may be attained in another way, which is more advantageous to the worker himself and which offers less ground for condemnation. Deliberate slackening of activity seems directly contrary to the principles of industry, and it alienates the sympathy of every one outside the wage-earning class. Diminution of working hours brings as great physical relief to the worker, and it offers social advantages which men of every class can appreciate. The enjoyment of home, the opportunity for intellectual cultivation, the possibility of stimulating new and higher desires—these things are visible to all and approved by all. (P. 820.)

Industrial Conference under the Auspices of the National Civic Federation. New York, 1902. The Eight-hour Day. Prof. George Gunton, *Institute of Social Economics. New York, The Winthrop Press, 1903.*

The factory system makes this (shortening hours) more and more necessary in proportion as it is perfected in its mechanism. It becomes all the time more and more exacting. The greater the perfection of the machinery or the method, the more attention is required. (P. 173.)

The remedy for this cannot be found in slackening up on the demands for economic output and effectiveness in the machinery. . . . The remedy for that must come on the other side, shortening the day, not slackening the effort. The tension may not be lessened, but the hours may be reduced. The exhaustion of the laborer must be avoided, but it cannot be avoided by reducing production . . . they must have relief by lessening the duration of the pressure every day. (Pp. 174-175.)

The Eight Hours Day. Sidney Webb and Harold Cox. London, Walter Scott, 1891.

In the large iron industries, again, constant alternations between fierce heat and the cold of the outer air are trying even to the most robust constitutions. Numberless industries also have specially noxious features, as, for example, the white lead industry, house painting, plumbing, fur pulling, etc., etc. And so we might go on through all the trades of the country showing the positive unhealthiness of the large majority of them. Doubtless in many cases a great deal of this unhealthiness might be removed by a little care on the part of the men, and a little expenditure on the part of the masters. But when all has been done in this direction that can be done, the great bulk of the manual work of the country must carry with it incidents of unhealthiness. Consequently the only way to diminish the ill effect on the human body is to diminish the period in each day during which the body is exposed to these noxious incidents. (Pp. 140-141.)

Canada Labor Gazette, August, 1903. Report of British Columbia Royal Labor Commission. Dawson. Ottawa.

The report concludes with a recommendation as to the shortening of the hours of labor. "In these days," say the Commissioners, "when the human energies are strained to their utmost amid whirling dust and machinery, long hours are a crime against nature. The machine should be the servant of man, and not man the slave of the machine. One of the most legitimate modes in which a legislature can aid in improving the condition of the workmen is by the shortening of hours." (P. 136.)

Eighth International Congress of Hygiene and Demography. Budapest, 1894. Vol. VII, Sec. V. Über das Verhältniss der Dauer des Arbeitstages zur Gesundheit des Arbeiters und dessen Einfluss auf die öffentliche Gesundheit. [The Length of the Working Day in its Relation to the Workman's Health and its Influence upon Public Health.] Dr. E. R. J. Krejcsi, *Vice-Secretary of the Chamber of Commerce in Budapest. Budapest, 1896.*

In branches of industry where machinery is used, the normal working day of which the worker is fully capable is shorter in proportion as machinery is more complicated and the demands made upon the intelligence, attention and memory of the worker are more incessant.

Such workers expend both their mental and physical strength in strenuous exertion, and thus their normal energy is sooner exhausted and the injurious results of overstrain become evident earlier than in simpler forms of labor. (P. 326.)

Archiv für Unfallheilkunde, Gewerbehygiene, und Gewerbekrankheiten. Bd. I. Über den Gesundheitsschutz der Gewerblichen Arbeiter. [*Protection of the Workingman's Health.*] DR. SCHAEFER. *Stuttgart, Enke, 1896.*

The more technic is perfected, the more complicated the machine and the more rapid its speed, the greater are the demands made upon the workman and the more important it becomes to shorten his hours of work. (P. 204.)

Die Pathologie und Therapie der Neurasthenie. [*Pathology and Therapeutics of Neurasthenia.*] DR. OTTO BINSWANGER, *Professor of Psychiatry and Director of the Psychiatric Hospital at Jena. Jena, Fischer, 1896.*

General prophylaxis will find its most pressing duty to lie in the protection of those members of society who are still healthy, from immoderate demands upon their strength. As, on account of the competition in all classes of society, it is hardly possible to relax intensity of work for any one individual without destroying his chances for success, a general plan of hygienic regulation of work must be adopted with a view to the preservation of racial vigor, and the working energy demanded shall be reduced enough to allow rest and recreation in ample extent for every one. (P. 358.)

Amtliche Mittheilungen aus den Jahresberichten der Gewerbe-Aufsichtsbeamten. XXII. 1897. [*Official Information from Reports of the (German) Factory Inspectors.*] *Berlin, Bruer, 1898.*

The demand for shorter hours of work is justified by the hardships in which modern industry has plunged the whole working class. In a comparatively short time, for instance, machinery of much greater speed has been installed in a number of branches of industry. Even the young, industrious workman must stretch every nerve to keep up with the speeding process necessitated by machinery. (P. 156.)

Machine work allows no time for rest and variety, the workman's nerves suffer, and when, as sometimes happens, his Sunday's rest is taken from him, he breaks down. Older workmen cannot accommodate themselves to this pace, and the rapidity of development has been such that a gradual adaptation to the altered conditions is for them absolutely out of the question. The result is that older people are excluded more and more from factory work. (P. 157). No unsatisfactory results appear to have followed in any instance where hours have been shortened. (P. 158.)

Gesammelte Abhandlungen. Bd. III. [*Complete works. Vol. III.*] *Die Volkswirthschaftliche Bedeutung der Verkürzung des Industriellen Arbeitstages.* [*The Economic Significance of a Shorter Working Day.*]. Ernst Abbe. *Paper read before the Economic Society at Jena in 1901. Jena, Fischer, 1906.*

On the one hand, it must be admitted that daily monotonous labor has a stupefying influence; on the other, that technical and scientific demands create a continuous strain upon intelligence; hence there is only one way to restore a balance:—by giving some opportunity for natural intelligence to develop, by concentrating daily toil into the shortest possible time and leaving the longest possible time for rest and intellectual stimulus, that people may not be made stupid, but, in spite of the monotony of their daily tasks, may retain the capacity for interest in other things. (Pp. 237-238.)

Jahresberichte der Gewerbe-Aufsichtsbeamten im Königreich Württemberg für das Jahr 1902. [*Reports of the Factory Inspectors in the Kingdom of Württemberg for 1902.*] *Stuttgart, Lindemann, 1903.*

But this reduction of hours does not keep pace with advances in technique . . . where there is an obvious tendency to make use of human power to the fullest possible extent. This is especially true in the textile mills, where certain older processes are modified by new contrivances. . . . The result now is, that, while the wages of skilled spinners (women) have risen about 12 or 13 per cent., the number of spindles, on which they must concentrate attention for 11 hours, has been raised from 500 to 750—an increase of 50 per cent. This is not quite the same as saying that the strain upon the spinners is 50 per cent. greater, since a certain number of helpers are provided, nevertheless the attention and skill demanded are much greater than was formerly the case. . . . Such examples make it plain that, with this increasing intensity of strain in work, the hours of work must be correspondingly shortened if the people are to be protected from ruin of health. (Pp. 74-75.)

Jahresberichte der Gewerbe-Aufsichtsbeamten im Königreich Württemberg für das Jahr 1903. [Reports of the Factory Inspectors in the Kingdom of Württemberg for 1903.] Stuttgart, Lindemann, 1904.

To-day the technical development of industry leads to ever and ever greater demands upon the intensity and attention of the worker. When the speed of the machine is greatest, then the workman has more given to him to attend to. This uncontested fact of rising claims upon the physical and mental capacity of the workman, which is more or less strikingly evident in every department of labor, has in recent years brought the question of shorter hours to the front. The necessity of compensation through shorter hours is not only recognized by the inspectors, but by many employers as well. (P. 96.)

Handwörterbuch der Staatswissenschaften. Bd. I. [Compendium of Political Science. Vol. I.] Edited by DRS. J. CONRAD, *Professor of Political Science in Halle;* L. ELSTER, *Ober Reg. Rath in Berlin;* W. LEXIS, *Professor of Political Science in Göttingen; and* EDG. LOENING, *Professor of Law in Halle. Arbeitszeit. [Hours of Work.]* DR. H. HERKNER, *Berlin. Jena, Fischer, 1909.*

The workman sees in reduction of working hours the surest remedy for all the dangers that arise from his work, and that menace him with premature exhaustion of his working power, his only capital. The more piece work and speeding stimulate the intensity of production, the more quickly a dangerous degree of fatigue is likely to appear, resulting from the one-sided exertion of certain nerves or muscles (a feature of the subdivision of labor). (P. 1204.)

Intensiveness of work means progress for the worker, so long as the tempo keeps within customary bounds; that is, while speed can be maintained without requiring continuous new impulses of will-power. If, in spite of shorter hours, intensiveness of work leads to chronic over-fatigue, then it is just as necessary to overcome that evil as the over-fatigue resulting from overlong hours of less intensity. (P. 1217.)

An das Schweiz. Industriedepartement, Bern, die Eidgenössischen-Fabrikinspectoren. [Report of the Swiss Factory Inspectors to the Swiss Department of Labor on the Revision of the Factory Laws.] Schaffhausen, 1904.

As technique becomes more developed, machinery more complicated, and the pace swifter, so much more insistent become the demands of the workers and the claims of hygienists for a shorter work day as a physiological necessity. (P. 23.)

When we consider the great material advantages of modern industry in being enabled to economize material by the use of water power day and night, by keeping its furnaces forever burning, and so on, it seems as if it might well be in place to economize also the strength of the people by shortening their shifts of work. (Pp. 34-35.)

V. ECONOMIC ASPECT OF REDUCING HOURS.

A. GENERAL BENEFIT TO COMMERCIAL PROSPERITY.

The experience of those manufacturing countries which have longest had the short working day, shows that commercial prosperity is not hampered by the curtailment of hours. The increased efficiency of the workers due to shorter working hours, together with the general improvement of industrial communities in physique and morals, reacts so favorably upon output that commercial prosperity is heightened rather than impaired.

The Employment of Children in Manufactories. Letter to the Earl of Liverpool. New Lanark. 1818. ROBERT OWEN.

Is it or is it not the interest of the master manufacturers that their operatives should be employed longer than ten hours per day?

The most substantial support to the trade, commerce, and manufactures of this and of every country, are the laboring classes of its population; and the real prosperity of any nation may be at all times accurately ascertained by the amount of wages, or the extent of the comforts, which the productive classes can obtain in return for their labor. It is evident that food must be procured by the working man and his family before he can purchase any other article. If therefore this class of our population is so degraded and oppressed, that they can only procure the bare necessaries of life, they are lost as customers to the manufacturer; and it is to be recollected that at least two-thirds of the population of all countries derive their immediate support from the wages of labor, and in this country chiefly from trade and manufactures. When ignorance, overwork, and low wages are combined, not only is the laborer in a wretched situation, but all the higher classes are essentially injured, although none will suffer in consequence more severely than the master manufacturer, for the reason which has been before stated. Let your minds dwell a little longer on this subject, and you will soon discover that it is most obviously your interest that your operatives should be well taught in infancy, and during their future lives rendered healthy, and put in possession of the means of being good customers to you. But they cannot be well taught, healthy, or competent to spend moderate wages advantageously for themselves, for you, and for the country, if they enter into your employment at a premature age, and are afterwards compelled to exhaust their physical powers by unreasonable labor, without proper relaxation and leisure. By such short-sighted practices you cut up your prosperity by the root, and most effectually kill the goose from which you would otherwise daily receive the golden egg.

I can have no motive to deceive you. My whole pecuniary interest is embarked in the same cause with you. I am one of yourselves, and should suffer more than the majority of you by any measure that really injured the manufacturing system. (Pp. 34-35.)

British Sessional Papers. Vol. XXIII. 1850. Reports of Inspectors of Factories for the Half-year ending April 30, 1850.

I am happy to be able to give some strong proofs that the Ten Hours' Act has not been productive of those ruinous consequences to trade which some predicted would inevitably follow, and that it has not had the effect of deterring persons from entering into the business and investing fresh capital in it, whether in building new mills or in extending works already existing, from an apprehension that ten hours' work could not yield a remunerative profit. There are many instances of additional machinery where there was previously unemployed power, and numerous instances of a change in the firm, implying also new investments of capital. And if we take into account the vast increase since 1834, not only of cotton mills, but of woolen, worsted, flax, and silk factories, it may be confidently maintained that the legislative restrictions imposed in that year and since, while they have vastly improved the condition of the operatives employed in them, cannot be charged with having thrown impediments in the way of a steadily progressive improvement in all these branches of trade. (Pp. 5-6.)

British Sessional Papers. Vol. XL. 1852-1853. Reports of Inspectors of Factories for Half-year ending April 30, 1853.

If those who in 1833 predicted (and there were some of great authority among our political economists who did so) the ruin of our manufacturers if the then proposed restrictions on factory labor were adopted, will now fairly and candidly look at the results of this great practical experiment in legislation, whether in relation to the improved condition of the factory workers, or to the increase of mills and to the fortunes since made in every department of manufacture subject to the law, they must, I think, admit that they have seen ground to make them pause before they in future condemn measures for elevating the moral and social condition of the humbler classes by the regulation of their labor, as being opposed to principle; for the factory legislation has been proved to be in entire accordance with principle, even with that of the production of wealth, when the term principle is understood in an enlarged and comprehensive sense. (P. 21.)

British Sessional Papers. Vol XVIII. 1856. Report of Inspector of Factories for Half-year Ending October 31, 1855.

. . . All the branches subject to the law have prospered and as regards cotton factories to an extent that they have been multiplied by at least one-fourth since the Act of 1833 came into operation. . . . The Factory Act of 1833 set the bold example to other nations of a great manufacturing country limiting in the face of formidable competitors the hours of labor in factories for the manufacture of textile fabrics. The example of England had followers on the continent. Other countries in which the evils of unrestricted and excessive labor in factories had become apparent, though the evils had become apparent to the Governments under different circumstances from those which excited attention in England, acknowledged that the limitation of the hours of labor within moderate bounds was as necessary for the welfare of the population as it had proved to be in England, and might be carried out with as little risk to the general prosperity of the manufacturer as it had been in England.. (P. 57.)

A vast number of the employers of labor assert the soundness of the principle of limiting the duration of labor and the development of the principle in this country has certainly attracted followers rather than created opponents. . . . The factory laws were enacted for the benefit of the employed, but under the full persuasion that they would prove innocuous to the interests of the employers, that anticipation, I believe, has in the main been verified; and in referring to the factory laws of France and their operation, I speak as fully persuaded that the uniform application of the principle of limited interference between employer and employed is advantageous to both, and certainly not mischievous to the former. (Pp. 76-77.)

British Sessional Papers. Vol. XII. 1859. Report of Inspector of Factories for Half-year ending 31st October, 1858.

It is most satisfactory to reflect that the experience of nearly a quarter of a century has proved the wisdom of Parliament in this humane legislation; that while the condition of persons employed in factories has been greatly improved by their protection from excessive labour, the restrictions have in no degree interfered with the prosperity of those branches of trade to which the

Acts apply, as I shall presently show by the clearest evidence. . . . It has been repeatedly said to me by mill owners and other persons living in the manufacturing districts that the Factory Acts have immensely improved the character, manners and general condition of the operatives. That they have in no way interfered with the progress and improvement of the branches of trade to which they apply is demonstrated by the following facts. . . . In 22 years the number of cotton mills is nearly doubled and the persons employed therein more than doubled; that the number of woolen and worsted mills has considerably decreased, but that the number of persons employed therein has more than doubled, showing that the larger mills have extinguished a considerable proportion of the smaller ones; that the same thing may be observed, although in a less degree, with regard to the flax mills; and that the number of silk mills has been doubled and the number of persons employed in them nearly so. (Pp. 8-9.)

British Sessional Papers. Vol. XXXIV. 1860. Report of Inspectors of Factories for Half-year ending October 31, 1859.

With regard to production, an analysis of the value of our exports in 1858 shows an increase of £21,231,032 over 1844, when the amended Factory Act came into operation. Of course I am not claiming this large increase on account of the Factory Acts, far from it, I only quote it to show that production has not been interfered with by them. (P. 53.)

British Sessional Papers. Vol. XXIV. 1866. Reports of Inspectors of Factories for Half-year ending 31st October, 1865.

Moreover, to assume that so to limit the hours of labour would be to destroy any branch of a particular trade is to assume that we have arrived at the end of mechanical and chemical science, and that there remains no more capital to be expended. . . . In no trade already under restriction from the longest possible hours to 60 hours' work a week, has production been diminished, or have the interests of the masters been injuriously affected; whilst it has become an axiom that overwork is never good work, seldom profitable, and always prejudicial to the physical and moral condition of the workers. (P. 82.)

British Sessional Papers. Vol. XIV. 1868-1869. Reports of Inspectors of Factories.

In conclusion we think we may point with satisfaction to the results of past legislation in this direction, seeing that in spite of the opposition, and deterring predictions hurled against it, our commercial intercourse and prosperity is extending with a corresponding increase of national wealth. (P. 314.)

The case for an Eight-Hours' Bill. London: Published for the Fabian Society by John Heywood, *1891. (Fabian Tracts, No. 23).*

Will shorter hours ruin our commerce? The capitalists and newspapers say so; but they ignore, as they have always ignored, the industrial advantages of the improved health and increased intelligence which follow upon the enjoyment of adequate daily leisure. Seventy-five years ago our cotton mills commonly worked ninety and one hundred hours per week. By successive stages these hours have been brought down to fifty-six and a half. At every stage it has been conclusively "proved" by the manufacturers that the proposed new restriction of hours would deprive them of all margin of profit, would raise the price of the commodity, lower the wages of the workers, and destroy the export trade. Yet the result has over and over again shown that manufacturers and theorists alike were wrong; the hours of work have been successively reduced, without diminution of production, fall of wages, rise of prices, or slackening of trade. (P. 10.)

The Eight Hours Day. Sidney Webb *and* Harold Cox, B. A. *London, Walter Scott, 1891.*

As regards the effect upon prices and the export trade, the following table is conclusive.

EXPORT OF BRITISH COTTON GOODS.

Average of Ten Years.	Quantities in Millions. Yards of Cloth.	Lbs. of Yarn.	Value in Thousands.	Per Inhabitant. Yards of Cloth.	Lbs. of Yarn.	Value in Shillings.
1821-30	340	39	£17,210	15	2	15
1831-40	589	90	21,390	23	4	16
Factory Acts, 1831, 1833, 1841-50	965	137	24,215	35	5	17
Factory Acts, 1844, 1847, 1850, 1851-60	1,988	171	38,030	70	6	27
Factory Acts, 1852, 1856, 1861-70	2,444	136	59,620	81	4	40
Factory Acts, 1861, 1863, 1864, 1867, 1870, 1871-80	3,693	222	71,930	110	7	43
Factory Acts, 1874, 1878....						

(Pp. 96-97.)

Shorter Working Day. R. A. Hadfield, *of Hadfield's Steel Foundry Co., Sheffield, and* H. de B. Gibbins, M. A. *London, Methuen, 1892.*

There are two very important sets of facts to be obtained upon this question of the previous effects of a reduction of working hours, and these facts come, not from Australia or any other country whose conditions we might grant were different from our own, but from England itself. We refer to the results shown in the working of the Factory Acts which reduced the hours of labour not by one or two, but by three, four, and even six hours per day, and which nevertheless, as everybody now admits, have been of immense benefit, not only to the working classes, but to the nation at large, and have caused no decline whatever in the rate of production. . . . During the successive reductions of working hours the price of cotton yarn has fallen from 25.71 pence per pound in 1821 to 12.82 pence per pound in 1884. (Pp. 102-103.)

As it is found that where labour is best paid that there are the best and, with certain qualifications, the cheapest products, so also will it probably be as regards reduced hours. (P. 114.)

Eight Hours for Work. JOHN RAE, M. A. *London and New York, Macmillan & Co., 1894.*

But the antecedent opinions of even the largest and most experienced employers cannot be set in the scale against actual experiment, and the teaching of experiment, as far as it has yet gone, seems certainly to indicate that an eight-hours day will strengthen us against foreign competition rather than otherwise, because it will strengthen that precise factor in production by which our industrial supremacy has been principally maintained, and on which apparently it must altogether depend in the future—viz., the high industrial energy of our workpeople.

The industrial competition of the nations is fast becoming a mere contest in the personal productive capacity of their labourers. The other conditions of the strife are getting equalized. . . . Improved machinery is no sooner made in one country than it is imported or imitated in another; and as the material elements of the competition are growing equal, the supremacy must obviously go to the nation that can turn these elements to most account—the nation with the most vigorous, the most intelligent, the most productive working class. . . . It is a great mistake, as I have already had an opportunity of showing, to imagine that the introduction of machinery has in any degree diminished the importance of the influence which differences in the personal efficiency of the labour of rival nations are capable of exerting on the results of the production of these nations and on their fortunes in mutual competition. Personal efficiency plays as decisive and controlling a part under machinery as it does in hand labour. (Pp. 144-146.)

This national characteristic of high productive energy, which has given us the superiority over Continental countries in the industrial competition, is itself the product of those high wages and short hours which are so commonly supposed to handicap us heavily for the race. (P. 150.)

Hours and Wages in Relation to Production. Lujo Brentano. *Translated by Mrs. William Arnold. London, Sonnenschein, 1894.*

. . . As a matter of fact, high wages and short hours are a cause of England's advance, while it is the contrary that causes our backwardness; and the same holds good of our relations to America and to Australia. (P. 72.)

How is it that it is not the countries which have the most perfect factory legislation, the shortest working-day, and the highest wages, that raise the cry that their competing power is threatened, but those in which the hours are longest and the wages lowest?

The experience of all nations teaches us that it is just those bad conditions of labour which they were anxious to retain that have caused their backwardness. Those conditions have acted like a prohibitive duty, checking technical advance, while on the other hand, high wages and short hours have conduced the leading countries to that advance which could only be attained with well-paid, strenuous workmen, in other words, with workmen whose standard of living was a high one; and this applies to all industries, not only to the textile ones. (Pp. 73-74.)

Schoenhof is no less right in saying that in the New World it is only the fittest who survive in the struggle to exist; in the Old it is hard to shake off the tenacious hold of the unfittest upon the industries in which they have once established themselves. For, in fact, low wages and long hours bring about a vicious circle from which, once one is within it, it is very hard to extricate oneself. For so long as labour is cheap, no technical progress seems necessary. It is bad labour conditions which are the main cause of the maintenance of inferior and long since antiquated methods. Then the employer appeals to the capital locked up in inferior processes of production and to the ruin with which he is threatened, in order to evade an improvement in the conditions of labour which would necessitate improved techn[illegible]. (Pp. 74-75.)

A History of Factory Legislation. B[illegible] L. Hutchins *and* A. Harrison. *Second Ed*[illegible] *London, King, 1911.*

. . . Accurate knowledge of the c[illegible]ions prevailing in an industry is an indispensable condition of legal regulation. For this reason the cotton trade [illegible]s the easiest to control, and having once established the principle of regulating hours and conditions of work in this trade, the Government had it continually before their eyes as a point of departure for further legislation. If it could be shown that this regulated industry, far from suffering in competition with others, went ahead, improved its machinery, and developed a higher standard of comfort than its rivals, then, although the improvement might not be due to the legislation, there would be, at all events, a strong presumption that good, and not harm, had been done. And this is what has taken place. No one has ever been able to get up in Parliament or out and say: "Here is your miserable textile industry, your deplorable cotton trade, drooping and ruined all because of Factory Acts—let us repeal them forthwith." What they had to say was that the improvement in the regulated industry was clear and conspicuous, whilst the irregularities in others remained a crying scandal. Gradually the conviction begins to appear in the utterances of public men that the evils of excessive labour and insanitary conditions, far from being peculiar to one or two industries, were, except under specially favourable circumstances, incidental to them all. (P. 121.)

The Case for the National Minimum. With Preface by MRS. SIDNEY WEBB. *London, National Committee for the Prevention of Destitution, 1913.*

Reduced Hours and Foreign Competition.—It follows that if production can be maintained as cheaply and as efficiently with reduced hours of labour, the bogey of foreign competition need not be raised. Indeed, Mr. A. H. Crosfield claims that in certain large and important branches of British industry the manufacturers have gained so largely by the introduction of the Eight Hours' Day that they [illegible] they will lose if their foreign competitors adopt the same system. This view is supported by the experience of the Tinplate and Chain and Anchor industries where the hours of work average forty-eight and forty-seven hours per week respectively. Yet these industries, with their short working hours, are the most successful of any British industries in their aggressive resistance to foreign competition, forcing their products beyond the most hostile tariffs specially constructed to exclude them. (Pp. 20-21.)

Report of Massachusetts Bureau of Statistics of Labor. 1881.

It is apparent that Massachusetts with ten hours produces as much per man per loom or per spindle, equal grades being considered, as other States with eleven or more hours; and also that wages here rule as high, if not higher, than in the States where the mills run longer time. (P. 457.)

Report of the Connecticut Bureau of Labor Statistics. 1886.

Down to a certain point, the nations who work shorter hours not merely do better work, but more work than their competitors. In Russia the hands work twelve hours a day; in Germany and France, eleven; in England, nine. Yet nine hours a day of English work mean more than twelve hours of Russian work.

The laborer receives better wages, and at the same time the manufacturer gets a larger product—so much larger that it is the Russian, the German, or the Frenchman who requires protection against his English competitor in spite of the longer hours and lower day's wages. (Pp. 16-17.)

Report of the New York Factory Inspector. 1894.

New York has about doubled its manufacturing resources and capacity in the decade referred to (1880-1890), notwithstanding the many laws which have been passed regulating the employment of the weaker elements of factory employees. To say that the passage of such laws and their strict enforcement injures trade or industry is a patent absurdity in the face of the facts shown, and is contrary to the history of all States and countries. . . . The gauge of the States' progressiveness and prosperity is not the wealth of its richest citizen, but rather the poverty of its poorest industrious laborer is a fairer test. When the conditions under which the latter strive are improved, the entire mass of citizens is benefited. Therefore, it is a reasonable proposition that factory laws, instead of being a detriment and a check to business, are in reality promoters of energy and productive of a greater earning and competing capacity. (P. 14.)

Report of the New York Bureau of Labor Statistics. 1900.

Fortunately, statistics are at hand which afford simple but fairly effective tests of the assertion that Massachusetts industries are threatened with ruin by restrictive labor legislation. In the first place, Massachusetts' cotton industry, the business chiefly affected by short-hour laws, has fully kept pace with that of rival States in the North. (P. 54.)

Certain facts appear with distinctness, one of which is that the cotton industry of Massachusetts has not only grown steadily throughout the period of short-hour legislation, but—what is far more impressive—has made larger gains than are shown by the adjacent States with less radical short-hour laws. In 1870, four years before the enactment of the ten-hour law, Massachusetts had 39.5 per cent. of all the cotton spindles in the North Atlantic States; six years after the passage of that law Massachusetts' proportion was 45 per cent.; in 1890 it was 47.5 per cent., and in 1900 53.5 per cent. It is difficult to see what clearer proof could be demanded of the beneficial results of the Massachusetts short-hour laws of 1874 (sixty hours a week) and 1892 (fifty-eight hours). (P. 55.)

Report of the United States Industrial Commission. Final Report. Vol. XIX. 1902.

Such progress as has already been made in the development of foreign trade has been made in spite of higher wages in this country, and as a result of the cheaper cost of production which has followed upon the possession of a more intelligent, better paid, and more energetic class of labor. The industries where the highest wages and fewest hours prevail are those in which the United States excels in marketing its products in foreign markets. A further reduction in hours will increase the efficiency of this labor and raise its intelligence. (Pp. 775-776.)

International Conference in Relation to Labor Legislation. Berlin, 1890.

Alone, the nations hesitate to reduce the hours of work for fear of competition, although, with modern machinery, experience has abundantly proved that the countries with the shortest working day attain the maximum of production. These are the countries that produce under good conditions most cheaply; that are most prosperous, and most feared as competitors in the world's markets. (P. 88.)

Le Travail de Nuit des Femmes dans l'Industrie. Rapports sur son importance et sa réglementation légale. Préface par ÉTIENNE BAUER. [*Night Work of Women in Industry. Reports on its importance and legal regulation. Preface by* ETIENNE BAUER.]

Dr. Fuchs, Factory Inspector, Baden:

No fact indicates that industry suffered any under the new régime. The production which had in some industries been slightly checked at first quickly recovered ground, thanks to the greater zeal of the workmen. The figures of the following table, taken from the statistics of German exports, do not in any case allow the assertion that the legislation exercised a paralyzing influence on the industry.

Kind of Goods	Value of Exports in Millions of Marks					
	1890	1891	1893	1894	1899	1900
Cotton goods	167.7	146.7	154.3	144.8	206.1	244.7
Woollens	246.8	227.8	217.9	186.7	217.2	235.8
Silks	175.9	146.5	152.6	103.9	142.7	139.5
Vestments, lingerie, etc.	121.3	67.6	61.7	60.4	92.3	99.6
Silver plate jewelry	36.1	31.3	23.9	25.4	48.7	73.5
Toys	26.8	28.4	30.3	29.4	43.0	53.4
Sugar	216.0	227.8	221.2	209.2	203.6	216.3

There resulted only certain difficulties and certain temporary disadvantages for some industries. . . . The limitation of the hours of work is especially felt by the export houses, though it is not possible to state that an industry has been injured. (Pp. 12-13.)

General Benefit to Commercial Prosperity.—Germany

Staats-und sozialwissenschaftliche Forschungen. Heft 138. [Researches in Political and Social Science. Vol. 138.] Edited by GUSTAVE SCHMOLLER *and* MAX SERING. *Höhere Arbeitsintensität bei Kürzerer Arbeitszeit, ihre personalen und technisch-sachlichen Voraussetzungen. [Intensification of Work in shorter Working-hours: its personal and technical basis.] Ernst Bernhard. Leipzig, Duncker & Humblot, 1909.*

Thus every reduction of the working day may raise the economic and intellectual forces of the nation. The gain in energy on the part of the individual sets itself against his exhaustion through labor; it strengthens power of resistance and lengthens life. The workingman can repay the economic costs of his bringing up by increased production. The industries save in coal, light, heat, wear on machines, polish and oil. Abbe, on the assumption that working-time is reduced from ten to eight hours, estimates this saving for Germany alone at 30-40 millions of marks.—Most important however is the moral and intellectual advantage of a shorter working-day. The intelligence of the people represents productive powers of the first rank, "a capital which for the most part lies fallow because conditions do not exist under which this intelligence could have full play." (Abbe). Above all does a technically developing industry, suited to a people of higher mental and moral development, have need of this capital. (P. 78.)

B. EFFECT ON PRODUCTION.

1. Examples of Superior Output in Shorter Hours.

The universal testimony of manufacturing countries tends to prove that the shortening of the workday acts favorably upon output. The introduction of a shorter workday does not result in lessened output.

Whenever reliable statistics of output have been kept, before and after the introduction of a shorter workday, they show that with rare exceptions the aggregate production under shorter hours has either equalled that of the long day, or risen above it.

These conclusions were long supposed to be true only of single individual manufacturing industries, such as the textile trade, in which the shorter workday was first established, over 70 years ago. The most recent investigations have confirmed the facts, and have shown that what was true of a single industry applies to practically all industries, and is thus not a special but a general rule.

a. SOME RECENT INSTANCES.

The Iron Age. New York, October 3, 1912. The Twelve-Hour Shift in the Steel Foundry. Results of its Abandonment in the Commonwealth Steel Company's Open-Hearth Department and the Substitution of an Eight-Hour Shift. R. A. Bull.

Hourly Wage Rate Higher for Eight-Hour Shifts.

The company with which I am associated some time ago inaugurated three eight-hour shifts as applying to the furnace and boiler crews, both of which had previously worked 12-hour turns. It had been my opinion and that of my immediate superior that such a revision of our working schedules in these departments would be accompanied with so much more efficient handling of the furnaces that if the rates per hour were reasonably increased to remove the natural disinclination of the men to receiving only two-thirds of their former monthly income, the final result would show economy. This was the purely business side of the question, whose humanitarian aspects received our first consideration. A careful adjustment of wages was planned which yielded an increase per hour of 22 per cent. to the first helpers, 18 per cent. to the second helpers and 16 per cent. to the third helpers. Even the door boy was included in the scheme, and was to receive an advance of 19 per cent. per hour. The boiler firemen were to be increased 19 per cent. per hour and the coalpassers 14 per cent. It should be borne in mind that none of the men affected had asked for a change in the shift hours, or an increase of wages, nor had any plant in our vicinity any such change in contemplation.

Permission of our principal executive officers was obtained to inaugurate the new plan, and when it was put into effect it came as a glad surprise to the various crews. No inducements were offered to them to render more efficient service, nor was any suggestion made that we proposed to keep comparative data. But it was an easy matter to make comparisons because we had a meter registering within ½ of 1 per cent. of accuracy by careful test, on each open-hearth furnace line to record the fuel oil consumption, a magnetic recorder to indicate the frequency with which the furnace burners were reversed, a system by means of which all extra pig iron used in each heat was weighed and recorded, a recording pressure gauge to show the steam pressure maintained in the boiler room, and finally the chemical analyses and physical tests customarily made for every heat to determine the relative qualities of the product.

Conditions of the Comparison Made.

. . . The first four weeks prior to the change and the first four weeks following were taken as those best for comparison, because working conditions for these two periods were as nearly identical as could readily be found in our plant. The melting stock, the fuel oil and the boiler coal were of uniform quality throughout, so far as the same grades or brands of these materials may possibly be. The demand made upon each 250-hp. boiler under fire was practically the same in each case, the air load being steady, but the electrical load extremely intermittent for the entire eight weeks, a chronic condition which in our case militates greatly against a desired uniformity of 125 lb. of steam pressure. The practice on the open-hearth platform had obtained for years of reversing the burners every 20 minutes when a furnace was charged and every 30 minutes when empty. It was, of course, the object to make the least possible additions to the percentage of pig iron charged, and the furnacemen were required to exercise such judgment in this respect as would keep the amount of extra pig within reasonable bounds and as low as possible. Naturally they were also expected to keep the burners nicely adjusted and to maintain the proper temperature of the bath at the lowest possible oil consumption. The furnaces were basic and 47,000 lb. of metal was charged per heat. The shift hours under the old plan had been from 6 to 6; under the new arrangement they are from 7 A. M. to 3 P. M., 3 P. M. to 11 P. M., and 11 P. M. to 7 A. M., these being the most convenient because of local conditions. The crews change their shifts the first day of each week, thus giving every three weeks the full daylight turn to each crew. Having made the above points clear, I refer you to the comparative record.

Improvement Under the Short Shift.

It will be readily understood that we were greatly gratified at the comparison, which indicates fully a more economical and efficient manipulation of both open-hearth and boiler furnaces. It will be observed that the differences in most cases are slight, but the pleasing and important feature is that the essential ones are in favor of the short shift.

It was not to be expected that the greatest improvement would take place immediately after the change, and had all working conditions been some months afterwards practically the same as they were previous to the adoption of the eight-hour shift, there could have been made a fairer comparison. Certain important working conditions have changed, it was advisable to compare periods as indicated. But it is interesting to know that in those instances where conditions remained constant there was a noticeable improvement the second month as compared with the first month after the new schedule was in force, as, for example, the reduction in the average amount of extra pig iron charged per heat, from 424 lb. to 137 lb.

Eight-hour Turn More Economical.

I do not know if any such comparisons as those made the basis of this paper have heretofore been made in a similar fashion. It is quite possible that the idea has some degree of novelty in certain of its details, for, notwithstanding the criticisms recently directed against the 12-hour shift, its prevalence is still almost universal in furnace operation in this country. And I feel satisfied that any careful comparison along the lines indicated by the record herein shown would convince any steel manufacturer of the wisdom of operating with three eight-hour shifts, purely from an economic standpoint. Speaking for the people with whom I am associated, we are greatly pleased over the change. And I can speak for the men in the same terms, for our furnacemen are enthusiastic in their praise concerning the new plan. And there is no small amount of inward satisfaction in the knowledge that we have done a humane thing. . . .

Therefore, viewed from any conceivable angle, I claim the change is justifiable and you will do well to make it so far as your open-hearth furnaces are concerned. As to your boiler firemen, each operating head must decide for himself. In our particular case it appeared to be, and finally proved to be, advisable from every standpoint. Conditions in certain other boiler rooms are very different from ours, practically the entire evaporation taking place during the daylight hours in many of them. Since the results are of some interest, however, I have included the comparisons made in our power plant. Reverting finally to consideration of the steel-maker, whose performance under both schedules is made the burden of this argument, the basic principle is absolutely sound and rests on the incontrovertible fact that you cannot expect any man to give you the best that is in him when you keep him employed without intermission for 12 hours per day, seven days per week, at work making a heavy demand upon his mental and physical powers, under conditions of high temperature such as obtain on a furnace floor. To expect the best results under such circumstances is folly and to continue operating under them spells, not the title of this paper, but the *costly* side of the 12-hour shift. (Pp. 808-809.)

Comparison of Results in Open-Hearth Department and Boiler Room with 12-Hour and 8-Hour Shifts.

Open-Hearth Furnaces.

		12-Hour Shift.	8-Hour Shift.
Average amount of extra pig iron charged per heat		556 lb.	424 lb.
Average amount of fuel oil consumed per heat		1,275 gal.	1,138 gal.
Average amount of fuel oil consumed per ton of metal charged		55 gal.	49 gal.
Average number of cracked castings per heat		0.49	0.37
Average of longest intervals between reversals of burners during 12-hr. periods		28 min.	26.7 min.
Average of chemical analyses of all heats	Carbon	Correct percentage	Correct percentage
	Phosphorus	0.011%	0.011%
	Sulphur	0.022%	0.022%
	Manganese	2 points under	Correct percentage
	Silicon	1 point over	Correct percentage
Maximum phosphorus in any heat		0.022%	0.018%
Maximum sulphur in any heat		0.025%	0.025%
Average physical tests of all heats	Yield point per sq. in.	13.0% over	15.5% over
	Tensile strength per sq. in.	5.9% over	5.8% over
	Elongation in 2 in.	4.6 points over	4.1 points over
	Reduction of area	7.9 points over	7.2 points over
Minimum physical tests of any heat. (Not combined results of one bar, but individual minimums of results covering all bars.)	Yield point per sq. in.	2.5% under	7.7% over
	Tensile strength per sq. in.	4.7% under	1.4% under
	Elongation in 2 in.	5 points under	3 points under
	Reduction of area	8.3 points under	7.6 points under

The term "point" means 1-100 of 1 per cent., where analyses are referred to, and elsewhere 1 per cent., but in all cases it refers to differences from works standard, being found by simple subtraction. In no case does it indicate relative or proportionate results. Where such are shown they are indicated by "per cent." followed by "over" or "under." "Over" and "under" mean respectively results more or less than those desired by plant requirements, and we have no reference to A. S. T. M. standard specifications, the requirements of which are fully met in all the minimum results obtained under the eight-hour shift. "Correct percentage" means exactly the composition desired. Lowest possible content of phosphorus and sulphur are demanded by plant requirements.

Boiler Room.	12-Hour Shift.	8-Hour Shift.
Number of times when steam pressure fell below 110 lbs.	77	42
Number of times when steam pressure fell below 105 lbs.	9	3
Number of times when steam pressure fell below 100 lbs.	1	0

On 12-hour shifts, from 6 a. m. to 6 p. m., one head fireman, two second firemen and two coal passers were employed; and from 6 p. m. to 6 a. m. one head fireman, one second fireman and one coal passer, at total expense per day of 24 hours of $19.50. On 8-hour shifts from 7 a. m. to 3 p. m., one head fireman, one second fireman and two coal passers were employed; and on each of the other two shifts one head fireman, one second fireman and one coal passer were employed, at a total expense per day of 24 hours of $19.12, or 38 cents less per day of 24 hours divided into three 8-hour shifts, despite the increased wages per hour.

As employers of labor we must look this question squarely in the face, realizing, if we do not understand as well as a layman may, the nature of work we require of men for 12 hours per day for seven days of the week, it is high time that we fully inform ourselves, and further, that having ascertained those facts, we will by no means benefit ourselves by attempting to disguise conditions.

Trying Conditions of Steel Furnace Work.

The question of the long shift, so far as the American Foundrymen's Association is concerned, crystallizes into a consideration of the melter and his furnace helpers, and has to do with the steel foundry. . . . Briefly, however, for the benefit of all others who may be interested in the subject, the work is distinctly arduous, physically and mentally, carries a responsibility which puts a man's nervous system in frequent high tension, and is especially trying on the physical system during the summer months. It can, however, be truthfully stated that the difficulties of the work are not constant but periodic, also that the Sunday shift in the steel foundry (not necessarily in the steel mill) is a very easy one. A furnaceman may have a considerable interval of comparative relaxation, when his furnace and heat respond nicely to his manipulation, and weather conditions prevail which do not make the working temperature a hardship. And again, he may, in spite of all the experience and skill at his command, have about as trying and exhaustive a day's work, without intermission and for several days in succession, as one can readily imagine. This latter fact being admitted, one can understand why our legislators are putting the furnaceman's occupation under scrutiny, in the interest of humanity. . . .

Injustice of the Long Turn on the Furnace Platform.

This paper does not purport to deal with the humanitarian side of the issue. But without stating in brief my own convictions, it might be claimed that I evade that phase of the question. . . . I do not hesitate to state my belief in the absolute injustice, humanely speaking, of the 12-hour shift on the furnace platform. I trust that I shall not be classified as a Socialist for having such a conviction. The question must be decided neither from the viewpoint of the plutocrat nor that of the walking delegate, and I claim to have formed my conclusions after consideration of the question from a conservative standpoint, and after many years of personal observation of working conditions surrounding the furnaceman's work. Furthermore, to offset any suggestion of bias, let me say that I do not now hold, and never have held, a union card, active or honorary, issued by any labor organization. (P. 808.)

British Association for the Advancement of Science. Section F.—Manchester, 1915. The Question of Fatigue from the Economic Standpoint.—Interim Report of the Committee, consisting of Professor J. M. Muirhead (Chairman), Miss B. L. Hutchins (Scorctary), Mr. P. Sargant Florcnco (Organizing Secretary), Miss A. M. Anderson, Professor Bainbridge, Mr. E. C. Cadbury, Professor Chapman, Professor Stanley Kent, Dr. Maitland, Miss M. C. Matheson, Mrs. Meredith, Dr. C. S. Myers, Mr. C. K. Ogden, Mr. J. W. Ramsbottam, and Dr. J. Jenkins Robb. (Report drawn up by MR. P. SARGANT FLORENCE.)

If we define fatigue in general as a "diminution of the capacity of work which follows excess of work or lack of rest, and which is recognized on the subjective side by a characteristic malaise," we at one and the same time put forward its most familiar symptom and its main external cause. (P. 2.)

That . . . the output of work may be expected to vary and to vary inversely with fatigue is suggested by the very definition of fatigue as a diminution in the capacity for work. (P. 17.)

Our figures agree with one another to such an extent, . . . that we are justified in speaking of a "normal" time-distribution of output. . . . The shape of the output . . . curves for a five-hour spell may for purposes of illustration be summarized as follows:

Hour of Spell	Output
1st . .	small
2nd . . .	very great
3rd . .	great
4th . . .	fair
5th . .	*small

In seeking an explanation of this 'normal' time-distribution of the . . . output in a spell of manufacturing work, let us concentrate on the illustrative table. Here we find the four same degrees: very great, great, fair and small, succeeding one another. . . . Now both output and accident immunity vary inversely to fatigue; these four decreasing degrees, therefore, may well be measuring an increase in fatigue. (P. 29.)

In the case of *output* there is in every table an increase of the second over the first hour of the spell except for a very slight decrease (Machine Sewing) in the afternoon. This almost general increase is as much as from 24 to 38 in soldering, Table III. and from 85 to 106 in Hand Chocolate-covering, Table II.

After the second hour of each spell there is generally a gradual decrease till the last hour, though in the third hour the output may be yet higher than in the second. (P. 26.)

* Where there are only four hours in the spell, strike out the last output . . . hour.

Table II.—Chocolate-covering Output.

Messrs. Cadbury, Bournville.

10 couples and 4 individuals for 10 days, in September, 1903.

Conditions.—Normal. Dinners supplied at cost price.

Workers.—Girls over eighteen. . . .

The Process.—Apparatus work (in couples): Handwork (singly). . . .

Relative Hourly Variation

Average of hour's output—100:

Time	Apparatus	Hand	Hour of Day	Hour of Spell
9-10	88.3 (1)	85.5 (2)	D1	S1
10-11	93.9	106.5	D2	S2
11-12	106.35	98.6	D3	S3
12-12.30	118.4 (4)	88.6 (5)	D3½	S3½
1.30-2	96 (2)	101 (3)	D4	S½
2-3	98.55	107.6	D5	S1½
3-4	94.4	107.4	D6	S2½
4-5	97	103.2	D7	S3½

NOTES.—Here (1) 15 mins., (2) 10 mins., (3) 5 mins. spent in "preparations" are averaged; and (4) 10 mins., (5) 5 mins. spent in "clearing up" are averaged. No clearing up included in the 4-5 figures since work ends at 5.30.

Table III.—Small Tin-box Soldering Output.

W. & R. Jacob & Co., Dublin. 10 workers for 10 days. Sept., 1914.

Workers.—Girls aged 17-25.

Work.—Standing up.

Cadbury Bros., Bournville. 7 workers for 1 day. Feb., 1915.

Boys aged 15½.

Sitting down.

Average rate of tins per hour per day.

Clock Time	Jacob's		Working Hour (D of Day, S of Spell)		Cad-bury's	Clock Time
8-9	24.3	(*)	D1	S1	46.8	7.45-8.45
9-10	38.42		D2	S2	52.4‡	8.45-9.30
10-11	35.29		D3	S3	47.1	9.30-10.30
11-12	35.03		D4	S4	44.4	10.30-11.30
12-1	29.74		D5	S5	43.7	11.30-12.30
2-3	26.62		D6	S1	45.1	1.30-2.30
3-4	37.39		D7	S2	48.7	2.30-3.30
4-5	37.06		D8	S3	42.9	3.30-4.30
5-6	34.93	(†)	D9	S4	40.8	4.30-5.30

NOTES.—(*) 7 minutes averaged for preparation. (†) 6 minutes averaged for clearing up. (‡) Averages to the hour. (P. 42.)

The afternoon's output is somewhat less than the morning's, but in both spells the maximum output occurs in the second, or, where the first period recorded is half an hour, as at Peek, Frean's (Table V.), in the first hour and a half, or second hour and a half. After this there is the gradual decrease of output, till the last hour's output may only total about 80 per cent. of the maximum for the spell, less if it is the fifth hour (as general in the morning), more if it is the fourth hour (as general in the afternoon). The total of the records of output of the three examples of soldering tins recorded at three different factories (Tables III. and V., Col. 3) is as follows:*

Hour of Spell	Morning	Hour of Spell	Afternoon
1st	114.06 tins	1st	119.43 tins
2nd	167.44 "	2nd	165.42 "
3rd	159.59 "	3rd	163.23 "
4th	157.27 "	4th	155.95 "
5th	138.96 "		

and the average hourly outputs added together of the three examples of hand-labelling of tins recorded at two different factories (Table V. and VI.) is as follows:†

* Weighted roughly in proportion to numbers and days at work; *i. e.*, Cadbury's ÷ 5, Peek, Frean's 1, Jacob's × 3.

†Table VI. Col. 1 is reduced to average per girl, but there is no other "weighting," since numbers × days at work are not very different in each case, *i. e.*, 8, 20, and 18.

Superior Output in Shorter Hours.—Great Britain.

Hour of Spell	Morning	Hour of Spell	Afternoon
1st	593.7 tins	1st	602.6 tins
2nd	669.0 "	2nd	622.9 "
3rd	687.9 "	3rd	611.0 "
4th	624.7 "	4th (not given in one case)	
5th	574.3 "		

(Pp. 34-35.)

Table V.—Processes at Peek, Frean & Co. April to June, 1915.

Work.—9 lb. Tin. Straightening.*	Tin. Labelling.	4 & 9 lb. Tin. Soldering.	Biscuit. Cream Stencilling and Sandwiching.
Numbers.—6 for 6 days.	3 couples, 6 days.	6 for 6 days.	6 couples for 6 days.
Workers.— Girls 21-24 years.	Girls 20-28 yrs.	Girls 17-24 yrs.	Girls.
Pay. — Piece-Bonus.	Piece-Bonus.	Piece-Bonus.	Piece-Bonus.
Surroundings. — Normal.	Normal.	Normal.	Normal.

Average rate per hour per day per individual:

	Of tins.			Of trays of biscuits.
8:00– 8:30	151	148.4	31.8	3.50
8:30– 9:30	170.4	165.2	41.7	3.99
9:30–10:30	171.25	162.7	44.3	3.92
10:30–11:30	168.75	156.3	43.3	3.95
11:30–12:30	138.6	147.3	41.0	3.62
Dinner.				
1:30– 2:30	160.6	144	39.55	3.63
2:30– 3:30	170.9	157	43.51	3.78
3:30– 4:30	165.4	150.2	43.47	3.87
4:30– 5:30	149.7	150.7	43.0	
5:30– 6:00	....	....	33.97	

* Each tin had different-sized dents differently placed, all to be hammered straight with mallet and wooden anvil.

Table VI.—Output. Hand-Labelling of Tin-Boxes. Report of Mr. Greenwood to the Fatigue Committee, 1914.

Hours of Day.	Total. 8 girls. One day.	Average. 4 girls. Average of 5 days.
7:30– 8:30	2,032	191.3
8:30– 9:30	2,123	238.4
9:30–10:30	2,282*	240
10:30–11:30	1,922	228.2
11:30–12:30	1,663	219.1
1:30– 2:30	1,921	218.5
2:30– 3:30	1,956	221.5
3:30– 4:30	1,938	218.6†
4:30– 5:00	1,430‡	

(P. 46.)

The following would be the psycho-physical diagnosis of a spell of factory work considered chronologically.

First hour: Fingers, arms, body and mind after their rest are working slow, but sure. To increase the pace and even perhaps to concentrate attention is uphill work and a fight against subjective feelings of sloth. In an emergency, however, muscles could be perfectly controlled.

Second hour: Body and mind getting into their stride again, are working very fast, but not perhaps so exactly. Feelings of sloth are conquered, but there is a terrible long prospect of work ahead. However, as work is running easily, the mind may think of pleasanter things: attention scatters.

Third or third and fourth hour: Body and mind running on, but attention lost. If any sudden danger threatens or emergency arises, it may not be quickly enough perceived, and when perceived muscles may not be quick enough to prevent an accident; they can con-

* Ten minutes (10-10.10) spent at lunch is average.
† For 4 days average.
‡ Rate per hour.

tinue rhythmically and automatically at the same work, but for any change of movement that may be suddenly called, there is insufficient *control.*

Last hour (fourth or fifth): Body no longer running automatically with the same ease, an effort of the will required (spurt) to keep speed up; but the end is ahead, with food and rest; the attention awakes and control over the muscles is braced up—danger is better perceived and more quickly avoided. At the very end, however, even this new attention and control may tire, as indeed the whole body is tired, and only a rest can bring recovery. (P. 31.)

The New Statesman. Vol. V. No. 129. Sept. 25, 1915. Men as Machines.

It is one of the most unfortunate characteristics of modern industry that the machine is no longer the implement or the instrument of the man, but the man is only an appendage or extension of the machine.

The unfortunate results of this development were well brought out in a report on "Fatigue from the Economic Standpoint" presented to the British Association and in the discussion upon it at Manchester. You may quite easily convert a human being into an extension of the feeding apparatus of a machine which stamps soap, and you will see him for a wage of some twenty shillings a week repeat the operations of inserting a cake of soap, pulling down a lever, and removing the cake of soap for eight or ten hours a day. But unfortunately, despite the efforts of employers and politicians to ignore the fact, the man obstinately remains a human being and not a machine. For it is characteristic of the human being that, unlike the cogwheel and the lever, in him repeated work, mental or physical produces fatigue. (P. 583.)

It is almost incredible that politicians, employers, and even economists should still believe that longer hours necessarily mean greater production. They believe it simply because they have come to regard the manual worker either as a machine or as an economic abstraction. But even statistics show that he remains a human being. The statistics are of two kinds, those relating to output and those relating to accidents. As regards the first, the most striking are those which show the difference of output in the different hours of spells of work. In nearly all industrial processes where investigations have been conducted the same phenomena are observed. If the work is divided into a morning and an afternoon spell of four or five hours each, then in the first hour of the spell a man's or a woman's output will be low, in the second hour it bounds up and usually attains its maximum, after the second hour there is a steady decrease in output until the last hour, in which sometimes there is again a slight increase. These facts show the exaggeration in much of the talk about the deliberate limitation of output by workers. They are found to exist when men and women are on piecework—that is to say, where the *incentive* to work is the same in the last hour as in any of the others. If, then, there was any very extensive deliberate limitation, one would expect to find no regular variations in the output of the different hours, because all through the spell the man would be producing deliberately less than he was able to produce.

But the true explanation of this regularity of variation is that the most important factor in limiting output is fatigue, which is scientifically defined as "a diminution of the *capacity* for work which follows excess of work or lack of rest." The smaller output of the first hour is due to the worker not being warmed up to his work; his muscles are stiff and he has not got into the swing of it, mind and body are working slow. In the second hour mind and body have got into their stride, the work is done easily and automatically, and the output is large; but after the second hour fatigue begins more and more to exercise its influence, and mind and body begin to work more and more slowly. But perhaps the most interesting fact of all is the cause of that increase of output in the last hour of a spell of work. It has two curious characteristics; it is frequently found in men's work, rarely in women's, and it can often be analyzed into a marked increase in the first half-hour of the last hour and a marked decrease in the last half-hour. The explanation is that a feeling of pleasurable excitement comes with the last hour of work: it is due to the thought of food and rest ahead; the consequence is that for a time the feelings of fatigue are thrown off, but very often this new and factitious strength does not last out the full hour and before the end of the spell fatigue reasserts itself with redoubled power. (P. 584.)

These facts suggest certain conclusions. In the first place, to treat the human being as a piece of iron or steel does not make even for industrial efficiency if that efficiency is measured by output. The amount of rest required if a man is to attain his maximum output has hardly been studied at all by employers, but where it has been studied the results were remarkable. There was a famous "Scientific Management" case at the Bethlehem Steel Works, in which by making a man rest for stated intervals during the day his output was increased by 60 per cent. In fact, there is good reason for saying that, if you want to increase production, you should tell the workers not to work more, but to rest more. Moreover, as Professor Benjamin Moore pointed out in the discussion at Manchester, at the present time people talk about the industrial slacker and "pay little attention to the man doing 70 hours a week." You get more work done in three eight-hour shifts than in two twelve-hour shifts. And men and women worked at high pressure for these long hours day after day inevitably break down, because "there is a physiological limit to which a man can be speeded up without injuring him." That, of course, did not matter very much to the employer when his human machine was cheap and plentiful, but it is hardly good policy, when Mr. Lloyd George is crying aloud for workers, by long hours and speeding up to lose those we have through an "accident due to fatigue" or merely because, unlike the machines, they have passed the "physiological limit." **(P. 584.)**

Superior Output in Shorter Hours.—Great Britain.

Engineering, Vol. C. No. 2599. London, October 22, 1915. Work-Weariness and a Three-Shift System. A Letter from JOHN E. GRANT.

Some months ago, before the war, I substituted a three-shift system in place of a two-shift system on account of shortage of some special machinery. It was so successful that it was retained and extended.

The original two-shift system was made up as follows:

A day shift from 7 a. m. to 5 p. m., with an hour's break—12 noon to 1 p. m. On Saturdays the week ended at 12 noon, and the total normal day-shift week was fifty hours. The night-shift ran from 6 p. m. until 7 a. m. next morning. There was a supper hour from 10 p. m. until 11 p. m., and a breakfast half hour from 3 a. m. to 3:30 a. m. The total night-shift week was normally 57½ hours. Also shop production was paid for on piece-work and bonus plan, and it was found that the output per man per hour on night-shift was 15 per cent. to 20 per cent. less than on the day-shift. The three-shift system which displaced the two-shift system was made up as follows: "A" shift from 7:30 a. m. until 4 p. m., with meal half-hour from 12 noon to 12:30 p. m.; "B" shift from 3:30 p. m. until 12 midnight, with meal half-hour from 7:30 p. m. to 8 p. m.; "C" shift from 11:30 p. m. until 8 a. m. next day, with meal half-hour from 3 a. m. to 3:30 a. m. The shifts for the week finish:

"A" shift, 4 p. m. Saturday.

"B" shift, 12 midnight Saturday.

"C" shift, 8 a. m. Sunday.

Any worker may obtain leave away on Saturday afternoons by obtaining a substitute willing to take his place from one of the other shifts, and we have no trouble from what appears at first sight to be a formidable obstacle.

There are thus three-shift weeks of 48 hours each, a total of 144 hours, compared with the two-shift weeks of 50 hours and 57½ hours—a total of 107½ hours; or, in other words, we obtain an increase in the normal weekly working hours of 34 percent. In actual fact it is worth more than this, as the output per man-hour is greater, and we soon found that each man in his 48-hour week was doing as much as he did before in the 50-hour day-shift week, and the output has increased 50 per cent. in view of the better value obtained from the night hours.

In the three-shift system we have each shift lapping over the other to the extent of half an hour, or equal to the meal half-hour. The half-hour is occupied in this way. During the first 15 minutes the incoming worker gets all his work and tools ready and clears up all obscurities before he begins. He then takes over the machine, and for the remaining 15 minutes of the half-hour the outgoing worker books in his work and attends to the various small duties necessary to be done before he leaves.

In changing the shifts at the end of every week, "A" shift becomes "C" shift, "B" shift becomes "A" shift, and "C" shift becomes "B" shift.

The shift itself therefore is run at high pressure, and the machine is kept running every possible minute. There is no time to think of weariness, and the workers are cheerful and energetic. . . .

Apart from the benefit of increased output, there is also a gain in economy, due to lesser overhead charges, even when increased maintenance cost, because of more machine hours per week, is taken into account. (P. 430.)

b. TEXTILE TRADES: COTTON, WOOL, LINEN, JUTE, ETC.

British Sessional Papers. Vol. III. 1816. Report from the Select Committee on the State of the Children Employed in the Manufactories of the United Kingdom. Minutes of Evidence. 25 April-18 June, 1816.

Testimony of Robert Owen:

You say you have tried the experiment, since the first of January, of only ten hours and three quarters per day; what was the result of that experiment?—The result of the experiment, with regard to the persons employed has been most favorable in every way; the result to the proprietors is much less unfavorable, under the most unfavorable circumstances which it could be tried, than could be supposed. The difference between our former time of working and the present, is an hour per day; for many years previous to the first of January last, the hours of work at New Lanark were eleven and three-quarters per day, exclusive of the time allowed for meals; since the first of January last the hours of work have been ten and three-quarters; and I find by actual practice, made from very accurate calculation, that the difference to the proprietors, taking every circumstance in the most unfavorable way in which they can be taken, will not be more than one farthing per yard upon the goods manufactured from the yarn spun at that manufactory; and I have every reason to believe, from the progressive increase in the quantity which has taken place regularly every month since this change took place, that before the end of the year the yarn will be manufactured as cheap, working ten hours and three quarters per day, as ever we manufactured it, working eleven hours and three-quarters per day. The present loss is not more than one farthing in twenty-pence. Nay, so convinced am I, from the very accurate calculations that have been made upon the subject, and viewing the consequences in the most extensive manner, which with all my experience I could view them, I do not hesitate now to say, that although no bill should be passed, although no restrictions should take place with regard to hours, or the limitation of the children being admitted into the works, in a pecuniary view only, I would not again alter the hours of the New Lanark establishment. (P. 90.)

You have expressed your opinion, that before the end of the year the loss of a farthing in twenty-pence, which you mentioned as accruing from the alteration in the hours of work, would vanish; from what did you form that opinion? On the increased strength and activity, and improved spirits, of the individuals, in consequence of being employed a shorter time in the day.

Have you found that cause already operates in lessening the loss which at first happened from the change of hours? Regularly every month, from the first of January last. (P. 93.)

Then the Committee is not to understand that the increased quantity stated to have been produced, in proportion to the hours of working, is solely to be attributed to a diminution of the hours of work? I believe, in the present instance, it is solely to be attributed to the difference in the hours of work, because I do not know that there has been the smallest alteration in any of the other circumstances; it is the same machinery, and, I believe, the same quality of raw material. (P. 93.)

Do you, as an experienced spinner, or a spinner of any kind, mean to inform the Committee, that the machines that you employ for throstle and water spinning can produce an additional quantity from any other cause whatever but the quickening of the motion of the machine? Yes, as an experienced spinner, I do say that it may.

Have the goodness to state from what cause it can proceed? From saving breakage, from the superior attention of the people to all their operations, from not losing a moment when the work commences, or when it ceases, and from the individuals in the previous process paying much more attention in the preparatory stages of the manufacture. (P. 94.)

If, therefore, the velocity of the machine has not been increased, how do you account for the produce per spindle being anything different from the proportion that would arise from the difference of the hours of labor? I have endeavored to explain those causes which I conceive would produce a difference. In addition, I can merely state, that I have before me a comparative statement of produce and prime cost, simply asked for by me from the clerk, who has been long in the habit of giving me these calculations; and these are the results, without, I believe, the smallest difference in this statement from any other statement which I have received for the last fifteen or sixteen years. It is far from my wish to deceive the Committee in any respect; and none of these papers have been made for any particular purpose. (P. 94.)

Eight Hours for Work. JOHN RAE. *London and New York. Macmillan & Co. 1894.*

The first great general reduction of hours was the reduction in the English textile trades by the Ten Hours' Act of *1847*, and it was regarded, not merely by employers, but by many even of its warmest promoters, with considerable trepidation as a leap in the dark. It is true that a whole generation before, the experiment of shortening hours on a very substantial scale had been tried with signal success by Robert Owen, the Socialist, in that great seedplot of fruitful social reforms, the famous cotton mills of New Lanark. He ran those mills 10½ hours a day for the twelve years from 1816 to 1828. The hours there seem to have been 16 at one time, and to have been 12½ about the date of his new semi-philanthropic partnership with Jeremy Bentham and William Allen in 1814. They were first reduced from 12½ to 11½, and then finally from 11½ to 10½ in 1816. And what was the result? One of Owen's own work-people, John Alexander, said to the Factories Inquiries Commission, that to his surprise the quantity produced after the reduction of 1816 did not sensibly fall off from the quantity produced previously, and that this was due entirely to the greater personal exertions spontaneously elicited from the operatives, among whom a general increase of cheerfulness and alacrity was very observable at the time, though, he added, it was not so great as the similar increase that occurred when the hours had been on a former occasion reduced from 12½ to 11½*. He makes no mention of any improvement or speeding of machinery, but attributes the whole result to the improvement in personal efficiency. Lanarkshire cannot stand the competition of Lancashire to-day though the hours are the same, but during those twelve years Owen successfully competed with all rivals, though he wrought two, three, or even four hours less in the day. He tells us himself that when he was in France in 1818, he was invited by the Duc de la Rochefoucauld to visit and inspect a cotton-spinning factory the duke had erected on his estate, and he examined the whole administration of the business. "I found by this investigation," says Owen, "that I was manufacturing the same numbers of fineness of yarn or thread, but of much better quality, at the New Lanark establishment in Scotland at 4d. per lb. cheaper than the duke. One penny per lb. upon the annual produce at that time at New Lanark was £8,000 Sterling, which when multiplied by four gives a gain upon the same quantity over the duke's of £32,000 a year."† The New Lanark mills continued to yield high profits. Bentham is said to have declared that that was the only successful speculation he ever embarked in, and Owen himself carried away from the place a considerable fortune, of which he lost £40,000 in his ill-fated attempt to found a community at New Harmony. If he conducted a profitable business not merely without the aid of "the last hour," from which other employers alleged all their profit accrued, but without the aid of the two last or even the three last hours, it must manifestly have been because there lay no real advantage in the long hours elsewhere prevalent, and because, as Mr. Alexander intimates, his work-people actually did as much in their short hours as the others did, or as they had done formerly themselves, in the longer day. Yet the world never seems to have discovered this remarkable fact, in spite of the extraordinary attention it then paid to the New Lanark institutions, and it kept on prating about "the last hour" for nearly a half century longer. (Pp. 15-18.)

* First Report, p. 96.
† Life of Robert Owen, by himself, p. 169.

Hansard's Parliamentary Debates. Vol. 74. 1844.

Lord Ashley:

"It is a mistaken notion," writes this gentleman, "to suppose that the produce of yarn or cloth from machinery, would be curtailed in an arithmetical proportion to the proposed reduction of working hours from 12 to 10, because in very many instances the workman can produce much or little during the day, as he feels disposed, or as his strength enables him; and in my own trade in which we employ at least 1200 hands, I have proved beyond a doubt, that whenever we have reduced the hours for working from 12 to 10 per day, which is equal to one-sixth the quantity of work produced has not fallen below one-tenth or even one-twelfth. . . . All men will be able to work much harder for 10 hours than they can for 12." (Pp. 901-902.)

The countervailing advantages of reduced time are so great, as compared with a reduction of wages, that they readily accept the loss, and find their interest in the improvement of health of body and mind; in social and domestic comfort; in the practice of household economy; and especially in the prolongation, by 3 or 4 years, of their working life, of their physical capacities to obtain a livelihood. (Pp. 904-905.)

British Sessional Papers. Vol. XXV. 1845. Reports of Inspectors of Factories from 1st October, 1844, to 30th April, 1845. ROBERT GARDNER, *Mill-owner.*

. . . I am quite satisfied that both as much yarn and power-loom cloth may be produced at quite as low a cost in 11 as in 12 hours per day; at least, that it has been so the last 12 months, in my mills at Preston. . . . It is my present intention to make a further reduction of time to 10½ hours, without the slightest fear of suffering loss by it. I find the hands work with greater energy and spirit; they are more cheerful, and apparently more happy. All the arguments I have heard in favour of long time appear based on an arithmetical question,—if 11 produce so much, what will 12, 13, or even 15 hours produce? This is correct, as far as the steam engine is concerned; whatever it will produce in 11 hours, it will produce double the quantity in 22. But try this on the animal horse, and you will soon find he cannot compete with the engine, as he requires both time to rest and feed. (P. 27.)

. . . It is, I believe, a fact not questioned, that there is more bad work made the last 1 or 2 hours of the day, than the whole of the first 9 or 10 hours. There can be no doubt but 11 hours are quite sufficient for any one to exhaust the whole of his or her strength in any one occupation, situation, or atmosphere, although the work is not laborious.

It can be no small gratification to any employer of a large number of hands to see them healthy and happy, with an opportunity of improving their minds. I beg to state that about 20 years ago we had many orders for a style of goods much wanted. To increase the quantity of the work, I requested they (his employees) would work, instead of 11, 12 hours. At the end of the week I found they had got a trifle more work done; but supposing there was some incidental cause for this, I requested they would work 13 hours the following week, at the end of which they had produced less instead of more work. The overlooker told me the hours were too long, and invited me to be in the room with them the last hour of the day. I saw they were exhausted, drowsy, and making bad work and little of it, I therefore reduced their time 2 hours, as before. Since that time I have been an advocate for shorter hours of labour. (P. 27.)

British Sessional Papers. Vol. XXIII. 1851. Reports of Inspectors of Factories for Half-year ending 31st October, 1850.

The unexpected and gratifying result mentioned in former reports of the amount of work turned off in 10 hours, having kept up so much nearer to the product of 12 hours than was conceived by any one to be possible, has been confirmed by many instances stated to me during the last half-year. This is accomplished partly by an increased speed of the machinery, but chiefly by the closer attention which the people give to their work, and are enabled to give by the shortened duration of the daily strain upon their physical powers. (P. 5.)

It is also worthy of note, that during a portion of the last period the greatest amount of restriction ever contemplated, either as to ages or as to hours of work, has been in operation. . . . the power of production has increased beyond that of any other period. (P. 65.)

British Sessional Papers. Vol. XL. 1852-1853. Reports of Inspectors of Factories for half-year ending 30th April, 1853. Letter to Leonard Horner from William Grant, concerning the effect of the ten-hour day.

We employ nearly 600 hands, and out of that number I have no hesitation in saying there is not one person would prefer to work even one hour per week longer than they do at present. By extra attention, knowing that their hours are shorter than formerly, and a little increase to the speed, they make quite as much money as ever they did. (Pp. 20-21.)

British Sessional Papers. Vol. XXX. 1876. Factory and Workshops Acts Commission.

Witness, Phillip Grant, representing operatives:

8582. During the agitation for the ten-hours bill in the year 1844 or 1845 he (a cotton-spinner at Preston) reduced his time voluntarily to eleven hours instead of twelve, and at the end of twelve months he reported, as Mr. Hugh Mason did, that he had got a better quality of work and more of it in the eleven hours than he had in the twelve, and that is obvious to anybody who understands the process of following a machine. (P. 418.)

Superior Output in Shorter Hours: Textiles.—Great Britain.

Lectures on the Labor Question. The Nine Hours Movement. THOMAS BRASSEY. *London, Longmans, 1878.*

A reduction in the hours of labor does not necessarily involve a corresponding reduction in the amount of work performed. . . . A few years ago M. Dolfuss, the great manufacturer of Mühlhausen, offered to reduce the working hours in his establishment to the extent of one hour a day, without reduction of pay, provided his work-people would undertake to do an equal amount of work in the shorter day. In a month after the offer was made the hands in the employ of M. Dolfuss had succeeded in making the production of the shorter day equal in amount to the production of their former longer hours. (Pp. 9-10.)

Overwork is equally undesirable from a moral and an industrial point of view. Adam Smith has said truly that the man who works so moderately as to be able to work constantly, not only preserves his health the longest, but in the course of the year, executes the greatest quantity of work. (P. 12.)

The Eight Hours Day. SIDNEY WEBB *and* HAROLD COX. *London, Walter Scott, 1891.*

The reduction in the hours of labor in the textile mills, which may be said to have begun in the United Kingdom from about 1817, has been continuous and considerable. Seventy-five years ago men commonly worked 90 and 100 hours per week. By successive stages these hours have been brought down to 56½. At every stage it has been conclusively "proved" by the manufacturers that the proposed new restriction of hours would deprive them of all margin of profit, would raise the price of the commodity, lower the wages of the workers, and destroy the export trade. Celebrated economists were found to demonstrate that the whole economic advantage of the running of the mill at all lay conclusively in the "last hour," and that its prohibition would involve, accordingly, the cessation of the industry. Yet the result has over and over again shown that manufacturers and theorists alike were wrong; the hours of work have been successively reduced, without diminution of production, fall of wages, rise of prices, or slackening of trade. (Pp. 94-95.)

British Sessional Papers, 1913. Report of the Chief Inspector of Factories and Workshops for the year 1913.

Mr. Wilson (Glasgow): "Many textile factories now start at 8 o'clock, and manufacturers inform me that better time is kept, and that there is less wastage and better work with the shorter hours, while the decrease in output is fractional only and in certain cases there is no reduction whatever." (P. 60.)

The most remarkable instance of a reduction of hours comes from Dunfermline, where an 8½-hours day has been established in all the linen-weaving sheds. Mr. Williams, after referring to a reduction of hours, which took place some years ago in some of the large textile mills in Scotland, gives the following quotation from the report of Mr. Sumner (Dundee):

An important change was made last July in the hours of labor of the Dunfermline linen trade, where there are ten factories employing between 4,000 and 5,000 workers, chiefly women. Dunfermline has a population of only a little over 28,000, and the linen manufacturers have to draw their labor from the surrounding districts. In some cases, workers were living seven or more miles from their factory, and owing to the bad train and tram service at that early hour had to leave home some time after 4 a.m. to get to work at 6. In consequence of a general request by the workers for a day of nine hours, divided into three working periods of three hours each, the occupiers as a body compromised to the extent of granting a day of eight and a half hours, namely, from 8 a.m. to 5.30 p.m., with only one break, from 12.30 to 1.30 for dinner. The weekly total of working hours was thus reduced 15 per cent. At the same time a 5 per cent. rise was allowed in the piecework rates, and the time workers were given the same weekly wages, although they had 15 per cent. less working time. From the workers' point of view the change has been an unqualified success. At first there was some grumbling by the pieceworkers because of the reduction in the total wages earned. The best and most industrious, who had worked hard under the old system, lost about 10 per cent.; the less industrious ones, however, found little change in their weekly total, as with the help of the 5 per cent. rise and a little better application they could earn the same wages as previously. Now that they have had longer experience of the new hours, and the winter weather has come, no one would like to revert to the previous conditions, and some say they would not go back to the longer hours even if they had the 5 per cent. rise in wages continued. There is not the same unanimity among the occupiers; some were favorable, others more dubious. One firm said they had increased their wage bill by nearly 12 per cent. and their turnover by 6.7 per cent., and instead of having to take any labor that offered they were getting all they wanted and of a better and more permanent class. They had less sickness, much less lost time, and better work, besides less expense of coal and gas. (Pp. 59-60.)

Report of the Massachusetts Bureau of Statistics of Labor. 1870-1871.

A man can work ten hours in the mill, and working with a will, and with the object of gaining one hour for himself, he will make a machine produce in ten hours as much as it will in eleven. He would be more attentive and try to make as much pay as in eleven hours. I think it will be found that much of the cloth made during the eleventh hour is of poorer quality than the rest, and that the necessity of looking it over the next day and fixing it all right, lessens the product of that next day. If we were to suppose two sets of operatives in the same business, one working 11 hours and one working 10 a day, other things being equal, there is no doubt that the 10-hour set would hold out more years than the 11-hour set. I certainly believe that the productive capacity of a set of work-people may be lessened by increasing the hours of their daily labor. (Pp. 499-500.)

Argument of Hon. WILLIAM GRAY *on Petitions for Ten-hour Law before the Massachusetts Committee on Labor. February 13, 1873. Boston.*

There are facts which . . . will show you . . . the actual result of the introduction of ten hours nearly six years ago. This corporation entered upon that change in June, 1867. (P. 17.)

The speed of the looms was increased about 4 per cent. the first month, and other machinery in about the same ratio. All work which could be made job work was so made . . . and the first month after the change showed these results.

Observe the time had been reduced from 10¾ hours to 10 hours; the product was reduced 4 to 5 per cent.; the cost of labor was increased 2¾ per cent.; the wages paid were not essentially changed. In three years and a half from the time of the change, the product of ten hours was fully equal to the product of 10¾ hours at the previous date. . . . With no material change in machinery, the following results appeared. . . .

First. We saw an improvement in the operatives directly after adopting ten hours—which improvement has been going on; and we have now the best set of workers that have been in the mill for fifteen years. . . .

Second. We have had more continuous and uninterrupted work throughout the year than before. (P. 18.)

Report of the Massachusetts Bureau of Statistics of Labor. 1873.

The overseer (of Pemberton Mills, Lawrence) informed us that they took the result of every half-hour's work, and upon inquiring the relative product of the different hours, he assured us that invariably the last hour was the least productive. (P. 246.)

Hon. William Gray, Treasurer of the Atlantic Mills. Lawrence, began the ten-hour experiment with the operatives in his employ, June, 1867, and his testimony concerning its practical and financial success may be regarded as nearly, if not quite, authoritative and decisive.

Superior Output in Shorter Hours: Textiles.—United States

Massachusetts Senate Documents, No. 33. 1874.

The Committee on the Labor Question to whom was referred so much of the Governor's address as relates to Labor Reform, having considered so much thereof as pertains to the enactment of a ten-hour law, and having also considered the petition of Wendell Phillips and others for the passage of such a law, report: . . . Your Committee find that the manufacturers of Fall River voluntarily adopted ten hours as the length of time their operatives should work, and continued on this basis for twenty-one months. They ceased only because the other manufacturers *in the State* would not adopt the same regulation. They find further, that the Atlantic Mills, in Lawrence, have long been run on these hours, and in both these instances the corporations have paid large dividends. Your Committee, therefore, are of the opinion that while the lessening of the hours of labor as contemplated may reduce the profits, it will not diminish them so much as to prevent a fair and honorable return for the capital invested. (P. 2.)

Report of Massachusetts Bureau of Statistics of Labor. 1881.

It is apparent that Massachusetts with ten hours produces as much per man or per loom or per spindle, equal grades being considered, as other States with eleven and more hours; and also that wages here rule as high, if not higher, than in the States where the mills run longer time. (P. 457.)

But perhaps the most emphatic testimony is that of another carpet mill employing about twelve hundred persons. This mill, which has been running but ten hours for several years, and has during this period tried the experiment of running overtime, gives the following results. The manager said: "I believe, with proper management and supervision, the same help will produce as many goods, and of superior quality, in ten hours as they will in eleven. I judge so from the fact that during certain seasons, being pushed for goods, we have run up to nine o'clock, and for the first month the production was increased materially. After this, however, the help would grow listless, and the production would fall off and the quality of the goods deteriorate." (Pp. 460-461.)

The reason is, the flesh and blood of the operatives have only so much work in them, and it was all got out in ten hours, and no more could be got out in twelve; and what was got extra in the first month was taken right out of the life of the operatives. (P. 461.)

Report of the Chief of Massachusetts District Police for the year ending December 31, 1883.

It has been stated by those who have specially watched the operation of the ten-hour law that "its enforcement has increased production and advanced the wages and moral standing of the masses." (Pp. 17-18.)

Ibid. for the year ending Dec. 31, 1886.

One manufacturer stated to me a short time ago that he had run his mill 66 hours per week, supposing that by so doing he increased the production nearly one-eleventh, but was persuaded last January to reduce his running time to 60 hours per week, and at the end of six months found that the production of his mill had increased nearly ten per cent., while the quality of the work done was more perfect. He also stated that no amount of argument could have convinced him that the results would be as they have proven. This shows that an operative can perform only a certain amount of labor though seemingly light when such labor is required every working day in the year. (Pp. 71-72.)

Report of the New York State Factory Inspector. 1887.

. . . As a rule, at the end of a year, they would not have so much working time to their credit as those who were not so overworked. It can be deduced from this that it does not pay even the employer to insist upon excessive hours of toil, and, indeed, the invariable testimony of the proprietors of those mills which, before the present law was passed, ran eleven hours a day, is to the effect that their product was not decreased by the reduction to ten hours, but that the quality of the work was superior, the employees worked more steadily, and were less interfered with by sickness. (P. 28.)

Fifteenth Annual Report of the National Consumers' League. New York, 1916. Some Practical Experiences in Shortening Hours of Labor. Address by MR. FREDERICK R. HAZARD, *President Solvay Process Company, Syracuse, New York, Cleveland, Ohio, November 4, 1915.*

I took occasion to inquire about the changes in hours at a woolen manufacturing establishment, and I found that their results were slightly more favorable after reducing their number of hours from eleven to nine and a half in some departments, ten in others. They got as much piece-work from weavers, for instance, in the shorter time, as they did in the longer time; and in the other departments . . . they found that they had increased the speed of the shafting which controlled the spinning, the carding, the combing and the other preparatory operations, so that they actually got as much work in the shorter time as they did in the longer time. The woolen industry is not upon an eight-hour basis, so far as I know, anywhere. The particular mill at which I made my inquiry is working on exactly as favorable conditions as any other woolen mill, but I think that industry could, in many ways, take advantage of the shorter hours, and I believe that it could be worked out to be an advantage.

Amtliche Mitteilungen aus den Jahresberichten der Gewerbe-Aufsichtsbeamten XVIII. 1895. [Official Information from Reports of the (German) Factory Inspectors.] Berlin, 1896.

The reports of amount and value of the work done in the reduced working day are also of interest. The fact that the value of the work is not in proportion to the hours of work is but slowly understood. A wool factory reduced their working day by one hour, in accordance with the law of June 1, 1891; subtracting the rest periods, it now amounts to ten and one-half hours. The owners assert that the amount and value of work done by both males and females remain the same, while calls upon the sick fund have greatly diminished. (P. 370.)

Ibid. for the year 1898.

In a jute spinning and weaving factory in Cassel the ten-hour day was provisionally introduced at the request of the hands in September. Thus far it has worked so well that the shorter day will probably be retained. (P. 106.)

Jahresberichte der Gewerbe-Aufsichtsbeamten und Bergbehörden für das Jahr, 1904. Bd. II. Baden. [Reports of the (German) Factory and Mine Inspectors for the year 1904. Vol. II. Baden.] Berlin, Decker, 1905.

It is satisfactory to find that many employers, instead of returning to the longer hours usual before the (recent) business depression, are keeping the shorter day permanently, because they have come to see that the longer hours formerly the rule do not mean a correspondingly larger output. So, for instance, a large textile manufacturer of the Oberland is retaining the 10 hours day, and it is so much the more noteworthy because he is doing it in direct opposition to most of his confrères, who all assert emphatically that every reduction of working time under 11 hours must, in the textile industries, involve a corresponding loss in output. (Pp. 5-41.)

C. METAL TRADES: IRON AND-STEEL; TIN PLATE.

A Shorter Working Day. R. A. HADFIELD *of Hadfield's Steel Foundry Co., Sheffield, and* H. DE B. GIBBINS, M. A. *Methuen & Co., London, 1892.*

Asked whether he adopted the eight hours system as an experiment or from conviction that it would be an ultimate success, Mr. Allan* said: "I adopted the eight hours first because, under the old system, where the men started work at six o'clock and worked till 8:30 in the morning, or what is called a quarter, this short morning division of the day, as I would call it, was so much taken advantage of by the men and the lads for 'sleeping in' that the actual time wrought throughout the week by men and boys, on a fair average, was something like forty-six to forty-eight hours per week. . . . Thinking over the whole question and the best mode of overcoming these irregularities and losses, I came to the conclusion that an eight hours day would be more satisfactory to myself as well as to the men. Besides, I had also in view the fact that by an eight hours day, commencing at 7:30 in the morning, it would be more beneficial to the men and the lads on physical grounds. Men who worked overtime could not be expected to keep regular time in the morning. Growing lads who went to night-classes or places of amusement could not be expected to turn out in the early morning. Hence it seemed to me the only successful way to ensure regularity in time-keeping, less possibility of loss, and better physical conditions for men and lads was to commence at 7:30 in the morning, and have only one break in the day, thus getting a full forty-eight hours' work in the week. For those reasons I was induced, with the approval of the men, to commence an eight hours day, agreeing with them that if the experiment proved itself a success in six months the wages which they agreed to forego—5 per cent.—should be returned to them at the end of that time."

* Allan & Co. Scotia Engine Works, Sunderland.

How It Has Worked.

"It must be borne in mind that in the management of an engineering factory, if the books are properly kept, the cost of each detail of an engine, and an engine as a whole, can be had at any moment, and be compared with other engines whether finished under a ten, nine, or eight hours day. Hence six months' trial was long enough to determine the labour cost of the engine finished under the new system as against the old. Therefore, from our costs, taken out very carefully and compared with similar engines fitted under the ten, nine and eight hours day, we found, much to our surprise, and paradoxical as it may seem, that the cost of the engines was in no way increased, in fact, if anything, rather decreased. It became, therefore, a duty to return to the men the wages which they sacrificed at the initiation of the system, as there has been *no diminution of output in the slightest degree*—rather the contrary. Our reason for that is simply this: that the men and lads are in better physical condition, and they lose no time now, while the machines are kept constantly going by the same men for a straight spin of 8¾ hours for four days of the week, 8½ hours another day and 4½ hours on Saturdays, overtime, unless in special instances, being thus dispensed with." (Pp. 172-174.)

Mr. Harrison, the manager of the works, gave some useful, practical information as to the success of the eight hours system. A certain quantity of work, he said, used to be turned out by each machine in a day's work under the nine hours system. Incredible as it may seem to some, he states that the same amount of work is turned out by the same machine while worked for eight hours only. He has only one explanation for this new state of things, namely, that much time that was formerly wasted is now utilized, and that the men go into their work with much greater enthusiasm. It is a very easy thing, he states, for men to do an additional hour's work in a day, for the men stick to their work instead of wasting five minutes here and there as formerly. (P. 179.)

The Eight Hours Day. Report on a Year's Work with a Forty-eight Hours Week in the Salford Iron Works, Manchester. (Mather and Platt, Ltd.) WILLIAM MATHER, M. P. *Manchester, Guardian Printing Works, 1894. Statistical Results.*

Piecework.—Piecework from the first has been a matter of considerable interest.

It was at the outset—perhaps naturally—assumed that men on piecework were already doing their best, and if their period of work were shortened, their earnings would be diminished in a corresponding degree.

This anticipation has not been realized; for, although there is a falling-off in the percentage earned by piece-workers over and above what they would have received as day wages, it is slight in comparison with the reduction in the time, and particularly so in the later portion of the year.

In order to judge better of the working out of the system as regards piecework, the year has been divided into three parts of approximately equal lengths.

In the first period the surplus over day-work rates was *1.76 per cent. less* than the standard piecework wages; in the second period *1.58 per cent. less* than the standard piecework wages; in the third period *0.78 per cent. less* than the standard piecework wages; the average for the twelve months coming out *1.41 per cent. less* than the standard.

These figures show that as the year advanced there was a steady adaptation to the altered conditions; and it is reasonable to expect that the small difference remaining at the end of the year will soon disappear.

It must also be noted that in no single instance during the year were piece-work rates advanced. In fact, some reductions were made in a few special cases where the rates were admittedly too high. Had these few changes not been made, the difference between the two periods would have been *0.5 per cent. only,* instead of 1.41 per cent., a difference which is not at all unusual between two years, as slight fluctuations in piecework earnings have occurred from one year to another under the old system. (Pp. 19-20.)

Conditions in British Iron and Steel Works. I. A Speech delivered to the Special Commission on Hours of Labour, International Association for Labour Legislation, June 11th, 1912. John Hodge, M. P.

As the result of negotiations between ourselves and the management of Bell Brothers, Port Clarence Works, Middlesbrough (this firm were members of the Employers' Association), it was necessary, after an agreement had been come to, that the consent of their Association should be obtained. The Employers' Association, however, absolutely refused to grant the permission. The management, however, were convinced that an eight-hour day was a necessity, and would be of very great advantage to the firm as well as to the men. It may be stated, in this connection, that this firm had introduced a hot-metal process: the pig iron from the blast furnaces, instead of being cast into pig, being transferred to the open-hearth furnaces in a liquid state; the work of the men was very laborious in this process, as all the other materials had to be handled without the aid of any machinery. In consequence of the refusal of the Employers' Association to grant permission, the firm resigned their membership, put the eight-hour shift in operation, and it is worthy of note that the change was successful.

So anxious were the workmen to obtain an eight-hour day in these works that the higher-paid men came to the determination, so as to remove every argument of the employers, that they would pay a percentage out of their own wages so as to give the lower-paid classes of labour an eight-hour day with themselves, and so get rid of the argument of increased cost of production; but added to this was a proviso that the average output of the melting shop should be ascertained, and such taken as a basis, and for every extra ton of output over that average a bonus should be given to the higher-paid men, so that what they had given to the lower-paid men would come back to them in greater volume as the output increased. To-day, I believe, the contribution of the higher-paid men is very small, if not entirely wiped out, as a result of increased output. (Pp. 2-3.)

In the Tin Plate trade of South Wales—and they have an enormous foreign export trade—the eight-hour day is universal. In the Sheet Mill trade in South Wales the eight-hour day is also in operation. That probably paved the way for us to a considerable extent, as in our agitation for an eight-hour day in that district with the Steel Makers, we have met with less opposition from the employers than has been the case in other districts; in fact, I might say a much more generous consideration than that shown by the employers in any other district. This will be evident as I go on.

Some six or seven years ago I discussed this question with Mr. Herbert Eccles, of Briton Ferry. Although the subject had been discussed many times previously, this time we came to an arrangement whereby he instituted an eight-hour shift on his Open-Hearth plant. The men whom this embraced were the smelters, the men who make the gas, the men in the casting-pit, and the crane-drivers, as well as the men who make up the ladles. Mr. Eccles made a concession of some extra wages to the ladle-men, so that the lower-paid men should not suffer, while he asked nothing from the higher-paid men to make up these wages. The experiment was to last for one year. Some six weeks before the expiration of the year, in an interview I had with Mr. Eccles, he stated that he was not quite satisfied of the success of the experiment, but he was not prepared to say it had been a failure, and he desired that we should enter into a new agreement for a second year, and that we agreed to do. Before six months had expired Mr. Eccles had arranged for an eight-hour day for every employee in his works.

Up to this point we had always been working for an eight-hour day without extra cost to the employer. Mr. Eccles, however, said this was impossible, as it would make certain men, such as engine-men, crane-men, and boiler-firemen such a low wage when divided by three, that he would not be able to retain the type of men he desired, and that in their case it would mean less than a living wage. He had prepared a scheme for the men in the rolling mills which, when totalled up, showed an estimated extra wages expenditure per annum of £586. My observations upon this acceptance by him of the universal eight-hour day are, that that experimental period had demonstrated that, if he had gained nothing from the change, he had lost nothing. In fact, I go further, and say that, if he had not been convinced that better results would accrue from the change, he would never have agreed to an addition to his wages bill.

Shortly after the establishment of the eight-hour day in these works, we asked for a conference with the Steel Makers of South Wales, which was held at Swansea some five years ago. Mr. Eccles was the Chairman of the Employers' Association, and, after a discussion upon the merits of the proposed change, as well as a discussion as to its effect upon the life, the health, and the physique of the workmen, the employers unanimously accepted the principle of an eight-hour day. (Pp. 3-4.)

Report of the Special Commission on Hours of Labour in Continuous Industries to the Seventh Delegates' Meeting of the International Association for Labour Legislation. Zurich, 1912. London. The Pioneer Press, Ltd., July, 1912.

In the United Kingdom there has been of late years in the iron and steel trade a marked tendency towards the eight-hour system.

Mr. J. Hodge, M. P., reported to the Commission on progress in the tin plate and steel industry. The British Steel Smelters' Amalgamated Society started a campaign in favour of an eight-hour day about 25 years ago. As a result all rolling mills (with 9,500 men) in the tin plate and steel sheet industry in South Wales now work eight-hour shifts. As regards the steel works of South Wales, the system was adopted in principle by the Employers' Association about five years ago, but they stipulated that it must be introduced gradually. It is now practically universal in the district. In the tin plate and steel works, work ceases at the week-end, and the average working week in South Wales ranges from 41⅔ to 44⅓ hours. In England, the eight-hour system is not yet so general, but a few months ago the men had a conference with the employers (England and Scotland), who have now asked the Society to draw up a practical plan for every individual firm in the Employers' Association, so devised that costs shall not be increased. The Society is accordingly now at work on a plan, which they are hopeful will be accepted. In the few steel mills where the eight-hour day is already in operation in England the average week is 46⅔ hours.

Mr. P. Walls, J. P., representing the blast furnacemen, informed the Commission that there are about 8,000 men in the continuous processes working on the eight-hour system (which is general in the North of England), and about 7,000 still on the 12-hour shift (mostly in the Midlands, Scotland, and South Wales). These latter work seven days a week, and 24 hours on end when the shifts are changed. The eight-hour system has been in operation in one district in the North of England for over 21 years, and in another for over 14 years, with excellent results. (Pp. 4-5.)

The reports and speeches of Mr. A. H. Crosfield, Mr. John Hodge, M. P., and Mr. Patrick Walls, J. P., contain evidence to the effect that within a comparatively short time after adopting shorter hours production has been found to increase to such an extent, on account of the more effective and accurate work of the men, that without any increase in the piece rates, the same weekly earnings were reached as had been received before with the longer day. (P. 10.)

Rational Hours of Work. I. The Case for Reduction. Shorter Hours and Greater Efficiency. A. H. Crosfield. *Reprinted from the "Manchester Guardian," June 27, 1913.*

Even more striking is the splendid progress which the eight-hour day has made throughout the steel trade, especially in the steel sheet and tinplate trades of South Wales. Mr. John Hodge, M. P., general secretary of the British Steel Smelters' Association, recently gave the International Association for Labor Legislation an interesting account of the adoption by Mr. Herbert Eccles of the eight-hour shift for his open-hearth plant at Briton Ferry. The eight-hour day was adopted there for men engaged in various classes of work, and for the lower paid men Mr. Eccles made a concession of extra wages involving an estimated extra expenditure of £586 per annum. Within less than two years of the introduction of the system Mr. Eccles was so convinced of its advantages that it was adopted for every single employee throughout his entire works. Conferences followed with the rest of the employers in the steel trade of South Wales, and the eight-hour day became the established rule in the industry, and is now by general admission a real and very substantial advantage both to employers and employed. With regard to the economic results, Mr. Hodge says, as a result of many conversations with them on the subject, that "managers in South Wales are agreed that, generally speaking, there has been an increase of output in the rolling mills of at least 20 per cent., but so far as the open-hearth melting process is concerned they would not place the increase of output at more than 12½ per cent." Mr. Hodge then quoted the opinion of Mr. Eccles to the effect that "if there had been no greater gain than reform of the habits of some of the men the change was worth it," the substance of his remarks being that it had made "bad men good and good men better."

Here, then, we have industrial undertakings on a very large scale which afford us striking practical evidence of enormous importance of the advantages of rational hours of work considered from every point of view, whether physical, ethical, or commercial. And this practical testimony is just what scientific investigation leads us to anticipate. (Pp. 3-4.)

The Eight Hours Day. SIDNEY WEBB *and* HAROLD COX, B. A. *London, Walter Scott, 1891. Appendix II. Memorandum of a conversation with Mr. T. W. Smith, of the firm of Caslon & Co., Typefounders, Chiswell Street, E. C., December 15th, 1890.*

The change to the Eight Hour System came about in this way: The improvements effected in type-founding machinery during the last twenty years have made it possible for our men to turn out the same quantity of work as formerly with much less exertion. We knew this and they knew it. . . . We thereupon had a friendly talk with the men in a general meeting, and told them that if they would undertake to send us down the same quantity of work as before, we were perfectly willing to reduce the hours, and still pay them the same wages. This arrangement was agreed to, and has worked perfectly since. (P. 257.)

Hours and Wages in Relation to Production. LUJO BRENTANO. *Translated by Mrs. Wm. Arnold. London, Sonnenschein, 1894.*

"In the parliamentary debate of the Miners' Eight Hours' Day, Chamberlain made the following statements: 'When I was in business—I am speaking of twenty years ago—my firm was working under great pressure, twelve hours a day. Shortly afterwards the Factory Acts were applied to Birmingham, and we reduced the hours to ten a day. Some time later we voluntarily reduced the hours to nine a day, after the experiment at Newcastle of a nine hours engineers' day. We were working self-acting machinery. All the workmen had to do was to feed the machines and see the tools were kept in order. In this case, if in any, the production should be directly proportionate to the number of hours worked. What is the fact? When we reduced the hours from twelve to ten—a reduction of 17 per cent.—the reduction in the production was about 8 per cent. When we again reduced the hours from ten to nine—a reduction of 10 per cent.—the reduction of production was 5 per cent.'" (P. 106.)

Report of the United States Industrial Commission. Vol. XIV. 1901. MR. WILLIAM C. REDFIELD, *Treasurer, J. H. Williams & Co.*

On January 2 last, after consultation with the leading workmen, notice was given that the works would, on March 1, be put on the basis of a 9-hour day with 10 hours pay, running 54 hours weekly for the wages theretofore paid for 60 hours. This concession, made voluntarily and unasked, was received cordially by the men, who have shown their appreciation by working closely up to the full 9 hours. Experience thus far has shown the 9-hour day to be profitable, for the output of the works is slightly larger than before. A comparison of a large number of orders executed on the 9-hour basis with the same number of orders for the same goods executed under similar conditions on the 10-hour basis shows a slight average gain in favor of the 9-hour day. There is a slightly larger average output for the 9-hour day than for the 10-hour day, though in every other respect the work was done under similar conditions. There is throughout an increased rate of hourly output and a total output somewhat larger for the shorter working time. (P. 659.)

The 9-hour day has been a gain and not a loss—demonstrably so where exact data can be had, satisfactorily so even where the full details can not be secured. This result is believed to depend in large degree upon the willing and helpful spirit that exists in the works. . . .

J. H. Williams & Co. believe that such success as has been obtained arises largely because and not in spite of the high and continuous wages paid to their working force, and recognize thoroughly the intelligence, efficiency, and, last but not least, the good will of that working force. While none can estimate exactly the difference in production in the same works between a force of men justly treated, earnest and zealous in their work, and a similar force working merely because they must live, the writer believes the difference between these two, under conditions otherwise similar, may be that between ruin and dividends.

Again, it should be said that the things above suggested are done not as charity, but as matters of justice, as privileges, and as sources of profit. The course thus far taken will be followed because it is both a pleasant and a profitable one. It pays because a man is more than a machine, and the policy which treats him as a machine ignores one of the greatest factors in production, viz., human nature. It pays because the rate of wages is not the chief factor in cost, but the rate of production. A clean man produces more in the long run than a dirty man. A well-informed man produces more than an ignorant man. A justly treated man produces more than an unjustly treated man. A contented man is a better and cheaper producer than a discontented man. A well-paid man is a more economic producer than an ill-paid man. It would often be well, when seeking to economize, to give less attention to the pay roll and more in other directions. (P. 660.)

The Eight Hour Day and Government Construction by Direct Labor. ETHELBERT STEWART. *Commons, Vol. 10. May, 1905.*

In the building of the two battleships, the Connecticut and the Louisiana, we have a concrete case offering opportunity for the study and comparison, not only of contract versus direct labor, but also of the eight-hour day versus the ten-hour day. The former battleship is being built by direct labor in the United States navy yards in Brooklyn under the eight-hour day and by union men. The battleship Louisiana is being built by contract by the Newport News Shipbuilding and Dry Dock Co., of Newport News, Virginia, employing its men ten hours a day. In chapter three of a report to Congress by the Department of Commerce and Labor, we find a comparative statement of the work on these two battleships up to November 1, 1904. The information for this chapter was gathered and compiled by Mr. Frank J. Sheridan, one of the most accurate and painstaking agents of the Bureau of Labor, and his figures may be depended upon. Mr. Sheridan says in his report: "No other factor is considered than the productive ability of the two bodies of men doing exactly the same kind of work, using the same kind of tools and the same kind of material. It is practically all hand work, as the output of the automatic machines, with their speed limitations in production per hour, does not enter into this work."

The keel of the Louisiana was laid February 7, 1903. She was launched August 27, 1904. On the date of launching, the percentage of the hull work completed was 54.5. The keel of the Connecticut was laid March 10, 1903. She was launched September 29, 1904. Percentage of hull work completed was 53.59. This is by far more rapid work than has ever been done by contracting firms building battleships heretofore, as it is well understood that there is to be a race between the direct labor in the navy yards and contract labor at Newport News. For instance, the elapsed time between the laying of the keel and the launching of the ship is 568 days for the Louisiana and 570 days for the Connecticut, whereas in the three battleships nearest the size of these two, the Georgia was 1,135 days from the laying of the keel to the launching, the New Jersey 957 days and the Virginia 684 days. These ships have a displacement of 14,948 tons, as against 16,000 tons of the two battleships under discussion.

At the date of launching, the gross weight of the structural material worked upon the Louisiana, the contract ship, was 14,295,965 pounds. The net weight worked into the hull was 12,216,154 pounds. The aggregate hours of all employes engaged upon the work was 2,413,888. The structural material worked into the hull of the Connecticut, the direct labor ship, at the date of launching, showed a gross weight of 14,173,894 pounds. The net weight of finished material worked into the hull was 11,391,040 pounds. The aggregate hours of employes engaged on this work was 1,808,240. In other words, the number of pounds worked in per hour was, for the Louisiana 5.0608; for the Connecticut 6.2995. The average number of pounds worked in for ten hours or one day, in the Louisiana was 50,608, while the average worked into the Connecticut in a day of eight hours was 59,396 pounds. The daily average of men working full time of ten hours on the Louisiana was 500.8. The number of men working full time of eight hours on the Connecticut was 470.9. This shows that the average production of a man per hour on the Connecticut exceeded by 24.28 per cent. the average production per man per hour on the Louisiana; which explains why the progress on the Connecticut, as shown in the report of percentage of work completed to the Bureau of Construction, has kept pace with the work completed on the Louisiana, namely: November 1, 1904, the Louisiana reported 60.7 percentage completed, while the percentage of completion of the Connecticut on the same date was 63.9. (Pp. 284-285.)

So far, the claim of labor leaders that the eight-hour day is productive of better work and just as much of it in the skilled trades as the ten-hour day, seems to be amply sustained. (P. 286.)

The Steel Workers. John A. Fitch. *The Pittsburgh Survey, Russell Sage Foundation Publication. New York. Charities Publication Committee, 1910.*

Some of the rolling mills in England are also operated on the eight-hour system. According to Mr. Hodge, one mill where the system has lately been introduced is now rolling as much steel in eight hours as it formerly did in twelve. There is little opportunity for such a comparison in this country, but in one case that came to my notice the same experience was reported, and I had opportunity to verify the report by the statements of both the company officials and the employes. The Sharon Steel Hoop Company, located at Sharon, Pennsylvania, is an independent company engaged in the manufacture of hoop steel and cotton ties. They employ about 1,200 men in their plant, about 150 of whom are engaged on the three finishing mills. These, from the time the plant was built up to 1904, had worked on the two-turn system. As in other hoop mills, a day's work was ten hours, the mill stopping three times during that period for about half an hour each time, to give the men opportunity to rest. The work required such speed and agility that it was held to be impossible for men to work continuously ten hours, consequently the finishing mills were idle five to seven hours out of the twenty-four.

But in 1904 a change was made. The finishers were, for the most part, members of the Amalgamated Association of Iron, Steel and Tin Workers. As usual the company signed their scale, but did so with something of a protest, for they said it was higher than that paid in non-union mills, with which they must compete. An officer of the union suggested that the company secure an advantage by putting on a third crew and eliminating the periods of idleness. This was a revolutionary suggestion, for there was no other hoop mill in the country operating with three crews. It was doubtful whether the plan were feasible or possible. When the men heard of it they objected. Their wages are based on tonnage, and they thought an eight-hour day would mean less output and lower wages. The company, however, decided to give the plan a trial.

When the men drew their first pay, they found that their earnings were not reduced. They had turned out as much tonnage in eight hours as they had previously in ten. It may have taken longer to convince the company that the plan was a good one, but it does not now care to go back to the old system. Instead of there being a period of idleness every day, the mills are operated continuously. There are no stops except to change rolls or to make repairs. The rest periods have been eliminated and the half hour for lunch as well. Instead, the company has provided "spell hands," so that the men are relieved in turn and each one has an occasional rest with plenty of time for lunch, without stopping the mill. This makes it necessary to employ larger crews than formerly so that the labor cost per ton product is larger than under the old system, but the general superintendent informed me that the saving in fuel is so great and the profits are so increased by the larger output per day that the extra labor cost is insignificant. . . .

Of course, this instance does not concern a large mill, and even if it did, it would hardly be safe to draw conclusions from a single example, especially with reference to an increased tonnage. However, it is an interesting case, and worthy of consideration. (Pp. 179-180.)

Superior Output in Shorter Hours: Metals.—Germany.

Jahresberichte der Gewerbe-Aufsichtsbeamten und Bergbehörden für das Jahr 1905. Bd. I. Preussen. [*Reports of the Factory and Mines Inspectors for 1905. Vol. I. Prussia.*] *Berlin, Decker, 1906.*

Hours of work have been reduced from 11 to 10 in a number of establishments—among others in all the day work departments of the Bochum Mining & Steel Company. The fact that this change was made during the height of the busiest season shows that the company did not fear any appreciable loss in output. (P. I. 296.)

d. MINES AND QUARRIES: COAL, SLATE, ETC.

Report of the United States Industrial Commission. Final Report. Vol. XIX, 1902.

Reduction of Hours in Mining.

The most important instance in recent years, of the adoption of the 8-hour working day, has occurred in the bituminous-coal mining industry. The strike of 1897 secured for the four leading Eastern coal States—Illinois, Indiana, Ohio and Pennsylvania—in the bituminous mines the 8-hour day, and a similar reduction has been obtained in other Western States. In Utah the 8-hour day was secured in 1896 by action of the legislature in a law applying to all mines and smelters. . . .

In the Pennsylvania district the period is 9 hours instead of 8, but includes the time spent in going to and from the mouth of the pit. Strictly speaking, the reduction is more nearly from 10 hours a day to 9 hours a day than from 10 hours to 8 hours. In Utah, however, in the case of the smelting works, the reduction is much more extreme, the hours, formerly 12 per day, being reduced to 8. This is a reduction of 33 1/3 per cent. in the time, and would make necessary an increase of the working force, provided there were no increase in efficiency, by 50 per cent.

There is a general agreement that the fewer hours in the coal mines have increased the energy of the workmen, and that there has been little or no decrease in the amount of work turned out during the day. The men are stimulated "to do a good, honest 8 hours' work"; the foremen do not find them asleep, as they used to, or lounging around or smoking. (Pp. 767-768.)

The two factors combined, namely, increased energy on the part of the employees and increased economy on the part of the employer, have certainly, in the mining industry, maintained a daily output equal to that which existed before the eight-hour day was introduced. This is shown in the following table, compiled from the reports of the United States Geological Survey and the Illinois Commissioners of Labor, showing the production of coal for the six years from 1895 to 1900:

Superior Output in Shorter Hours: Mines, etc.—United States

Bituminous Coal Mining.

Year.	Output. Short tons.	Average days active.	Average number employed.	Total days worked.	Average output per day. Short tons.	Per cent. mined by machines.
COUNTRY AT LARGE.						
1894........	118,820,405	171	244,603	41,827,113	2.84	....
1895........	135,118,193	194	239,962	46,232,628	2.90	....
1896........	137,640,276	192	244,171	46,808,832	2.72	19.17
1897........	147,609,985	196	247,817	48,572,132	3.03	16.19
1898........	166,592,023	211	255,717	53,956,287	3.09	20.39
1899........	193,321,987	234	271,027	63,420,318	3.05	23.00
1900........	212,513,912	234	304,975	71,364,150	2.98	25.15
OHIO.						
1894........	11,909,856	136	27,105	3,686,280	3.24	....
1895........	13,355,806	176	24,644	4,337,344	3.08	....
1896........	12,875,202	161	25,500	4,105,500	3.13	26.16
1897........	12,196,942	148	26,410	3,908,680	3.12	31.51
1898........	14,516,867	169	26,986	4,560,634	3.18	35.76
1899........	16,500,270	200	26,038	5,207,600	3.17	41.35
1900........	18,988,150	215	27,628	5,940,020	3.19	46.53
PENNSYLVANIA.						
1894........	39,912,463	165	75,010	12,376,650	3.22	....
1895........	50,217,228	206	71,130	14,652,780	3.43	....
1896........	49,557,453	206	72,625	14,960,750	3.31	12.29
1897........	54,417,974	205	77,272	15,840,760	3.44	16.40
1898........	65,165,133	229	79,611	18,230,919	3.57	25.34
1899........	74,150,175	245	82,812	20,288,940	3.66	29.67
1900........	79,842,326	242	92,692	22,431,464	3.56	33.65
ILLINOIS.*						
1894........	16,429,032	183.1	35,398	6,481,527	2.53	....
1895........	17,026,429	182.2	35,539	6,475,315	2.63	....
1896........	18,995,160	186.0	34,069	6,336,915	3.00	19.57
1897........	19,365,847	185.5	31,084	5,766,260	3.36	19.66
1898........	17,855,327	174.7	32,223	5,629,518	3.17	18.36
1899........	22,497,067	205.7	34,031	7,000,324	3.21	24.90
1900........	24,147,771	214.0	36,233	7,753,921	3.11	19.73
UTAH.						
1894........	431,550	199	671	134,329	3.21	....
1895........	471,836	203	670	136,010	3.47	....
1896........	418,627	202	679	137,158	3.05	0.18
1897........	521,560	204	704	143,616	3.62	....
1898........	593,709	243	739	179,577	3.30	....
1899........	786,049	265	743	196,895	3.99	....
1900........	1,147,027	248	1,308	324,384	3.54	....

* Figures used for Illinois cover 92 per cent. of total employees and 96 per cent. of total output for all years, this being the proportion belonging to shipping mines. (Pp. 770-771.)

While the 8-hour day was introduced universally in the bituminous mines in 1897, it applied to more than half of the output of the entire country.

From this table it can be seen that during the two years 1895 and 1896, under the ten-hour system, the average output per workingman per day was 2.9 and 2.72 tons; while in 1897, during the latter three months of which the eight-hour day prevailed, the average output per man was 3.03 tons per day; and for 1898, 1899 and 1900, three years of the eight-hour day in the majority of the coal mines, the average output ranged from 2.98 to 3.09 tons. Each year of the eight-hour day shows for the country as a whole a larger output per day for each workman than the highest output of the ten-hour day. The table also shows the increase in the use of machinery already referred to.

Individual States, where there has been a great increase in machinery, and where since 1897 the 8-hour day is universal, such as Ohio and Pennsylvania, show an increased output per day per man, as will be seen by the same table. There is one State, Illinois, where the proportion of coal mined by machines has remained fairly constant, standing at 19.57 per cent. in 1896, increasing to 24.9 per cent. in 1899, and falling to 19.73 per cent. in 1900. The table shows that in this State the highest output per day for each workman was in 1897, when it reached 3.36 tons. This was a year operated partly under 10 hours and partly under 8 hours. Comparing the two 10-hour years, 1895 and 1896, with the three 8-hour years, 1898, 1899, and 1900, it can be seen that the output for each working day has considerably increased, the 10-hour years showing an average output per day for each employee of 2.53 to 3 tons, while the 8-hour years show an average of 3.11 to 3.21 tons. This must be ascribed solely to the increased energy and promptness of the workmen, since, as already stated, the proportion of coal mined by machinery in that State has remained constant.

In the case of Utah, where the law went into effect in June, 1896, it will be seen that there is for the four complete years of the 8-hour day, 1897 to 1900, an actual increase in the output per day above the figures for 1894, and that three of the four years show an increase above the output for 1895.

These tables bring statistical evidence to support the testimony of witnesses before the Industrial Commission that in the industry of coal mining the shorter working day has increased the efficiency of both the workman and the management. (Pp. 770-772.)

A Handbook of Political Questions of the Day and the Arguments on Either Side. SIDNEY BUXTON, M.P. *11th Edition. London, John Murray, 1903. Legal Limitations of Hours.*

The Eight Hours' Bill for Miners is also specifically supported on the grounds:

13.—(a) That the output depends largely on the efficiency of the miner; and with shorter and fixed hours he could and would increase his individual output. He would be healthier and stronger, would work harder and more regularly. (b) That, with a re-arrangement of hours waste of time would be avoided, most of the time now lost over meals could be saved; and the saving thus effected, would in many cases more than compensate for the nominal reduction of hours. (c) That the short-time miners turn out the most coal per man.

For instance, in Lancashire, where the men work nine and a half hours, the output is estimated at 350 tons per worker per annum; in Yorkshire, with eight hours, the output is 350 tons; in Durham and Northumberland, with seven and a quarter hours, the output is 420 tons.

14.—That, thus, neither the output produced, nor the wages earned, would in the end be affected. (Pp. 191-193-194.)

The Eight Hours Day. SIDNEY WEBB *and* HAROLD COX. *London, Walter Scott, 1891.*

The Eight Hours Day was established in some of the South Yorkshire coal mines about 1859. In 1860 the General Secretary to the Masters' Association stated as "a fact that cannot be disputed, that the production under the eight hours system that has been introduced into the South Yorkshire district this last twelve months, at some of the largest collieries, is greatly in excess of what was ever produced by an equal number of men when the men worked twelve or thirteen hours.'' He went on to attribute this to the greater energy and steadiness with which the men worked on the shorter shift.* (P. 100.)

British Sessional Papers. Vol. XXIV. 1892. Royal Commission on Labor. Précis of Evidence. Group A. Vol. I.

Testimony of Mr. Alfred Onions, Secretary for the South Wales and Monmouthshire Miners' Federation.

He did not believe that the cost of production would be really increased by shorter hours, or that the output would be diminished. Such had not been the result of similar reductions in Northumberland and Durham, where the shortest hours are worked and the output is largest. In 1872 a man produced 279 tons of coal per annum. He can now produce 317 tons.† (P. 24.)

British Sessional Papers. Vol. XXXVI. 1893. Part I. Royal Commission on Labor.

Testimony of Mr. W. A. Darbishire, Managing Director of the Penyr-orsedd Slate Quarry Co., Ltd.

9084 . . . I should doubt very much whether eight hours would be desired, but I stated in my proof, and I wish to state it distinctly, that it would not make any material change in the business. I believe that exactly the same amount of work would be done in eight hours that is at present done in ten. I may say that as a matter of fact, whenever we have worked what is called short time—for five days—the production has been as much, if not more, than when we have been working six days.

---

* Report of Social Science Association on Trade Societies, 1860, pp. 45, 268.

† The "Times" Report on "the home coal industry in 1891" states: "The mines, generally, have been working shorter time in 1890 and 1891 than in previous years. Their average output per employe in 1890 was only 302 tons, as compared with 320 tons in 1888."

Eight Hours for Work. John Rae. *London and New York. Macmillan & Co., 1894.*

M. C. Grad states that, according to the President of the Corporation of Miners in Germany, miners there attain their maximum productivity with eight hours effective work, and that when temporary prolongations occur the product is only augmented to some extent for the first three or four weeks, and after that it begins to fall off till no more is got in ten hours than was got before in eight. (Revue des deux Mondes, 1877, p. 132.) (P. 53.)

In the Cleveland iron mines the men send out more stone in the day now in their eight hours under ground than they did formerly in their twelve hours, and this result is in no way due to the introduction of machinery, for machines are not used in more than five mines out of the twenty-three, and the increase of production has occurred in all, whether machines are used or not. (P. 54.)

e. GRANITE AND STONE CUTTING.

United States Congress. Senate Document No. 1124. 62nd Congress. 3rd Session. 1913. The Eight-Hour Day. Various Articles, Arguments, and Bills relating to the Eight Hour Law. (Letter from WILLIAM J. CRAWFORD, *President, William J. Crawford & Co., Inc., to Mr. James Duncan, International President Granite Cutters' International Association. December 19, 1912.)*

Dear Sir: For several months the writer has wished to write to you and explain some facts which we are sure will interest you and your fellow members.

There are few firms in the country who have kept a comprehensive cost system extending over a period of more than 30 years. Just 32 years ago, in January, 1880, we commenced to keep this record of the value of each man and the exact cost of each piece of work, and we have kept this ever since. In the part of this work which will interest you we have a page for each granite cutter, and following each entry of the piece of work he takes up is the day and hour commenced, the day and hour finished, the entire time consumed, the wages we have paid, the quarry bill, and a column for loss and a column for gain. In this way we are able to raise a man's wages from time to time as he proves his worth. We do this without request from the men, and in this way we obtain the highest efficiency, and we can not remember when a man has asked us to raise his wages.

Now about the fact that I think will be of particular interest to you. This cost system extends back to the time when the day was 10 hours, and it shows that the same man under identically the same conditions, accomplished more, of exactly the same kind of work when he was working 9 hours, than he did when he was working 10 hours, and again when the hours were reduced to 8 hours this same man accomplished still more in an 8-hour day than he did in a 9-hour day, or a considerable amount more than he did when the day was 10 hours long.

My observation of the condition, and I am with our

men from 8 a. m. until 5 p. m. is this, that as men work to-day at the granite cutting trade, an 8-hour day is too long, and I believe that any good granite cutter (and I mean by this a man who uses his brains as well as his muscles every minute) could do just as much work in 7 or even 6 hours as he does in 8. This may sound radical, but from close study I find that 16 hours for "rest and refreshment" to a granite cutter is not sufficient to make him approach his work in the morning in a perfectly rested condition.

We are glad to watch the efforts of a Matthewson, Johnson, Joe Wood, or any of the other star pitchers, and we would think McGraw, Griffiths, or Stahl, beside themselves to put any one of these men in the box for two consecutive days, of about two hours each day. Now what granite cutter does not put as much of his brains and muscles into his work every day as these stars exercise? The shrewd manager knows he can get the best results from a man whose brain and body are not fatigued. We employers of granite cutters can learn a lesson from them. Once in a while there is an Edison who can work long hours profitably; but they are conspicuous by their rarity. The short life of the granite cutters is due not to the dust alone, but to the hard work incident to the trade. (Pp. 16-17.)

Jahresbericht der grossherzoglich-badischen Fabrikinspektion für das Jahr 1903. [*Report of the Factory Inspectors of Baden for the year 1903.*]

In many instances the efficiency of workmen has so improved under shorter hours that where piecework wages have remained unchanged they have been able to earn as much as before.

In the Mannheim Granite and Sandstone Works belonging to Georg Hartman, employing on an average 120 men, the employers and men agreed to establish an 8½-hour day while doing away with the half-hour rest pauses formerly customary in the morning and afternoon. The canteen, which had previously had an active trade in beer, was abolished. The firm states that so definite an increase in working capacity and application has resulted, that the output is scarcely, if at all, less than it was before with a working day of from 10 to 11 hours, while the quality of work has noticeably improved. The sandstone cutters are delighted with the restriction and hope much from it in the way of improvement in the very bad conditions of health hitherto prevailing among them. (P. 38.)

Jahresberichte der Gewerbe-Aufsichtsbeamten und Bergbehörden für das Jahr 1904. Bd. I. Preussen. [Reports of the (German) Factory and Mine Inspectors for the year 1904. Vol. I. Prussia.] Berlin, Decker, 1905.

A noteworthy instance of reduction of hours is found in a large stone-working plant in Trier. The working time formerly was from 7 a.m. to 6 p.m. for the day shift and from 6 p.m. to 5 a.m. for night shift. . . . The experiment of eight-hour shifts was tried. One shift was from 5 a.m. to 1 p.m. and the second from 1 p.m. to 9 p.m. . . .

The result was surprisingly satisfactory for those working with machinery on piecework. The output and wages suffered a slight decrease for four weeks only, and after that they rose, slightly with the inferior piece workers, and with the most expert ones, to as much as 11 per cent. over that under the longer hours. This has been the average for six years. The same satisfactory results were observed with the other workmen. . . . They now easily complete in eight hours the full amount of work formerly done in the longer day; wages naturally remain the same. Inquiries made of the men as to whether they preferred the old arrangement were answered in the negative throughout. (P. I. 485.)

f. GLASS AND OPTICAL INSTRUMENTS.

The Eight Hours Day. SIDNEY WEBB *and* HAROLD COX. *London, Walter Scott, 1891.*

Herr Heye, the proprietor of the large glass works of Gerresheim, near Düsseldorf, Germany, reduced the working day from eleven, and in some cases twelve hours, to a normal eight hours. He reports that in a very short time there was produced, without increase of staff, as much as before the reduction.* (P. 101.)

Gesammelte Abhandlungen. Bd. III. [*Complete Works. Vol. III.*] *Die Volkswirthschaftliche Bedeutung der Verkürzung des Industriellen Arbeitstages.* [*The Economic Significance of a Shorter Working Day.*] ERNST ABBE. *Paper read before the Economic Society at Jena in 1901. Jena, Fisher, 1906.*

Beside the effect on production and international competition involved in shorter working hours, the question arises as to the effect of a shorter day on the workman's strength. If he produces as much in shorter hours, does he do this at the cost of his reserve energy? In a word, does he use up his strength sooner by more intensive work? If he did, this fact would be of far-reaching social and economic import. (P. 204.)

The experiment made in the optical works in whose management I had a part, and where the working day was abruptly reduced from a nine to an eight-hour day at a time of the most active production, . . . confirms, in the most important and leading points, all that the far more extensive experiences of England had demonstrated as to the effect of shorter hours on output.

Our researches proved that this reduction from nine to eight hours, that is, of more than 10 per cent. at one bound, brought about not the least diminution of the daily output, but increased it demonstrably even if only to a slight extent. . . . It would not be worth while to add our testimony to that of England, if it were not for

* Revue des Deux Mondes, November, 1887, p. 132.

the fact that we worked out our results in exact figures. (P. 205.)

Our inquiries have this further credit, that they give a decisive answer to the question: Does reduction of hours mean a greater expenditure of strength for the individual? Is the work more wearing to the workman or not?

Our observations enable us to reply with certainty in the negative: the workmen are subjected to no greater strain by executing in eight hours what they used to do in nine, although they do, certainly, work with greater intensiveness during the shorter period. We gained an insight into the actual factors that enable efficiency to rise with shorter hours, and to rise in such degree that the results are the same. To the question whether the difference is accounted for by such special motives as good-will or ambition for personal interest (as in piecework), we say, decidedly: no. The satisfactory result is obtained independently of such motives. And I regard this as one of the most important points that our experience has brought to light.

Finally, our observations have enabled us to explain the connection between rapidity of work and shorter working hours, and to show how the equalizing of efficiency is brought about. I am under the impression that this has never been explained. (P. 206.)

Our working hours were first reduced gradually through a period of 30-35 years, from 12 hours to nine, then to eight. . . .

Some slight differences in output were noticeable from the standpoint of the age of workers, but so insignificant that they are negligible. The youngest workmen had, to be sure, the best results, yet in no instance was there any lagging worth mentioning among the older ones. (P. 211). From our results it may be concluded: Success under shorter hours is attained equally, with but slight variations, by older and younger workmen. (P. 212.)

The testimony of different individuals on time work agreed that after the first few days no conscious effort had to be made to keep up the pace of work. . . . Many were unconscious that they had done more until I proved it to them. . . . All, even the older ones, averred that the work was not more wearing; the last half-hour was not harder than before. (P. 218.)

Piece workers, who, at first, made an effort that they could not keep up, found that they had at first in reality attempted to do much more than they had ever done before. After relaxing to the pace that was permanently endurable, they discovered that their output and earnings were the same as previously, or slightly more. (P. 219.)

(*Condensed from original.*)

1. Reduction of working hours is not followed by a reduction of output. Frequently a distinct increase in output results. In our works, in a year, 30 men have done as much under the 8 hours as 31 men had done in the year before under 9 hours. (P. 222.)

2. In spite of good-will and obvious self-interest, increased output is only temporarily attainable by lengthening the hours of work, and after a short time the output under lengthened hours falls back to what it was in the shorter day.

3. Even where workmen have no interest in doing as much in the shorter hours; where on the contrary they have interests in *not* doing as much, nevertheless the same result is obtained:—no diminution of product occurs.

4. This seems to me conclusive evidence that the rate of speed (short working hours resulting in heightened intensity and long ones in diminished intensity) is an automatic and involuntary adjustment not realized by the individual; that many persons have no idea of it, and indeed do not believe it until the proofs that they have accomplished more in a short day are shown to them. (P. 223.)

In saying that recuperation must equal fatigue, I am speaking of real things. . . . We may discern three plainly separable factors in the production of fatigue, and these, when added together, make an important total.

I. The first is the amount of the daily output, quite independent of the time in which it is produced. When, for instance, a man at a turning lathe, one who is distinctly skilful, has about 50 similar objects to make, he must make a certain number of motions of the hand in sequence and must exercise a certain number of sense perceptions in order to control his work. He needs also to exercise a certain number of impulses of the will. Now, if instead of 50 objects he makes 100, then he has done all these things twice as often—quite independent of whether he has worked 5, 6 or 10 hours.

The amount of output gives an estimate by which to measure the amount of strength expended. This is different with different persons. Greater experience, skill, or quickness enables one to work with less expenditure of strength than another. . . . Yet on the whole, with persons who are working under similar conditions, there is always a large number whose expenditure of strength in the daily working hours is wholly proportionate to the amount of their output.

II. The second factor in fatigue depends on the speed with which work is done. In general it might be supposed that when a given piece of work was performed in a shorter time, a greater exertion of strength would be necessary. But this is only true beyond certain limits. Within certain reasonable limits, the same piece of work can be done somewhat faster without increased outlay of strength. If, for instance, one walks, say, four kilometres, it is quite the same whether one walks a little faster or slower, so long as one does not actually run. This second factor, speed, is an important one in producing the same result with a shorter work day. (P. 229.)

III. The third, however, is the most important, in my opinion, and is entirely analogous with what is called in technical language concerning machinery, "waste of power," when the machines are running dead. (Kraftverbrauch für Leergang.) . . .

The consequence of the previously mentioned division of labor is that, with few exceptions, all details of industry are performed by persons who must either sit or stand all day; few have any chance for change within the limits of their working time. If we picture to ourselves what it would be for a man to be obliged to sit, or stand, without doing any work, but maintaining a fixed position of the body for 8 or 10 hours, we know at once that he would be fatigued even though he had done nothing. My contention is that, as this fatigue represents an outlay of strength required solely by sitting or standing in the position needed by his work, and in the environment of work (with noise, confusion, the need of attention to protect himself and others from danger)—as this purely passive fatigue, I repeat, forms a large part of the day's work, every reduction of hours which results in concentrating the usual output within the shorter working day is a clear gain for the worker's strength.

If a man can do a certain day's work in 8 hours, and he is compelled to spend 10 hours at it, then it is just as if we said to him: you may do your work in 8 hours, but then you must sit here for 2 hours more, in the same position, listening to the same noise, paying the same attention, being careful to avoid danger, but without doing anything. And I maintain that, just as the shorter time has been a definite saving for the "wasted power" of the machine, so the shorter day is a corresponding saving of human strength, avoiding a waste of power in men. (P. 230.)

The length of working hours, therefore, comes up for consideration three times—twice in estimating the expenditure of energy (1. Shortened hours and increased intensity; exertion the same if certain limits of speed are not exceeded. 2. In estimating the "wasted power" of man, analogy with the machine), and thirdly in considering recuperation (shorter work—longer time for rest). (P. 232.)

Without pressing mathematical conclusions further it is evident that, when this relation of work to rest is correctly grasped, the shorter day not only leaves the day's output unchanged, but may improve it. (P. 232.)

It must be true that, if we could accurately gauge the mathematical relation, we would find that there was an "Optimum" for each person, namely, the shortest possible time in which the largest possible product could be achieved. Where this lies will depend largely upon the thoroughness with which the single elements of fatigue are studied.

How great the outlay of strength in lost time, wasted energy, and speed is in individual cases, is essentially a question of investigation. (P. 232.)

INCREASE IN EFFICIENCY UNDER THE EIGHT-HOUR DAY OF 233 PIECE-WORKERS AT THE ZEISS OPTICAL WORKS.—CLASSIFIED BY AGES.

(Ages were reckoned from April 1, 1900. Length of service reckoned according to years spent in the firm's employ after the eighteenth birthday.)

Ages	No. of Work-men	Average Ages	Average Length Service	Average Piece-Rate Earnings per Hour in Pf. 9 Hr. Day	8 Hr. Day	Ratio of Increase
22-25	34	23.5	5.5	55.3	65.2	100 : 117.9
25-30	69	27.3	7.9	62.2	72.6	100 : 116.7
30-35	69	32.2	10.1	65.1	74.8	100 : 114.9
35-40	40	37.7	12.7	60.6	70.2	100 : 115.8
Over 40	21	45.3	15.3	63.3	74.3	100 : 117.4
Total	233	31.6*	9.6†	61.9	71.9	100 : 116.2

* Maximum 53, minimum 22 years. † Maximum 33, minimum 4 years.
(P. 159.)

Superior Output in Shorter Hours: Glass, etc.—Germany.

INCREASE IN EFFICIENCY OF THE 233 WORKERS. CLASSIFIED BY OCCUPATION.

Occupation	No. of Persons	Average Age	Average Length Service Years	Earnings per Hour in Pf. 9 Hr. Day	Earnings per Hour in Pf. 8 Hr. Day	Ratio of Increase
Optical Operations:						
1. Lense - setters: Fine hand work	21	31.1	12.7	72.8	84.9	100 : 116.6
2. Microscope grinders, etc.	20	33.2	13.8	79.1	86.5	100 : 109.4
3. Other hand grinders and centerers, entirely hand work	59	26.1	7.5	60.4	70.5	100 : 116.7
4. Machine grinders, entirely machine work	19	32.1	5.8	52.2	62.0	100 : 118.8
Mechanical and Auxiliary Work:						
5. Adjusting rooms, entirely hand work	22	31.7	8.2	65.5	76.7	100 : 117.1
6. Mounting rooms, chiefly hand work	20	36.9	11.6	66.6	78.5	100 : 117.9
7. Turning and milling, entirely machine work	23	35.2	11.1	57.6	68.0	100 : 118.1
8. Polishers and lacquerers, entirely hand work	17	34.7	11.2	53.8	63.3	100 : 117.7
9. Engraving, entirely hand work	5	27.2	6.8	56.1	66.9	100 : 119.3
10. Molders, entirely hand work	6	36.2	9.7	56.4	64.8	100 : 114.9
11. Carpenters, part hand, part machine	15	35.2	10.5	52.3	62.9	100 : 120.3
12. Case makers, chiefly hand work	6	30.4	6.4	55.7	62.8	100 : 112.7
	233	31.6	9.6	61.9	71.9	100 : 116.7

(P. 160.)

Association Nationale Française pour la Protection Légale des Travailleurs. La Réglementation du Travail dans les Usines à Marche continue. Rapport de F. FAGNOT, *Enquêteur à l'office du Travail. [National French Association for Labor Legislation. Regulation of Working Hours in Continuous Industries. Report of* F. FAGNOT, *Investigator for the Bureau of Labor.] Paris, Felix Alcan, 1913.*

(M. Wagret, head of a number of glass factories in the north of France, spoke in the discussion as follows:)

The system of three shifts is in use in the factories for window glass and glass bottles in the north. . . . In the second [illegible]: we have three eight-hour shifts with seven and a half hours' effective work. This has been going on ten years. I must acknowledge that the men produce just as much, if not more, in their seven and a half hours' actual work than during the ten hour day that preceded it.

This method of work, then, is very favorable. (P. 91.)

g. CHEMICALS.

Jahresbericht der grossherzoglichen badischen Fabrikinspektion für das Jahr 1901. [Reports of the Factory Inspectors of Baden. 1901.] Karlsruhe, Thiergarten, 1902.

The chemical works in Durlach resolved not to dismiss any workmen in a certain slack season, shortening the hours of labor instead. But the expected decrease in output did not occur, so that occasional closing for a day had to be resorted to. After this experience the firm resolved to retain the shorter hours even in recurring seasons of full orders, believing that they can institute an even shorter day without any reduction of product worth speaking of. (P. 22.)

Fifteenth Annual Report of the National Consumers' League. New York, 1916. Some Practical Experiences in Shortening Hours of Labor. Address by Mr. Frederick R. Hazard, *President Solvay Process Company, Syracuse, New York, at Cleveland, Ohio, November 4, 1915.*

I remember distinctly, and I think many of you must also, when it was the rule for both men and women, in almost every factory, to work twelve hours a day, beginning at half past six in the morning and working until half past six at night, with a poor half hour at noon, usually spent in the plant, eating a cold lunch which they had brought with them.

In my first experience in studying the business with which I afterwards became identified, I went abroad to the foreign works, and the system there was eleven hours work for day time, thirteen hours at night. It is a twenty-four hour job, a three hundred and sixty-five day job, it doesn't stop any more than a blast furnace. The method of changing shift, in order that one man might not be compelled indefinitely to work the thirteen hours at night, was for him to continue and work eleven hours in the day time, making twenty-four hours of continuous work. Meantime his partner had had a rest, and he came on comparatively fresh, much more so, certainly, than the man who had just finished twenty-four hours. I personally made that change a great many times, in the course of my apprenticeship, and I can assure you that for the last few hours my work was not worth what I got paid, or what I would have got paid. It was not worth anything, and my observation led me to the belief that most of the men that worked on the basis were equally worthless with myself before the end of their long turn. It was also noticeable that accidents, to the work and to the workmen, were more frequent on the twenty-four hour shift than at any other time.

After my experience abroad, coming home, we established the industry, which has since grown, and we followed the practice of the foreigners, because we didn't know any better, for a few years. We found also, on inquiry, that it was a very common practice in this country to work on that same basis, eleven hours in the day time and thirteen hours at night, and that practically continues to this day in some industries and in some localities. We came to the conclusion, however, twenty-three years ago, that it would be possible to establish three shifts of eight hours each and thereby much improve the results both for the corporation and for the workman. Now, please bear in mind that this is only one phase of the problem; this is the phase in which you are considering twenty-four hours' work, not a day's work, when the plant may be idle for sixteen hours, but where the plant must be kept up to its utmost efficiency twenty-four hours in each day.

Again, our problem differs from that which many have to face, in the fact that we are dealing with large units, large weights. The raw materials going in are measured by tons, even by the hundred tons, the finished products coming out are measured by the same units; it is a question of handling large things rather than small. By small, I mean the kind of pieces which would be handled in an automobile factory, or, smaller still, pieces which would be handled in the manufacture of clothing. The problems of fatigue are necessarily quite different from those found in the other cases, and I do not pretend to speak of those problems which would be presented in the handling of the smaller things; but I can from experience speak somewhat of those problems of handling—the larger units, the problem of dealing with the fireman who handles his tons of coal per day, with the lime-burner who handles his tons of limestone and of the burnt lime, and with the packer who handles his tons of the finished product. In those respects I know that we have made an advance by going to the eight-hour basis.

Comparing the results attained in the first two years after making the change, we find that there was some increase in cost, total cost, per unit of product handled. It was not increase of cost in material. There was of course an increase in wages, since we decided that we could not ask the men to materially reduce their income. Since that time wages per unit of time, per hour, have increased very greatly. In spite of that increase, the total time consumed has decreased so that the result in cost is less than it was before the eight-hour change was made.

Instituts Solvay. Travaux de l'Institut de Sociologie [Sociological Publications of the Solvay Institute.] Une Expérience Industrielle de Reduction de la Journée de Travail. Par L. G. FROMONT *avec une Préface de* E. MAHAIM. *[An Industrial Experiment in the Reduction of Hours of Labor.* L. G. FROMONT, *with Preface by* E. MAHAIM.] *Brussels, Misch et Thron, 1906.*

The experiment which Mr. Fromont has carried on for more than twelve years at the Engis Chemical Works, of which he himself is the founder and managing director, is free from the possible objections indicated (vagueness, inexactness of record, difference of conditions, etc.) I know none of greater value as evidence.

The work in question is that at the furnaces where ore is roasted. . . . The productivity of the workman is measured with absolute exactness, since his work is, so to speak, weighed. Wages remained fixed by piece work, by the ton, that is, of roasted ore; equipment has not been altered but simply better utilized. In short the general conditions of work have remained the same.

The results have been as follows: In an 8 hours' day ($7\frac{1}{2}$ hours' actual work) the same men at the same furnaces with the same tools and raw material have produced as much as before in a 12 hour day (10 hours' actual work.)

It goes without saying that the cost of production per ton is less, that wages are the same, and that both employer and men are benefited. It is also not without interest to note that the company, the Engis Chemical Works, has not ceased to be financially successful. (Preface, pp. XVI-XVII.)

The cause of the reduction of daily hours of work is, theoretically, a victorious cause. It would be difficult to find an economist worthy of the name who would maintain that reduction of working hours meant, always, or necessarily, a reduction of output on the part of the worker.

It is, on the contrary, generally held that the "day" can be reduced, in many industries, without increasing cost of production. Variations arise from kind and number of industries, extent of reduction and, above all from the manner of its establishment; but the principle itself is scarcely any longer contested.

It is worthy of note that this victory . . . was not gained by theorists.

It has come as a result not of deduction from abstract reasoning but of induction by men of affairs from observed facts of experience. . . . (Preface, pp. XIII-XIV.)

Every demand upon the sick benefits' fund left a deficit which increased month by month. This fund was established to pay not only for medical attendance and medicines, but also a part of the wages of sick workmen during non-employment. . . . We are considering solely the legitimate charges on the funds, arising chiefly from the fatigue and exhaustion from which the furnace men suffered. (P. 47.)

Concerned as we were by the alarming deficits in the sick benefit fund, we were still more alarmed by the manifest and daily increasing debility of our men. It was precisely the most industrious and loyal who gave most evident signs of overwork and exhaustion. Every one was growing discouraged. (Pp. 48-49.)

In the presence of these alarming difficulties . . . it was necessary to take counsel. . . . Must we have recourse to a foreign labor-supply, and import stronger work men from more favored countries? (Pp. 49-50.)

We decided to retain the same men, but to shorten their hours of work. The new organization of industry was planned for three shifts of men, each one being on duty for eight hours, 7½ of which were actually spent at work. The first shift worked from 6 a. m. to 2 p. m. with half an hour of rest at 10; the second from 2 to 10 p. m. with half an hour off at 6; the third from 10 p. m. to 6 a. m. with half an hour at 1:30. In order that the same men should not always work at night, a rotation was established by which the second relay stayed on for 16 hours on Sunday night, leaving at 6 a. m. instead of at 10 p. m. This new system not only gave the men more daily time, but also more Sunday rest than before. (Pp. 54-55.)

Under the old plan the mills were working 20 hours and shut down for four hours, while under the new system they are working for 22½ hours, and work is interrupted for only 1½ hours. The gain is thus 2½ hours in 24, or 10.5 per cent. During the 7½ hours of actual work the gain in activity is

$$\frac{10.5 \times 7.5}{100} = 0.7875 \text{ hour} = 48 \text{ minutes.}$$

(Pp. 62-63.)

What increase in productivity of plant and workman was to be expected?

The old production per man for 10 hours' actual work

was 1,000 kilos, that is 100 kilos an hour, which was equivalent to 750 kilos for 7½ hours' actual work.

The old production, briefly stated, averaged 750 kilos for 7½ hours of actual work. Now, a daily gain of 2½ hours gives us a daily increase of 2.5 x 100 = 250 kilos, which, distributed among the three shifts, gives to each $\frac{250}{3} = 83$ kilos. Each shift should then attain output of $750 + 83 = 833$ kilos in 7½ hours of actual work, or $\frac{833}{7.5} = 111.1$ kilo per hour.

Figuring in another way, we reach practically the same result. We have seen that the 10.5 per cent. gain in activity is equivalent to 48 minutes for 7½ hours' actual work. This 48 minutes corresponds to a production of $\frac{100 \times 48}{60} = 80$ kilos, which added to the 750 as the minimum expected would give a total of 830 kilos which we hoped might be produced, that is for each shift $\frac{830}{7.5} = 111$ kilos per hour. (Pp. 63-64.)

Eight hundred and thirty kilos was to our mind a minimum that ought to be greatly exceeded, and which might easily reach the figure of 890 kilos. (P. 65.)

The workmen were at first opposed to the new system, seeing in the shorter hours a diminished output and consequently lowered wages. (P. 72.)

Patience and strict discipline were necessary to enforce ample trial . . . At first they began to realize the benefit to their health and vigor . . . their confidence returned and with their renewed zeal our expectations were surpassed. Almost imperceptibly, the daily output increased, and in less than six months from the beginning of the new time scale the men had succeeded in producing, in 7½ hours of actual work, as much as they had formerly turned out in 10. And their wages . . . for the eight hours on duty came to be as high as formerly when they spent 12 hours in the mill. (P. 75.)

We have represented in dotted lines the curves we expected to obtain and in solid lines the curves actually achieved.

Superior Output in Shorter Hours: Chemicals.—Belgium

Chart I, showing output per man, and per day, gives us the curve M R instead of the lower curve estimated N R.

I.

In Chart II, showing earnings per man, and per day, the estimated curve N'R' has become M'R'.

II.

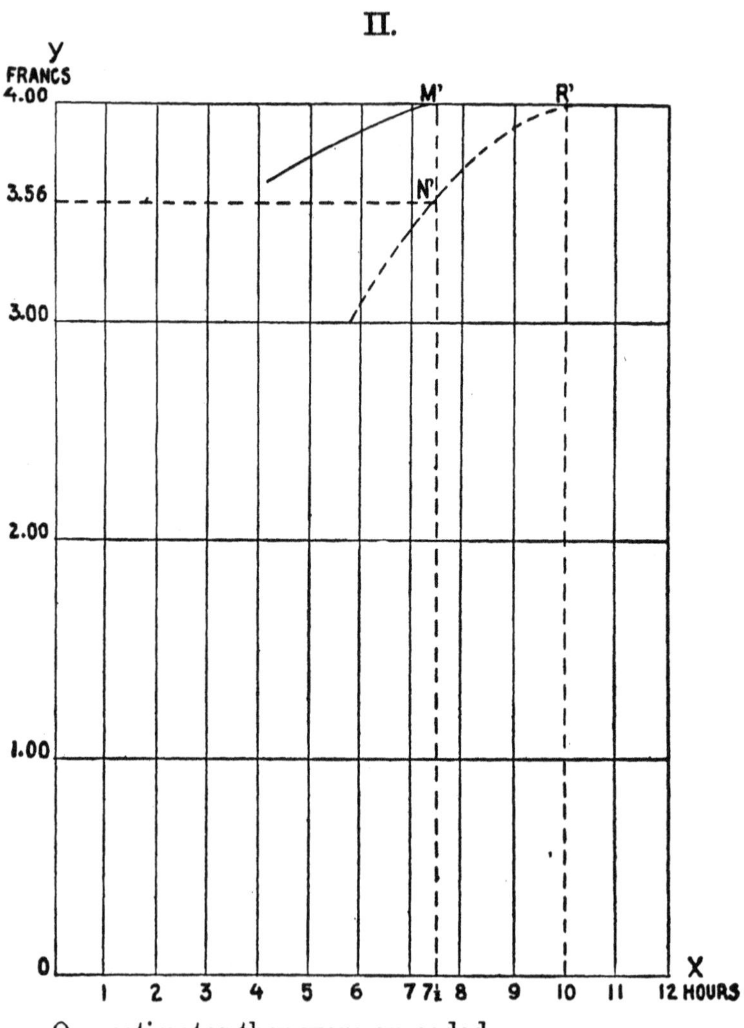

Our estimates then were exceeded

for production, by $\frac{110 \times 100}{890}$ } = 12.4%

for wages, by $\frac{44 \times 100}{356}$

(Pp. 77-78.)

Chart III, showing output per man, and per double day, gives us an ascending curve S P, much more accentuated than the estimated curve S Q.

III.

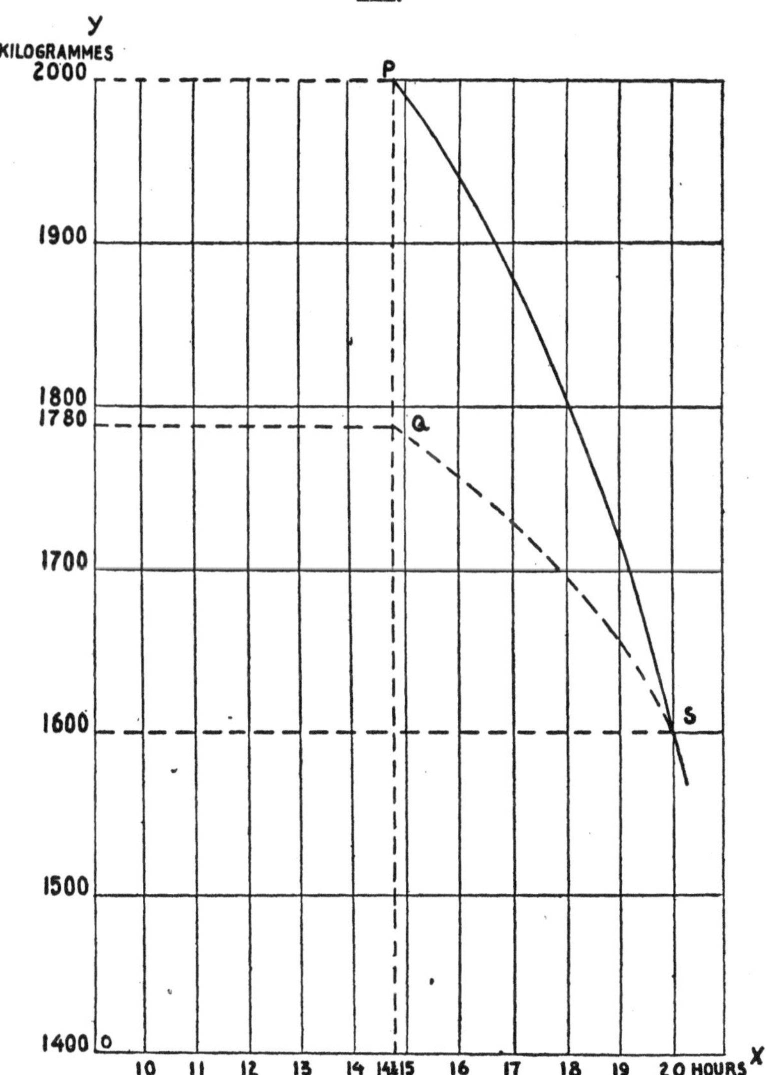

Similarly Chart IV, of wages earned per man, and per double day, gives the more marked curve S'P' in place of the expected curve S'Q'.

IV.

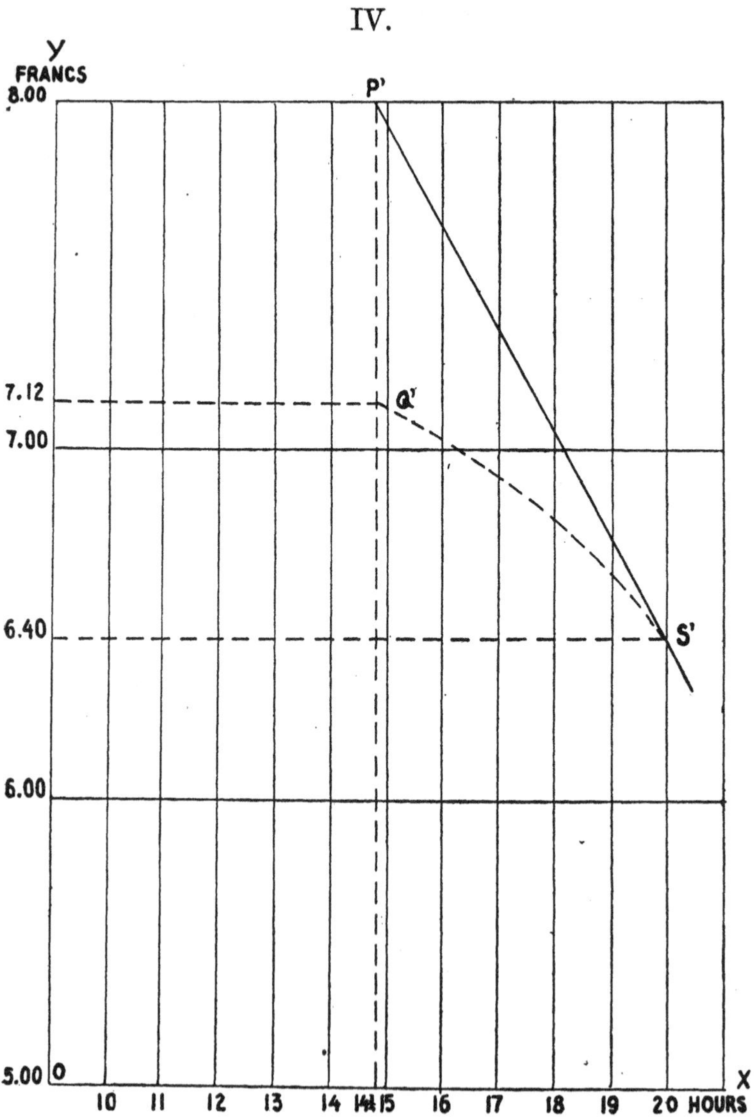

Here, too, our estimates were exceeded

$$\left.\begin{array}{l}\text{for output, by } \frac{400 \times 100}{1{,}600} \\ \text{for wages, by } \frac{160 \times 100}{640}\end{array}\right\} = 25\%.$$

Chart V, showing output per man and per hour, gives us the curve H K instead of the expected curve H L.

Similarly Chart VI, showing wages per man per hour, gives us curve H'K' instead of the estimated curve H'L'.

Our estimates are accordingly exceeded

$$\left.\begin{array}{l}\text{for output, by } \frac{33.33 \times 100}{100} \\ \text{for wages, by } \frac{133.33 \times 108}{400}\end{array}\right\} = 33.33\%.$$

V.

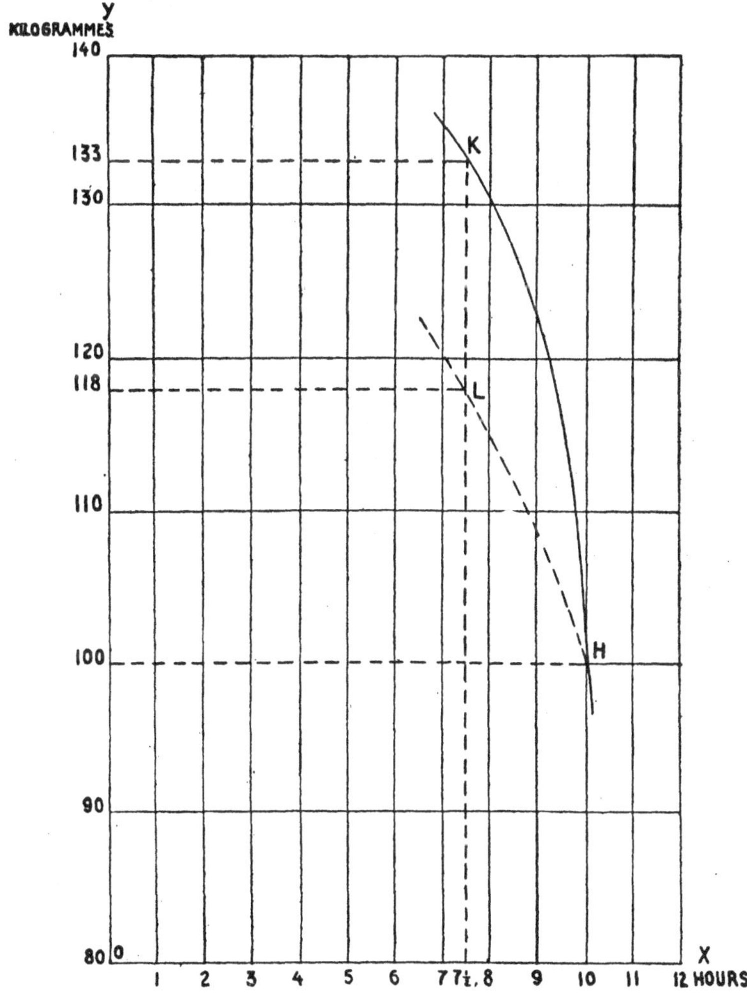

VI.

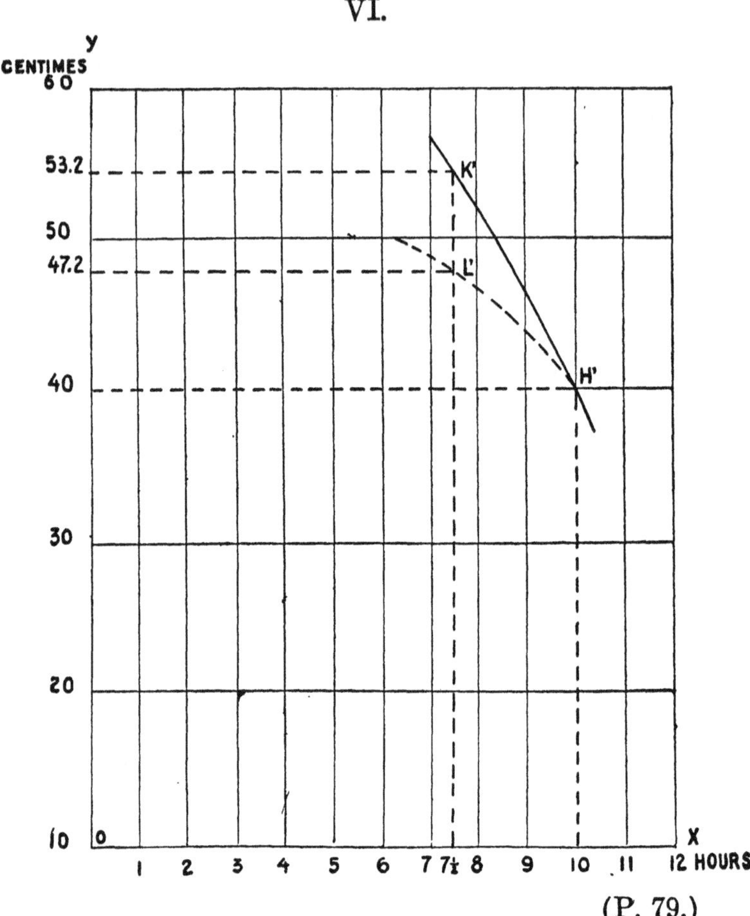

(P. 79.)

Committee of One Hundred on National Health. Bulletin No. 30. July, 1909. Report on National Vitality, its Wastes and Conservation. Prepared for the National Conservation Commission. Professor Irving Fisher, *Yale University. Washington, Government Printing Office, 1909.*

The Solvay Process Company, of Syracuse, installed in 1892 a system of three eight-hour shifts in place of the two previous shifts of eleven and thirteen hours, respectively. It was stated by the assistant general manager in 1905 that the change had considerably lessened the wear and tear on the men, and that they could be called on to do their work at their highest state of efficiency, which had not been possible on the two-shift basis. President Hazard of the company writes:

In general, I can say that the results of the change from a twelve-hour shift for an eight-hour shift were very satisfactory and have continued to be so. While the immediate result was to considerably increase the cost per unit of product, the efficiency of the men gradually increased, so that at the end of about one year the first increase had been overcome and the cost per unit of product fell to a point even lower than had been obtained under the twelve-hour shift, and further the time consumed per unit of product has since been so reduced that we are today and for some time have been operating with a smaller number of hours per unit of product than we had under the twelve-hour shift.

Further proof of the benefits of the change to the three-shift day is furnished by the records of the Solvay Mutual Benefit Association for 1891 and 1904. The days lost per man by sickness each year fell from seven and one-half days in 1891 to five and one-half days in 1904. (P. 46.)

Report of the Special Commission on Hours of Labor in Continuous Industries to the Seventh Delegates' Meeting of the International Association for Labor Legislation. Zurich, 1912. London. The Pioneer Press, Ltd., July, 1912.

Mr. A. H. Crosfield (who was for many years a leading member of the firm of Joseph Crosfield & Sons, large manufacturers of soap and chemicals at Warrington) said that while the adoption of the eight-hour shift throughout the continuous process of Messrs. Crosfield's business had been absolutely justified in the result from a commercial and economic standpoint, the employees had benefited by it enormously, both in mind and body; indeed, he added that the same might be said of the results of working shorter hours in all the branches of Messrs. Crosfield's business where they had been introduced, both those which were continuous processes and those which were not. Referring to the experience of men who had worked both the 12-hour and eight-hour shifts in continuous processes, and to the contrast between the state of affairs in those parts of the country where the long hours were worked and those where the eight-hour shift had been adopted, Mr. Crosfield summed up and emphasized the comparison by saying that it reminded him of nothing less than the difference between barbarism and civilization. (P. 9.)

Brunner, Mond & Co. state that the increase in output and more regular and better work resulting from the shorter shift more than counterbalance the increase in wages. Sir Alfred Mond writes:

"If my own personal view is of any value, I have no doubt in expressing the opinion that for furnaces requiring continuous labor, the eight-hour shift is the right system, and that with proper organization, better results will be obtained from a manufacturer's point of view by men working a number of hours which enables them to keep their minds and bodies fresh for work rather than by attempting economy on the wages, by working men beyond the limit of their best capacity." . . .

That positive economic advantages are accredited to the eight-hour shift, at least in some manufacturing quarters, is shown by Mr. Crosfield's statement to the effect that certain English employers with experience of the three-shift system had said to him that they were not at all anxious to see the same system introduced on the Continent; they would prefer to keep the advantages of it to themselves.

h. CIGARS.

Archiv für Soziale Gesetzebung und Statistik. Bd. VI. 1893. Ein Experiment mit dem Achtstundentage. [*An Experiment with the Eight-hour Day.*] Dr. OTTO PRINGSHEIM. *Berlin, 1893.*

That production remains at the same height when working time has been reduced by 18.4 per cent. has been recently proved in Holland. In a cigar factory in Gouda, with 26 workers (7 of these minors), the hours in accordance with the law passed in 1889 were shortened from 11½ to 9½. At the end of 1890 it was shown that the output was even greater than before and the wages as high also—in some cases higher. (P. 14.)

Amtliche Mittheilungen aus den Jahres-Berichten der Gewerbe-Aufsichtsbeamten. XVIII. 1893. [*Official Information from Reports of the (German) Factory Inspectors.*] *Berlin, 1894.*

In most establishments the working day was eleven hours, but the ten-hour day was introduced in certain ones. The shorter day turned out well in all cases. (Liegnitz.)

In a cigar box and wrapper mould factory all adult workers were given uniform working hours in summer and winter—a nine-hour day, from seven to six, with two hours free time at noon. The owner asserts that in this shorter time no less work is done than formerly in the longer time, the eleven-hour day. (Kassel.) (P. 155.)

Jahresbericht der grossherzoglich-badischen Fabrikinspektion für das Jahr 1900. [*Reports of the Factory Inspectors of Baden for the year 1900.*] *Karlsruhe, 1901.*

A cigar factory in Bühl was forced by the workmen to establish the 9-hour day. The employer found that the diminution in product was an entirely negligible quantity. He is now convinced that, in cigar making, the 9-hour day, if generally established, will, after a certain transition period, give as abundant an output as is now had with the 11 hours. (P. 20.)

Jahresberichte der Gewerbe-Aufsichtsbeamten und Bergbehörden für das Jahr 1904. Bd. I. Preussen. [*Reports of the (German) Factory and Mine Inspectors for the year 1904. Vol. I. Prussia.*] *Berlin, Decker, 1905.*

The owner of a cigar factory employing chiefly women had, by experimentation, become convinced that the introduction of a shorter working day would not influence output unfavorably. He therefore established the 9½ instead of the former 10-hour day. As the piece workers were afraid their earnings would be lessened, he could only get them to accept the new time by agreeing that the factory should be open half an hour earlier for those who preferred working ten hours. But after a very few weeks' time, all—both men and women—were convinced that no loss of earnings was to be feared from the shorter day. (P. I. 483.)

i. SHOES.

Report of New Jersey Bureau of Statistics of Labor and Industries. 1905. The Eight-hour Movement: How reducing the Hours of Labor has affected the cost of Production.

The other experience is the case of a large shoe manufacturing firm, located in Boston, Mass., where it employs nearly 3,000 people in its factories. The working hours in this great establishment had been, up to July 1st, 1898, 59 hours per week. A change was made then which brought working hours down to 53½ per week; no change was made in daily wages, and the result was a reduction in the labor cost of one per cent., and at the same time, the product per employe increased 2½ per cent. . . . (Pp. 226-227.)

The firm managers reasoned that an active 9-hour day would be superior to a more or less inactive 10-hour day; these expectations were fully justified by the fact that a larger volume of work was turned out, and the workmen averaged larger earnings in 9 hours than they did in 10; there were fewer of them late starting in the morning, and a steadier application to work was maintained during the day than was the case formerly. (P. 227.)

Jahresberichte der Gewerbe-Aufsichtsbeamten und Bergbehörden für das Jahr 1903. Bd. I. Preussen. [Annual Reports of the (German) Factory and Mine Inspectors for 1903. Vol. I. Prussia.] Berlin, Decker, 1904.

The so-called English time has been introduced in several shoe factories: The resultant reduction from 10 to 9¼ hours has not brought about any reduction in output. Employers and workers are both pleased. (P. 219.)

Employers seem more and more inclined to establish the ten-hour day; various mills which formerly had long hours, have adopted the ten-hour day without having experienced any disadvantage; others intend to introduce it. (P. 275.)

The prejudice against a ten-hour day is fast disappearing, as it comes to be understood that the productivity of the worker in the eleventh hour is proportionately low. (P. 295.)

Jahresberichte der Gewerbe-Aufsichtsbeamten und Bergbehörden für das Jahr 1904. Bd. III. Hesse. [Reports of the (German) Factory and Mine Inspectors for the year 1904. Vol. III. Hesse.] Berlin, Decker, 1905.

Strong efforts are being made to secure the 9-hour day generally in the shoemaking trade. The opinion of a manufacturer of shoes has been given in the following words: "The 9-hour day, which has been in force for 3 years in my factories, gives excellent results. I have succeeded in abolishing the morning and afternoon pauses with their accompanying inevitable beer-drinking. The men keep sober and steady, and turn out quite as much work in nine as formerly in ten hours, as I had, indeed, thoroughly convinced myself, in some weeks experimentation, would be the case. The power needed for the machines is reduced 10 per cent. as a result of the shorter hours; one hour less of artificial light is needed in winter; two advantages, in my opinion, which of themselves are enough recommendation for shorter hours. The workmen gain one hour more for themselves at the same wages, and do not have the occasion to spend their money during working hours." (Pp. 6. 58-59.)

Jahresberichte der Gewerbe-Aufsichtsbeamten und Bergbehörden für das Jahr 1907. Bd. III. Hesse. [Annual Report of the (German) Factory and Mine Inspectors for 1907. Vol. III. Hesse.] Berlin, Decker, 1908.

An important example of reduced hours while wages remained the same was given last year by the biggest employer in the district. (C. Heyl.) Now, also, the large leather works of Doerr and Reinhart have carried out their long contemplated plan of a shorter working day, with the result that 4,615 leather workers or about one-third of the entire working population of Worms have gained the advantage of an 8¾ hours working day.

The firm has come to the conclusion that a more economical use of machine power, daylight, and working time will be attained, quite aside from the benefit to the men. With day wages raised somewhat, the workman will earn quite as much as before, or even rather more. With punctuality in beginning and stopping work the pieceworkers will produce and will earn as much as before. (Pp. 6.[32] and [33].)

j. MISCELLANEOUS INSTANCES.

American Labor Legislation Review, June, 1914. Working Hours in Continuous Industries. Eight-Hour Shifts in the Milling Industry. S. THURSTON BALLARD, *Ballard & Ballard Milling Company, Louisville, Ky.*

While on two shifts we had twenty-two men on each watch, making forty-four men to pack our output in twenty-four hours. When we changed to the eight-hour basis we required only fifteen men to a crew, or forty-five men in all, so that practically the same number of men were able to do the same work when they worked only eight hours as they had before done when each man worked twelve hours. Therefore, I have come to the conclusion that, for any considerable length of time, a man doing active or laborious work can do as much in eight hours as he can in twelve. . . .

Therefore, from our personal experience, although we pay our men the same wage for eight hours' work as we formerly paid for twelve, and in a few instances have found it necessary to employ extra men, I feel sure that in the quality of output and steadiness of running—in dollars and cents—it has been a profitable investment. (Pp. 117-118.)

The Eight-Hours' Day. SIDNEY WEBB *and* HAROLD COX, B. A., *London, Walter Scott, 1891. Appendix II.*

Memorandum of a Conversation with Mr. Mark Beaufoy, M. P., Manufacturer of Vinegar, British Wines, and Jams.

When I first obtained control of the business, I found that during the months of October and November overtime was habitual. The men often worked till 8 or 9 at night, and sometimes even till 11. I realized that they were doing no good to themselves or to me, for such long hours rendered them physically incapable of doing good work. I put a stop to the system, and in order to compensate the men for the loss of overtime pay, I revised the scale of wages in their favour. It was some years later before I began to think of an Eight-Hours' Day. . . . We have one complete year's experience. During this year, from September 1889 to September 1890, we did more business than in almost any year I can remember, but *not one hour of overtime was worked.* The work was done by the same staff as before, with the exception of three or four men added to relieve the gate porters and watchmen, who had previously been on duty 12 hours at a time, and were now reduced to 8 hours. (Pp. 262-263.)

Eight Hours for Work. John Rae. *London and New York, Macmillan & Co., 1894.*

Herr Freese, window-blind maker at Hamburg and Berlin, having first abolished Sunday labour and overtime and found it advantageous, then reduced his regular hours of work to nine a day in 1890, and finding that again advantageous, tried the experiment of eight hours a day in his Berlin factory for two months last year, and with such satisfactory results that he adopted the eight-hours system as a permanent arrangement in 1892. . . . He employs various kinds of skilled labour, but the result has been the same with all alike. . . . The majority of the hands therefore earned better wages in eight hours' work than in nine; when they earned less there was no instance in which the decrease was as great as the reduction of hours, 11-1/10 per cent., and the general average of earnings was higher. More work, therefore, was done in an eight-hours' day than in a nine-hours' one, and the result is attributed to greater punctuality in attendance and greater energy in working. The improvement in punctuality was attested by the marked diminution in the fines for lateness in the morning and for absence on the Monday. . . . The old men found it more difficult, however, to keep up the more energetic rate of work than the younger men, and probably some of the cases of decreased earnings may be due to that cause. The machines wrought in the machine rooms were circular saws and fluting planes, quite as automatic, one may presume, as Mr. Seaton's lathe, but the improvement in the product was more remarkable in the machine work than in hand work, though it is stated the speed of the machines was not increased and could not be for fear they should get too hot. To this it must be added that Herr Freese says that while the quantity of the product has increased, the quality has in no way fallen off, and that he has made no inconsiderable saving in gas and fire. (Pp. 80-82.)

British Sessional Papers. Report of the Chief Inspector of Factories and Workshops for the year 1913.

In pickle factories in the Metropolitan area Miss Constance Smith found the fact established that in nearly all the hours worked are below those permissible, e. g., 8 a. m. to 7 p. m., 8 a. m. to 6 p. m. (with Saturdays 8 a. m. to 1 p. m.).

Miss Smith.—Several employers have reduced hours within the last two or three years, and were confident that they, as well as their workpeople, had benefited by this reduction. A partner in one large firm whose hours were formerly 8 a. m. to 8 p. m., and are now 8 a. m. to 7 p. m., stated that, although obliged to engage extra hands on making the change, the firm have found their annual cost of production slightly diminished while their output has considerably increased. The head of another considerable firm where the hours are 8 a. m. to 7 p. m. in winter and 7 a. m. to 6 p. m. in summer, and no "overtime" has been worked by women for 10 years, was strongly against any extension of these hours. (P. 97.)

The Economy of High Wages. Jacob Schoenhof. New York and London, Putnam, 1892.

Close attention to speeded machinery is a much greater nervous strain than was required by the humdrum of old routine and hand work. I have the statement of one of the largest dye-works in Zurich (mostly hand work, of course) to the same effect. The works employ some 450 hands. They formerly worked thirteen hours, with two hours for meals. The senior partner had hard work to obtain the consent of the other members of the firm to a reduction of the hours to twelve a day, or ten working hours. They figured out to him that it would entail a loss of 15,000 f. a year. The reduction of hours was introduced more as a trial than a determined policy. But after the first year it was found that not only was no loss sustained, but, on the contrary, the results were more satisfactory than those of the preceding year. The facts were not so astonishing as men's obstinate resistance to their application. (P. 393.)

Jahresberichte der Gewerbe-Aufsichtsbeamten und Bergbehörden für das Jahr 1905. Bd. I. Preussen. [Reports of the Factory and Mines Inspectors for 1905. Vol. I. Prussia.] Berlin, Decker, 1906.

A manufacturer of insulating apparatus reduced the hours in one department from 8 to 7, leaving wages for piece work the same, in spite of objections from the men, who thought their earnings would be diminished. However, after a few days they found they could turn out just as much as before with the longer hours. This instance is the more remarkable because this company has reduced hours of work from ten to seven, in the course of about eight years, while maintaining the price of piece work unchanged. They now seem to have reached the utmost limits of their workmen's speed and their machines' capacity, for they find it is impossible now to do overtime for any length of time, as the output then falls off in a quite marked degree. (P. I. 40.)

A number of large manufacturers have adopted the plan of running their factories with two shifts of men, closing only from midnight to 6 a. m., in order to utilize the plants to the full extent. There is a general tendency toward a simultaneous attainment of increased intensity with correspondingly shortened hours of work.

The experiments mentioned in last year's report, by two of the largest industries in the district [a rubber works of the General Electric Company at Oberspree and Borsig's machine shop], reducing the hours of labor respectively from 10 to 9 and from 9½ to 8½ hours, have been declared to be thoroughly satisfactory. (P. I.[40].)

The efforts of workingmen to obtain shorter hours of work are continually resulting in success. Hours of 9, 8¾, 8½, or even 8, daily, are now not at all uncommon in Frankfurt a. M. The employers are in general not opposed, as they find that the output of the shorter day is quite equal to what it was before. (P. I.[344].)

k. GENERAL COMMENTS.

Fourth Annual Convention of the International Association of Factory Inspectors of North America. Boston. Wright and Potter, 1890. The Restriction of the Hours of Labor in Factories and Workshops. L. R. CAMPBELL, *Maine.*

The history of all successful movements for less hours to constitute a day's work, as a rule, is that they have been followed by a greater production in their several lines; and, also, these reductions in the hours of labor were generally followed by an increase of wages. (Pp. 43-44.)

In my State, since the adoption of the ten hours in lieu of the eleven hours, in mills and factories where machinery is employed, it is the universal verdict of manufacturers that their product is as great under the ten-hour system as it was under the eleven-hour system, and I think that the same answer comes from every State that has adopted the ten-hour system. (P. 47.)

Report of the New York Factory Inspector. 1894.

It must be said that not only was the time reduction (60 hours a week) hailed with satisfaction by the hands in the factories, but their employers, within a short period from the date on which the law took effect, almost unanimously acknowledged that there was no reduction whatever in the amount of labor performed or the product of their plants. (P. 32.)

Report of the Pennsylvania Factory Inspector. 1895.

I have come in contact with a number of operators who state that their experience in working long hours had been detrimental to their business, and injurious to the employees, and by working shorter hours they get a better production per hour, and a superior article, and are now running their establishment less than the sixty hours a week required by law. (P. 6.)

Report of Chief of Massachusetts District Police. 1899.

One question has been raised from the beginning, which is, whether or not legislation of this kind does not make it impossible for our manufacturing industries to compete successfully with those of other States of the Union not having laws fixing the limit of hours of labor for women and minors. . . . To shorten the hours of labor, it was said, would reduce the production of our factories, and increase the running expenses, unless wages should be cut down to meet the changed condition. The evils predicted have not come to pass. It is at least probable, if it cannot be claimed as an ascertained fact, that, taking a reasonable period for the basis of comparison, better work and more of it is done by the operatives than under the former system of unrestricted hours of labor. . . . It may be assumed that no legislation in this Commonwealth would insist upon maintaining a policy whose effect would be the destruction of our manufacturing supremacy. . . . It cannot be shown that the laws in question have wrought injury to any interest; but it is true that they have been highly beneficial to those most deeply concerned. The condition of operatives, of women and minors as well as men, has been greatly improved. (Pp. 11-12.)

Fourteenth and Fifteenth Annual Conventions of the International Association of Factory Inspectors of America. Indianapolis, 1900. Niagara Falls, 1901. (Bound in New York State Department of Labor Report, 1901.) The Shorter Workday in its Effect upon the Personal Character of the Worker. JOHN HOLBROOK, *Deputy Commissioner of Labor, Michigan.*

. . . It was feared by employers that to reduce the hours of labor was to reduce the quantity of products, and that in the competition for markets the longer hours would have a decided advantage over the shorter hours; but it has been demonstrated that the lessening of the hours of labor does not, within certain limits, result in a decrease, but rather in an increase of products instead. (P. 562.)

Report of the New York Department of Labor: On Factory Inspection. 1901.

Another phase of the subject has also come to the front gradually in the course of this agitation for a shorter work-day. It is that quality of product may be improved by a shorter day, and by this improvement in quality of the product has come to be considered the improvement of the quality of the laborer himself. (P. 562.)

Report of the United States Industrial Commission. Final Report. Vol. XIX. 1902.

. . . . A reduction in hours has never lessened the working people's ability to compete in the markets of the world. States with shorter work-days actually manufacture their products at a lower cost than States with longer work-days. (P. 788.)

Getting a Living: The Problem of Wealth and Poverty—of Profits, Wages, and Trade Unionism. George L. Bolen. *New York and London, The Macmillan Company. 1903.*

The longer the day the more the rest that must necessarily be taken as the work is done. With a day of fourteen hours, workers would need to be very slow to avoid breaking down. A man who works every night, often the case with a person doing his own work, accomplishes something extra the first few days, but afterward weariness usually makes his product smaller than it would be if he worked only ten hours a day. Working seven days a week, as in some industries and many localities of Continental Europe, tends to make people very slow and very dull. Then they are resting all the time as well as working. (P. 405.)

In any work not fixed in speed by steadily running machinery, less is done in the tenth hour, by reason of weariness, than in other hours; and the work of the last hour, like overtime work at night, weakens a person for the next day. It is this weariness that causes accidents to occur two or three times as frequently in the last hour as in other hours—a fact proved by accurate European statistics. With the steady machinery too, weariness, as a rule, either lowers the quality of the work done, or by frequent stoppage lessens its amount—often causing both these losses. Therefore, with the encouragement of gaining their demand, with the intelligence to be acquired in leisure time, and by avoiding the weariness caused by working long days, a force of men might turn out as much value in product in nine hours as previously in ten, leaving wage cost per unit of output as low as before. It was for these reasons, apart from improvement of machinery, that daily output per worker was even increased by shortening the factory day from twelve and eleven hours to ten, with the result that there was a rise of wages. (Pp. 407-8.)

Eleventh Special Report of the United States Commissioner of Labor. 1904. Regulation and Restriction of Output.

Considered solely with reference to speed or intensity of exertion, a moderate reduction in the number of hours of labor each day usually tends to increase the speed rather than to restrict it. From the standpoint of exertion a reduction of hours is exactly the opposite from a restriction of output. (Pp. 15-16.)

The Eight Hours Day. Sidney Webb *and* Harold Cox. *London, Walter Scott, 1891.*

The reduction to eight hours has taken place without any fall in wages, and with great advantage to all employed. In some cases production has not diminished at all, nor cost of production increased. Prices have in no case been affected, or the volume of trade reduced. In some cases a reduction of profit has taken place, but this is attributed to the fact that business rivals are left free to work the longer hours. In no case does the adoption of the Eight Hours Day appear to have been followed by any economic disaster. (P. 102.)

The successive reductions of the hours of labour which this century has witnessed have been attended, after a very short interval, by a positive general increase in individual productivity. In many cases it has been found that the workers did more in ten hours than their predecessors in twelve. The effort to get more than a certain amount of work out of a man defeats itself. Even if an increase in quantity can be dragged out of that terrible "last hour" immortalized by Senior and Marx, it is often at the expense of the quality of the whole. And the speed of work lessens as the day advances. The shunters of goods trucks in busy railway centres, working twelve-hour shifts, do, as a matter of fact, dispose of 50 per cent. more trucks in the first six hours than in the second. It is calculated that in one large station this fact implies that the substitution of three eight-hour for two twelve-hour shifts would enable two hundred more trucks to be disposed of daily by the same actually working staff, at an additional cost in wages per truck of only 25 per cent. (P. 103.)

Eight Hours for Work. John Rae. *London and New York, Macmillan & Co., 1894.*

The whole history of the short-hours movement and the special history of the eight-hours experiments seem strongly to suggest . . . that if masters and men both do their part aright, we can in the great run of occupations, get as good a day's work done regularly in eight-hours as in any longer working day. This suggestion is strongly supported (1) by the large number of experiments in which the eight-hours system has succeeded compared with the small number and indecisive character of those in which it has failed; (2) by the great variety of occupations in which it has been successfully tried; (3) by the number of cases in which production has been even increased by it, and sometimes without piece-work, or any other special spur: In this last respect the record of the eight-hours day is really more striking than the record of either the ten-hours day or the nine-hours day. (Pp. 93-94.)

A History of Factory Legislation. B. L. Hutchins *and* A. Harrison. *Second Edition. London, King, 1911.*

. . . In such work as brass-stamping or pattern making, for instance, any master will explain the loss in economy of material and machinery that ensues from fatiguing the hands. Mr. Arthur Chamberlain, though himself an extreme opponent of legislative interference, requires only forty-eight hours work a week in the Kynoch Company's works, and considers the reduction of hours profitable to the manufacturer. At Mr. Cadbury's works at Bourneville the working day is only seven hours and forty minutes long. After half a century's experience of regulation, the best of the manufacturers, who may surely be supposed to know their own business, are found voluntarily reducing the working day to one, two, or even three hours less than the maximum permitted by law. (P. 198.)

Work and Wages: In Continuation of Earl Brassey's 'Work and Wages' and 'Foreign Work and English Wages.' Part III. Social Betterment. Sydney J. Chapman, M. A. *London and New York. Longmans, Green & Co., 1914.*

Other things being equal, the more effective the instruments of production are the better. In the instruments of production labour is included. The physical and mental vigour of the workers is therefore a national concern, even if regard is paid solely to the output. (P. 5.)

Roughly generalising from the totality of evidence, we may affirm as follows. No instance appears in which an abbreviation of hours has resulted eventually in a proportionate curtailment of output, and production in the shorter hours has seldom fallen short, by any substantial amount of production in the longer hours. In some cases the product, or the value of the product, has actually been augmented after a short time and even before machinery could be improved or speeded up. For some industries—for instance, for the Lancashire cotton industry—a series of observations reaching back about three-quarters of a century have been preserved, and it would seem from them that the beneficial effects wrought upon output by the shortening of hours were substantially repeated, though, of course, in different degrees, at each successive reduction of the working day. It must be borne in mind, moreover, that not only speed of work but a rise in the quality of the output and a more careful use of machinery (materially reducing the cost of repairs and time lost in repairs) are effects to be expected ultimately from the shorter working day. (Pp. 235-236.)

Jahresberichte der Gewerbe-Aufsichtsbeamten im Königreich Württemberg für das Jahr 1901. [Reports of the Factory Inspectors in the Kingdom of Württemberg, 1901.] Stuttgart, Lindemann, 1902.

The productivity of the workers in the (previously mentioned) trades where shorter hours have been established has not fallen with the reduced hours of work, and thereby fresh proof has been given that the quantity of output does not rise and fall with length of working hours. (P. 13.)

Ibid. for the year 1902.

Special report made on questions as to the possibility of shortening hours.

Industry would suffer no injury from shortening the working day for women by an hour. (Legal day 11 hours.) Such a reduction would finally bring about a general 10-hour day in all industries where men's and women's work was correlated, and, while some diminution of product and wages might take place for a time, output would finally be restored to its former level by greater activity and improved devices, and wages would also tend to return to their previous rate. (P. 179.)

Jahresberichte der Gewerbe-Aufsichtsbeamten im Königreich Württemberg für das Jahr 1905. [*Reports of the Factory Inspectors in the Kingdom of Württemberg, 1905.*] *Stuttgart, Lindemann, 1906.*

Earlier fears that the Saturday half holiday would bring reduced output and lower wages have not been realized.

The unanimous verdict of the employers affected by the Saturday closing is rather a repetition of the opinions given upon the shorter working day—that the working capacity of the women improves with the shorter hours, and that, as a result, the interests of neither employer nor employee are damaged. (P. 41.)

Many employers say that, with shorter hours, "blue Monday" has almost disappeared, and that men are more punctual. Amount of production is hardly if any less, and the saving in light and heat is considerable. (P. 51.)

Jahresberichte der Gewerbe-Aufsichtsbeamten und Bergbehörden für das Jahr 1906. Bd. III. Elsass-Lothringen. [*Reports of the (German) Factory and Mines Inspectors for the year 1906. Vol. III. Alsace and Lorraine.*]

The ten-hour maximum working day is coming more and more to be generally approved. Wherever hours have been agreed upon by collective bargaining they are even shorter. With shortening of hours comes generally, too, the concentration of time spent in the factories (by cutting out the pauses). It is repeatedly stated by employers that the output under shorter hours has not fallen off, and that, on the other hand, the costs of production are lessened. (Pp. 26. 63-64.)

Jahresberichte der Gewerbe-Aufsichtsbeamten im Königreich Württemberg für 1911. [*Annual report of the Factory Inspectors of Württemberg, for 1911.*] *Stuttgart, Lindemann, 1912.*

First District: In the larger industrial plants working hours exceeding 58 per week are exceptions, since the fixing of the maximum day for women, at that limit. The efforts of the working people to obtain shorter hours have by no means ceased, and are evinced in various trades by agitations which have resulted in their favor. In the larger industrial centers such agitations have had greater publicity, although the movement for shorter hours. . . . has also made progress in regions more largely agricultural. In order to preserve his efficiency longer, a workingman stands much in need of shorter hours than have hitherto prevailed, in proportion as greater demands are now made on him with regard to his output. The observation might also be made that in the trades with shorter hours, the workers after the day's work do not make the impression of overtired people without interest in anything, and probably are still ready to seek opportunities for furthering their mental development. An employer who introduced the 8½-hour day some time ago, and who is a keen observer, is said to have stated that when longer hours were the rule, the output of his workers suffered both in quantity and quality, and that the maximum degree of productivity is attained for the average worker in a day of about 8 hours. (Pp. 5-6.)

Second District: . . . The municipal gas works (in Feuerbach) has introduced a three-shift in place of the former two-shift system for furnacemen, thereby reducing the working day from 12 hours to 8. . . . Especially noteworthy is the advance made in many factories of Feuerbach in the direction of Saturday half holidays, especially as the employees in nearly all the trades in question are exclusively or at least predominantly men. There are now some 20 factories with about 2,000 employees which close on Saturday at 12 or at the latest 2 o'clock. This reduction, it is true, is effected in most cases at the cost of protracted hours on the remaining days of the week. (P. 6.)

Fourth District: A large noodle-factory in Plüderhausen reduced the working day from 10 to 9½ hours. In the gas works of Heilbronn the three-shift system was introduced for furnacemen. Every shift lasts 8 hours; the first begins at 6 a. m., the second at 2 p. m., the third at 10 p. m. Every week there is an alternation of shifts, effected by letting two shifts work 12 hours each over Sunday, while the third has 24 hours free. (P. 7.)

Le Premier Mai et la Journée de Huit Heures. [*The First of May and the Eight-Hour Day.*] *With Préface by Jules Guesde. J. B. Coriolan and J. Mortair. Paris, G. Crépin, (1891?).*

One of the delegates of the French Government to the "Conference of Berlin," M. Delahaye himself, has shown that wherever the shorter working day exists production has increased.

This fact moreover is no longer a mystery to any serious student of economy; investigation, indeed, of labor conditions in other countries has proved for example that in the mines of Germany where the eight-hour day is established, production instead of decreasing has notably increased. In the Massachusetts mills where they have the nine-hour day the average yearly production per workman is 9,136 francs. In New Jersey where the working day is only 8½ hours long the average production per workman is 13,500 francs.

Even in Paris, in the mills where the working time is 12 hours the production per workman averages 4,000 francs; in the mills where the working time is only 10 hours it rises to 5,600 francs.

Experience then proves that reduction of hours far from decreasing production actually increases it. The reason is very simple: on the one hand the manufacturers and mill-owners, forced to accelerate output to meet the demands of their customers, must increase their number of employees, enlarge their factories, and perfect their equipment; on the other hand the workmen, no longer exhausted by 12, 16, or 18 hours' work, work with more energy, more briskness, and do more work. (Pp. 17-19.)

La Revue de Paris. T. V. Sept.-Oct., 1907. La Journée de Huit Heures. [*The Eight-Hour Day.*] MAXIME LEROY.

In his testimony during this inquiry (1902) M. Grillet, a factory inspector in Brittany, said: "If we do not go below a certain limit, say 8, 9, or 10 hours, according to the different industries, we find that the reduction of working hours has produced no appreciable loss of production, and on the other hand, it has brought about an often striking improvement in the quality of the product."

He adds: "It is certain that in proportion as working hours lengthen, the hourly output of the worker diminishes. What does the employer want to have from his employee? Work, not simply his presence during so much time. And what does the employer need to do? To utilize the workman's strength to the best advantage." (Pp. 838, 839.)

An das Schweiz. Industriedepartement. Bern. Die Eidgenössischen Fabrikinspektoren. [*Report of the Swiss Factory Inspectors to the Swiss Department of Labor on the Revision of the Factory Laws.*] *Schaffhausen, 1904.*

. . . We have to examine the effects of shorter hours upon our industry to find out whether they can be introduced without injury to business. The statements and opinions expressed by the various factory inspectors in the course of recent years, as to the results of experience in shortening the working hours wherever this has been tried, have brought us to the conclusion that a generally shorter day may be introduced without injury. (P. 23.)

It will be readily seen that these two questions,—the extension of legislation to workers now unprotected by law and the reduction of working hours are the most important for revision. As to the latter we here state our conviction that Swiss industry is well able to substitute a ten-hour for an eleven-hour day. This has indeed been done in the majority of factories now subject to the law and is moreover required by law in various cantons without, indeed, having brought ruin upon industry. (P. 5.)

In no case where the 10-hour day has been introduced is there any tendency to return to the 11 hours, because both employers and workers find advantages in the shorter time. Not only from individual branches of industry, but even from the ranks of the cotton factory owners, who constituted the majority of the opposition, the sentiment of all who have established the 10-hour day is favorable to it. (P. 26.)

2. Shorter Hours Increase Efficiency.

The increased productivity of workers under shorter hours is due to their heightened efficiency. Such efficiency springs from improved physical health and energy, together with a change of attitude toward work and employer. Greater promptness in starting in the morning and at noon, more interest and application on the part of the workers and the elimination of "soldiering" and lost time contribute to the increased output under shorter hours.

*Bulletin of The Society to Promote the Science of Management. Vol. I, No. 6, November, 1915. Personal Relationship as a Basis of Scientific Management**. Richard A. Feiss.

1. Given two establishments in the same industry, in the same locality, build for them the same buildings, equip them with the same machinery and establish for them similar methods of handling equipment and materials—yet, in the course of a short time, there will be a difference in both the quantity and the quality of their output. This difference in result will be caused by the difference between the two in the quality of their personnel. For this reason alone the question of personnel must ultimately be considered the real problem of management. . . .

5. The old type of management would at the best consider expenditures for the development of personnel as an unnecessary outlay forced upon it by unintelligent public opinion, or would consider it a politic expenditure which would bring a certain amount of cheap advertising at the expense of fair wages. The enlightened, or scientific type of management would consider expenditures of this kind not only wise, but also an invest-

* A paper read before the Society to Promote the Science of Management, Philadelphia, Pa., October 23, 1915.

ment bringing proportionately larger and more permanent returns than all other kinds. Full value of all expenditures or investments for upkeep and improvement of a plant can be realized only when sufficient investment of both time and money has been made for the purpose of improvement and upkeep of the personal side. In fact the management which has the correct viewpoint will find that the mechanical and material side of the organization will be better developed as a necessary incident to *personal* development than it would be where this point of view is reversed. This is well illustrated in the Clothcraft Shops and The Joseph & Feiss Company, where this philosophy has been the basis of its development of Scientific Management. (P. 5.)

63. Results cannot be accomplished in the spirit of charity, but must emanate entirely from a sense of justice. It must be understood that work along the lines described above can never take the place of wages. Such work must have as a reason for its existence not only increased efficiency, but the increased reward to which increased efficiency is entitled. Figure 6 is a chart showing the progress of the Clothcraft Shops in respect to wages and efficiency from June, 1910, to January, 1915. This shows during this period an increase in production of 42%; an increase in the average individual hourly wages of 45%, weekly wages 37%; and a decrease in total manufacturing cost of about 10%. During this period the weekly working schedule was reduced from fifty-four to forty-eight hours. (P. 15.)

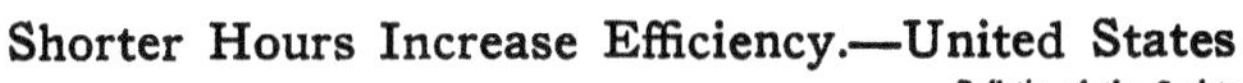

Shorter Hours Increase Efficiency.—United States

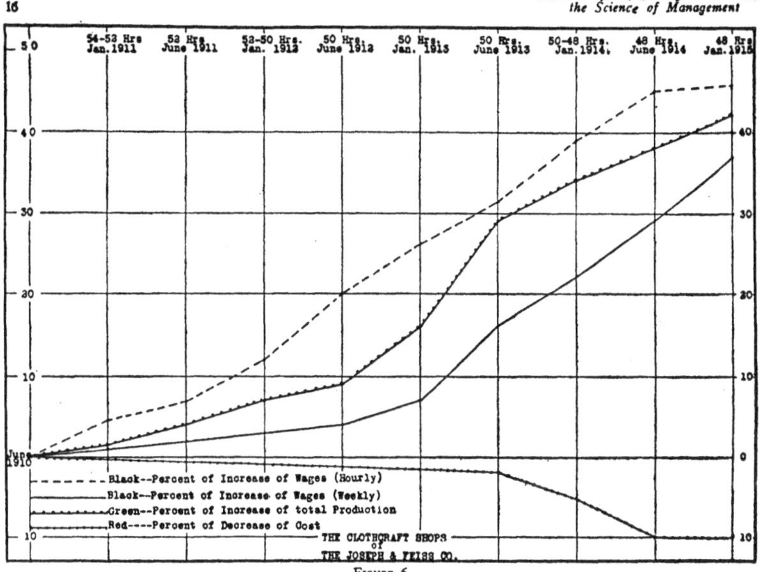

FIGURE 6.
RECORD OF PROGRESS.

American Labor Legislation Review, March, 1914. Working Hours in Continuous Industries. Introductory Address. WILLIAM C. REDFIELD, *Secretary of Commerce.*

Long years ago, before the agitation for the reduction to the nine-hour day took place, my associate in business came to the conclusion that there was what he called "a tired hour," that it would be in his judgment undesirable and unprofitable to continue running the factory as long as it was then run; and after mature reflection, unasked and unexpected, he reduced the hours of the shop from ten to nine, simply on the ground that he believed it would be profitable to do so. The event, in his judgment, proved his opinion to be sound; and at the end of a very considerable period he was satisfied that he had gained both in quantity and quality of output as well as in the unconscious discipline which, in his judgment and in my own, is self-enforcing upon an adequately paid and properly treated working force. He often expressed to me the view that a further reduction of time to eight hours was inevitable, merely on the ground of its being profitable to do so. . . .

Only ten days ago, or less, I had the privilege of meeting a very large manufacturer who has 6000 men at work upon the eight-hour basis, competing actively with other concerns which are running nine hours and even longer. He tells me that nothing would induce him to go back to the longer hours; that he does not understand why his competitors do not see the profitableness of the eight-hour day; that both he and his men are entirely content to be running in a strictly competitive business at eight hours per day, while all their competitors are continuing to run nine hours; and that in his judgment, as the leading manufacturer in the business, it would be far better for their pockets, as well as for their peace, if they also would take up the shorter day.

My own experience with manufacturers, and I have known a great many of them and talked with many hundreds of them in past years, has been that this subject, like most of our human subjects, has been treated almost altogether from the arithmetical point of view. . . .

A hundred times manufacturers have said to me, "Take off one hour from nine and you reduce your output one-ninth"—just as they had said to me before, "If you take off one hour from ten, you reduce your output one-tenth." But as a matter of fact, we did not; we increased our output more than one-tenth. Therefore the thought that seems to me essential on this whole subject is to get away from mathematical dealings with mankind, and try to deal with them on the human side, as they are. (Pp. 105-106.)

The Survey. January 3, 1914. Can American Steel Plants Afford an Eight-Hour Turn? WILLIAM B. DICKSON, *Former First Vice-President United States Steel Corporation.*

A more specific question is: Can the manufacturers afford an eight-hour day?

741

Shorter Hours Increase Efficiency.—United States

I believe the advantages to be derived from more efficient, because less exhausted, workmen will, to a great extent, offset whatever additional cost may be involved; but aside from this, I am of the opinion that the steel companies can today afford to change from a twelve-hour to an eight-hour day in all those processes which are necessarily continuous. In other departments a ten-hour day is practicable, and perhaps advisable. (P. 376.)

A Documentary History of American Industrial Society. Edited by John R. Commons, Ulrich B. Phillips, Eugene A. Gilmore, Helen L. Summer, *and* John B. Andrews. *Vol. VIII. Labor Movement. Cleveland, The Arthur H. Clark Company, 1910. "New York Weekly Tribune," Oct. 16, 1847.*

No, my friend! your *must* is very positive, but it is confuted by mountains of experience. Robert Owen ran a whole village of cotton-mills for some twenty years, working only ten hours per day, while his neighbors and competitors all around ran from twelve to sixteen, yet he made money as fast as any of them—made all he wished. The same experiment has been tried a thousand times in a thousand ways, and with a uniform result. Great Britain is now trying it by a law imperatively forbidding more than eleven hours' work in a day in factories during the present year, or more than ten hours after this year. Does anybody believe her manufactures will be ruined under this law by American, German and French rivalry? We are confident that very nearly as much work would be accomplished in ten hours as in twelve or thirteen, while a great saving would be effected in lights, fuel, etc. You can't get more work out of a man than there is in him; and if ten hours' active, faithful labor per day is enough, protracting the hours of toil to twelve or thirteen will effect no good purpose. It is just like giving workmen liquor in order to extract work from them; for a few days it may seem to answer; but after that the liquor only serves to extort as much work as was formerly done without it, and hardly that. (Pp. 196-197.)

Maine Senate Document 19: Public Documents, 1848. Report on Petition Praying Passage of Law Making Ten Hours Legal Day's Work.

Everyone knows by observation and experience, that a man can endure a certain amount of labor every day, and that he must have a certain amount of rest; and that if he is compelled to toil on day after day from early morning till late at night, he may for a few days do more work, but if long continued, he actually becomes unable to accomplish as much per day as he could do if permitted to divide his time more equally. . . . And your committee are firmly of the opinion, from all the facts and information they can procure, that men accomplish more work in ten hours, where that system is reduced to practice, than where they work as long as they can see. (Pp. 2-3.)

Massachusetts House Document No. 153. 1850. Minority Report of the Special Committee. Re Limitation of Hours of Work.

Nor is it difficult to see, that the restriction of the hours of labor, will harmonize with the true interest of the manufacturing capitalist and employer. . . .

The employing manufacturers will generally find, that, the higher the degree of intelligence which pervades the mass of their workmen, the better work they will perform, and they will do their work to more advantage and profit for them. . . . Let, then, their hours of labor be reduced, and their general condition and well-being thereby improved, and a better and more intelligent class of persons will offer their services for this kind of employment; and while remaining in it, they will, with time and opportunity (which they do not now have) for improvement, continually advance in general intelligence, as it is the nature of the human mind to do under proper circumstances. . . . The operatives would thus become more valuable, as members of the community, and at the same time, render a more profitable service to their employers, by producing improved fabrics. When it is taken into consideration, that, in many articles of manufactured merchandize, it is the best goods which command the markets, it will be seen how important it is to the manufacturing interest, that such regulations should be adopted, as will permanently secure intelligent operatives in all its branches. . . . (Pp. 28-29.)

Report of the Massachusetts Bureau of Statistics of Labor. 1881.

We have large mills, employing in the aggregate several thousand persons, which have voluntarily adopted ten hours in eleven-hour districts, bearing witness emphatically that they find the product of ten hours a day, in the long run, so nearly or quite the same as that of eleven hours, that their mills are as profitable to them under the shorter as under the longer time. In addition to this fact, and as partly explaining it, may be recorded the words of great wisdom spoken by the managers:

"Skill in management and thoroughness in discipline are more important than the eleventh hour in the product of a mill; and thorough discipline is much more attainable under ten than under eleven hours. For men and women are flesh and blood, and they cannot be held up to such steady work during eleven hours as during ten; the overseers are flesh and blood, and cannot hold them up."

As incidentally illustrating the improvement that may be made by "good management" joined with a reduction of hours, we relate the experience of a manager of a cotton mill as he gave it to us. He said, "I took charge of this mill about fifteen years ago, having already purchased an interest in it. The mill had been running thirteen hours per day. Soon after I took charge, I persuaded the rest of the directors to allow me to reduce the hours to eleven. Before this the weekly product of the mill had been ninety thousand yards of print cloths. After it, with the same machinery, the weekly product rose to a hundred and twenty thousand yards."

Now granting, as should doubtless be done, that a part of that increase was due to improved management, yet it is clear that this improvement could not have been made nearly so effective without the improved physical conditions which so great a reduction of the hours of labor afforded; for it is impossible to secure as thorough order, steadiness, and efficiency of work, under thirteen as under eleven hours. Flesh and blood cannot endure the strain. And the same principle applies to a reduction to ten. (Pp. 461-462.)

Report of the New York State Factory Inspector, 1890.

. . . Every important manufactory in this state, which formerly required sixty-six or more hours of labor as a week's work, is now running on sixty or less hours' limit, and the testimony of the proprietors thereof is to the effect that their production increased instead of diminished at the same time. This enhancement of the productiveness of their employees has not come through increasing the speed of machinery, as some people suppose, but it is believed that it has grown out of the more contented minds and better rested bodies of the operatives. (P. 26.)

The Eight-hour Movement. An Address Delivered Before the Brotherhood of United Labor at the Armory in Chicago, February 22, 1890. Judge P. Altgeld.

It is urged . . . that shorter hours mean reduced production. . . .

To this it is replied that it cannot be shown that there will in the end be less production. On the contrary that under shorter hours the laborers will have increased vigor and higher intelligence, feel more interest in their work—and will, in the end, accomplish not only as much work but a higher grade of work, that, in fact, this is no longer an open question, it having been settled by experience; that when in England the reduction was made from twelve and fourteen hours to ten—as soon as things had adjusted themselves to the new conditions it was found that there was not only as much work done in ten hours as had been in the longer hours, but that it was a higher grade of work, and that when subsequently a further change was made from ten to nine while there was some falling off at first, yet owing to the introduction of better machinery and the improved condition of workmen, the product soon increased to what it had been, and that when in the New England States about the middle of this century the manufacturers voluntarily reduced the hours of labor from twelve to ten, there was scarcely any falling off in the production after the new system was in full operation, while the condition of the laborers and their families greatly improved in every respect. (Pp. 4-5.)

Discussions in Economics and Statistics. Vol. II. Francis A. Walker, Ph. D., LL. D. *The Eight-hour-Law Agitation. New York, Holt, 1899.*

There is little doubt that all the successive reductions in the working day which have thus far taken place among certain laboring populations have resulted in an immediate gain to productive power in the generation following. It has probably never occurred that a reduction of working time has been all loss, since a somewhat increased activity, a somewhat enhanced energy, has characterized each part of the time remaining. (P. 387.)

Report of the New York Bureau of Labor Statistics, 1900.

In these days mere muscular strength is becoming a minor qualification of a successful wage-worker, but nervous force and energy are taking its place. The machinery which now does the heavy work requires the most careful and undivided attention, which wears upon the workman's vitality with tremendous effect. Such work demands even more of relaxation and leisure than the manual toil that it supersedes, if the man is to preserve his usefulness.

And modern industry demands not only a heavy expenditure of nervous force on the part of the artisan, but also a larger intelligence, which shall continue the succession of inventions that, united with its unrivaled material resources and the organizing ability of its business men, has made the United States so formidable a rival of European industrial countries. . . . All experience . . . teaches . . . that a stronger and more skilful and intelligent body of workmen will, either by greater energy or by improved methods and apparatus, more than make up for the loss of time. The foremost industrial nations are those which have short hours, and they do not fear the competition of long-hour countries. (Pp. 80-81.)

United States Congress. House Report, No. 1793 (4405). Hours of Laborers on Public Works of the United States. Report from the Committee on Labor. Fifty-seventh Congress, First Session. 1901-1902.

No reasonable person would, for a moment, entertain the proposition that the work day should again be lengthened to fourteen or twelve hours. . . It is nowhere claimed, so far as your committee is aware, that any reduction in the hours of labor has had a detrimental effect on business, on manufacturers, on labor as a unit, or individual laborers. The advocates of the short-hour theory, on the other hand, trace the moral, social, and financial improvement of the laborer to this cause, and allege that business was at no time injured, but improved, if affected, and that production was stimulated and consumption increased. (P. 9.)

Report of the United States Industrial Commission. Final Report, Vol. XIX, 1902.

A representative of a large drop-forge establishment,* testified, after three months' experience with the nine-hour day, that there is a slightly larger average daily output than there was for the ten-hour day in both day work and piece work, though in every other respect work was done under similar conditions. This has not been due to the fact that methods were lax previously, for

* Reports Industrial Commission, Vol. XIV, p. 659, et seq.

there was rigid supervision under the ten-hour system. A part of the gain has been made by reason of the fact that under the nine-hour system the men go promptly to work on the minute and work up to the very close of the day; also that a man can work normally at a higher rate of speed without pushing himself for nine hours than he can for ten hours. The fundamental reason, according to this witness, for the keeping up of the amount of production is to be found in the spirit of the men themselves. If the machines were operated at the highest rate of speed and were in perfect condition, and were continuously fed, a workman could not maintain his output up to the same amount if the hours of labor were shortened; but these perfect conditions are rarely, if ever, found. It cannot be demonstrated mathematically just how it happens that a man can produce as much in nine hours as he formerly could in ten hours, but as a matter of fact it has been the experience of almost every manufacturer, says this witness, that "a man can and will and does do more the moment he is justly and fairly and liberally treated." . . . (P. 765.)

A representative of the Chicago bridge and structural iron workers' union holds that the eight-hour day has so increased the efficiency of the laborer that there is actually more work done in eight hours than was formerly done in ten hours.

A boiler manufacturer, having adopted the eight-hour day, testifies that he does not think his men do as much in eight hours as they did in nine hours, taking one day as the basis of comparison; but that at the end of the year he believes he would find that they had done just as much as they did when they were working an hour longer. . . . A manufacturer of mining machinery holds that it is to the interest of the manufacturer to employ his men only eight hours, since he gets better services out of the men. Formerly, when the hours of machinists were reduced from twelve to ten, and again when they were reduced from ten to nine, the same alarming predictions were made as now, when it is proposed to reduce them from nine to eight; yet the inventions in machinery have made it possible for manufacturers to reduce their hours and still make as much money as they did formerly in the longer workday. This witness holds that the eight hours in this industry are needed not so much to relieve the men of severe exertion as because a better educated man is required to do the work. (P. 766.)

Organized Labor. JOHN MITCHELL. *Philadelphia, American Book and Bible House, 1903.*

Owing to the fact that the work of the modern world is becoming more and more a matter of nervous energy, of skill, and intelligence, and less a matter of mere brute force, the reduction of hours is not only of advantage, but of absolute necessity. Even when work is simply and purely physical, it is not economical to work long hours, but a shorter day of labor is imperative when work is intense or when intelligence, ingenuity, and inventiveness are required. You cannot get more out of a man than is in him, and if you take too much one day, there will be so much less to obtain on succeeding days. As stated by Professor Clark of Columbia University: "If you want a man to work for you one day and one day only, and secure the greatest possible amount of work he is capable of performing you must make him work for twenty-four hours. If you would have him work a week it will be necessary to reduce the time to twenty hours a day; if you want him to work for a month a still further reduction to eighteen hours a day. For the year fifteen hours a day will do; for several years, ten hours; but if you wish to get the most out of a man for a working lifetime, you will have to reduce his hours of labor to eight each day."

The English mill owners in the beginning and middle of the nineteenth century claimed that they would be ruined if hours were reduced; and the same complaint was made by the New England manufacturers in the seventies and is being now repeated by the Southern mill owners. Wherever the reduction has been made, however, the result has been a decided benefit not only to the workman but to his employer. In a succeeding chapter I shall endeavor to show how short hours, like other demands of trade unions, have benefited employers, and how an absolute increase in the amount of work performed during a day has frequently resulted from a shortening of the working day. (Pp. 123-4.)

Getting a Living: The Problem of Wealth and Poverty —of Profits, Wages and Trade Unionism. GEORGE L. BOLEN. *New York and London. The Macmillan Company. 1903.*

By diminishing the worker's fatigue, and by raising his efficiency through use of improved machinery, the increase of his product has balanced both the successive shortening of the day, at least down to ten hours, and the repeated rise of his daily wages. . . .

Perhaps in all the trades shortening the day from ten to nine hours, little or no diminution of product has been noticed. Whether there is some diminution may not be after all a serious matter to the employer generally, since if he cannot preserve his profits by raising prices, or by lowering wages, he can do so effectively by taking up the slack in his methods, by hiring better men, by driving them a little faster, and not by undertaking the less profitable work. In the latter particular, though he does not maintain his aggregate of business and of profit, he does maintain the profit rate. So far as faster and steadier work is secured, the burden of maintaining a shortening of the day falls on the workers. So far as methods are improved and better machinery adopted, the burden falls on the employer. Generally a share is thus borne by each, as in the case of raising wages by union demand, and in both cases there is with each side a strong inducement for progress. Hence, as a rule, the shorter the day and the higher the pay, the greater is each side's efficiency, and the better is the outfit of machinery. When by extension of the British factory law about eight years ago the sweated laundry women of London, too poor and ignorant to save themselves, were rescued from toil of inhuman length per day, machinery was at once put in that kept prices and profits unchanged. (Pp. 420-22.) . . .

So far therefore as further shortening of the day takes place, it will come about gradually as heretofore, in those trades suited to it, mainly by desire and demand of the workers, but largely by realization among employers that natural conditions make a shorter day better for all concerned. . . . The customary short day of bankers and professional men, working under mental strain, was found by all concerned to yield best results. A shift of only four hours on duty, followed by eight hours off, is willingly conceded to firemen on steamships, such an arrangement being found necessary to keep up steam and save men from breaking down. For the same reason night work on daily papers was long ago limited to about seven hours. . . .

The short day in building trades has been successful, not only because of their local monopoly, but also because it spreads over a longer time an amount of work that seldom lasts all the year. Repeated shortening of the factory day has come because it was found that strength was saved, intelligence promoted, and that product and wages were even increased, though there has generally been some diminution of output for a while at first. (Pp. 423-4.)

United States Congress. Senate Document, No. 110. Report on Conditions of Employment in the Iron & Steel Industry in the United States. Vol. III. Working Conditions & the Relations of Employers & Employees. 62nd Congress, 1st Session, 1911. Washington, 1913.

. . . Past experience indicates that considerable increases in efficiency may be expected as a result of the 8-hour system. It is impossible to demonstrate this statistically from the records of mills that have changed their hours, for in every case for which accurate records were obtainable some change either in equipment or in method of operation was made at the same time the mills went on the 8-hour system. It may be noted, however, that the steel company quoted above, in changing its blast furnaces to the 8-hour system, found it possible to reduce the number of men on each shift sufficiently to counterbalance the increase of 28.6 per cent. in their hourly wages. Seven British blast-furnace operators stated before the recent international conference on continuous industries* that the increase in output per employee had compensated for the increased hourly rates paid their employees on the introduction of the 8-hour system and that they would not willingly return to the 12-hour system. As the rate of production of a blast furnace is influenced in a less degree by the exertions of its labor force than other departments of the industry, it would seem theoretically to be the least likely to give improved results under the 8-hour system. The Bessemer converters and the rolling mills on the other hand respond readily to increased exertions on the part of a crew of workmen, and it is principally in these departments that the 8-hour day has been introduced hitherto. Furthermore, in these departments the workmen who work 12 hours in the most exhausting positions are usually relieved after 30 minutes' work and rest for 30 minutes (*i. e.*, two men are provided for each job). Experience has shown that with an 8-hour day 15 minutes' rest is sufficient to allow full recuperation in such cases. In a great many cases arrangements can be made to allow three men for every two of such exhausting positions so as to provide this rest of 15 minutes out of every 45 minutes. In all such cases the change would more than compensate for an increase of 25 per cent. in the hourly rate of wages.

Numerous illustrations of increases in productive efficiency following the substitution of the 8-hour system for the 12-hour system might be cited from other industries. It seems sufficient, however, to call attention to the fact that the sheet and tin mills, in which most of the material is handled by hand, were many years ago

* Report of the Special Commission on Hours of Labor in Continuous Industries, London, July, 1912. (P. 14.)

changed to the 8-hour system by the voluntary action of the manufacturers in order to secure increased efficiency and continuous operation of their mills. . . . The significant fact is that practically every mill of this kind in the United States is operated with three shifts of 8 hours each and there is no desire on the part of either the manufacturers or the workmen for the substitution of the 12-hour system. (Pp. 185 and 186.)

With regard to the effects of seven-day work on the efficiency of the workmen very little direct evidence could be obtained except in one case. In one plant the records for ore unloading day by day are available over a long period of years. The records for the earlier years in which the ore was handled on every day in the week show practically a dead level throughout the week, no one day being appreciably higher in the amount of ore handled than any other. During 1910 no ore was stocked on Sundays. The records for this year show that 7 per cent. more ore was unloaded on Monday than the average for the remaining five days of the week. The foreman of this plant stated that the men are fresher and do more work on Monday after a full day of rest on Sunday than on any other day in the week. (P. 383.)

The Limits of Efficiency. An Address before the Cleveland Chamber of Commerce, November 19, 1912. William C. Redfield. *Cleveland, 1912.*

Some have perhaps resisted the idea of a shorter working day, with sincerity, indeed, believing it to be a matter of mere arithmetic that the shorter day must cost more for labor than the longer did. But talk some day with your family doctor and ask him what science teaches about fatigue. He will tell you that fatigue is the result of a definite poison, because the wastes in the human body from exertion have accumulated faster than the powers of nature can remove or replace them. It is no dream, but a commonplace fact, known to physicians, that fatigue is a form of poison. We should not think that poisoned men could do good work, and yet the fact that men may be weary has possibly never occurred to us as a reason for shutting the shop down a half hour sooner. Yet, if by a shorter day men and women can go without exhaustion to their homes, their work upon the morrow will be better.

A great cement plant, with painful misgivings, caused by arithmetic, went from the ten-hour day to the eight-hour day without changing the wage. At the end of the year they were glad, for they were doing better than before. The same is true of a paper mill in New England and of a shipyard in Scotland; another in Massachusetts has now made the change. Men wonder why it is so, when it is quite in accord with the laws of the human body and mind that it should be so. Men who are innocent of precise knowledge of the human frame, have had strong opinions about the shorter working day, yet this, after all, is a question of exact knowledge of the human machine.

Suppose some group of manufacturers, resisting the eight-hour day, had employed a commission of physicians to advise thereon, and these had reported that the ten-hour day was better for men, that the longer work was helpful to their bodies, and that a thorough study of the human frame showed that the greater exertion meant stronger men, and that fatigue was nothing of moment. Then the resistance of the manufacturers would have some scientific basis. But suppose, on the other hand, the fact to be that fatigue is a cumulative thing, that it is not always worked off, if it be excessive, in one night's rest, but as a matter of fact it is a shortener of life and has the same definite action towards reducing the span of life that a planer has in finishing a casting. These are or are not facts, and they are the controlling facts, if they are facts at all. I suspect that our own ignorance of the laws of fatigue has held back our efficiency and that overtime has sometimes meant a temporary profit at a permanent loss. (Pp. 10-11.)

The New Industrial Day. WILLIAM C. REDFIELD. *New York. The Century Co. 1912.*

We are the most efficient people in the world, yet are but beginning to be efficient. We have yet to learn to utilize the brains of our workers as we utilize their hands. The best plants anticipate and avoid waste so far as may be by designing, making, operating, protecting their machinery in accord with the laws of its being. When we treat our men in the same way, using each of them at the work he is fitted to do, training each in mind and hand to use efficiently the best appliances under working conditions that develop his mental and physical manhood, then we shall save human waste and reach a quality and quantity of product that will free us from all doubts of our power to meet on equal terms the men of any land. So long as we look first at the wage rate and the past or present cost instead of at the product rate and the possible cost we shall all be cowards. (P. 72.)

We may think well to crowd our machinery to its limit and scrap it in a few years because a new invention shall have then replaced it; but we must learn not to crowd men that way, for we cannot scrap men. (P. 74.)

Another manufacturer says: "When the time comes, and I think its approach is near, that as much thought and study and as big brains are devoted to the problem of labor as have heretofore been devoted to and absorbed by the problems of financing, selling, and equipment, when we study the man behind the machine as closely as we do the machine, we shall see ways of making the one fit the other more closely than we do now."

All about great mills are instruments regulating machinery; means are provided that machines shall not be overstrained, that their product shall be within their power regularly to produce without damage to the machine; we even care lest machines get overheated and, in a true sense, lest they get overtired. We know that a tired machine gives out and its life is neither so long as it should be, nor its product so large nor so good as it ought to be. We protect it against dust, we lubricate it, we even let it rest, yet that machine is dead, inert. When shall we learn that to be most productive a living, responsive man needs also not to be overstrained, that he needs rest, that his product must for economy's sake be always within and not beyond his powers? Until the course we take with our machinery is recognized as of equal application to our men and women workers we shall not have solved the problem of production. So long as we extract from men and women the most possible for the least return to them, we are working against the deepest laws of nature and of finance; our sight is short; we are but blind leaders of the blind. The normal resistance of a working force to pressure under conditions of a narrow wage and long hours is not an element that leads to continued profit. And here, once for all, let it be said that no management is scientific or permanently profitable which either promotes or permits human overstrain. (Pp. 142-143.)

If we may argue from English statistics, it seems probable that about three million people in the United States are seriously ill at all times, and we are told that half of this can be avoided. The number who are slightly ill, sick enough to reduce their efficiency, but not enough so as to give up their work, is probably larger, and the presence of such men and women in our mills is a real drain upon our industries. Time your machines ever so carefully, a half-sick operative will not get the best results from them. Indigestion or a severe cold or a bad headache does not allow him who endures it to do the full work of a well person. Everyone knows also that he cannot work efficiently when eyes or brain or hand are fatigued. The factory in which the average of health is high has at the same wage rate an advantage in labor cost over similar plants in which health conditions are poor, because of the greater and better product of well men. Goods cost more which are made by tired hands. For these reasons the management which has for years given care to machinery, materials and methods begins now to give thought to men, not merely as to their skill or wages, but as to their physical fitness to earn their wages to the full. . . . No employer can make his men so behave outside of working hours as to keep themselves in health. Nevertheless, it still remains "up to him" to prevent their being over-strained nervously or physically during the hours of toil. . . .

The present trend towards saving effort and keeping the human mechanism in our factories in good working order does not arise from altruistic motives, but from economic ones. In actual practice in a mill it makes a difference in the financial results whether among a thousand men one hundred or three hundred or more are out of health. Any large amount of impaired vigor among his operatives is a condition whose continuance an intelligent manufacturer should know that he cannot afford. Still less can he afford to permit conditions to prevail in his works that cause ill health, for that injures all parties to industry. It pushes costs up, it pulls wages down; it enhances prices by diminishing both quality and quantity of output. . . . (Pp. 157-8-9-60.)

We take great care of race horses because success depends on their health and their ability to endure strain. In the race of modern commerce the same is true of men and the interests at stake are such as make it vital that the human factor in our industries shall be fit. Some far-sighted employers, having seen that it is profitable so to do, have led the way in caring for their operatives and the contagion of their example is spreading. What is called "scientific management" aims to save waste of human effort in unnecessary motions. It is quite as important to save the loss to workers and employers arising from needless weakening of physical powers by causes which we know how to avoid. . . . (Pp. 162-163.)

Many of us have stopped too soon on the path of scientific development of our industries. The man is infinitely well worth study and infinitely more difficult to study than the machine. . . . We all believe in clean shops, but do we think enough of the human element to be careful to avoid sweeping when the men are about because of the well-known fact that dust carries all manner of disease germs which men breathe? The working out of the machine has been a long evolution and the working out of the study of men may also be a long evolution.

It cannot be hastily done. It requires patience; so did the machines. Your machines are complex; how much more so the man with his human mind and heart. But if patience is exercised, there is in the man the responsive spirit the machine lacks, and that spirit led and not driven, guided and not abused, is a power in industry of which the wisest of us do not yet dream. Without it, we may be able, or we may not, to profit temporarily. With it, the age of industrial conquest opens. (Pp. 208-209.)

Fifteenth Annual Report of the National Consumers' League, New York, 1916. Some Practical Experiences in Shortening Hours of Labor. Address by Mr. Frederick R. Hazard, *President Solvay Process Company, Syracuse, New York, at Cleveland, Ohio, November 4, 1915.*

I have regarded the shortening of the hours of labor as really a part of the general problem of maintaining efficiency. The wise manufacturer will always endeavor to lay his plans ahead, to look forward into the future as far as he is able, in order to plan his campaign of production to meet the contract which he has with the public by reason of the fact that he is in business. He owes it to the public to deliver as much of his product as the public demands, and it is as binding a contract as if it were written in letters of gold. He must do it. In order to do it, he prepares his buildings, he fills them with the necessary machines and apparatus of all kinds required to produce his particular merchandise. He goes out and lays in stocks of the raw material required. He buys those under as good conditions as possible and for what appears to him a reasonable time ahead. He takes all these material precautions. But how many of the manufacturers of this country or of any other country look to the supply of labor, without which all efforts to produce any given article are without value? How many, having a present supply of labor, examine the supply with a view of conserving it, of keeping it up to the same efficiency that is required from machinery built of iron, steel, wood, or other materials? An inanimate steam engine is subjected to a periodical examination, and, if found defective, is shut down for repairs, in order that it may be put in the most efficient working order. We have our repair establishments for the human frame, in hospitals, clinics, dispensaries, and all the agencies of a sanitary character. But does the average manufacturer make full use even of those? Is the problem brought home to the average employer as it ought to be? Does he consider that his labor is of greater importance—I think I speak advisedly—than his plant? Does he give to his employee the careful attention that he gives to his steam engines and his pumps? I think not, I fear not. But it is an idea which is growing. There is a great deal more of that care and attention than existed even a few years ago. Whether it is merely through self-interest or through a broad-minded view of the necessities and the duties, is somewhat immaterial to me, provided only the idea shall spread and become more universal, provided that the manufacturer, the employer of labor, shall actually give to his employees the same careful supervision and attention that he gives to the inanimate engines and pumps in his plant. I think there is the most important point of maintenance which we can conceive of. I think in that line we shall make the most important progress, the truest conservation of energy, the truest advance toward a more enlightened and prosperous industrial and commercial activity.

Under the present emergency conditions with which this United States is struggling, it may be a little difficult in the minds of some to do very much more than to just keep ahead of the game and push and strive to get out the goods that are required and drive everybody up to the limit. But if the human engine is driven beyond its limit of endurance, it breaks down, and repairs to it are not always possible, and they always are more costly, both in time and in pain than the repairs to the inanimate object. I therefore sincerely hope that we shall be in this country sufficiently wise to avoid that kind of overstrain, which is so easy to indulge in, and especially so under the emergency conditions. I hope we can avoid it, and I hope that we can do more than that—establish ourselves firmly in the way of maintaining our existing supply of labor and in safeguarding the continuance of that supply.

Address to the Superintendents of Manufactories, and to those Individuals generally, who, by giving employment to an aggregated population, may easily adopt the means to form the sentiments and manners of such a population. ROBERT OWEN. *London, 1813.*

Like you, I am a manufacturer for pecuniary profit. But having for many years acted on principles the reverse in many respects of those in which you have been instructed, and having found my procedure beneficial to others and to myself, even in a pecuniary point of view, I am anxious to explain such valuable principles, that you and those under your influence may equally partake of their advantages. (P. 259.)

From the commencement of my management I viewed the population, with the mechanism and every other part of the establishment, as a system composed of many parts, and which it was my duty and interest so to combine, as that every hand, as well as every spring, lever, and wheel, should effectually co-operate to produce the greatest pecuniary gain to the proprietors.

Many of you have long experienced in your manufacturing operations the advantages of substantial, well-contrived, and well-executed machinery.

Experience has also shown you the difference of the results between mechanism which is neat, clean, well-arranged, and always in a high state of repair; and that which is allowed to be dirty, in disorder, without the means of preventing unnecessary friction, and which therefore becomes, and works, much out of repair.

In the first case the whole economy and management are good; every operation proceeds with ease, order, and success. In the last, the reverse must follow, and a scene be presented of counter-action, confusion, and dissatisfaction among all the agents and instruments interested or occupied in the general process, which cannot fail to create great loss.

If, then, due care as to the state of your inanimate machines can produce such beneficial results, what may not be expected if you devote equal attention to your vital machines, which are far more wonderfully constructed. . . .

Will you then continue to expend large sums of money to procure the best devised mechanism of wood, brass, or iron; to retain it in perfect repair; to provide the best substance for the prevention of unnecessary friction, and to save it from falling into premature decay?—And when in these transactions you estimate time by minutes, and the money expended for the chance of increased gain by fractions, will you not afford some of your attention to consider whether a portion of your time and capital would not be more advantageously applied to improve your living machines? From experience which cannot deceive me, I venture to assure you, that your time and money so applied, if directed by a true knowledge of the subject, would return you, not five, ten, or fifteen per cent. for your capital so expended, but often fifty, and in many cases a hundred per cent.

I have expended much time and capital upon improvements of the living machinery; and it will soon appear that time and money so expended in the manufactory at New Lanark, even while such improvements are in progress only, and but half their beneficial effects attained, are now producing a return exceeding fifty per cent., and will shortly create profits equal to cent. per cent. on the original capital expended in them.

Since the general introduction of inanimate mechanism into British manufactories, man, with few exceptions, has been treated as a secondary and inferior machine; and far more attention has been given to perfect the raw materials of wood and metals than those of body and mind. Give but due reflection to the subject, and you will find that man, even as an instrument for the creation of wealth, may be still greatly improved. (Pp. 260-261.)

. . . Let us not perpetuate the really unnecessary evils which our present practices inflict on this large proportion of our fellow-subjects. Should your pecuniary interests somewhat suffer by adopting the line of conduct now urged, many of you are so wealthy that the expense of founding and continuing at your respective establishments the institutions necessary to improve your animate machines would not be felt. But when you may have ocular demonstration, that, instead of any pecuniary loss, a well-directed attention to form the character and increase the comforts of those who are so entirely at your mercy, will essentially add to your gains, prosperity, and happiness, no reasons, except those founded on ignorance of your self-interest, can in future prevent you from bestowing your chief care on the living machines which you employ. And by so doing you will prevent an accumulation of human misery, of which it is now difficult to form an adequate conception. (Pp. 261-262.)

British Sessional Papers. Vol. XXIII. 1850. Report of Inspectors of Factories for Half-year ending April 30, 1850.

I continue to receive favorable accounts of the working of the Ten Hours' Act. That great experiment, dangerous as it appeared to many, and to myself among others, because of so sudden a change from twelve to ten hours, has succeeded, so far as it has yet been tried, beyond what the most sanguine of those who were favorable to it ventured to anticipate. Where the law is fully carried out, according to its true intention, the workpeople appear to value the limitation more and more in proportion, as they have longer experience of its effects; and the masters appear to be getting daily better reconciled to it; partly by finding that, by the increased alertness of their workpeople, by the closer application they are now enabled to give, together with some additional speeding of the machinery not before tried, the produce is much nearer to that of twelve hours than it was conceived possible it could be brought up to, but partly also by the marked change for the better which they see in the health, appearance, and contentment of their workpeople. (P. 5.)

The Half-holiday Question. JOHN LILWALL. *London, Kent, 1856.*

. . . It is a well-ascertained fact that the amount of work done, whether in the case of a man who makes an article or of him who sells it, does not depend so much on the extent of time devoted to any given employment, as upon the degree of application, energy, and cheerfulness of spirit which are brought to bear thereon. The human frame and the human mind are so constituted that they are capable of only a certain amount of continued effort. Let the natural bounds be but systematically extended, and so far from such excess being productive, it will ordinarily be found that there will be really less work done than when due regard is paid to the capacity of the agent, and that it will also be of an inferior description. This statement is borne out by the experience of many scientific and practical, observant men, who have recorded their opinions on the subject.

. . . Mr. Robert Baker, surgeon, of Leeds, also observes:

"There is more work done now in ten hours and a half in the factories in England than ever was in twelve or fourteen, and there is no greater fallacy in the employment of physical strength than to suppose that long hours are conducive to its profitable use." . . .

Mr. Leonard Horner, Government Inspector of Factories, says:

"It will be satisfactory to you to learn that the last year has afforded fresh proofs that the restrictions now regulating the labor of children, women, and young persons in factories, which have immensely improved their condition in many respects, have not been attended with the injurious effects upon trade which were apprehended.

Shorter Hours Increase Efficiency.—Great Britain

. . . This is accounted for, partly by the increased stimulus given to ingenuity to make the machinery more perfect and capable of increased speed, but it arises far more from the workpeople, by improved health, by absence of that weariness and exhaustion which the long hours occasioned, and by their increased cheerfulness and activity, being enabled to work more steadily and diligently, and to economize time, intervals of rest while at their work being now less necessary."

Mr. Henry Millward, of the firm of H. Millward and Sons, extensive needle manufacturers, of Redditch, writes:

"In reply to your note, I cannot have the slightest difficulty in your stating . . the excellent effect I have found the Saturday half-holiday and a general short time in the week, has had on my people. I have adopted it now more than two years, and it is valued by the men. I have no hesitation in saying that *my orders are got out quicker and better than they were previous to it.*"

I think this varied testimony, considering its distinctness of character, and the practical and highly respectable parties from whom it emanates, must be admitted as conclusive by proving two points: First, that a curtailment of the period of labor does not necessarily involve a diminution of the work done; and secondly, that such curtailment as is advocated in these pages would, as a rule, be advantageous to the employers of industry. (Pp. 34-37.)

Factory Act Legislation. The Cobden Prize Essay for 1891. VICTORINE JEANS. *London, T. Fisher Unwin, 1892.*

"The great improvements," wrote one of the inspectors in 1858, "made in machines of every kind have raised their productive power very much. Without a doubt the shortening of the hours of labor . . . gave the impulse to these improvements. The latter, combined with the more intense strain on the workman, have had the result that at least as much is produced in the shortened (by 2 hours, or one-sixth) working day as was previously during the longer run.''

We may fairly conclude, then, that the first result of the Factory Act was this—it fostered the growth of the factory system.

. . . The second great result,—the increase in the vigor and intelligence of the laborer, and therefore, to some extent at least, in his capacity for work. . . . It is perfectly certain that a fair portion of the increased production may quite justly be put down to the improved physical and mental energy of the mill-hands themselves. That was Lord Shaftesbury's great argument. . . . He brought forward a great many cases of equal or increased production arising simply from improved vigor on the part of the workmen in mills where owners had voluntarily reduced their hours by way of experiment.

''I could not understand,'' one master wrote, ''how it was that our men could turn off as much work (and some a little more) in 11 hours as ever they did in 12. I said to one of them, 'John, will you tell me how it is that you can do more work in 11 hours han you did in 12?' 'Why,' said he, 'we can lay to in 11 hours a day better than we could in 12, because we get more rest at night and we are in better spirits all the day through, and besides, the afternoons were not so long.' ''

''He could spin, he said, 10 years longer if Mr. G. would keep on 11 hours.'' . . .

The truth is, there is a law of ''Diminishing Returns'' from labor as from land. . . . Dr. Cunningham's verdict is concise and to the point. ''There is an amount of tension,'' he writes, ''which the human frame can bear, and to prevent men from going beyond it was really to establish the textile industries of Great Britain on a far firmer economic basis.'' Factory legislation thus helps forward production in the textile industries in two ways: by hastening the development of production on a large scale or the factory system, and, secondly, by heightening the efficiency of each individual worker. But . . . the first result has always a certain tendency to weaken the force of the latter. (Pp. 31-34.)

Shorter Hours Increase Efficiency.—Great Britain

British Sessional Papers. Vol. XXXIV. 1892. Royal Commission on Labor. Minutes of Evidence. Group A. Vol. 1.

Testimony of Mr. Joseph Toyn, Cleveland Miners' Association.

1072.—He works very much harder, I quite agree with that, than he used to do. His working time in the face is seven hours, and he can certainly work better, brisker and freer in the seven hours than he could before.

1078.—Do you think there is as great an output now as there was when the hours were longer? There is a larger output.

1079.—A larger output arising from the number of men? Per man.

1080.—That is, you think a man does more work and better work in the short time than he did in the nine or ten hours? He does.

1081.—There is less exhaustion and more energy in his work? He works harder and freer than he did then, of course.

A Shorter Working Day. R. A. Hadfield *of Hadfield's Steel Foundry Co., Sheffield, and* H. de B. Gibbins, M. A. *Methuen & Co., London, 1892.*

It is almost a universal opinion in the colony that the men work harder now while they are at their work, and that they turn out work of a better quality, than they did under the long hours system. (P. 73.)

It is a well-known fact that when physical exertion is necessary, the longer the day the slower the workman becomes. It may not be easy to find out the exact number of hours that an average healthy man can work with the least possible detriment to himself, and with the greatest possible advantage in the production of that upon which he is engaged, but . . . it seems to be an established fact that a reduction of hours invariably results in better work, and that it does not necessarily of itself diminish production. (P. 109.)

However much it may be objected to by certain employers on the ground of lessened production, or of the bogie of Continental competition, I fearlessly assert there would be no diminution of the output, but rather the contrary; since the men will be in a better physical condition, and thus be enabled to do practically more work, as I find in our own experiment. It is pitiful to me to hear employers talking of dread and fear of 'foreign' competition. Why, the longer hours men work on the Continent the better it is for us, as they are in a worse physical condition to turn the work out. If long hours meant increased production, why are they not sending coals to Newcastle? (Pp. 175-176.)

The writer has some diffidence in referring to the case of his own firm, Hadfield's Steel Foundry Co. When, however, one can speak from actual experience, it seems specially advisable to mention the results. . . . The working hours per day were reduced from nine and a half to nine, or the week's time from fifty-four to fifty-one hours. . . . The wages remained as before.

That the change has been eminently satisfactory will be seen from the results quoted, for although alterations of method and organization were introduced about the same time, no doubt contributing much to the satisfactory results, still the writer, from many facts that have come under his personal observation, considers that one of the chief factors has been the better tone and morale amongst the men. It is the old tale, that human nature is not irresponsive to more trust and confidence being placed in it. . . .

. . . As far as can be determined, practically the reduced hours have not added to the cost of production. The management on its side has perfected better methods, and the workers on their side have shown more intelligent interest in carrying out the work to be done, the result being that as much work has been done as in the former long hours. The costs show, after carefully comparing the time spent in the same class of work under the old and new systems, that there is little or no appreciable difference between the amount of work turned out per man.

One important improvement has been noticed. Taking the comparison haphazard, viz., for the months of January 1891 and 1892, in the former case out of about 500 men seventy-two averaged half an hour late each morning during the month, twenty-two averaged a commencement of work at 9 a. m. In January, 1892, the whole of the men, except a daily average of nineteen, were in at work punctually at the starting time—6:30 a. m. The company has therefore clearly saved time, which under the old régime must have been highly wasteful through absence of the workers and foremen, to say nothing of the demoralization under the old system. (Pp. 147-8-9.)

The engineering foremen report that owing to the men all starting together, instead of the previous desultory system, much better results are obtained in the work. In fact they consider the same jobs were turned out in less rather than more time, and several cases of this were instanced. Also that the men were making the work more a personal matter; in other words, as the masters showed more interest in them they are showing more interest in the masters' welfare. Similar results are reported from all the departments, while the better supervision of the foremen and the commencement of work with only 4 per cent. of absentees instead of 20 per cent. must in itself be a considerable monetary saving. (P. 149.)

The Eight Hours Day. Report on a Year's Work with a Forty-Eight Hours Week in the Salford Iron Works, Manchester. (Mather and Platt, Ltd.) WILLIAM MATHER, M. P. *Manchester, Guardian Printing Works. 1894.*

I attribute the full maintenance of our production through the trial year solely to the unimpaired and cheerful energy on the part of every man and boy throughout the day. We seem to have been working in harmony with a natural law, instead of against it. (P. 25.)

Of this I am assured, that the most economical production is obtained by employing men only so long as they are at their best. When this stage is passed, there is no true economy in their continued work. (P. 26.)

Ibid. Appendix. Extracts from Reports of Foremen of Different Departments.

"Moral tone greatly improved, also greater capacity for, and more general eagerness to commence work at once."

"Promptitude in starting work. In this connection there is a very decided improvement, the men are brighter and come to their work apparently feeling fit for work and with powers of endurance quite equal to the reasonable day before them. They seem to work altogether more willingly, and having got over the overtime bogie, are ready at any time to exert a little extra effort rather than run the risk of working after hours."

"From conversation with the men, and personal knowledge of many, I think the eight hours day is highly appreciated by them, and is conducive to their advancement physically and morally, and as one of your foremen, should view with serious apprehension a return of the old state of things."

"There is more life and spirit about commencing work than under the old system, and it seems to give a better tone to the whole day's work."

"During the past twelve months I am glad to be able to report none of my men have come to work under the influence of drink. Therefore, there has been no occassion to turn them back in consequence."

"There has been less illness and less time lost through the same. The men are also more punctual in their habits." (Pp. 27-28.)

Eight Hours for Work. John Rae. *London and New York, Macmillan Co., 1894.*

In the great mass of the staple industries of any country, on the contrary—the industries requiring physical or mental exertion—it is possible by improvement in the personal efficiency of the laborer to compress more work into any definite space of time than was done in it before; and positive experience can safely be said to encourage rather than discourage the hope that most men will do as good a day's work in 8 hours as they can do at all. This hope will appear more and more reasonable as we consider the diverse sources from which the improvement in the working powers of the laborer has come in the past, and the unexhausted reserves of personal efficiency on which we may still call in the future. (P. 95.)

The increase of product per hour, which we have seen so generally accompanying the reduction of the hours of work, has in some cases been aided by the improvement or speeding of the machinery in use, but the aid derived from this quarter has been after all surprisingly small, and in all cases much the greatest part of the effect, in many cases the whole of it, must be ascribed to the improvement and speeding of the personal agent in production. I have quoted the case of cotton mills in Lancashire, of which the details are given by Mr. Horner and in which out of £22 worth more work done in the ten hours only £5 worth, or one-fourth of the result, could be ascribed to increased speeding of machinery, and the remaining £17, or more than three-fourths of the whole, came from closer attention and greater accuracy of work on the part of the operatives. In Switzerland, the usual increase of speed in the machinery was only 2½ per cent., while the increase of product per hour was 8 per cent. . . . The change from which that mainly accrued was a change in the physical and mental energies of the work-people themselves. Indeed in many factories, and in some whole trades, no other change had taken place.

Various expedients, no doubt, were often practised for the purpose of whipping up these energies to their utmost exertion. Piece-work may have been substituted for day-work, or overlookers been paid a premium on the output; but after all is told, there remains the great fact without which no amount of whipping would have been effectual, that under the shorter hours the workpeople themselves brought with them every morning a greater store of energy to respond to such stimulation, and that it flowed out more freely and readily into their labor than before. (Pp. 96-97.)

The improvement in production obtained under shorter hours is not obtained by working harder so much as by working better and more accurately. It is a fruit of the mind, of increased intelligence in working, not of increased physical exertion. (P. 107.)

Mr. W. Glennie, an engineer, explained to the Labor Commission that the reason Messrs. Allan and Co. get as much work done in their eight-hours day as they got before in their nine-hours one is "not because the men work harder, but because they lay their mind to their work better and work more intelligently." . . . Indeed, intelligence and method are always the great reducers of strain, the great savers of labor; and it is ever the unskillful stroke that uses up the strength most. (P. 108.)

It is a common mistake to suppose that it is impossible for any improvement in personal efficiency to tell on the product of self-acting machinery, and that mistake is at the bottom of much of the opposition of employers on the proposal of an eight-hours day. . . .

It must be admitted that nothing does seem clearer before we examine into the facts than that such a thing is impossible, but nothing is better established by the fact than that it is done constantly every day. What can be nearer clockwork than a textile mill?—yet the Ten Hours Act stopped this clockwork in every mill in the country for 11 hours a week without making any material difference in its weekly product. In some mills the machinery was neither changed nor speeded and yet it gave out the same quantity in 10 hours it used to do in 12, in consequence of nothing but the improved personal exertion of the work-people. (Pp. 109-110.)

Our first false impressions on this subject, in which so many of us remain, come from simply failing to observe two things: first, that with the most automatic machinery in common use there is always plenty of room for the "ability and push" of the workman, of which Mr. Whitwell speaks, to tell decisively on the result; the second, that the short-hour workman is a being of more push and ability than the long-hour workman. (P. 111.)

The personal factor really counts for more in machine work than in mere hand work, and if shortening the daily span improves the push or ability of the personal factor, that improvement will tell more on the product of the machine than on the product of the hand, because there is much more product to tell on. It may be true enough that a lathe will not do as much work in 8 hours as it will in nine, *if it is properly worked on both occasions;* but the employer who made the statement, and thought it so conclusive against the eight-hours day, did not realize in the least the great practical importance of the conditional clause in his sentence. The eight-hours workman will necessarily work it better than the nine-hours one, and the difference in the result may be really very considerable. (P. 113.)

The world takes a long time to appreciate adequately the enormous productive value of mere contentment and cheerfulness of mind. . . . One of the first and most marked effects of shortening hours has been the greater satisfaction and cheerfulness which the laborers feel in their work. They come back to it in the morning with a new spring and relish and they leave it in the evening with hope and spirit. . . . The cheerful mind carries a spontaneous vigor into labor and dispenses with much of the necessity of constant superintendence and goading. (Pp. 123-125.)

If we are justified in expecting the gift of leisure to spread an active desire for mental improvement, we are even better justified in expecting this spread of mental improvement to result in very substantial gains in industrial efficiency. We have seen employers remarking a certain quickening of the intelligence in their men immediately after the shortening of their working-day. The faculties which seem to have been somewhat torpid and wandering under the long hours, concentrated themselves with more purpose and interest in their work and produced better results. But I speak now of the increase of intelligence to be expected from the larger opportunities for mental instruction afforded by the shorter day. We have begun to grow alive to the value of technical education, but for the ordinary workman the fruitful thing is general education. (Pp. 136-137.)

Hours and Wages in Relation to Production. LUJO BRENTANO. *Translated by* MRS. WM. ARNOLD. *London, Sonnenschein, 1894.*

Where, however, a rise in the standard of life has come about as a consequence of increased wages and shorter hours, experience shows that it induces greater intensity of labor, since men whose requirements are larger and their hours shorter are compelled to greater industry, and that at the same time it makes that intensive labor possible, owing to the fact that favorable bodily circumstances and greater pleasure in labor make the greater industry easier to such workmen than to those whose requirements are small and who are badly nourished, weary and depressed. (P. 48.)

Life and Labour of the People in London. Edited by CHARLES BOOTH, *Vol. IX, Pt. III, Ch. VII. The Hours of Labour.* ERNEST AVES. *London and New York, Macmillan, 1897.*

One great hindrance will have been removed when the lesson of the elasticity of the power of human response has been fully learned; when it is realized, for instance, that, even when machinery is used, and its speed and capacity remain the same, output may often be maintained, even though hours be diminished. Even in factories, in which the operative is sometimes regarded as of secondary importance to the machine, this "reserve of personal efficiency," to quote Mr. Rae's phrase, may tell: while in the case of all skilled labour, in which machinery plays no part, the possible effects of this subtle, unknown, and often unexpected expansion of individual power, may be still more important, though more difficult to measure. . . .

The differences between one man and another are

hardly greater than those that may be discovered between a man and himself. Who, for instance, can measure the difference, even in productive efficiency, between one who is overworked, physically tired, and morally embittered and degraded, and the same man, strong, keen, alert and interested? Few more fatal fallacies have hindered the path of industrial reform than this superficial assumption, happily dying with the century, that return can be safely measured in terms of the hours of employment. (P. 288.)

A Handbook of Political Questions of the Day and the Arguments of Either Side. Sidney Buxton, M.P. *11th Edition. London, John Murray, 1903. Legal Limitation of Hours.*

The legal limitation of hours is supported on the grounds: . . . 27. (a) That shorter hours, even though not followed by any, or a proportionate reduction of wages, would not in the end affect profits. (b) That during the last thirty or forty years, the hours of labour have been shortened and wages have largely risen, yet profits have increased. (c) That the restrictions imposed by the Factory Acts, the Mines Acts, etc., have not injured but have improved the condition of the industries to which they have been applied. (d) That the prophecies of the ruin that would result from the limitation of hours in factories have all been falsified. While the condition of the workers has been greatly bettered, the commercial position has been improved, not impaired.

28. (a) That a shortening of the hours of labour is compatible with the maintenance of the present aggregate product of labour. (b) That each reduction or curtailment of hours, whether brought about by Factory Acts, or by agreement in a particular industry or business, has been followed by an actual increase in the productiveness of individual workers. (c) That experience has shown that shorter hours mean more profitable labour and more economical working. The speed and efficiency of work diminishes as the day advances, and

the great majority of accidents occur near the close of the day's work; weariness makes a man less apt and less careful. (d) That an individual worker might, and very likely would, produce more in a single day of ten or twelve hours, than another would do working eight hours only; but, by the end of the year, the latter would have produced more and better work.

29. (a) That there would be a considerable saving in the extra payments now made for "overtime"; a system of work uneconomical to employer and hurtful to employed. (b) That the workers would begin work more punctually. (Pp. 166-7.) . . .

30. (b) That attention would be turned towards the improvement of machinery, and production would be more rapid and less costly than before.

31. That thus, while the probable economic effect cannot be accurately ascertained, on the whole it is probable that the amount of production would not be diminished, nor its cost increased. (Pp. 167-8.)

Industrial Efficiency. A Comparative Study of Industrial Life in England, Germany, and America. Arthur Shadwell, M. A., M. D. *London, New York, and Bombay. Longmans, Green & Co. 1906.*

Probably no one will seriously deny that hours of work may be too long or too short. They may be too long because human nature has limits, as the saying goes; rest and recreation are physiological needs; the brain cells, which are the motive power of all action, become exhausted and faculties fail after a time, with the result that bad work is produced. They may be too short, because the power present is not fully utilized, with the result that insufficient work is produced; in the end it would be bad work too, for powers disused atrophy and the less people do the less they can do. (Hours, V. 2. P. 105.) . . .

The question is evidently complicated; but perhaps some general principle can be laid down. I beg to offer these suggestions: (1) prolongation of work becomes disadvantageous from the point at which the quality begins to fall off or the speed begins to slacken; (2) shortening of work becomes disadvantageous from the point at which full powers are left unutilized. Experience can alone determine when these points are reached. They will evidently vary in different branches of industry, in different countries and at different periods, as the pace of working changes with improved machinery.

Turning to the lessons of experience we have strong evidence of the advantage of shortening in the gradual substitution in England of 8-hour for 12-hour shifts, and in the tendency, noted above, towards reduction both in Germany and in the United States. This is, to a great extent, a voluntary movement on the part of manufacturers, and if they did not find it advantageous they would not follow it. Even in those cases in which employers have been forced more or less against their will to shorten hours, as, for instance, in the case of railway servants, it has been found advantageous, and no one proposes to return to the old practice of keeping signalmen or engine drivers on duty for 20 hours or more. (Pp. 106-7).

The eight-hour shift has unquestionably proved economically advantageous in England. (P. 112.)

A question here arises which has a very important bearing on industrial efficiency. . . .

I refer to the relative energy put into their work by the workers. This will obviously affect the number of hours which can be worked with advantage. (P. 107.)

There is no doubt at all that men do work harder in America. (P. 108.)

My belief is that with such a rate of work the longer hours, though advantageous in some respects, are disadvantageous in others. (P. 111.)

The general tendency to shorten hours will doubtless continue. Apart from the efforts of organised labour and sympathetic reformers to effect reduction as a thing desirable in itself, it will be inevitably brought about by economic pressure, if the principles I have stated are correct. For mechanical invention constantly increases speed of working, which in turn involves more constant and concentrated attention, making greater demands on the brain: and as the demands increase the time during which they can be fully satisfied without exhaustion diminishes. In other words, extent varies inversely with intensity. A reduction of hours becomes a condition of efficient work and is therefore inevitable in many branches of industry. But in those in which there is no change of intensity, such as ordinary unskilled labour, reduced time may mean diminished efficiency. (P. 113.)

The Case for the National Minimum. With Preface by MRS. SIDNEY WEBB. *London, National Committee for the Prevention of Destitution, 1913.*

. . . The practical possibility of the Eight Hours Day (or alternatively the Forty-eight Hours Week) depends on three factors:

(i) The improved health and productive capacity of the worker;

(ii) The more efficient arrangement of shorter hours;

(iii) The fact that production depends on the wages paid rather than on the length of time worked.

These are not the theories of the arm-chair economist; they are based on a wealth of experience so great that it is difficult to select specific instances for quotation. Past reductions of hours from fourteen to twelve, from twelve to ten, and from ten to nine hours per day have resulted in greater output and increased wages. Where reductions have been carried still further, to forty-eight hours per week, similar results have followed.

Efficiency of Shorter Hours.—It is difficult to separate the first two factors in the economy of the shorter day, viz., the greater productive capacity of the worker and the more effective arrangement of his working day. Two spells of work of four hours each would appear to produce the greatest output with the least expenditure of energy. This arrangement eliminates the slow and ineffective spell of work before breakfast; it cuts out one break of work per day with its waste of time in stopping and re-starting; it almost eliminates loss of time from various causes, and it saves the energy of the worker to the extent of one journey home and back. The Royal Small Arms Factory at Enfield found that this system reduced time lost by unpunctuality from *five per cent.* to less than *one-half per cent.* while the engineering firm of S. H. Johnson & Co., Stratford, found its economies so great that it was able to pay the same wage for *eight* hours' work that it had previously paid for *nine* hours. In other words, wages per hour were advanced 12½ per cent.

Workers' Response to Improved Conditions.—Perhaps the most effective factor ensuring the success of the Eight Hours Day is the fact that in the manufacture of material goods, the employer purchases and the worker sells, not time but a certain amount of skill and energy. Time is introduced only as a convenient method of calculating wages. Output need not diminish with reduced hours if the weekly wage is maintained at the original level. The productive energy of the worker responds readily to the changes of wage. If it is made possible for the worker to earn the same wage for shorter hours, his output will speedily attain its former level, though a short period must be allowed for adjustment to the new conditions. (Pp. 18-19-20.)

Die Arbeiterfrage. [*The Problem of Labor.*] Dr. HEINRICH HERKNER. *Berlin, Guttentag, 1894.*

Chap. I, Part III. The relation of wages and hours to production.

The raising of wages and the reduction of hours which have taken place in the last few decades are not due solely to state intervention and the pressure of labor unions. Increasing competition at home and abroad continually demands increasing efficiency. Experience has proved that really good work can be permanently given only by well paid workmen who are not overworked. Schoenhof and von Schultze-Gaevernitz have amply demonstrated that the heightened demands made upon the workman by the pressure of competition in the markets of the world have also been instrumental in procuring more favorable conditions for him. Keen-sighted employers have long understood that the highly paid workers, not the cheap ones, are the most economical ones in the long run. Similar experiences have been collected in regard to hours. Under modern conditions of production it is not the long, exhausting work day of 13-14 hours, but the moderate day of 8-10 hours, that yields the best output. (P. 186.)

So, in every instance w[illegible]s have been raised and hours reduced it has b[illegible]ed that none of the fears of those opposed to the change have been realized. (P. 187.)

Deutsche Vierteljahrsschrift für öffentliche Gesundheitspflege. Vol. 43. 1911. Zur Phyziologie und Pathologie der Arbeit, mit besonderer Berücksichtigung der Ermüdungsfrage. [Physiology and Pathology of Work, with Special Reference to the Fatigue Problem.] Dr. E. Roth.

The shortening of the work-period as such has a most favorable influence, not only on the health and well-being of the workers, but also upon their physical working-capacity, as shown by the good results obtained in all countries, through the diminution of the work-period. Not only the hygienic but also the economic effect was favorable, for the cost of production was not increased, nor were the wages lowered. The timely shortening of the day's work represents the equivalent of a greater activity. *Practice* and *habit* lead to this goal. The increased output is then no longer a conscious activity, but it takes place unconsciously, so that the speedier work involves no greater effort. Routine practice leads to progressive adjustment of the muscles and nerves of the workers and especially of their central organs, to the action of the machines in factories. The effect of practice does not uniformly increase with the duration of the activity, but it is most marked at first, and then gradually diminishes. (P. 651.)

Shorter Hours Increase Efficiency.—Austria

Eighth International Congress of Hygiene and Demography, Budapest, 1894. Der Physische Rückgang der Bevölkerung in den modernen Culturstaaten mit besonderer Rücksicht auf Oesterreich-Ungarn. [The Physical Degeneration of the Population in Modern Civilized Countries with Particular Reference to Austria-Hungary.] Dr. Julius Donath, *University of Budapest. Budapest, 1896.*

Not only is the he[illegible] of the labourer protected, more leisure left him for [illegible]e and for the satisfaction of mental and moral r[illegible]ents, (for man does not live by bread alone, the Scriptures say)—but, as is undoubtedly most surprising to one unacquainted with the subject, his productivity is actually increased. A less exhausted workman who is not, so to speak, a victim of chronic fatigue in consequence of long continued overwork, accomplishes more in a shorter period, does it better and more surely, and at the same time, owing to his less impaired power of attention, protects himself more effectively from accidents while at work, and is less subject to illness. And it requires no further explanation to demonstrate that a population thus raised to a materially and mentally higher plane offers also a less favorable field for tuberculosis, alcoholism, and syphilis,—these three fertile scourges of humanity. (P. 617.)

Berichte der eidg. Fabrik und Bergwerkinspektoren über ihre Amtstätigkeit in den Jahren 1898-1899. [Reports of the (Swiss) Factory and Mine Inspectors. 1898-1899.] Aarau, Sauerländer, 1900.

The reductions of hours from 12 to 11 has justified itself; it has had none but good results; it has contributed largely to restore order and regularity to industry.

The adversaries of the 11-hour day who predicted the total ruin of many industries have had to abandon their prejudices; they now see, as we do, that instead of being ruined our industries are developing in a most gratifying way. We hope soon to have a similar experience with the 10-hour day.

Shorter Hours Increase Efficiency.—France

The man who works 11 hours per day will probably produce more on a given day than he who works 10, but this advantage is more apparent than real, and vanishes with time, since prolonged work results in fatiguing the workman.

Workers who are overstrained by long hours are less efficient and less skilful than others, and in the end they produce less.

. . . It is also an incontestable fact that reduction of hours has a good moral effect. It is generally admitted by employers that the deplorable habit of not working on Monday is tending to disappear more and more among the employees with reduced hours of work. (P. 146.)

La Revue Socialiste. T. XLI. Jan.-Juin. 1905. La Journée de Huit Heures. [*The Eight Hour Day.*] ÉTIENNE BUISSON. *Paris.*

The seemingly paradoxical result of equal production with shorter hours of work can be attained, at least to a certain degree, in industries where human labor plays the most important part,—in a word, in all those lines where the worker is not simply an attendant for a machine which performs the work. In such industries the product may remain equal, in spite of shorter hours, by reason of the worker's increased application to the work. This augmentation of output is quite possible. Physical strength and concentrated attention cannot be exerted during 10 or 11 hours with equal intensity. According to the time of day, or the feelings of the moment, the worker has more or less energy for his work; nevertheless he is human; he is not a machine, and he is liable to ups and downs. Then, in the workshop itself there are causes for distraction; in brief, without going into details, there are various causes for inattention, or interruption, which constitute waste time or a loss of output. These losses in many trades may easily make a total of 45 minutes, or an hour, or even more in a day of 10 or 11 hours. This is true of day work; and a comparison of day work with piece work in the same kind of trade will always prove it. (Pp. 642, 643.)

3. Shorter Hours Lead to Improvement in Management.

The introduction of the shorter working day has acted as a stimulus to heightened efficiency on the part of employers as well as on the part of workers. The curtailment of hours has led to a new scrutiny of methods and organization in manufacture. It has proved possible for instance to lessen or eliminate "lost time" by securing a steadier flow of work and materials through the factory. An added incentive is provided for installing improved machinery and new processes of manufacture so that output may be maintained under shorter hours.

The Establishment of Minimum Rates in the Tailoring Industry under the Trade Boards Act of 1909. R. H. Tawney. *London. G. Bell & Sons. 1915.*

In Hebden Bridge, for example, the order of the Board of Trade making the minimum rates obligatory was followed by a reduction of hours, in all except two firms, from 58 to 52, and the general opinion is that the women, who are employed on piece-work, turn out as much in the shorter as they did in the longer week. Thus the influence of the Trade Board upon hours, while indirect, has been real. It led employers to look for ways of turning out their work without interruptions; and when they had discovered them they found that they could produce as much as before in a shorter time. (P. 64.)

The question of overlapping between departments, which is mentioned in this instance, is, indeed, a crucial one. Owing to the high degree of sub-division which obtains in a clothing factory, the workers engaged upon one process are dependent for work upon the workers engaged in another. If a business is well managed there is a regular flow of work through all departments, so that none are congested and none are without employment.

But to arrange the work so that it will go forward smoothly and without interruption requires careful organization, and there is a constant tendency for one group of workers to be overwhelmed with work while another group is slack. The hardship which this inflicted on the piece-workers who might have to wait for some hours in the factory without earning any wages has already been noticed. . . . Such defective organization is extremely uneconomical from the point of view of the employer, part of whose machinery and other capital is standing idle. As the evidence already presented suggests, business is largely governed by custom and defective organization has been tolerated. (Pp. 146-147.)

An assumption which is still not uncommon is that the self-interest of competing employers is the guarantee that the most efficient methods of industrial organization will be adopted.

. . . In reality, except in a few strongly organized industries, no assumption could be farther from the truth. What is true is that competition does keep competing employers up to the mark *in those matters which come within their immediate purview*, and the significance of which needs no special effort either for their understanding or their application. . . . But there are a large number of matters which do not ordinarily come within the purview of more than a small number of exceptionally enlightened employers, because they have not any immediate competitive significance, and, with regard to these, the actual practice of employers is no guide to the practice which is either economically or socially most beneficial. (Pp. 156-157.)

The ordinary barrister does not spend time in considering how legal procedure can be improved. On the contrary he finds Jarndyce *v.* Jarndyce a gold mine. The ordinary employer of labour does not spend sleepless nights reflecting whether by raising wages he could not increase the efficiency of his employees, or whether he could not meet the extra cost of better organization and machinery, until the need of attending to such matters is forced upon his attention. While to the outside observer such matters appear fluid, to those actually engaged in the industry they usually present themselves as conditions which are more or less fixed, which "will last our time" and to alter which would involve capital expenditure and the tiresome work of reorganization. . . . In fact there are probably not many industries where the actual product is identical with the potential product under good conditions of labor and management. (P. 158.)

Fifteenth Annual Report of the National Consumers' League. New York, 1916. Some Practical Experiences in Shortening Hours of Labor. Address by MR. FREDERICK R. HAZARD, *President Solvay Process Company, Syracuse, New York, Cleveland, Ohio, November 4, 1915.*

It is not possible, however, to say that the total reduction (in cost of production) is caused by reason of the change in working hours; many other factors come in. The changes in the rate of the wages and hours is always an incentive to the engineers and others in charge, to devise ways and means of making labor more efficient, by putting in mechanical contrivances; and you can readily conceive that in our problem, handling material by the hundred ton lot, it was possible to devise mechanical means of handling which would be cheaper than the hand methods. That was done in very many cases, so much so, in fact, that, looking over a composition of a group of workmen who before the change might have been taken as representing an average rate, and then looking at the corresponding work some years after the change, I find that the unskilled laborer has to a great extent disappeared; his place is taken by mechanical contrivances, and the more highly skilled laborer, receiving a greater rate of wages, has become a more important factor in the group.

Now, that does not mean that the men so eliminated necessarily lose their positions. In a great many cases and I think the majority of cases, those men really step up into a better position, and it is only the less worthy of them who are allowed to depart from a given plant and must find their employment in other places at approximately the same level of intelligence.

Report of the United States Industrial Commission. Final Report, Vol. XIX, 1902.

It is true also that the higher the wages and fewer the hours the greater is the pressure upon the employer to substitute labor-saving devices and to be more careful in his selection of high-grade workmen. No doubt it is true that often a given automatic machine will not run faster per hour in 8 hours than in 10 hours, but industry has by no means reached the limit of invention. Invention will cease only when the employer ceases to adopt new labor-saving machinery, and every reduction in hours and in wages keeps the employer further and further away from the sluggish policy. While a particular machine will not go faster in 8 hours than in 10 hours, the substitute for that machine, which the 8-hour day presses upon the employer to adopt, will go faster. Less hours in this way have an indirect as well as a direct compensating effect. Not only do they make it possible for the workman to keep up his intensity of personal exertion during each hour of the day and to work more days at a high rate of speed, but they cause the employer to economize his labor at every point and to improve its quality by better selection. One advantage to the employer in less hours is the smaller number of breakages and injuries to machinery, owing to more alert attention on the part of the workmen. For the same reason it is often true that the quality of the work is better. (Pp. 765-766.)

On the side of the employer there is abundant evidence that the shortening of the working day in the mines has strengthened the motive to greater economy of time and better use of machinery and labor-saving devices. . . .

While the introduction of machinery in bituminous coal mining has for some time been advancing, the greatest advances have occurred in the past four years, following the time when the 8-hour day was introduced. The number of tons mined by machines in the entire United States in 1891 was 6,211,732; this had increased under the 10-hour day system to 22,649,220 in 1897, an increase of 16,000,000 tons in six years. On the other hand, from 1897 to 1900, a period of three years under the 8-hour system, the number of tons mined by machines rose to 52,790,523, an increase of 30,000,000 tons. The proportion of the output mined by machines increased from 6.66 per cent. in 1891 to 16.19 per cent. in 1897, and then to 25.15 per cent. in 1900. It is doubtless true that the use of machines would have increased whether or not the eight hour day had been introduced, and it can not be shown statistically that the fewer hours have stimulated the introduction of machinery; but individual witnesses who have appeared before the Commission have asserted this to be the fact, and the large increase in machine mining seems to substantiate the claim. (Pp. 769-770.)

Report of the Wisconsin Bureau of Labor and Industrial Statistics, 1903-1904.

Wherever a uniform standard of wages, hours of labor, and wholesome sanitary conditions have been uniformly enforced, the result has been that laborers have been stimulated to render greater services to their employers, and, in turn, employers strive to excel in improved machinery and devices for the protection of employees, sanitation, and methods of production in general. (P. 138.)

That the enforcing of a certain standard in regard to hours of labor, wages, and sanitary conditions compels employers to continually seek more improved machinery and methods of production is as true in practice as in theory. (P. 140.)

British Sessional Papers. Vol. XII. 1859. Report of Inspector of Factories for Half-year ending 31st October, 1858.

But the increase in the actual number of mills is not the only measure of progression, for the great improvements that have been made in machinery of all kinds have vastly increased their productive powers, improvements to which a stimulus was doubtless given, especially as regards the greater speed of the machines in a given time by the restrictions of the hours of work. These improvements and the closer application which the operatives are enabled to give have had the effect as I have been again and again assured of as much work being turned off in the shortened time as used to be in the longer hours. (P. 10.)

Factory Act Legislation. The Cobden Prize Essay for 1891. VICTORINE JEANS. *London, T. Fisher Unwin, 1891.*

Each succeeding experiment has proved legislation to be justifiable not only on grounds sanitary, educational and moral, but also when judged by the "strictest rules of Political Economy." All the English economists were against the Act of 1844; probably there is hardly a single writer of note who would wish to see that or any subsequent act repealed today. The expected economic results nowhere came to pass, because, wherever legislation penetrated it acted as a stimulus to "invention" in the best and widest sense of the word.

. . . Production will increase with the improved vigor of the work-people and the use of better appliances, wages will rise, foreign trade can be only temporarily injured; the whole basis of the industry must in the end be made wider and stronger. (Pp. 83-84.)

The Eight-Hours Day. SIDNEY WEBB *and* HAROLD COX. *London, Walter Scott, 1891.*

"Press of work arising at recurring seasons of the year" does not necessarily involve the permission of overtime. Such press can also generally be met, either by taking more people into employment when the pressure comes or by getting stock ready beforehand. Either of these ways is preferable to overtime working. Moreover, as a matter of fact, there is a great deal of superstition about the necessity for overtime working at certain seasons. No better illustration of this could be found than that of Mr. Beaufoy, related in the Appendix.

An important part of Mr. Beaufoy's business is the manufacture of British wines, and, as everyone knows, British wines are consumed more freely at Christmas than at any other time of the year. Consequently, here appears a clear case for a season of overtime. And in fact when Mr. Beaufoy succeeded to the business there was no limit to the amount of overtime worked during the months of October and November. But Mr. Beaufoy on general grounds thought the system was bad, and determined to put it down. He has put it down absolutely and completely, and his business has benefited by the alteration. (P. 160.)

A Shorter Working Day. R. A. HADFIELD *of Hadfield's Steel Foundry Co., Sheffield, and* H. DE B. GIBBINS, M. A. *London, Methuen, 1892.*

Yet production has not suffered. The reason is that necessity, here as always, showed herself to be literally the mother of invention, and the decrease of hours was amply compensated by an increase of new machinery, appliances, and devices which have brought the development of the manufacturing industries up to the present point. Some fear that we have gone as far in our inventions as it is possible for us to go, and that if we were to reduce the hours of labor now we could no longer compensate by increased facilities of production. But we can hardly believe that this is the case. To take but one example: The steam engine alone is as yet practically in its infancy, and one can hardly believe that there is no room for further invention when we remember that only 10 per cent. of the power generated by coal in the steam engine is utilized while the remaining 90 per cent. is wasted. (P. 88.)

One might say, almost without doubt, that as regards many trades, by more systematic arrangement of work and better organization, an extra hour might readily be saved without any reduction in the amount of work turned out. There is now often sheer waste of time. There seems no reason why the workers should continue to suffer from bad management, for they are in no way responsible for this, though all the same they do now suffer for it. It is the directing hand of the employer or manager, who has had, or should have had, more facilities by means of technical training, education and other advantages, that is responsible in this direction. (Pp. 120-21.)

British Sessional Papers. Vol. XVII. 1893. Report of Chief Inspector of Factories and Workshops.

As far as this district is concerned, the only demand for this overtime comes from an inconsiderable minority of manufacturers. . . . Although there are more than 4,000 who could claim to make it (overtime) not more than 200 . . . apparently do so. I am persuaded that in a majority of instances in which overtime has been made by these 200 employers, it has been brought about either by greed, tyranny, or incompetence of the managers or employers. I believe that much of the apparent necessity for working overtime is simply the result of want of forethought and organization on the part of the employers and their managers. . . . I came across a very large firm employing several hundred work-people on work of an exceptionally important and public nature. It has been the custom in the works at the end of each month to keep all hands, young and old, at work for two days and nights. . . . They said their arrangements could not possibly be interfered with without causing serious public inconvenience. . . . I answered that I would allow them two months to rearrange their system of working. . . . Before the two months were over I met the manager of the works, who said that my visit had been the best thing that had happened to them for years, that the strain of working under the old system had been almost unbearable as much to the managers as to the work-people, that since my visit they had gone carefully into the whole matter, had laid the facts before their customers and had so rearranged the system of working that they could commence their undertakings early in the month, and that there was now no further necessity for the great strain at the end. If such a change as this could be brought about in a case of such apparently exceptional difficulty, it is fair to assume that most of the seasons of pressure which beset certain trades can be provided for by forethought and arrangement, but I am afraid that such forethought and arrangement will never be exercised while the mischievous expedient of overtime is made so easy. (Pp. 89-90.)

How little actual demand there is for overtime on the part of protected hands, I think the return of this district will show. Out of nearly 9,000 occupiers of factories and workshops, only about 200 apparently avail themselves of the permission to work overtime. (P. 91.)

British Sessional Papers. Vol. XXXIV. Appendix CXXIX. 1893. Royal Commission on Labor. Group C. Summary of Evidence of Mr. C. B. Bowling, *Her Majesty's Inspector of Factories.*

. . . I am persuaded that in the majority of instances in which overtime has been made by these 200 employers (out of 4,000 in the district who could claim it), it has been brought about either by the greed, tyranny, or incompetence of the managers or employers.

I believe a large proportion of it results from want of forethought and organization; a good deal from an insatiable greediness and striving to steal a march on their neighbors, which prompts many manufacturers never to refuse an order, however unprepared they may be to fulfill it. . . .

Of course the principal argument in support of this allowance of overtime to the trades named in the schedule, is that they are season trades, subject to recurring pressure at certain times.

To a more or less degree this may be urged with regard to the vast bulk of manufacturing industries of the country, and if under a law framed for the protection of young people from an undue strain on their mental and physical powers, you are going to sanction any overtime at all, I confess I cannot see where, without great injustice, you can draw the line. (P. 724.)

British Sessional Papers. Vol. XXXIX. 1893. Royal Commission on Labour. Minutes of Evidence.

Testimony of Mr. Tom. Mann.

2657.—As you know very well, all over the country three years ago, the Gas Workers' Union very successfully promoted a movement for eight hours amongst gas stokers? Yes.

2658.—Do you know that since then there has been such a development in machinery for doing stokers' work as there never was before? I believe that is so, and I am very pleased to hear it.

2659.—That machinery was first introduced or first proposed, or the first patent was obtained by Best & Holden in 1860, and the matter has been dragging on for thirty years doing little or nothing, but since 1889 the gas undertakings throughout the country cannot get it made quick enough? I am glad to hear it.

2660.—If I should see that by the application of the eight hours' principle, the chief result would be the stimulating of invention, then for that reason alone I would go for it.

British Sessional Papers. Vol. XXXV. 1894. Royal Commission on Labour. Fifth and Final Report. Part I. General Review of the Evidence.

In favor of intervention by the Legislature the chief arguments put forward were as follows: . . .

(a) To diminish the hours of work in any trade is not necessarily to diminish production. Experience shows that in many industries reduction of hours is consistent with maintenance, and even increase of output, and consequently that in those trades the same number of men working shorter hours can earn at least as much as when they worked longer hours. This result may be due either to the men working harder during the shorter hours and wasting less time, or to the employer under stress of competition introducing improvements in machinery or in the organization of work. (P. 61.)

Short Hours and Management.—Great Britain

Eight Hours for Work. John Rae. *London and New York, Macmillan & Co., 1894.*

In some trades much of the time of the day used to be taken up merely in waiting for work, and that time was, after the Act of 1867, saved for actual work. A female bookbinder said to the Factory Inspector in 1876, "The work is now given out during the day in the factory more regularly and more promptly, and we never lose time waiting for it as we used to do. I find I can earn more money under the Factory Act than when we had no regulations, and in book-sewing we are all paid by piece-work." Complaints of this kind of unnecessary waiting for orders or for materials were laid before the Labour Commission by some of the Sheffield trades. The "makers up" in the Britannia metal trade—a class comprising three-fourths of the persons engaged in the industry—are said to spend not less than a third of their whole time, or about two days a week, in merely waiting in this way for orders or materials without any reason except the dilatory or indolent habits of management of those they work for. Shorter hours generally cure this evil, and sometimes raise the amount of the week's production into the bargain, by merely compelling employers into greater regularity. (P. 117.)

A shortening of hours has always two immediate effects—it improves the mettle of the masters, and it improves the mettle of the men. The masters set themselves at once to practice economies of various sorts, to make more efficient arrangements of the work, to introduce better machinery or to speed the old, to try the double shift and other expedients to maintain and even augment the production of their works. The men return to their toil in better heart after their ampler rest, reinvigorated both in nerve and muscle, and make up in the result sometimes in part, sometimes wholly, by the intensity of their labour for the loss of its duration. (P. 291.)

Hours and Wages in Relation to Production. Lujo Brentano. Translation by Mrs. Wm. Arnold, *London, Sonnenschein, 1894.*

But more important still is the influence of high wages and short hours on the practical application of inventions already known. It is an old-established economic maxim, to which the lectures of Hermann and Helferich in particular have given emphatic expression, that it is not the greater technical perfection of a process of production, but merely its greater cheapness, that settles its practical employment in industry. It is not enough to invent a labour-saving process of production to ensure its adoption; its application must cost less than the labour it replaces. So the first result of a rise of wages and shortening of hours is the practical application of better methods of production, which from a purely technical point of view have long been possible. Conversely these perfected technical processes, in particular the faster, more delicate machines which with fewer workmen turn out a far greater production, are for the first time physically possible with superior workmen, well paid, well fed, intelligent, strenuous, and eager. (Pp. 51-52.)

Thus high wages and short hours are the occasion and condition of an increase in production by means of improved technique. (P. 52.)

British Sessional Papers. Vol. XIX. 1895. Report of the Chief Inspector of Factories and Workshops.

. . . Where organization and economy of management exist, the necessity for overtime does not exist; and that workrooms conducted under the apparent necessity for overtime can prosper under its withdrawal is shown by the fact that overtime has entirely ceased, under the control of a new manager, in workrooms in which under other management it had been excessive, and that the development of business rather than its diminution had been the result.

Various employers of labour have shown it to be possible to satisfy the demands of a thoughtless public and at the same time to guard the health of their work-people. (P. 12.)

The Case for the Factory Acts. Edited by MRS. SIDNEY WEBB. *London, Richard, 1901.*

But the exemption from regulation is also responsible for corresponding deficiencies in the technical administration of the industry. The very fact that the employers are legally free to make their operatives work without limit, and to crowd any number of them into one room, makes them disinclined to put thought and capital into improving the arrangements.

. . . We might indefinitely prolong the list of examples of the effect of the Factory Acts in improving the processes of manufacture. (P. 53.)

British Association for the Advancement of Science. 73rd Meeting. 1903. Women's Labour: Third Report of the Committee . . . appointed to investigate the Economic Effect of Legislation Regulating Women's Labour. London, Murray, 1904.

So far as legislation has furthered the reduction of hours to the period of greatest output, it has promoted efficiency; and in many cases the Acts have only made generally compulsory what the firms with most capital and best management had already practised. (P. 339.)

History of Factory Legislation. B. L. HUTCHINS *and* AMY HARRISON. *Westminster, King, 1903.*

If it could be shown that this regulated industry, far from suffering in competition with others, went ahead, improved its machinery, and developed a higher standard of comfort than its rivals, then, although the improvement might not be due to the legislation, there would be, at all events, a strong presumption that good and not harm had been done. And this is what has taken place. . . . The improvement in the regulated industry was clear and conspicuous. (P. 121.)

British Sessional Papers. Vol. XII. 1903. Report of Chief Inspector of Factories and Workshops.

There is a growing disposition on the part of a number of employers to relinquish the habit of overtime as not "worth the candle." . . . It is significant that where one occupier in a given trade avails himself of the permission, there are several others, apparently engaged in identical work, who never work overtime from year's end to year's end. There may sometimes be exceptional circumstances to account for this, but I am inclined to believe that it is more often a question of management and methodizing work. (P. 29.)

National Conference on the Prevention of Destitution. 1912. Papers and Proceedings. London. P. S. King & Son, 1912. The Limitation of the Hours of Work. GEORGE N. BARNES, M. P.

It is true that shortened hours of labour, other things being equal, must be accompanied by increased productivity per man per hour if price is to be maintained at about the level as before the reduction. Experience has shown that this increased productivity has always followed, and that, indeed, long hours with cheap labour are generally accompanied by slovenly management and lack of organisation. Long hours and low wages benefit nobody, because they relieve employers from the necessity of proper organization and of the use of machinery and scientific appliances. As wages are increased or hours lessened employers immediately begin to increase output by the introduction of labour-saving methods and appliances. That is why the best organized trades are also the most productive and successful trades, the improved methods more than making up the relatively high labour cost. As instances of this, one might cite the textile industries which have been subjected for many years to legislation as well as to the pressure of strong trade unionism. As a result, industry has been organized on such a high plane of efficiency that it has now become one of the staple industries of the country, and exports into the markets of the world in competition with long hours and low wage countries. The same might be said of the ship-building industry. (P. 447.)

Der Acht-Stundentag (*The Eight Hour Day*). A. Koechlin-Geigy. *Basel, Werner-Riehm, 1893.*

The decisive factor for shorter hours is something more powerful than manifestations, processions, and revolutions—something beside which laws themselves are only scraps of paper. This factor is industrial progress. The slowly growing training of the people in industrial work, their practice in the discipline and precision of great industries, the replacement of the old hand tools by machines, of primitive machines by improved types, of hand work by the almost unlimited speed of mechanical power—these are the factors which are working for reduction of hours. (P. 9.)

Drucksachen des Kaiserlichen Statistischen Amts, Abth. für Arbeiter Statistik, Erhebungen Nr. 3, Teil I. 1903. [*Publications of the German Imperial Office of Statistics, Department of Labor Statistics, Inquiry No. 3, Part I. 1903.*] *Uber die Arbeitszeit der Gehilfen und Lehrlinge in Handelsgewerbe und Kaufmännischen Betrieben.* [*On the Hours of Shop Assistants and Apprentices.*] (*Investigation made in 1901.*) *Berlin, 1904.*

The blame for many bad conditions must be ascribed to the absence of adequate legal restrictions on length of working time. So long as working hours are not limited, the employer does not meet extra work by bringing in extra help, but by overworking his staff by overtime . . . for the work must be done. (P. 34.)

It is often hard to define "overtime." The line between "working time" and "overtime" is not easily drawn unless "working time" is specifically limited by law. . . . The testimony shows that many business firms keep their employees busy until near midnight or even 1 a. m. Such overtime is often due to inadequate accommodation or to poor management, and disappears when these are improved. From Düsseldorf the reports stated that this excessive overtime, often persisting for months and running until late in the night, was complained of by all who were affected by it as the greatest hardship they had to endure. (P. 41.)

The chief complaint of employees as to late overtime is not entirely of the overwork itself, but of the fact that it is almost always avoidable. The causes of late work are actually poor arrangements or insufficient personnel. (P. 43.)

4. Relation of Short Hours to Cost of Production.

The introduction of the shorter workday has not led in the long run to an increase in the cost of production. This is due to two causes: first, because the labor cost is only one item, and often a small item, in the total cost of manufacture; second, because the heightened efficiency of both employers and workers under shorter hours stimulates output and thus tends to equalize or even decrease the total costs.

Fourth Report of the New York State Factory Investigating Commission. Vol. V. February 15, 1915.

Statement of N. I. Stone, former Chief Statistician, United States Tariff Board.

The United States Tariff Board made an exhaustive study of the cost of production in the paper, woolen and cotton industries. The reason for the creation of the Tariff Board and the object of its investigations was to find the cost of production of various commodities as compared with that in foreign countries, in order to furnish Congress with a measure of protection for American industries against the competition of the cheaper labor of Europe. In every instance, the Tariff Board found that there was no such thing as *a* cost of production; that costs varied not only in the same industry and in the same city, but in the same plant; last, but not least, that neither the total cost, nor the labor cost varied in a direct ratio with the rate of wages paid.

Highly Paid Men Working Eight Hours Per Day Are Cheaper Than Lower Paid Men Working Twelve Hours a Day.

Thus in the paper and pulp industry it was found that the labor cost of making a ton of news-print paper in the United States varied from $2.19 to $7.26 per ton.*

* U. S. Tariff Board Report on Pulp and News Print Paper Industry, 1911, p. 39.

The most remarkable fact about it was that the mills paying the lowest wages and having a twelve hour day had a higher labor cost per ton of paper than those paying the highest rates of wages and having an eight hour day.

The solution of this puzzle lies in the chapter of the report dealing with the "Efficiency of Equipment in Paper Mills." Mills were found to vary greatly in this respect. Some had machinery thirty years old, while others boasted of machines with latest improvements. The older machines had a capacity of 17 tons in 24 hours, while the newer machines could produce 50 tons. The result was that the machine cost of labor per ton of paper was $1.84 on the old machine and only 82 cents with the new, the same rate of wages being paid to the machine tenders in each case.*

But important as the machine equipment is in determining the efficiency of labor, the human equation is subject to no less variation under certain conditions.

When the agitation for the removal of the import duty on news-print paper resulted in an inquiry by a special committee of Congress, a representative of one of the largest paper mill companies in the country pointed to the fact that they had recently reduced the hours of labor from twelve to eight, without reducing the weekly rate of wages, with the consequent increase of 33 per cent. in their labor cost. The figures secured by the Tariff Board from the books of several mills, including those to which reference was made before the Committee of Congress, showed a reduction in the labor cost per ton of paper from $4.35 to $3.73 in 1909 under the eight hour system. In other words, an increase in the hourly rate of wages to the extent of 33 per cent. not only failed to result in a corresponding increase in the cost of labor per ton of paper, but, strange as it may seem, was accompanied by an actual reduction in cost. While the figures of $4.35 in 1908 happened to be the highest in ten years, there was not a single year in that decade under the twelve hour system which showed as

* Ibid., p. 52.

low a cost as in 1909, the first year under the eight hour system.* On the other hand, when it is remembered that during a large part of the year 1909 the mills were idle, owing to the strike for shorter hours and that costs are usually above normal when a plant is started up after a long period of idleness, there is every reason to believe that the labor cost was still further reduced after 1909.

Yet it can not be said that there was a radical change in the equipment of the mills to which these figures relate, immediately following the introduction of the eight hour shift. The change was due largely to the increase of the personal efficiency of the workers under the shorter day. The duties of a machine tender in a paper mill consist chiefly in watching the thin sheet of paper as it first appears on the large cylinder of the machine. A slight twist at the outset will result in reams of paper being torn on the cylinder, with a mad rush of all the tenders in an endeavor to set things right and will frequently require a complete stoppage of the machine, all of which greatly increases the cost of production. The fatigue caused by twelve hours of such nervous and physical strain resulted in a much greater proportion of damaged paper and interruption of work than was the case after the adoption of the eight hour day. With the hours of labor cut down from twelve to eight, the machine tender was relieved from duty during the last four hours, when he used to be tired out most and when his alertness and general efficiency were at their lowest ebb. The change in working hours not only enabled him to leave the mill less fatigued than formerly, but with the resting period increased by four hours a day, the recuperation was more thorough, so that his alertness of mind and body was greater upon his return to work than it used to be even during the first eight hours under the old system. With his mind more alert, he was able to detect in time imperfections which formerly escaped his attention. This resulted in so great an increase in the relative time the machines were in actual operation (free from breakdowns and stoppages), accompanied by a re-

* U. S. Tariff Board Report on Pulp and News-Print Paper Industry, p. 79.

duction in the quantity of damaged paper on which labor had been expended in the preceding stages of production and therefore wasted, that the labor cost of production of paper declined in spite of the increase in the hourly rate of wages. (Pp. 657-659.)

The Survey. Vol. 31. New York, January 3, 1914. Three Eight-Hour Tours in the Paper Mills of America. Charles Sumner Bird, *President F. W. Bird & Son.*

I doubt very much whether the increased cost of labor due to a change from the two-tour to the three-tour system in a paper mill representing as it does, I think, approximately not over 2 per cent. of the average value of the product, would be sufficient to drive any one out of the paper business. Furthermore, I doubt whether it is true that it costs even that amount, because I believe that mills that run on the eight-hour basis or three tours as compared to the twelve-hour or thirteen-hour basis, produce more paper and better paper, due to the improved spirit among the men and due to the physical capacity of the men to do better work.

It wouldn't take much better spirit or much better physical capacity on the part of the men to produce enough better and enough more paper in any paper mill to make up the difference between the labor cost of three-tour as against two-tour systems. Furthermore, if it is necessary for any mill in order to exist to employ men seventy-two hours a week year in and year out, then the sooner the mill is removed from the state and the country the better for the men and women of the country.

The public is becoming more alive each year to the economic waste of excessive hours of labor. It will demand legislation to correct these evils for they can be remedied satisfactorily in no other way. (P. 377.)

Short Hours and Cost of Production.—United States

United States Congress. Senate Document, No. 110. Report on Conditions of Employment in the Iron & Steel Industry in The United States. Vol. III. Working Conditions and the Relations of Employers and Employees. Sixty-second Congress, 1st Session, 1911. Washington, 1913.

Maximum Cost of Change to Eight-hour Day.

The estimates show that the increase in the cost of production of a ton of pig iron would be only 2.6 per cent. of its cost if the workmen were paid the same wages for 8 hours that they now receive for 12 hours and if absolutely no variation followed the change. Similarly the maximum increase in the cost per ton of the principal products of the steel works and rolling mills would be only 6 per cent. The reason for the small increase in the cost of production as compared with the assumed increase of 50 per cent. in the hourly rates of wages lies in the fact that labor constitutes only a very small part of the cost of production. In the production of pig iron labor constitutes only 6.4 per cent. of the total cost and for the five principal products of the steel works and rolling mills only 17.1 per cent. of the total cost.

Probable Cost of Change to Eight-hour Day.

If the workmen were given an increase of 25 per cent. in the hourly rate of wages at the time of the change to the 8-hour system instead of the 50 per cent. assumed in the preceding discussion, the increase in the cost of production per ton of pig iron would be only 1.3 per cent. and in the cost of the principal steel products only 3 per cent., even if no change in the efficiency of the workmen occurred as a result of the change.

There is, however, every reason to expect that an increase in efficiency sufficient to at least offset this estimated increase in cost would follow the adoption of the 8-hour system. As a basis for this statement there is not only the experience in other industries, but in the iron and steel industry there are the statements of the British blast-furnace owners and the conclusive results of tests of the 8-hour system in American steel plants. These tests have shown that there is not only no increase in the cost of production, but that where the success of the process can be readily affected by the attention and physical condition of the employees the quality of the product has been greatly improved as a result of the shorter working hours and numerous immediate economies have been effected which more than compensate for the cost of the change. (Pp. 18-19.)

As, however, it is impossible to foretell with any accuracy the influence of shorter hours on efficiency, the following estimates as to the cost of introducing the 8-hour day are made on the assumption that efficiency would not be affected by the change. . . .

Maximum Cost of Change to the 8-hour Day.

This estimate of the maximum cost of introducing the 8-hour system is based on the assumption that in making the change wages are so readjusted that the workmen would receive the same amount for working 8 hours that they now receive for 12 hours. . . .

Increases in Rates of Wages Per Hour, Cost of Production, and Selling Price Which Would Be Required to Introduce the 8-Hour System in the Blast Furnaces, on the Basis that Each Workman in Continuous Processes Earned the Same Amount for 8-Hours' Work that He Now Receives for 12 Hours and that Productive Efficiency Was Unchanged.

	Amount under 12-hour system	Amount under 8-hour system	Required increase Amount	Required increase Per cent.
Average hourly earnings..........	$ 0.172	$ 0.242	$0.07	40.6
Labor cost of production per ton	.770	1.080	.31	40.6
Total cost of production per ton	12.100	12.410	.31	2.6
Average selling price per ton....	18.000	18.470	.47	2.6

Increases in Rates of Wages Per Hour, Cost of Production, and Selling Price Necessary to Introduce the 8-Hour System with Certain Other Changes in Hours in Blast Furnaces, Steel Works, and Rolling Mills, on the Basis that Each Workman in Continuous Processes Earned the Same Amount for 8 Hours' Work that He Now Receives for 12 Hours and that Productive Efficiency Was Unchanged.

	Amount under 12-hour system	Amount under 8-hour system	Required increase Amount	Required increase Per cent.
Average hourly earnings..............	$ 0.22	$ 0.30	$0.08	34.7
Labor cost of production per ton	4.22	5.68	1.46	34.7
Total cost of production per ton	24.79	26.25	1.46	6.0
Average selling price per ton......	34.24	36.29	2.05	6.0

Probable Cost of Change to the 8-hour Day.

In the preceding statements have been presented the maximum increases which could be reasonably supposed to follow the introduction of the 8-hour system in the industry. It seems certain, however, that the steel manufacturers would not offer nor would the employees demand the same earnings for an 8-hour day that they now receive for working 12 hours . . . Most of the workmen interviewed said that while they would not be able to accept 8 hours' work at their present hourly rates, they would gladly secure an 8-hour day if they were given the equivalent of 10-hours' pay at the prevailing rates per hour. This would mean that the hourly rates must be increased 25 per cent. . . .

It seems fair, therefore, to accept as a basis of estimate for determining the probable cost of introducing the 8-hour day into the industry generally that the hourly rates of men now working 12 hours per day would have to be increased approximately 25 per cent. and that the rates of other workmen whose hours would be changed would be increased proportionately. . . .

Increases in Rates of Wages Per Hour, Cost of Production, and Selling Price Necessary to Introduce the 8-Hour System in the Blast Furnaces, on the Basis that Each Workman in Continuous Processes Earned the Same Amount for 8-Hours' Work that He Now Receives for 10 Hours and that Productive Efficiency Was Unchanged.

	Amount under 12-hour system	Amount under 8-hour system	Required increase Amount	Required increase Per cent.
Average hourly earnings....	$ 0.172	$ 0.207	$0.035	20.3
Labor cost of production per ton	.770	.935	.165	20.3
Total cost of production per ton	12.100	12.265	.165	1.3
Average selling price per ton......	18.000	18.235	.235	1.3

Increases in Rates of Wages Per Hour, Cost of Production, and Selling Price Necessary to Introduce the 8-Hour System in the Blast Furnaces, Steel Works, and Rolling Mills, on the Basis that Each Workman in Continuous Processes Earned the Same Amount for 8 Hours' Work that He Now Receives for 10 Hours and that Productive Efficiency Was Unchanged.

	Amount under 12-hour system	Amount under 8-hour system	Required increase Amount	Required increase Per cent.
Average hourly earnings..............	$ 0.22	$ 0.26	$0.04	17.4
Labor cost of production per ton	4.22	4.95	.73	17.4
Total cost of production per ton	24.79	25.52	.73	3.0
Average selling price per ton......	34.24	35.27	1.03	3.0

(Pp. 176 ff.)

Short Hours and Cost of Production.—United States

The Economy of High Wages. Jacob Schoenhof. *New York and London. Putnam, 1892.*

The length of the working-day is an index of the productive ability of a nation. The application of the most improved methods to production (implying a better paid and better conditioned laborer) makes a shortening of hours practicable and even necessary, because of both the physiological fact stated above and the economic necessity. Production must go hand in hand with consumption. If, by the too rapid introduction of labor-saving devices, production runs ahead of demand, it must adapt itself to the altered conditions by shortening the working time. . . . The great advances made in the economy of production in the highest developed industrial states have led directly to the short working day, to the material, intellectual, and political advancement of the labor[illegible] hence are the cheering and elevating signs of a great and bright future. (Pp. 394-395.)

The question of the relation of labor to the cost of production resolves itself entirely to one of equipment. Whether labor be equipped with all the improvements and inventions or not, whether labor be well conditioned and fed, or underpaid and overworked, decides the contest, not the relative difference in day wages. It is the output after all that makes the price of a commodity. (P. 102.)

Getting a Living. The Problem of Wealth and Poverty—of Profits, Wages and Trade Unionism. George L. Bolen. *New York and London. The Macmillan Company. 1903.*

Wages have not varied according to the length of the work day. Generally they have been highest where the day was shortest. Wages depend less upon time than upon skill and speed, upon the difficulty of doing the work, and upon the machinery equipment for turning out a large product value. (Pp. 405-406.)

In view of these facts it may be concluded with some

certainty that the lowest cost of product, reaching, with the price lowering involved, the greatest aggregate of sales, and affording the largest total of net proceeds to divide with workmen in wages—is obtained in the longest work day through which the best average speed of continuous labor can be kept up without exhaustion to the close of the last hour. . . . Making the day include all these hours the workman of average strength can bear without injury, reduces interest on capital, and other fixed charges, to the lowest point per yard of product that does not increase other expenses. (P. 409.)

American Labor Association Review. March, 1914. Working Hours in Continuous Industries. WM. C. REDFIELD, *Secretary of Commerce.*

It is well to enumerate briefly the advantages of the eight-hour system.

In the first place, all the records of actual experiment to which I have had access, show that it promotes efficiency and actually gives a lower cost of production and a better quality of work than the twelve-hour system, in spite of the higher immediate wage cost. This arises from the fact that under the shorter schedule of hours the men work not only harder and faster, but also more accurately so that the saving in material alone in some cases has more than paid the extra wage bill.

Second, as a result of the better condition the men are more regular, which in turn increases their efficiency.

Third, the eight-hour system is very flexible. (P. 112.)

Annals of the American Academy of Political and Social Science. Vol. LXIII. January, 1916. The Work of the Federal Bureau of Labor Statistics in its Relation to the Business of the Country. ROYAL MEEKER, *United States Commissioner of Labor Statistics.*

The studies made by the Bureau of Labor Statistics also show that shortening the hours of labor has not thus far meant lengthening the labor cost sheet. Quite the contrary result has followed cutting out the seven-day-week, granting the Saturday half-holiday, and nipping off the last hour or half-hour from a long, fatiguing day. Yet in the face of this experience in the best factories, many employers run their businesses as if profits depended upon driving their employees at the maximum speed for the maximum number of hours per week. (P. 267.)

The Eight Hour Day. Sidney Webb *and* Harold Cox. *London, Walter Scott, 1891. Appendix II. Letters, etc., received from firms which have already adopted an Eight Hours' Day. From Burroughs, Wellcome & Co., Importers, Exporters and Manufacturing Chemists, Snow Hill Building, London, E. C. 16th December, 1890.*

Replying to your inquiries of the 11th inst., regarding our experience with the Eight-Hour System, we beg to say that our impressions are:

First.—We believe the amount of work produced in a week is very nearly, if not quite, as great as when we were working nine hours a day.

Second.—We think that the cost of production is not materially increased.

Third.—At first there was a considerable amount of overtime work. . . . Now, however, we have been able to avoid overtime work almost entirely.

Fourth.—Wages. We are glad to have been able both to reduce the hours of work and to increase the amount of wages at the same time. Of course, in the first instance, this was money out of pocket and a loss to us, but it is our opinion that in the long run the loss will be made good to us on account of the hearty and friendly interest which all our employés manifest in our business. (Pp. 255-256.)

British Sessional Papers. Vol. XXXVI. 1892. Part I. Royal Commission on Labour.

Testimony of Mr. J. Keir Hardie, Ayrshire Miners' Union.

12,876. . . . I am speaking as a man with a practical knowledge of mining in all its phases, and knowing what does tend and what does not tend to increase the cost of production, and the eight hours day so far as Scotland is concerned, would not add to the cost of production.

Testimony of Mr. Patrick Walls, National Association of Blast Furnacemen (Cumberland and North Lancashire District.)

14,425. . . . Another reason why it did not cost very much more to place the men on the eight hours was that the men can work proportionately harder in the eight hours than they could in the twelve hours. It is well understood that when a man is kept at work continuously for twelve hours, and is working eighty-four hours a week instead of fifty-six he can not do as much work proportionately in each hour of the longer time. Consequently the employers were able to do with less men per shift on the eight hours shift than they formerly required on the twelve hours, and when it takes about 2s. 3d. in labor at the present time to produce a ton of pig-iron it formerly took about 2s. It has scarcely made 3d. a ton difference.

14,431. . . . Our men receive practically the same wages, if not more, taking the average day's wages, than the men in other districts do receive for twelve hours.

A Shorter Working Day. R. A. Hadfield, *of Hadfield's Steel Foundry Company, Sheffield, and* H. de B. Gibbins. *London, Methuen & Company, 1892.*

. . . In speaking of the value of overtime it must not be forgotten that men generally work then under bad supervision. Probably overtime from five to seven is only worth some 80 per cent. of the normal, which with the time and a quarter charges equals an increase in cost to the employer of some 50 per cent. over the normal. When time and a half rates are in force the cost is probably 70 to 80 per cent. in excess of the normal, to say nothing of the inferior quality of the work. In other words, if overtime is of regular occurrence, it would really pay to increase the plant and employ more men, which is what the workers wish. (P. 164.)

An eight hours day, with overtime reduced as much as conveniently possible, would, for many reasons, possibly be found to act as ballast, being a steadying rather than a disturbing element. Once get employers by actual experience to see the matter in this light, and probably they would benefit as well as the workmen. (P. 118.)

(Messrs. S. H. Johnson and Co., of the Engineering Works, Carpenter's Road, Stratford, England, stated in reply to questions):

1.—"They found no increase in cost of production, but on the contrary a decrease.

2.—"It is much appreciated by the men, their zeal and efforts show it has given the greatest satisfaction.

3.—"*We have a more intelligent set of men.*

4.—"There are many incidental savings by shorter hours.

5.—"We get out more work.

6.—"Also more time being afforded to the men and lads to improve themselves, they attend technical classes in the evening. Messrs. Johnson considers that the workers secure a good two hours extra for recreation and improvement.

7.—"The cost of production is not increased, and from our experience of Continental workmen we do not think they, working longer hours, could hold their own with our men working shorter ones."

Note.—At this time they had been having the eight-hour day 3½ years. (P. 140.)

Ibid. Letter from Mr. William Allan. William Allan and Co.

"Scotia Engine Works, Sunderland,
"February 26th, 1892.

"Dear Sir:

"Your favor received, and I beg to reply to queries seriatim:

1. "So far as I can judge from the books and wages bill, I believe the cost of production will be less than formerly.

2. "The men are all in favour of the change and exhibit what I would call a healthier tone, so much so that we have had no 'sleepers in' since the new system was adopted.

3 and 4. "In fact the change is so much appreciated by all that the results will be in favor of an employer. The foremen are all at their posts regularly so that the work goes on briskly.

5. "Paradoxical as it may seem, *I get fully more work* out than formerly; in fact I am surprised at how the work is going ahead, having believed—like so many employers—that there would be a corresponding decrease in output. *This is a fallacy,* as the human machine when in good order and contented can do more work than when otherwise.

6. "Foreign competition is a 'bogie.' Long hours do not mean greater output or lessened cost, else we would be importing coals from Germany, etc. In some goods, such as watches, clocks, hurdygurdies, etc., etc., it may affect us, but in our staple industries, never—for, while they have conscription abroad, our young fellows are getting inured to the hammer and chisel instead of the rifle, so we thereby produce better workers.

"I feel sure all adopting the eight hours system will be in pocket by the change.

"I have given you my views from results and observations and have no reason whatever to regret the change. To me it is really astonishing how my old views are demolished and fears dissipated by the new order of things.

"Yours truly,
"WILLIAM ALLAN."

Since writing the above Mr. Allan has (June, 1892) advanced the wages of his workmen 5 per cent. without being asked. This is a very practical proof of how well a shorter day pays him. (Pp. 144-145.)

Ibid. Letter from Messrs. Short Bros., Shipbuilders of Sunderland.

"Sunderland, Feb. 26th, 1892.

"GENTLEMEN:

"In reply to yours of the 25th inst., we have as you know only worked on the eight hours since the 4th January, but from our short experience I can answer your first question by saying we are satisfied it will *not* increase the cost of production.

2. "The men appreciate the change.

5. "We have every reason to believe that our production will be *more.*

7. "My opinion is the long hours which the foreigner works destroy his chance of competing with us in manufacture. Men become dawdlers if compelled to work longer than their physical strength will allow. I believe we can produce at less cost in eight hours than the foreigner (or Englishman) can in *twelve* hours.

"I may say *last week* our *wages bill was more* than any week during the last year, showing that our men were working better and more regularly.

"Yours faithfully,
"JOHN Y. SHORT."
(Pp. 145-146.)

The Eight Hours Day. Report on a Year's Work with a Forty-Eight Hours Week in the Salford Iron Works, Manchester. (Mather and Platt, Ltd.) WILLIAM MATHER, M. P. *Manchester, Guardian Printing Works, 1894. Statistical Results.*

We commenced the 48 hours system on Monday, February 20th, 1893; but, for convenience, the period of the experiment is comprised in the twelve months commencing March 1st and terminating February 28th, 1894.

Wages Cost.—The figures we have taken as the standard with which to compare results are the averages per year of the preceding six years, during the earlier portion of which the number of hours worked per week was 54, and 53 hours per week during the later portion.

The production during the two periods has been similar in character, and the turnover in the trial year has approximated to the average of the six years so closely as to be practically the same. As regards quantity of production, there was actually a larger output in the trial year; but owing to the prices in that year being considerably lower than in the six preceding years, the turnover did not increase with the amount of production. This fact must be borne in mind in studying the following statement as to the cost of wages.

On making up the books, we found that comparing the ratio of wages to turnover in the trial year with the ratio of wages to turnover in the six preceding years, there was an increase of 0.4 per cent. in the former. But as in the trial year selling prices were considerably lower, the actual quantity produced, as represented by the equal turnover of that year, was considerably larger than in the six preceding years; therefore the ratio of the cost of wages to the turnover in that year must have been proportionately less. Had prices ruled the same, the turnover in the trial year would have been greater, and the wages cost, instead of showing an increase of 0.4 per cent., would have shown a decided decrease.

We have given no credit for this fact to the side of the trial year, but show the actual result as given on the comparison we have instituted, viz., *an increase of 0.4 per cent.* in the ratio of the wages cost to the turnover.

This, however, does not exhaust the changes made by the reduction of the hours. . . . We have found a marked economy in gas and electric lighting, wear and tear of machinery, engines, gearing, etc., fuel and lubricants, and miscellaneous stores. On the other hand, we have examined the increased fixed charges due to interest of plant and machinery, rent and taxes, permanent staff on fixed salaries being employed 5 hours less per week.

The balance of debtor and creditor account on these expenses is unmistakably in favor of the trial year. The credit from these items to be carried to the trial year is an amount *equal* to 0.4 per cent. on the net amount of the year's turnover. Thus, by a remarkable coincidence, *a saving of 0.4 per cent.* is secured as a direct consequence of the shorter hours, which counterbalances the debit of 0.4 per cent. in the increased wages cost.

Lost time.—The improvement in respect to lost time is very marked. The proportion of "time lost without leave" to the total time worked averaged in the 53 hours period 2.46 per cent., whereas in the 48 hours period it is only 0.46 per cent. (Pp. 17-18.)

The chief points of interest arising out of the comparison made between the two periods for wages-cost of work produced may be thus epitomised:

	In favour of 48 hours.	Against 48 hours.
Comparison of wages to turnover, made simply on the net value of production and the wages thereupon....	....	0.4%
Balance of account for "wear and tear," fuel, &c., as against increased cost per hour worked, for fixed charges, which must be credited to wages account	0.4%	....
Proportion of "lost time" to total time..............................	.2%	....
Difference in the amount of piece-work production as shown by piece-work balances, in 3 periods of the year:		
1st period	....	1.76%
2nd period	....	1.58%
3rd period	....	0.78%
Difference of piece-workers' earnings after equalising prices for fair comparison with preceding years for the whole trial year..	....	0.5%

It will be clear from these figures that the wages-cost of production in the forty-eight hours system remains the same as it was under the fifty-three hours system, when the new system is credited with the saving in consumables, wear and tear, fuel, etc., which is the direct consequence of the change without diminishing the output of the Works.

The piece-workers have lost slightly on the year, but the later months show this loss to be a vanishing quantity. (P. 20.)

Even after a few months of its workings, I felt so assured of the mutual benefits accruing both to Employers and Employed from our trial, that I felt it to be a matter of public duty to apprise the heads of the Government Departments—the War Office, the Admiralty, and the Post Office—of the advantages that would be derived by the adoption in them of the forty-eight hours week.

The Secretary of State for War, Mr. Campbell-Bannerman, the First Lord of the Admiralty, Earl Spencer, and the Postmaster General, Mr. Arnold Morley, respectively invited me to meet the chiefs of their construction departments from the Woolwich Arsenal Works, the Dockyards, and the Post Office, to give the results of the trial at the Salford Iron Works, and to state my reasons for advising the immediate adoption of the 48-hours week in their departments.

These responsible chiefs of important Government departments, in which many thousands of men are employed in the mechanical trades, naturally required convincing proofs that they would be justified in adopting the 48 hours week on economic grounds, and on those grounds alone. They approached the subject at our interview with open minds, but with serious doubts as to the possibility of accepting the advice I ventured to offer, that they should at once adopt the new system. After the conferences only a few weeks elapsed before the Woolwich authorities heartily adopted the 48 hours week, and since then the Dockyard authorities have announced their determination to do the same. (P. 21.)

Great Britain. Board of Trade Labour Gazette, July, 1905. Eight-Hour Day in Government Workshops.

In 1894 the hours of labor of about 43,000 work-people in certain Government factories and workshops were reduced on an average of 48 per week. . . .

The reduced hours affected 18,641 work-people in 1894, whose working time was reduced 5¾ hours per week on the average. . . .

When the 48 hours week was first adopted it was anticipated that there would be a saving of time in stopping and re-starting work at the breakfast hour, work not beginning till after breakfast under the new system, and also a saving of light and fuel.

It was also expected that a later hour of starting work would ensure greater regularity of attendance, that there would be an improvement in the physical condition of the men and an increase in their power of production.

The fact that the reduction in the hours of work had not reduced the output, or increased the cost of it, in private factories in which the experiment had been tried, also led the War Office to assume that the cost of production would not be increased in their workshops.

It is stated that these anticipations have been justified, and that it is clear that no extra cost has been incurred by the public on account of the reduction of hours, nor has the output of work been diminished. On the other hand, the majority of the workmen being on piecework, the average weekly earnings per man have not been sensibly altered, although piecework prices have not been increased. The day workers received an increased hourly rate of pay to make their earnings per week of 48 hours equal to those per week of 54 hours. It was not found necessary to increase the number of day-workers. (P. 196.)

Eight Hours for Work. John Rae. *London and New York, Macmillan & Co., 1894.*

Sir Charles Tennant and Co. (now of St. Rollox Alkali Co.) have been working on the three eight-hour shift system for the last 25 years in the vitriol department of their works on the Tyne and for a shorter period in the same department of their works in Glasgow, and in both cases with such complete satisfaction that they have now decided to extend the system to all the other departments. (P. 78.)

Messrs. Thomas Bushill and Sons are printers as well as bookbinders in Coventry, and when they reduced their hours in 1892 from 54 to 50 a week—not quite to the eight-hour limit, but close on it—they experienced no diminution of production whatever. Mr. Bushill informs me by letter that now, after eighteen months' trial, the results continue to be as favorable as at first, and that though the old rate of wages has been maintained there has never been any increase in the cost of production. (Pp. 84-85.)

Report of the Special Commission on Hours of Labour in Continuous Industries to the Seventh Delegates' Meeting of the International Association for Labour Legislation. Zurich, 1912. London, The Pioneer Press, Ltd., July, 1912.

Mr. Dyson (Secretary of the Amalgamated Society of Paper Makers). Only one paper mill is at present known to be working eight-hour shifts, starting at 12 midnight on Sunday and ceasing at 12 o'clock on Saturday night, each shift working 48 hours per week. (Pp. 4-5.)

Mr. Dyson certified that after reducing the working hours in one paper mill where he was employed from 12 to 8 on each shift, it was found possible to increase the speed of the machines gradually to such an extent as to make (within nine months) the weekly wages equal to what they were before with the same rates. (P. 10.)

Conditions in British Iron and Steel Works. A Speech delivered to the Special Commission on Hours of Labor, International Association for Labor Legislation, June 11th, 1912. ALDERMAN P. WALLS.

The question of cost seems to be a great obstacle, but when the matter is fully considered this disappears. A man can do more work per hour when working eight hours than when working twelve hours. He is more alert and physically fit.

Again, the furnaces benefit by being regularly filled. There is an improvement both in quantity and quality. I venture to assert that after a full experience of the eight-hour system no employer would return to the twelve hours. There has always been some additional cost at the outset, but it has been compensated for later on.

Jahresberichte der Gewerbe-Aufsichtsbeamten und Bergbehörden für das Jahr 1904. Bd. I. Preussen. [Reports of the (German) Factory and Mine Inspectors for 1904. Vol. I. Prussia.] Berlin, Decker, 1905.

The majority of employers are becoming more and more convinced that, when overtime is worked regularly, output does not increase in proportion to the lengthened hours of work and additional wages. On the contrary, it tends to decrease gradually so that finally overtime becomes too expensive to be worth while. (P. 241.)

Instituts Solvay. Travaux de l'Institut de Sociologie [Sociological Publication of the Solvay Institute.] Une Expérience Industrielle de Reduction de la Journée de Travail. Par L. G. FROMONT *avec une Préface de* E. MAHAIM. *[An Industrial Experiment in the Reduction of Hours of Labor.* L. G. FROMONT *with Preface by* E. MAHAIM.] *Brussels, Misch et Thron, 1906.*

After having brought out both the social and moral advantages of the eight hour day, it remains for us to establish its industrial advantages. The cost of production has in its turn undergone improvement, and it is easy to gather from the figures quoted above what the importance of this may be.

In all costs, we can distinguish between two distinct kinds of charges, that is, the fixed daily overhead expenses irrespective of the amount of output; and the variable charges which are dependent upon and generally proportionate to the amount of output. (P. 87-88.)

The new cost of production amounted to 80 per cent. of the old cost; that is to say, the total fall in cost of production was 20 per cent. of the original cost. (P. 93-94.)

5. Long Hours Reduce Efficiency and Thus Result in Inferior Output.

With excessive hours of labor, the efficiency of the workers is so much reduced that output deteriorates both in quantity and quality. Overfatigue results in "spoiled work" which must often be done over again the next day. The early belief that profits were dependent on the last hours of the working day has long been proved a fallacy. On the contrary, the output of the last hours shows a steady and marked decline.

American Labor Legislation Review, March, 1914. Working Hours in Continuous Industries. Work Periods in Continuous Day and Night Occupations. Basil M. Manly, *United States Bureau of Labor.*

There is reason to believe that experience will show the twelve-hour day to be one of the costliest things in industry, not only in its direct effects as a cause of accidents, but in its direct effects as a prime cause of inefficiency and waste. (P. 114.)

Report of the Massachusetts Bureau of Statistics of Labor, 1871.

The operatives vary in perfectness and productiveness as the day progresses; and if there should be a reduction to ten hours there would not be a loss of one-eleventh of the product. . . . I think it will be found that much of the cloth made during the eleventh hour is of poorer quality than the rest, and that the necessity of looking it over the next day and fixing it all right lessens the product of that next day. . . . I certainly believe that the productive capacity of a set of work-people may be lessened by increasing the hours of their daily work. The question is not legitimately one of arithmetic, nor can it be settled by argument about one-eleventh less or one-tenth more. It is a question to be settled by actual results on long-continued trial. (Pages 499-500.)

Report of the Chief of Massachusetts District Police for the Year Ending December 31, 1885.

It must of course be admitted, that there is a limit to human endurance. If one labors twelve hours a day, it cannot be maintained that he will do as much work in the last two hours, nor do it as well, as in any previous two hours of the same day. Jaded by excessive toil, the brain becomes sluggish and the fingers clumsy. It is not an assumption, but an acknowledged fact that under the improved condition resulting from shortening the number of hours of labor, operatives produce in the shorter period at least the same amount of work; and many manufacturers admit that in the last two hours in any given day under the old system, work so much inferior was produced, that what was gained in quantity was lost in quality. The shortening of the number of hours of labor, if the time thus gained for leisure is used for proper purposes, becomes one of the best means for the elevation of the people thus affected. (Pp. 19-20.)

The Economy of High Wages. Jacob Schoenhof. *New York and London. Putnam, 1892.*

Once recognize the fact that, after all, man is the great wealth-producing machine, the source of all wealth, then all our efforts will be directed to the elevation of this machine to the highest potentiality.

What is labor? Physical and muscular exertion. It becomes economically valuable by intellectual guidance. . . . But to this we must add the further and most important fact, that labor, be it ever so intelligently conducted, will always remain physical exertion. This is to say that labor is an expenditure of vital force. Unless this is replaced by wholesome nutrition (air, light, sanitation, and even cheerful surroundings, are part of wholesome nutrition), the frame will work itself out, and labor will become economically of smaller and smaller value.

Another fact of vital importance is the time during which the human frame is capable of its best exertion. In going over the contentions, not of fifty years ago, but of the present day, we find the assertion, by the defenders of long hours in factories, that the last hour is the one that gives all the profit. This is not borne out by the facts. It is found by all who employ machinery that the work of the last hour is the least satisfactory, and the work of the first hour the best and most copious. I frequently found that after working extra hours many of my help came late the next morning or stayed away a day; others showed a lack of spirits and less efficiency. The spirit was wanting, the frame was tired. I gave it up after repeated experiments, and reaped better results with regular hours and premiums for any quantity beyond the daily averages of output. (Pp. 392-393.)

Getting a Living. The Problem of Wealth and Poverty, Profits, Wages and Trades Unionism. George Lewis Bolen. *New York, Macmillan, 1903.*

Chap. 15. Shorter Workday.

If in the tenth hour as much work has been done as the average for the previous nine hours, a reduction of time to nine hours per day, at the same pay, would be an increase of wages by eleven and one-ninth per cent., unless the extra hour of rest increased the hourly product. But in any work not fixed in speed by steadily running machinery, less is done in the tenth hour, by reason of weariness, than in other hours; and the work of the last hour, like overtime work at night, weakens a person for the next day. It is this weariness that causes accidents to occur two or three times as frequently in the last hour as in other hours—a fact proved by European statistics. With the steady machinery, too, weariness, as a rule, either lowers the quality of the work done, or by frequent stoppage lessens its amount—often causing both these losses. (Pp. 407-408.)

Long Hours Lead to Inferior Output.—United States

Report of the Nebraska Bureau of Labor and Industrial Statistics. 1907-1908.

Of his experience . . . one manufacturer . . . says: "When the business first came under my control, the men were working a nominal nine-hour day. But the real day was much longer. Recourse was had to overtime on the slightest provocation, and during the months of October and November overtime was the daily rule. In those months we have to get ready our goods for Christmas consumption, and the men used to be at work night after night till 8 or 9 o'clock. I have known them to leave the factory as late as 11 o'clock. When I complained of the system I was told that it was absolutely necessary; that the work could not be gotten through otherwise. However, I knew that it was bad for myself as well as for the men. A man who has done a reasonable day's work is not fit to give good work at night, and if he makes the attempt his work next morning suffers. So I put my foot down and stopped the practice almost entirely." (P. 189.)

Bulletin of the United States Bureau of Labor Statistics. Number 118. April, 1913.

Ten-Hour Maximum Working-Day for Women and Young Persons.

It has not infrequently been contended that the effect of shorter working time in increasing output is not to be found in Oriental countries, but this doubt has recently been removed. In three factories in Calcutta electric light was introduced in 1907, and the number of hours worked, which was formerly 11½ to 13½, was increased to 14½. This led to a decrease of output. The productivity of these factories per hour was greater in 1906 than in 1907. The amount of work performed is shown in the table following:

Long Hours Lead to Inferior Output.—Great Britain

DIFFERENCE IN PRODUCTIVITY BETWEEN SHORT HOURS IN 1906 AND LONG HOURS IN 1907.

Hours per day	Per cent. of production in 1906 over 1907 in: Factory No. 1	Factory No. 2	Factory No. 3
Production in:			
13½ hours' work over 14½ hours' work........	8.87	15.85	4.49
13¼ hours' work over 14½ hours' work........	17.32	26.54	5.04
13 hours' work over 14½ hours' work........	9.14	22.19	4.56
12½ hours' work over 14½ hours' work........	....	....	10.96
12¼ hours' work over 14½ hours' work........	12.08	19.21	....
12 hours' work over 14½ hours' work........	10.09	15.65	5.68
11½ hours' work over 14½ hours' work........	4.61	9.36	17.17

(P. 46.)

British Sessional Papers. Vol. XIII. 1843. Children's Employment Commission. JOHN LAWSON KENNEDY, ESQ., *Lancashire.*

408. . . . Practically it has been found that the attention of the workman, on which the application of his skill and the productiveness of the machine under his care depend, cannot be sustained beyond a certain daily period. From this cause, namely, the impossibility of keeping up the attention, care, and skill of the workman in applying the machinery, night work has been generally abandoned in the cotton-spinning trade; and it is, moreover, an important fact that those establishments in this district which resorted systematically to night work have almost without exception become bankrupt. I have been assured by printers themselves that the rule as to the unprofitableness of long hours of work for long continued periods is equally applicable to the (calico-print) trade. I have been favoured by an influential house in the print trade with an inspection of those books which show the rates of production in their roller printing machines during a period of 4 months when they worked unusually long hours, *viz., 15 hours a day,* under a peculiar stress of business. The machines never stopped from morning till night and there was no intermission at the dinner hour. From the beginning of the first month to the middle of the second the production kept

very steady, scarcely varying from week to week, with a comparatively low proportion of spoiled work, towards the end of the second month a gradual decrease in the proportion of the machines was perceptible, attended by increased proportion of spoiled work. Towards the end of the third month, and throughout the fourth, the production of the machines arrived at their minimum, and the proportion of spoiled work its maximum. The proportion of spoiled work from the beginning of the first to the end of the fourth month actually doubled itself, whilst the average production of the machines decreased from 100 to 90 per cent. during the same time. In fact the amount of spoiled work increased to such an alarming degree that the parties referred to felt themselves compelled to shorten the hours of labour to avoid loss, and as soon as the alteration was made the amount of spoiled work sunk to its former level. The men were paid extra wages for their extra exertions, and there was no intention or motive on their parts to produce this result. It is, I am informed, the general experience of this branch of trade that under whatever circumstances night work is tried the produce is distinguished by a larger share than ordinary of spoiled work. (P. 72.)

Hansard's Parliamentary Debates. Vol. 73. 1844.

Mr. Vernon Smith:

But he would venture to say, that though the diminution of time was one-sixth, the diminution of profitable labour would be much less because the last 2 hours would be the least efficient owing to the exhaustion caused by the previous 10 hours of labour. But he could not think that the commerce of this country was really in so ticklish, hazardous and perilous a state, as to depend upon so small an amount, more or less, of additional labour. . . . If the proposed diminution of labour should induce some evils as regarded our commerce, it appeared to him that the change would be attended, on the other hand, with great advantage to the country. (Pp. 1404-1405.)

Long Hours Lead to Inferior Output.—Great Britain

Hansard's Parliamentary Debates. Vol. 74. 1844. Letter in Bolton Free Press (April, 1844).

"There is also another consideration for employers, namely, that in a day's work of 12 hours, the last hour by reason of the exhaustion and listlessness of the workers, is the least productive in quantity, and the least satisfactory in quality." (P. 911.)

"The probability is, that the twelfth hour produces more spoiled work than any other 2 hours of the day." (P. 911.)

Hansard's Parliamentary Debates. Vol. 92. 1847.

The Earl of Ellesmere:

. . . Deductions are made, when the article is brought in by the operative, for waste and spoil. . . . From such information as I can obtain, it is my firm belief that nine tenths of that spoiled will arise in the last weary hour of the operatives' present average toil. I have never met with any man of any class, conversant with the subject, who has not laid much stress on this circumstance. (P. 898.)

The Bishop of Oxford:

Could they for a moment conceive, that by limiting the labour of the factory worker to 10 hours a day instead of 12, they would sweep away all the manufacturers of the country, and drive them abroad? . . . Could their Lordships believe that upon the last 2 hours' labour . . . tending upon that machinery after long, unceasing, and heart-consuming attention, when nature almost refused to perform her functions—could their Lordships believe that upon those 2 last hours depended all the profits and accumulations of the manufacturers? He believed that the work done in those 2 last hours was infinitely inferior in quality to that which was done in any other portion of the day. It was demanding work when nature refused the power of working. (Pp. 939-940.)

British Sessional Papers. Vol. XXIX-XXX. 1876. Factories and Workshops Acts Commission.

Witness, A Manufacturer. Vol. XXX.

10,947. . . . I think there is very little advantage in overtime, people are worn out at night and do not work with the same vigor in the morning. (P. 535.)

British Sessional Papers. Vol. XXIII. 1877. Reports of Inspectors of Factories.

. . . There was such a brisk demand for bricks, that they wanted to increase their production, and determined to work half an hour overtime 3 nights a week. After trying it some little time they found the number of bricks turned off decreased, that on mornings succeeding the days on which they worked half an hour after the usual time for ceasing work the men invariably came late, and worked less time and less assiduously than when they worked regularly, and so they returned to regular hours. (P. 15.)

A Shorter Working Day. R. A. HADFIELD *of Hadfield's Steel Foundry Co., Sheffield, and* H. DE B. GIBBINS, *London, Methuen & Co. 1892.*

Moreover, even from an employer's point of view, overtime and long hours are often even in the ordinary way not economical. . . .

Let the unsolicited testimony of one of the cleverest and best of our shipbuilding engineers in this country speak for itself. The managing director of one of the largest shipbuilding firms in the North of England (Earles), which employs a capital of some half million sterling, and has 3,000 or 4,000 hands, stated publicly, "that he considered overtime was the curse of the trade." This is a plain matter-of-fact statement, and most masters who know anything about cost of work must admit that it is true. (P. 162.)

Long Hours Lead to Inferior Output.—Great Britain

British Sessional Papers. Vol. XXI. 1894. Report of the Chief Inspector of Factories and Workshops.

Some employers, too, hold the opinion that in proportion as work-people suffer in health their work suffers in execution, and that in addition to this consideration has to be reckoned that of an extra expenditure in gas, which considerably weakens an already doubtful advantage. (P. 11.)

It is not likely that work done during these . . . hours of overtime, or on days following overtime, will equal either in quantity or quality that done when regular hours only are worked. (P. 15.)

In connection with overtime I think that very often the occupiers and managers of works object to it while they take advantage of the privilege. They naturally recognize that after a spurt comes reaction and that late hours tell against good work the next day. (P. 301.)

Eight Hours for Work. John Rae. *London, Macmillan, 1894.*

But for the last 60 years we have been slowly learning the lesson that all this successive prolongation of working hours, which was near eating the heart out of the labouring manhood of England, was also, from the standpoint of the manufacturers' own interest, a grave pecuniary mistake. In their haste to be repaid their expenditure on machinery, the manufacturers were really wearing down the most precious machine they had got —their great *machine mère,* as Blanqui called it, on which the success of all the rest depended. They found that with this flesh and blood machine an hour's more running in the day did not mean an hour's more product in the day, but that really, after a certain limit, an extra hour of repose has much higher productive value than an extra hour of work. . . . A French manufacturer once said to Guizot: "We used to say it was the last hour that gave us our profit, but we have now learnt it was the last hour that ate up our profit," and though we still hear much fright expressed about the competition of the pauper and long hour labour of other countries, we are coming more and more to perceive that Mr. Mundella is probably right in saying it is really their long hours that save us from their competition, because their long hours impair the personal efficiency of their labour and the competition between the nations is growing every day more and more to be mainly a competition in personal efficiency. (Pp. 11-12.)

To all these diverse economies of time we have still to add the saving of the time spent in repairing spoiled work, caused through excessive hours, and of the time sometimes wilfully wasted through ill-feeling arising from the same source. Mr. Thomasson, of Bolton, we are told by Lord Shaftesbury, used to say there was more spoiled work done in the last hour of the twelve-hours' day than in any other two hours; and a manager said to Mr. Horner that it generally took the first hour of the day to put to rights the things that had been done wrong in the last hour of the preceding day. The mere saving of materials in cases like these is of course very important, for the price of raw material constitutes constantly a larger and larger share of the value of commodities, as compared with the price of labour, and a little less waste of raw materials every day will soon tell on the profitableness of the business. When we add to it the saving of gas and fuel, and in the yearly expenditure on repairs of machinery, arising from the greater care which employers admit is bestowed on the machinery by the men under a short-hour system, the whole economy amounts to a very considerable gain. But at present I am speaking merely of the saving of effective working time, and the time wasted in avoidable repairs of bad work is one item worthy of attention.

Then think of the time intentionally wasted. Mr. Spill, an India-rubber manufacturer, informed the Children's Employment Commission that he found working overtime extremely unprofitable, because his men used to loiter over their work in the regular hours in order to get better pay for it by doing it during overtime. (Pp. 121-122.)

Long Hours Lead to Inferior Output.—Great Britain

Hours and Wages in Relation to Production. LUJO BRENTANO. *Translated by* MRS. WM. ARNOLD. *London, Sonnenschein, 1894.*

Before the passing of the Ten Hours Act, individual manufacturers who were agitating for that law had set on foot experiments in their factories, with the view of testing the assertion that the lowering of the working day from 12 to 10 hours would ruin the cotton industry. These cases made it quite clear that the question was not merely the arithmetical one,—if 12 hours produce *x*, what will 10 produce? It was found that the work done in the last two hours was so small that in the experimental shortening of the working day from 12 to 10 hours the output was not one-sixth but only one-twelfth less than formerly. In addition to this, it was found that just in those last two hours a great deal of material was spoiled by the wearied and therefore careless operatives. When, therefore, the Ten Hours Act was actually passed,—it became generally apparent that, as Ernest von Plener said in his work on factory legislation, "the mere lengthening of the working day of a workman was not equivalent to the increase of his productive capacity; the operatives, especially the younger ones, no longer exhausted by excessive bodily effort, produced the same amount, and frequently even turned out more in the shorter time." (Pp. 29-30.)

It has been everywhere observed that the workmen in countries where work-time is short produce more than in those where it is long. . . . I myself was told in March, 1890, by an overseer in Mr. Mathers' machine works in Salford, . . . that he had worked in Dresden, England, and America; and he said that the greater efficiency of the American workman was a result of his shorter hours. In the same way he had observed an increase of production in Salford as often as the work-time was shortened; in Saxony, on the other hand, one of the chief reasons of the inferior efficiency of labour was the length of the working-day. . . . And Brassey says of the Russians, that one English workman produces as much in ten hours as two Russians in sixteen.

In complete harmony with the above, it has been further observed that in one and the same country, workers with regularly short hours outstrip those who regularly work longer. (Pp. 32-33.)

At the Congress of Hygiene at Vienna, in 188' .ne Swiss factory inspector, Schuler, reported that in Switzerland experience had shown that the legal reduction of the working day from twelve to eleven hours, *i. e.*, by 8½ per cent., had led, in short, to a falling off in the less well-equipped cotton-spinning factories of only 3 per cent. in production, while in the well-equipped ones it was only 2 to 1½ per cent. In Mühlhausen, Dolfuss reduced his working day from twelve to eleven hours, and promised his operatives that their wages should remain unaltered if they produced the same quantity of work as before. At the end of a month it was seen that not only as much work was done in eleven hours, as formerly in twelve, but 5 per cent. more. (Pp. 35-36.)

Life and Labour of the People in London. Edited by CHARLES BOOTH. *Vol. IX. Pt. III. Ch. VII. The Hours of Labour.* ERNEST AVES, *London and New York, The Macmillan Co., 1897.*

In the case of overtime . . . many employers, while accepting the necessity of occasional spells of it, are strongly opposed to its more prolonged use. They find that "it does not really pay;" that after a very short time "the extra hour you get at night is taken off the next morning; and that you "do not get a *consistent* extra hour for the extra hours, even on machines although they depend less on the physical state of the man." (P. 289.)

British Sessional Papers. Vol. X. 1901. Report of Chief Inspector of Factories.

I hope and believe that employers are at least beginning to recognize that employment of their hands overtime is a short-sighted policy and really bad economy.

Some, I know, think so. There is also a waning inclination, I believe, on the part of the employed to grasp at the chance of making extra wages by overtime. If so, it is, I think, a healthy sign on both sides; health and full efficiency while at work being better than extra wages and long hours, better also in its results to the employer. (P. 158.)

British Sessional Papers. Vol. XII. 1902. Report of Chief Inspector of Factories.

I think employers are beginning to look askance at overtime because it has to be paid for and sometimes at enhanced rates, resulting often in poorer work and less output the following days, and damage to the power of the work-people. (P. 34.)

Report of the 72nd Meeting of the British Association for the Advancement of Science. 1902. London, Murray, 1903. Women's Labour: Second Report of the Committee . . . appointed to investigate the Economic Effect of Legislation Regulating Women's Labour.

. . . The Factory Acts, after being bitterly opposed by the manufacturers, taught them a valuable practical lesson of the bad economy of excessive work. Mr. Baker has recorded a case of a Birmingham firm of button-makers who in 1866 became so dissatisfied with the conditions and mode of life of their work-people that they voluntarily applied the provisions of the Factory Act for textiles (1844) to their own factory and found its advantage. . . . The tendency is evidently in the direction of a still further shortening of hours in some quarters. "There may be a limit to which hours can be profitably reduced, but we haven't found it yet" was one remark. . . . (Pp. 296-297.)

Long Hours Lead to Inferior Output.—Great Britain

Report of the 73rd Meeting of the British Association for the Advancement of Science. 1903. London, Murray, 1904. Women's Labour: Third Report of the Committee . . . appointed to investigate the Economic Effect of Legislation Regulating Women's Labour.

. . There is a general consensus of opinion that overtime is wasteful and expensive, entailing higher wages and fixed expenses for inferior work, and hence its diminution tends to efficiency. Very few, indeed, seriously desire to increase the length of the week's work, and many by their action have shown that it is best kept below the legal maximum. (P. 339.)

Journal of State Medicine. London, October, 1914. Occupational Fatigue. Professor Sir Thomas Oliver. *University of Durham; late Medical Expert Home Office Committee on Dangerous Trades.*

It goes without saying that too long hours are a source of fatigue. In a large factory which I recently visited in the United States, where work of a specialized character is carried on, requiring careful and steady use of the eyes, the manager informed me that when the firm was unusually busy, the men had occasionally worked overtime. When one hour was added to the day's work without a break, the results, after a few days' trial, began to dwindle, also when the men left the factory at the usual time in the evening, went home, had a meal and returned to the factory and did two hours' extra work, not only after a time did production diminish, but on the following days so many mistakes occurred, and so badly was the work done, that in consequence of the amount of the material spoiled and the reduction in the wages which this entailed, it was found not to be worth while working overtime. The strain upon the eyes was more than the men could bear. . . . (P. 344.)

Long Hours Lead to Inferior Output.—Great Britain

Work and Wages: In Continuation of Earl Brassey's 'Work and Wages' and 'Foreign Work and English Wages.' Part III. Social Betterment. SIDNEY J. CHAPMAN, M.A., *London and New York, Longmans, Green and Co., 1914.*

Let us suppose that the following table represents at a given time the value of labour of a given kind per week, in relation to the length of the working day, when all the reactions, as regards, for instance, the efficiency of labour and the provision and arrangement of other agents, have taken place:

Hours per day.	Value of labour per week in shillings.
6	34
7	38
8	40
9	41
10	40
11	39
12	37

The fall in the value of labour, after the working day exceeds nine hours, is due to the fact that diminished weekly productivity more than counteracts the direct effect of the extension of the daily time for work. The diminished weekly productivity may be due to impaired vitality—physical, mental, or moral—or to some extent to irregularity, where that is possible, as in the case of colliers. The damage to productivity may be inflicted directly by excessive work, or it may be indirectly consequent upon it, the prime cause consisting in the use of stimulants, or recourse to unhealthy excitement in periods of leisure, reactions which are only to be expected when work is very exhausting or very dull. The use of leisure affects, of course, mental vitality, culture and character, and it will therefore be observable as a rule that labour which has had its hours reduced will be capable after a time—when the use of leisure has been improved and the improvement has produced its effects—of managing satisfactorily more complicated machinery; and will be generally more responsible and trustworthy, and therefore less in need of continuous watching and directing. (Pp. 239-240) . . .

Suppose the efficiency of labour at the time is that associated with a customary working day of ten hours. The product of the tenth hour would not be zero. The ultimate effect of extending the working day beyond nine hours is loss, in the case put above, not because the product of the last fraction of the ninth hour is zero, but because the product of the last fraction of the ninth hour just equals the ultimate reduction of the product of the other hours that would be occasioned by the lengthening of the working day. (P. 241.)

A rough calculation for a particular industry of the saving in hours which might be effected by the continuous running of plant will not be altogether irrelevant, though actually any further adoption of the shift system would usually take the form of two shifts only, the works being closed for eight hours or so during the night, instead of continuous running. In the industry for which figures have been obtained, interest and depreciation would be reckoned ordinarily at 10 per cent. on the capital—about half for each—while wages would be in the neighbourhood of 12½ per cent. Now, it being assumed provisionally that the depreciation charge varies as the hours worked, that the rate of interest is a constant, that the equipment of the industry remains as before and labour tends neither to leave the industry nor to flood into it, and that other costs of production are not affected, we find that hours could be reduced from ten to eight without any loss of wages, were the continuous running of plant substituted for the ten-hours day. Similarly, it can be shown that two shifts of little more than eight and a half hours each would yield the same wages, on the assumption stated, as the ten-hours day under the single shift system. (Pp. 248-249.)

Without a more general recourse to shift systems, there seems to be little immediate prospect of such additional leisure for the mass of the population. (P. 251.)

Long Hours Lead to Inferior Output.—Great Britain

British Sessional Papers. Report of the Chief Inspector of Factories and Workshops. 1914.

Emergency Overtime.*

. . . With the outbreak of war questions immediately arose as to what amount of latitude ought to be sanctioned. . . . Not only was there extreme pressure in factories engaged in the manufacture of the ordinary munitions of war, untold quantities of clothing of all kinds were required; there was an instant demand for camp equipment. . . . The problem at once arose, how was the situation to be met? On the one hand unrestricted overtime was clearly impossible; it could only result in a serious breakdown of labour; on the other hand the greatest possible output was required to satisfy the country's needs. Where was the line to be drawn? . . . The sole problem now was to determine what the need of the different branches of industry were, what amount of overtime could properly be worked in each, and what scale of hours was likely to give the largest amount of production. (P. 55.)

Woollen and Worsted Industry.

At the end of two months the whole situation was reviewed, and further conferences were held both in Yorkshire and in Scotland. There was still the same need for overtime, but the fact that production had been gradually falling off suggested that some reduction of hours ought to take place. A number of firms both in Yorkshire and in Scotland had already found it necessary to reduce their hours, and the workers' representatives in Yorkshire were strongly in favour of reduction.

Boots.

In many cases the periods of employment for which sanction was sought were beyond all reason, and the claims had evidently been put forward without proper consideration as to what was physically possible, or as to what the results of excessive hours might be in rela-

* Since this was written it has been found possible in some industries, e. g., wool, clothing, boots, to reduce the overtime still further or even discontinue it.

tion to production. At the conferences, however, it was generally recognized that, as the work consists largely of manual labour of a rather heavy character, little advantage is to be gained from long spells of overtime which only result in undue fatigue. . . . After some discussion, during which different totals of hours were suggested for different departments, it was agreed that a weekly total of 60 hours (exclusive of meal-times) would meet all requirements, if this limit were accompanied by certain provisions allowing some elasticity in the arrangement of the daily hours of work. (P. 57.)

The effects of continued overtime on production are so intimately connected with those bearing on the health of the workers that a separate analysis of this side of the question is almost uncalled for; yet the period under review has not been without its lessons. Though it has been found impracticable to give the results statistically, since the variations in work from week to week make comparisons most difficult, instances have repeatedly come to light where it has been found that production has gradually fallen away when long spells of overtime have been worked. Thus in the woollen trade it was found advisable, after overtime had been worked from Monday to Friday each week for nearly three months, to knock it off on one day in the middle of the week; in some of the largest ordnance factories where work has been going on day and night for seven days a week, it has been found desirable if not to abolish Sunday work, at least to reduce it to a minimum. "The men get stale," it is said, "and their tempers are upset." Again a remarkable instance is afforded by the clothing trade. When the pressure first arose it was noticeable that whereas no applications for latitude were received at all from some of the largest manufacturers, others desired to work overtime for two hours every evening of the week. Amongst the former were some of the most experienced in the trade, who believed they could obtain a maximum of output by working within the limits of the ordinary statutory hours. The others commenced their overtime but quickly learned that they had over-estimated the capacity of their workers and readily agreed to material reduction of their orders. And so too, in other trades, there has been noticeable a general tendency to reduce the overtime. The whole experience of these last months leads unquestionably to the conclusion that while long and even excessive hours can be worked with advantage for short periods, continued overtime, if not kept within proper limits, soon fails in its object and ceases to aid production. (Pp. 59-60.)

The testimony of the Inspectors on the whole has gone to show that the main resistance to excessive overtime in the greater normal industries, comes more from the employers' side than from any other, although there have been marked exceptions to this rule, and the method of approach to the problem of obtaining the best output has varied greatly among them. It is highly satisfactory to lead off the account of the employers' work in this matter with the example of a crown factory where the experience is, says *Miss Squire,* that any lengthening of the day beyond 6 p. m. and a total of 8½ hours' work daily exhausts the workers and is of no advantage in increasing output. . . .

Miss Squire.—A well-known wholesale clothier employing 1,000 women on Government contracts gave it as his well-considered opinion that the full period allowed under the Factory Act, 8 a. m. to 8 p. m., is sufficient, and "any work beyond this is quite useless: it exhausts the workers and does not pay." (P. 40.)

Miss Constance Smith.—In the month of October, when applications for orders were general in London, the great Bristol clothiers were for the most part carrying out their contracts within the Factory Act day. Two firms only had emergency orders, and they were not using them to the full. Where overtime was worked at all, it was under Section 49; but in several instances this had been tried and discontinued, the managers finding that an hour and a-half's overtime after 8 p. m. on three nights in the week had an injurious effect upon output, as well as upon health if carried on beyond a fortnight at the outside. In one case, where this bad effect showed itself at the end of the second week, the manager persuaded the directors to return as an experiment for a week to normal hours; the output and quality of the work improved so much during this week that the firm decided to keep to normal hours altogether. It would appear as if the question of carrying out contracts within the Factory Act day, if not within the normal clothier's day (some of the Bristol factories worked 9-7) were largely one of thorough organization and complete knowledge on the part of the managers of the rise or fall of output in each week, in proportion to hours worked and number of hands employed. Certain keen-sighted managers found their disapproval of overtime strengthened by the results of the short time worked in the early weeks of the war. One responsible for a factory employing over 2,000 women and girls, where the normal day is 7-6, told me that when this day had to be reduced to 8-5 by reason of cancelled orders, he found the girls' output remained the same.

Miss Taylor.—The outstanding feature was the refusal of the great majority of the occupiers of the largest and the better conducted factories in Leeds to entertain the idea of systematic overtime beyond the ordinary period of employment allowed by the Factory Act. Their reasons were, I gather, two-fold. In the first place, overtime beyond the usual limits is never financially beneficial for the output decreases relatively, while the standing charges for power, light, &c., remain the same. . . .

Miss Vines in Glasgow found considerable divergence of opinion among manufacturers. One member of a large firm making military uniforms informed her that overtime did not pay, but that as it increased his workers' earnings he was obliged to continue it lest his workers should leave for another factory. The manager of a powder bag factory on the other hand found after some weeks' experience that the pieceworkers were making less during overtime than during the normal period of employment. The experience of this occupier is more than matched by that reported by several during the short-time period e. g. (a) a cardboard box manufacturer who told me he had put his workers on shorter hours only to find that their output and earnings were equal to those on the full factory day; (b) a biscuit manufacturer, (c) an apron manufacturer who reported a similar result to *Miss Constance Smith* and *Miss Squire* respectively. (P. 41.)

Berichte über die Fabrikinspektion. 1884: 1885. [Reports of the (Swiss) Factory Inspectors, 1884-1885.] Aarau, Sauerländer, 1886.

The argument that hours of work, if prolonged beyond a certain point, result in increased production has been disproved by the experience of a factory where . . . to avoid over-production the hours were reduced to one-half the usual number during the summer. According to calculations the output should have been reduced by 50 per cent.; actually it only fell 10 per cent. True that in this factory hand work played an important part: yet does not this result prove that workmen, overstrained by excessive toil and worn by fatigue in excess of their strength undergo a deterioration of their productive facilities? In proportion as fatigue enfeebles in them that master faculty—application—they come in fact to produce less and less in the same extent of time. (P. 65.)

Berichte der eidg. Fabrik- und Bergwerkinspektoren über ihre Amtstätigkeit in den Jahren 1898-1899. [Reports of the (Swiss) Factory and Mine Inspectors for 1898-1899.] Aarau, Sauerländer, 1900.

The upholders of a shorter maximum working day all energetically oppose the frequent and widespread legal exemptions for overtime, and in this campaign they are often supported by employers who have come to regard overtime as unprofitable and who therefore do not use it. (P. 57.)

Long Hours Lead to Inferior Output.—Germany

Archiv für Soziale Gesetzgebung und Statistik. Bd. VIII. 1895. Zur Verkürzung der Arbeitszeit in der Mechanischen Textilindustrie. [The Reduction of Working Hours in the Mechanical Textile Industry.] RUDOLF MARTIN, *Referendar in the Statistical Office of the Kingdom of Saxony.*

The mechanical textile industries of Germany suffered greatly after 1830, because, protected by a high tariff but with no protective labor laws she sought her economic salvation through long hours of work and low wages—in a word, through defective conditions of labor. Depending on her long hours and low wages she neglected to improve her technic, whilst England, with a ten-hour day for women and children established as far back as 1850, and higher wages . . . made vast strides. . . . The melancholy result was that the history of cotton mills . . . in the '70's was a history of bankruptcy. (P. 261.)

Gesammelte Abhandlungen. Bd. III. [Complete Works. Vol. III.] Die Volkswirthschaftliche Bedeutung der Verkürzung des Industriellen Arbeitstages. [The Economic Significance of a Shorter Working Day.] ERNST ABBE. *Paper read at the meeting of the Economic Society at Jena in 1901. Jena, Fischer, 1906.*

The more clearsighted of our overseers had often said that, when there was great pressure of work and overtime was necessary—perhaps rising from 9 to 10 hours daily, the results were only satisfactory for a short time —perhaps 14 days, not longer. After that a corresponding rate of output was not obtainable even though there was a 25 per cent. increase in the rate of wages. The men got listless and surly and things did not go well.

I had doubted this, and made an experiment to test it. . . . The men were anxious to please me, and had promised to work overtime . . . being glad of the extra income before Christmas. . . . After one week the extra output began to fall, and by the third and fourth week it had practically fallen to nothing.

It is therefore impossible, even with good will and self-stimulation to increase output over and above the regular day's work, except for a short time.

I am glad to see that this is corroborated by the factory inspector of Brandenburg in 1900. In his report we find the testimony of a factory owner, who had found that it was only worth while to work overtime when work pressed, for about 14 days. After that the working capacity flagged. Fourteen days was our limit also, as we found.

From all this I estimate the importance of good will and initiative as follows: Workmen are incapable of maintaining increased productivity during a lengthened working day, beyond a certain short time; and likewise, the individual's ill will alone does not cause a lessened output under shorter hours. (P. 220.)

The English examples of work under trades unionism have shown that even when the men felt an interest in doing less work in a given time, from the viewpoint of making more work for the unemployed, their efficiency and output under reduced hours were nevertheless the same. I therefore regard it as settled, that no motive is necessary, no will power, no driving of self interest is needed, to bring about this adjustment of rapidity of work to the shortened working hours, but that it is automatic and would occur even if the workers were discontented. (P. 221.)

Jahresberichte der Gewerbe-Aufsichtsbeamten und Bergbehörden für das Jahr 1903. Bd. III. [Annual Reports of the (German) Factory and Mine Inspectors for 1903. Vol. III.] Berlin, Decker, 1904.

Mecklenburg Schwerin.

Abnormally long hours of work are gradually disappearing, partly by the influence of the trade unions and their demands for a shorter day, partly because of the legal restrictions, but also because employers are generally beginning to realize their ineffectiveness. (P. 7.5.)

Jahresberichte der Gewerbe-Aufsichtsbeamten und Bergbehörden für das Jahr 1904. [Reports of the (German) Factory and Mine Inspectors for 1904. Vol. III.] Berlin, Decker, 1905.

Alsace Lorraine.

The abandonment of extremely long hours in Lorraine is due less to the efforts of the unions than to the effect of legislation. It is due most of all to the steady if slow increase of insight among employers, that a permanently long working day is useless. . . . Only force of habit and the stupidity of some employers—also of some workers—explain the persistence of long hours in the face of all the favorable testimony for the shorter day. (P. 26.62.)

Jahresberichte der Gewerbe-Aufsichtsbeamten im Königreich Württemberg für das Jahr 1905. [Reports of the Factory Inspectors in the Kingdom of Württemberg, 1905.] Stuttgart, Lindemann, 1906.

Employers agree that overtime work is, essentially, irrational, because as a rule wages for overtime are higher, while the productivity of the worker retrogrades with longer hours. (P. 53.)

Revue Internationale de Sociologie, November-December, 1895. Le Travail Humain et ses Lois. [The Laws of Human Work.] Francesco S. Nitti, *University of Naples. Paris, Giard et Brière, 1895.*

The workman who persists in working despite his fatigue not only makes a greater organic effort with more trouble but produces an inferior mechanical result. (P. 1029.)

. . . These facts explain how it is that people subjected to long hours of work finally produce inferior output; and they explain, too, what seems at first an economic paradox, that the whole cost of industry is ordinarily less in countries where the hours of work are short than in those where they are long. (P. 1029.)

One of the most intelligent of the Swiss factory inspectors said long ago on this point, "Germany and France, apparently will not reduce their hours of work; Austria has an animated opposition going on to reduction of hours; Italy retains night work. Their workmen will become less and less capable of productive labor whilst ours will advance and then we shall see once more what we have seen several times before, namely, that we shall excel our neighbors." (P. 1029.)

Bulletin de l'Inspection du Travail. Ministère du Commerce, de l'Industrie, des Postes et des Télégraphes. Fasc. 5 and 6. Travaux originaux des Inspecteurs. [Original Contributions by the Inspectors.] Etude sur l'Influence de la Réduction de la Journée de Travail sur le Rendement Industriel. [The effect of Shorter Hours on Production.] M. Grillet, *Inspector at Rennes. Paris, 1892.*

The most striking and happy results of the reduction of hours effected within the last four years (brought about in two steps: first to 10½, then to 10 hours) has been, that many employers are more ready to agree to the principle of limiting the adult worker's hours of labor; that the general and uniform application of a shorter day has been facilitated, and that upright and reliable employers are able to affirm that this reduction of 1/22 in the length of hours has not brought about any sensible loss of output. (P. 425.)

One thing is certain: in proportion as the daily duration of working hours is prolonged, the production per hour decreases. What does the employer want of his workmen? Hours of work, not hours of presence. What does he need? To secure the best possible use of his workman's strength. Now, to attain that, it is essential that the worker should have rest periods sufficiently long to completely repair his vitality. (P. 426.)

M. Rivière in a report to the International Congress for Labor Legislation in Paris, July, 1900, set forth in masterly fashion the disadvantages of long hours of work from the industrial, not the sentimental point of view. We have reached the same conclusions by a different route.

Now, if workmen are employed steadily eight hours a day for a certain time, say two months, then nine hours for an equal period and then in succession for 10, 11, 12, 13, 14 hours, it can be shown that the production per hour is at first nearly the same (in 6, 7, 8 or 9 hours of work) and that, consequently, the daily output is directly proportioned to the length of the working day. After that, in proportion as length of working time increases, production per hour decreases and as a result, daily output does not keep pace with daily hours of work. (P. 426.)

It can be stated positively that the workman's daily output diminishes progressively, starting with such a period as we have just mentioned, and becomes stationary after from 8 to 15 days have elapsed. It is natural that it should be so. Taking one single day, after a certain number of hours have elapsed fatigue comes on (later, if the workman is fit; sooner if he is already fagged by previous work) and his productive capacity sinks. The hourly output decreases toward the end of the day while at the same time duration of work is prolonged. Then, when the workman resumes his work on the following day, his fatigue of the day before has not all disappeared. His daily output, is then, a little less every day than it was the day before, working hours being the same, until finally at the end of a certain period, an equilibrium is arrived at.

It is evident that the contrary will be true if hours of work are reduced. The output per hour will rise until, again, an equilibrium is established.

The result is, that when the employer increases working hours considerably, and for a considerable length of time, the final hours of every day bring him a certain loss, varying in different industries.

The personal interest of the employer, then, is, not to overpass the "maximum day," that duration of time during which the worker's productivity is at its best. (P. 426.)

Our observations enable us to say positively: If it is not carried beyond a certain limit of hours, eight, or nine, or ten a day according to the industry, reduction of working hours has not only *not* caused any sensible diminution in output, but instead, has resulted in an often notable improvement in the quality of the product. (P. 428.)

These results have not only been demonstrated in hand work, where the workman's share in production is direct but also in machine work, where the workman's part is primarily to supervise the machine. For then, by reason of the shorter sojourn in the factory the workman is more alert, more ready; he loses less time; feeds his machine more rapidly, and this quite unconsciously, just because he feels more able. (P. 428.)

M. Benedict B—having successfully tried the 12, then the 11, 10, and finally the 8-hour day in his factories, definitely established the 8-hour day because it assured him not only the best hourly output but also the best daily output. . . . Naturally (he told us) one of his women could produce more in 9 or 10 hours, but only temporarily. According to his opinion, every industry has its maximum day which ought not to be overpassed and . . . in his, this maximum is eight hours. If a rush of work comes, he requires his workwomen to work for nine hours, and the output keeps up if two conditions are observed: 1. that supervision is good; 2. that overwork does not last for a long stretch of time. (P. 434.)

M. Moussard, carriage maker, said:

In our shop the men do as much in 10 hours as formerly in 12, because, with 12 hours they became fatigued and worked without energy. In 10 hours they work steadily. (P. 135.)

Long Hours Lead to Inferior Output.—Belgium

Royaume de Belgique, Conseil Supérieur du Travail, 9e Session, 1907. [*Belgian Higher Council of Labor, Ninth Session, 1907.*] *Réglementation de la Durée du Travail des Adultes.* [*Regulation of Hours of Work for Adults.*] *Discussion.*

M. G. Helleputte:

It has been established by figures which it is impossible to disregard that what is lost in time is regained in work-intensiveness, and this is not surprising. It is impossible that product should be proportioned to the number of hours, for the work of a fatigued organism is not as effective as that of a fresh and able organism. We have but to recall our own experiences to see this. If one could trace from hour to hour the curve of effectiveness of the workman, one would very probably find that it rose in the morning, rapidly attained a maximum, and fell toward evening to a point which descended as the working day increased in length.

Cut off the last hour experimentally and you do not reduce, proportionally, the output of a given workman; cut it off permanently and the workman, thanks to the longer rest, becomes more alert and vigorous. His curve of work will be enlarged. It is understood, of course, that this reduction is not carried to extremes. (P. 13.)

C. RELATION TO WAGES.

Statistical evidence tends to show that wages are not decreased by the reduction of hours. In some cases there may be temporary decrease for a short time, before industry adjusts itself to a change in hours, but after a short period the gain in the workers' efficiency from shorter hours and their consequent increase in output tends to balance completely the curtailment of their working time. Wages are almost universally higher in industries in which the short workday has been established than they are in wholly unregulated trades.

Moreover, even when the shorter day has resulted in a slight temporary decrease in wages, the majority of workers have willingly suffered the reduction, in order to gain the increased health and leisure consequent upon shorter hours of labor.

United States Bureau of Labor Statistics Monthly Review. Volume II, No. 2. February, 1916.

Reduction of Hours of Labor in the Machine Trades.

A movement for the reduction of hours of labor, notable for its rapid progress, has taken place in the machine trades since late in the summer of 1915. It has chiefly affected the firms having contracts for making war munitions, though not exclusively restricted to such establishments. The demands for reduced hours have usually come from machinists, although other occupations have joined, and in most establishments all employees have received the benefits in the reduction of hours which have been granted to machinists. Reduced hours of labor have in practically all cases been effected with no reduction in weekly wage, and in many cases with increased wages. (P. 37.)

Report of the Massachusetts Bureau of Statistics of Labor. 1871.

I have worked what is called ten hours a day, and the ten-hour system always has a good influence on the work-people. We don't lose one-eleventh of the pay—everybody knows that. I didn't lose a single cent, because I didn't get so much exhausted. (P. 498.)

To prove the soundness of the ten-hour claim, the operatives instance the reduction in the past, from sixteen to fourteen, to thirteen and to twelve, and from twelve to eleven hours. They also point to the twenty-one years' experience in Great Britain, where the reduction was made in 1850 from twelve to ten, a reduction of one-sixth of the working day. (Pp. 557-558.)

Report of the Massachusetts Bureau of Statistics of Labor. 1881.

It is apparent . . . that wages here rule as high if not higher than in the States where the mills run longer time (*i. e.,* than ten hours a day). (P. 457.)

Still another case is that of a carpet mill employing about seventeen hundred persons. Twenty-five years ago the hours were reduced directly from twelve to ten. . . . The establishment has been run by the same management from then till now, without a break and with great success; and yet the average pay in it is higher than in any other mill, with possibly one or two exceptions, which we found. (P. 460.)

The Willimantic Linen Company of Connecticut ran its mills eleven hours per day till about two years ago, when it was determined as an experiment to run ten hours. . . . Wages have remained intact so far as the hours of labor are concerned. (P. 461.)

. . . It was quite generally conceded (by manufacturers) that even if, at first, there was a reduction of wages, yet by a year's time (only one person said more) the market would have readjusted itself, and the wages for ten hours would have become the same as they were before for eleven. A half-owner of six mills stated the case thus: "If all the mills would run but ten hours, there would be a diminution in the product of perhaps five per cent. That slight diminution would after a while so empty the market that prices would rise much more than five per cent., and so we could pay the same prices for ten as now for eleven hours' work, and then make more money than we are now making." And the principle involved in this statement was very generally conceded by manufacturers. . . . That is, a large portion of the manufacturers have come to see, what is undoubtedly true, that the width of the margin between cost and price, and so the possible amount of wages which can be paid, are not so much determined by the volume of the product alone, as by the relation between the amount produced and the amount consumed. (Pp. 462-463.)

Within a year's time the market would adjust itself entirely to the shorter day, the operatives would have as good a living with ten, as now with eleven, eleven and a half, and twelve hours. (P. 464.)

Nearly all of the operatives who can bear a cut-down, and live, that is, those above five or six dollars a week, would prefer to take a *pro rata* loss of wage, if necessary, to get ten hours. Ten hours anyway, and run the risk of less pay—this is the general position. The piece hands would spur themselves to more close attention to their work. Every one in the mill would expect and help maintain a more thorough discipline. To gain an hour a day, an hour and a half, and in the case of many hundreds two hours a day, year in and year out, what exertions would they not put forth? and whatever of the product of the time over ten hours they could not make up if the market went against them, so that the mill could not pay the full amount of the old wage, that small reduction they would rather submit to, than to work more than ten hours, for, as one of them most aptly said, "if we didn't have it in our pockets, we'd have it in our bones." (P. 465.)

A Documentary History of American Industrial Society. Edited by JOHN R. COMMONS, ULRICH B. PHILLIPS, EUGENE A. GILMORE, HELEN L. SUMNER *and* JOHN B. ANDREWS. *Vol. VIII. Labor Movement. Cleveland, The Arthur H. Clark Company, 1910. Nile's Register, Sept. 26, 1840, p. 59. Letter from President Martin Van Buren to certain political inquirers.*

The ten-hour system, originally devised by the mechanics and laborers themselves, has by my direction been adopted, and uniformly carried out at all public establishments, and . . . this mitigation of labor has been accompanied by no corresponding reduction of wages. I also caused it to be distinctly intimated in the month of March last, to the officers of such of these establishments as might contemplate a reduction of wages, that in my opinion the present peculiarly uncertain state of things, which it is believed results from circumstances that cannot be permanent in their operation, does not present a just and proper basis for a reduction of wages. (P. 85.)

Massachusetts House Documents No. 153. 1850. Minority Report of the Special Committee Re Limitation of Hours of Work.

Already, even with the powerful example of the corporations against them, in many places the mechanics and laboring people, in various trades and employments which are carried on by individual enterprise, have established by mutual arrangement with their employers the "ten hour system" of labor. In the city of Boston, in many branches of industry, laborers work but ten hours a day. By this arrangement they have secured to themselves more time for relaxation and mental improvement, and without a consequent reduction of wages. They receive on an average as high, and in some cases higher daily wages, than those who work more hours. In these cases of reduction of the hours of labor, the inexorable law of supply and demand, as fixing the rate of wages, has been vindicated; for the reduction of the hours of labor did not reduce its daily wages, but in some cases, a reduction of the hours was followed by an increase of wages. (P. 26.)

The Industrial Situation and the Question of Wages. Jacob Schoenhof. *New York. Putnam's, 1885.*

Hand in hand with increasing earnings has gone a corresponding reduction in the hours of labor. It is a very reassuring fact that the working hours are shortest today in countries where wages and productiveness are highest. While the week in England averages 54 to 56 hours, Germany's and France's week still averages 72 hours, with many industries at 78 hours. Switzerland has sometime ago adopted a normal working day of 11 hours. The report of the Factory Inspectors for 1882 and 1883 finds much to say on the improvement the act has worked in the condition of the working people. As with all innovations of this kind, of course, many manufacturers express disparaging opinions, while a great many more make favorable comment on the results achieved thereby. Massachusetts has fixed 60 hours by statute without having experienced any incursion by competing neighboring States, which still adhere to longer hours. It has been the common experience, wherever tried, that shorter hours enable the workman to put more energy into his work. . . .

In the United States the extent of the working day in cotton-mills is quoted by Mr. Atkinson as having been 13 hours in 1840; this was by degrees reduced to 11 hours, and since 1883 to 10 hours in Massachusetts, with other States beginning to move in the same direction, the State of Rhode Island having adopted a 10-hour day within a month of this writing. (Pp. 127-28.)

Report of the New Jersey Bureau of Statistics of Labor and Industry. 1886.

The Factory Acts were believed to be the death-blow to English manufacturers, and they have made labor more efficient, more intelligent, more decent, and more continuous without trenching on profits. (P. 231, footnote.)

In 1851 and 1852 those who advocated that ten hours should be a legal day's work were denounced as demagogues, and the ten-hour plan as a humbug which could only tend to reduce the wages proportionately, while all kinds of evil results were sure to follow its application, especially to agricultural labor. But we have seen ten hours become the rule; wages have not fallen, and many of those who prophesied disaster are now as loud in their praises of its beneficence as the friends of the change. (P. 232.)

Report of the New York Factory Inspectors. 1894.

This material reduction (from 10 to 15 per cent. in many industries) in the working time was not accompanied by any reduction in the pay of those interested. (Pp. 31-32.)

Report of New York Bureau of Labor Statistics. 1900.

In all those departments of the factory in which wages are paid by piece-work—and these constitute probably not less than four-fifths of the whole, the proportion to fixed daily wages being daily on the increase—it has been found that the quantity produced in ten and one-half hours falls little short of that formerly obtained from twelve hours. In some cases it is said to be equal. This is accounted for partly by the increased stimulus given to ingenuity to make the machines more perfect and capable of increased speed, but it arises far more from the work-people by improved health, by absence of that weariness and exhaustion which the long hours occasioned, and by their increased cheerfulness and activity, being enabled to work more steadily and diligently and to economize time, intervals of rest while at their work being now less necessary. (Pp. 49-50.)

The Arena. Vol. XXIV. 1900. New York, Alliance, 1900. The Eight-Hour Day by Legislation. EDWIN MAXEY, *Southern Normal University, Tenn.*

According to the best authorities wages are more likely to be raised than lowered, though it is possible they may remain stationary. . . . New York State witnessed, in 1887, 2,256 strikes for shorter hours, and in every one of the trades where a reduction of hours was obtained a positive increase in wages is also reported. In 1860, six years after the enactment of the ten-hour law in Massachusetts, as a result of an argument made before the legislative committee by Edward Atkinson, who had always been an active opponent of the law on the ground that its operation was injurious to the working man (as they had to work for one-eleventh less than similar laborers in other States), the legislators ordered the Labor Bureau to investigate the hours of labor and wages paid in Massachusetts, the other New England States, and New York. This was done, and the result was as follows:

In Maine, average hours	66 1/8	; average wages per week,	$7.04
In New Hampshire "	66 1/7	; average wages per week,	7.44
In Connecticut "	66 1/4	; average wages per week,	7.81
In Rhode Island "	66	; average wages per week,	8.01
In New York "	65 1/4	; average wages per week,	7.57
In Massachusetts "	60	; average wages per week,	8.32

The result of this investigation—proving as it did that the average wage in Massachusetts was 65 cents more for 5½ hours less per week than the average in Maine, New Hampshire, Connecticut, Rhode Island, and New York—was far more eloquent than any words Mr. Atkinson could utter. (Pp. 236-237.)

United States Congress. House Report No. 1793. Hours of Laborers on Public Works of the United States. Report from the Committee on Labor. 57th Congress. 1st Session. 1901-1902.

Economists who advocate the eight-hour day contend, with great plausibility, that the shorter day results in an increase of wages without an increase of price, as greater consumption enlarges production, and the larger the scale of production the cheaper the given article is produced; that the laborer, when he has the leisure resulting from the shorter hours, has new aspirations, ambitions, and greater personal self-respect, and, as before stated, wants a better house, better furniture, better clothes, better food, and becomes a great deal better consumer; that the scale of wages is controlled by the wants of the laborer in any given state of society rather than by the "iron law of wages"; that modern men cease to work under normal conditions if the proceeds of their labor do not satisfy their normal wants; that therefore the social status of the laborer controls the law of wages to as great an extent as the law of wages controls the status of the laborer. (P. 9.)

Report of the United States Industrial Commission. Final Report. Vol. XIX. 1902.

Furthermore, a reduction of hours is not accompanied by a permanent reduction in the daily rates of pay. Doubtless it is good policy for labor organizations, in demanding a reduction of hours, to concede a temporary reduction in the rate of pay per day, which might be consistent with an increase in the rate per hour. The granite cutters adopted this plan, and when their hours were reduced from 10 to 9 they accepted a drop of 25 cents a day in wages. One year later they regained the wages of the 10-hour day, again they dropped 25 cents in order to get the 8 hour day, and in another year they regained the 25 cents. A reduction of hours is the most substantial and permanent gain which labor can secure. (P. 773.)

Bulletin of the United States Bureau of Labor, No. 80. January, 1909. Woman and Child Wage-Earners in Great Britain. VICTOR S. CLARK, Ph.D.

It is no longer argued by people familiar with industrial history that shorter hours necessarily mean lower wages. But this argument was used extensively when the earlier British acts were passed. Here again, as in case of the shortening of hours, it is difficult to separate the effect of state regulation from the effect of other causes, but the upward tendency of the wages of women and children during the past century is a matter of statistical verification. The following table gives the most authoritative statement of the increase of the wages of women since 1820. The table shows the average relative wages of all women wage-earners, by decades, as stated in percentages of the average wage during the ten years ending with 1900. To show that there was more than a normal increase in women's wages, as compared with the wages of unregulated men's labor, the relative wages of workers of both sexes combined, using the decade ending with 1900 as the base, is given in a parallel column.

Relative Wages in the United Kingdom, 1820 to 1900.

Decade Ending	Relative Wages of Women Employees	Relative Wages of Employees of Both Sexes
1830	58	65
1840	56	60
1850	58	60
1860	62	65
1870	75	75
1880	93	95
1890	95	90
1900	100	100

Between 1830 and 1850 women's wages may have declined less than those of men because they were already near the subsistence level. An English authority, to whom these statistics are due, says: "Factory legislation has not lowered wages, but has been accompanied by a decided and progressive increase." It is not to be understood that factory laws are given as the cause of this increase, but they may have contributed to it by improving the efficiency of workers.

The wages of women in industries regulated by the factory acts are generally better than those in unregulated industries. Among the best-paid women factory workers of England are the cotton operatives of Lancashire. This condition, however, is probably less an effect of the law than of the fact that the law happens to apply to a better grade of workers. (Pp. 53-54.)

Trades may be mentioned, like some kinds of decorating and polishing, where neither machinery nor labor unions have influenced conditions, in which wages have risen as working hours grew fewer. But workers in these trades were benefited by the rising standard of living of their fellow-workers in other industries, and their rate of compensation was affected by the competition for labor caused by high wages in other occupations.

The statistics available indicate that the enactment of the successive laws shortening the hours of labor did not, in the particular industries affected, interrupt the progressive improvement of wages that has marked the last century. (P. 55.)

Bulletin of the United States Bureau of Labor Statistics. Number 118. April, 1913.

Ten-Hour Maximum Working-Day for Women and Young Persons.

Since 1895 wages have increased by nearly 24 per cent. When we remember that it is precisely during the last 15 years that American industrial activity has increased to the greatest extent, we are bound to acknowledge the importance of these figures. It is now a well-known fact that the adoption of a 10-hour or a 9-hour day has not affected the amount or value of the output even in the case of establishments where machinery is predominately used.

The necessity of diminishing the hours of labor is still more apparent in the case of establishments where workers who are subject to increasing pressure of work are unable to transfer some of the pressure to a machine. For instance, when the Norwegian Factory Act of 1909 was under discussion, the director of the Norwegian State workshops declared that approximately the same amount of work was done in 53 hours per week as was formerly done in 60 hours. It was reported that in other industries in which the work is done at piece rates, the difference in the wages earned by persons working 8 and 10 hours daily was almost inappreciable. (P. 47.)

Annual Report of the Secretary of Internal Affairs of Pennsylvania. Part III. Report of the Bureau of Industrial Statistics. 1913-1914. The Henry Ford Plan.

This co-operative relation has enabled the Ford establishment to increase the average wage of its 15,000 employes from 29 cents per hour to 61 cents per hour, with prospects of still greater increase after the more perfect mobilization of its immense forces. The increase of wages was attended by reduction in the hours of labor per day, to permit the working of three shifts of eight hours each, if necessary. Nevertheless, the daily Ford earnings are still more than those of a ten hour day in many establishments, under the old system. These conditions are due largely to very superior organization and the extraordinary efficiency attained by the men whose co-operative spirit is well-nigh invincible. This is all the more surprising when we are told that these working people were not employed because of their exceptional skill or experience, but were mainly and simply ordinary workmen, with various grades of intelligence, and more than one-half are foreigners, drawn from about fifty nationalities. (P. 57.)

The appeal to worth and manhood was squarely made and the result has usually been a new man, living among new environments with a strong inclination for all the privileges of American citizenship. There has been a marked increase of naturalizations and extraordinary improvement in the habits, living conditions, health, mentality and morals of the working people. . . .

The Ford plan has made it possible to increase the production efficiency by at least 20 per cent. (P. 59.)

Principles of Labor Legislation. JOHN R. COMMONS. *University of Wisconsin. Former Member Wisconsin Industrial Commission.* JOHN B. ANDREWS, *Secretary of the American Association for Labor Legislation. Harper & Brothers. New York and London. 1916.*

This increase of output through increased efficiency probably largely explains why wages have seldom fallen, but have frequently even risen after a reduction of hours, and why the industries in which wages are highest are often those in which hours are shortest. Practical experience, therefore, gives weight to the old eight-hour league slogan:

> Whether you work by the piece or the day,
> Decreasing the hours increases the pay.

(P. 203.)

British Sessional Papers. Vol. X. 1840. First Report from Select Committee on the Act for the Regulation of Mills and Factories.

Witness, L. Horner, Inspector of Factories:

1616.—You are aware that the persons working in factories have for a succession of years petitioned Parliament for a reduction of the hours of labour in factories to 10; are you also aware that in all the petitions they have ever sent they have never expressed any opinion whatever as to what the wages would be, but they have constantly complained of the hardship they had to endure by being worked longer than their physical powers afforded them means of doing compatibly with their health, and that they have been willing to make the experiment of limiting it to 10 instead of 12, provided an Act was passed for that purpose regardless of the consequences that might befall them in the rate of wages?—I am strongly impressed with the belief that the workers who have come forward in that way, have done so under a conviction that there would be no reduction in wages eventually, although it might take place at first, but that they would get in a short time as much for 10 hours' labour as they at present get for 12 hours' labour. (P. 121.)

A Few Words on the Ten Hours Factory Question. Edmund R. Larkin, M. A. *London, Richardson, 1846.*

It is consolatory and encouraging to find that so far as experience can be a guide to us in determining this important question, it goes to prove that the diminution of profits and wages would not be so great under a system of shortened time, as to deter us from making trial of this great social experiment. . . . The trial has been made, not indeed of reduction to Ten, but to Eleven hours of work; and the result has been not merely so slight a diminution of produce as to justify a further experiment, but no diminution whatever thereof, nor, consequently, of the wages of the producers. (Pp. 21-22.)

British Sessional Papers. Vol. XXII. 1849. Reports of Inspectors of Factories for Half-year ending 30th April, 1849.

Referring more particularly to the Cotton district, it may be premised that, shortly before the passing of the Ten Hours Act, a general reduction in the rate of wages, to the extent of 10 per cent., was adopted by the masters, and submitted to by the work people; but this did not produce, even at that critical moment, any remonstrances on the part of the work people against the law, which was then impending over them, for further limiting their hours of work, whence it may be inferred that they had calculated not only what would be its effects upon their earnings *in the factories,* but also how it would affect their condition *in other particulars.* . . .

From the inquiries which I have made, I find it indeed, to be generally represented that, notwithstanding this reduction in the rate of wages and the abridgment of the hours of work, the Ten Hours Act has not effected any diminution in the earnings of the work people which is not practically counterbalanced by some equivalent advantages which they gain from the shortening of the working day. In the first place, it would seem that the diminution in the amount of net wages, actually received in cash at the end of the week or fortnight, is by no means proportioned to the reduction in the number of the hours of labour; for it is stated that the "two last" hours of the 12 were not those in which the greatest energy, activity, and vigilance were available; that, by shortening the day, the hands are now enabled, in 10 hours, to do more work, and do it better, than they could in the first 10 hours of a longer working day; that by improvements in the construction as well as by accelerating the speed of the machinery, a greater amount of work is turned off in the same time than before, that, in fact, they get through their work with more hearty good-will, with greater care and attention, and in better spirits, and that, by turning their work better out of hand, their earnings are not diminished by so many abatements, stoppages, and fines for negligence and for bad or damaged work, as used to curtail their receipts under the system of longer hours. . . . (Pp. 19-20.)

Ibid. Appendix. Evidence of the Opinions of Persons Employed in Factories, Respecting the Ten Hours Act, Collected in September, October, and November, 1848.

Cotton Mill A. No. 2, Manager, and No. 3, Bookkeeper, spoken together: . . . added, that the spinners are making nearly as much (in 10 hours) as they did when working 12 hours, partly by a little increased speed, partly by some improvements in the machinery, but chiefly by greater attention and economy of time; that by shortening the hours they are able to keep up their exertions. (P. 27.)

Nos. 29, 30, 31, 32. Adult males. Mule spinners. All said they would much rather work 10 hours with less wages than go back to 12 with higher. "No one who has felt the good of the 10 hours would willingly go back to 12." They said that they have better appetites and better health. (P. 28.)

Cotton Mill F. No. 16. Manager. . . . Many of the hands in this mill make nearly as much as they used to do; there has been no alteration in the speed of the machinery, "but they stick closer to their work." (P. 27.)

Nos. 75 and 76. Adult males. Weavers. Say, that there is not so much difference in the amount of work they can turn off, so that their wages have not been much less than when they worked 12 hours; they make it up by increased exertion, and they do not find themselves so much fatigued by thus working more closely as they were by the long day's work. (P. 29.)

Cotton Mill W. No. 89. Owner. Afterwards added since the 10 hour restriction began, they have paid the overlookers by piecework instead of fixed wages as formerly, and they are making nearly as much in the 10 as they did in 12. That by their greater vigilance in looking after the workers the produce has been increased. (P. 30.)

Cotton Mill E. No. 14. Mill-owner. Extract from letter tô Mr. Horner, dated 18th October, 1848:

. . . My weavers do not suffer in their wages to the extent of reduction in the working hours. I pay more money now than I formerly did in proportion to the time worked. I account for this by unusual exertion on the part of the work people, coupled with greater strength for the work, from having more time to recruit themselves. (P. 37.)

No. 143. Overlooker of the card room. . . . He was not averse to the reduction either in time or wages, and remarked that "towards the close of the 12 hours' day, he could not do his duty satisfactorily, as the hands were too much jaded to attend to their work, and many of them fast asleep." He added, "that there is not half the number off sick since the 10 hours have been worked, that the hands work more cheerfully, and that there is less trouble in keeping them up to it." He had never heard one express a wish to return to longer hours. For his own part, he declared, that although he now has less money to spend, there is much greater happiness in his family. (P. 72.)

British Sessional Papers. Vol. XXXIV. 1860. Reports of Inspectors of Factories for half-year ending 31st Oct., 1859.

Two other arguments formerly in great repute with the opponents of any Factory Bill these Acts have entirely refuted; the one the certain reduction of wages concurrent with the reduction of the working hours; the other, the "pro-rata" limit which the same reduction of hours would place upon the textile production of the country to the disparagement of our commerce. In no branch of textile labor are wages reduced since 1833, but there is an average increase of 12 per cent. and in one instance of 40 per cent. I do not mean to say that whole branches of manual labor have not ceased, nor to deny that machinery has replaced it here and there, but if it has other branches of industry have supervened. (P. 53.)

The Eight Hours Movement. Tom Mann. *London, William Reeves, 1889.*

Employers and employes alike continue to use arguments about the effect of shorter hours and higher wages, which have, again and again, been confuted by the experience of our own and other countries. It is said, now, that the Eight Hours Bill would raise the price of labour, and, consequently, the cost of production, to such an extent that the trade of the country will be destroyed, and masters, as well as men, be involved in one common ruin. Exactly the same cry was raised by the opponents of the Ten Hours Bill and of the Nine Hours Movement. Yet in those cases, it is certain that not only have the operatives reaped considerable benefit in the shape of shorter hours and higher wages, but also that the cost of production has enormously *decreased*, and that the manufacturers, nevertheless, have obtained a larger aggregate profit than before, though their proportion of the greater output may have diminished. Improved methods of production have so increased the output, that the employers can pay a higher wage for fewer hours work, sell the articles cheaper, and still obtain a larger income for themselves. There is no reason to doubt that similar results will follow a further reduction of hours, and increased demand for commodities owing to a greater purchasing power among the workers. (P. 6.)

British Sessional Papers. Vol. XXXIV. 1892. Royal Commission on Labour. Précis of Evidence. Group A. Vol. I.

Testimony of Mr. W. H. Lambton, Sec'y of the "Durham County Colliery Enginemen's Mutual Aid Ass'n" and Sec'y of the "National Federation of Colliery Engineers."

One-third of the men work eight hours; when this was granted no reduction of wages followed, but the men refused an offer of 33⅓ per cent. advance rather than work again twelve hours. (P. 11.)

Testimony of Mr. Enoch Rees, Agent for the Anthracite Miners' Ass'n.

When the system of working nine hours a day was adopted many of the men thought that the change would diminish their earnings; but, as a matter of fact, they have since obtained better wages, and are more active, healthy and intelligent than when they toiled long hours under ground. Since the change their work has been observed to be more methodical. (P. 26.)

A Shorter Working Day. R. A. Hadfield, *of Hadfield's Steel Foundry Co., Sheffield,* and H. de B. Gibbins, M. A. *London, Methuen & Co., 1892.*

Another instance, the Huddersfield Corporation Tramways may be cited. . . . Formerly the trams ran fourteen hours per day, and the men worked twelve hours (two hours off). Under the new system two shifts are employed, each working an eight hours day. The manager states that by the change he has, in the first place, obtained a good reserve of experienced hands in case of emergency, and that the work is certainly done better. . . .

The wages previous to the alteration were, drivers 32s., conductors 23s. per week, based on a twelve hours actual working day. Now they stand at 26s. and 21s. per day of eight hours. In other words the advance on the old rate per hour has been 25 per cent. and 50 per cent. respectively. Here is another of those proofs that long hours often mean not only positive degradation to the human being enslaved by them, but proportionately lower wages too. . . . By giving more leisure time you will get a better class of men, as Messrs. Johnson found, who will make themselves worth the higher wages. (Pp. 142-143.)

British Sessional Papers. Vol. XXXII. 1893. Royal Commission on Labour. Précis of Evidence.

Testimony of Mr. C. S. Caird, a shipwright employed in Her Majesty's Dockyard at Pembroke, representing the Pembroke branch of the Ship Constructive Association.

An analysis of the earnings of the men uniformly employed at piece work shows that they earn, and, therefore, produce, as much during the short days of winter as during the long days of summer. The Ship Constructive Association, therefore, considering the day of eight hours to be sufficiently long, has officially declared itself in favour of the eight hours' movement. (P. 60.)

Ibid. Vol. XXXIV. Royal Commission on Labour. Précis of Evidence.

Testimony of Mr. George Mitchell, Scottish Chemical Worker.

Mr. Thomas Steele represented the Tyneside and National Labourers' Union. Two modes of working prevailed. In some factories on the Tyneside there were three shifts of eight hours each; and in others two shifts, the day shift consisting of eleven hours, and the night shift of thirteen. . . .

There was practically little difference in the wages earned by the eight-hour men and twelve-hour men, because they were on a piece-work system, and the piece-work prices in the eight-hour factories were at least one-fourth higher than in the twelve-hour works. The cost of production was not materially increased, because the output for the twelve hours was very little larger than for the eight hours. Where the eight-hour shifts were employed, improved machinery was used, and this enabled the men to turn out the same amount of material in a shorter time. . . .

Only one factory on the Tyne still adhered to the two-shift system, the others had all adopted the three-shifts, either through the voluntary action of the employers or under pressure from the Union. (P. 20.)

Ibid. Vol. XXXIX. Part I. Royal Commission on Labour. Minutes of Evidence.

Mr. Henry Meyers Hyndman:

The trades which are best paid to-day are precisely those that work the shortest hours, and as was got out by one member of the commission on inquiry of Mr. Giffen, it appeared that during the last 20 years, although undoubtedly the hours have been consistently reduced, especially in the higher skilled trades, such as the engineers and so forth, the amount of wages which have been paid has increased. (P. 595.)

Eight Hours for Work. John Rae. *London and New York, Macmillan & Co., 1894.*

The surest inference as to wages that we can draw from the actual facts is that wherever production has not been diminished by the shorter hours, wages have not been diminished, and that when wages have been reduced in the expectation that production would be reduced, they have afterwards been raised again on discovering that production was fully maintained. . . .

The result is due solely to the circumstance, which we know from the factory inspectors and other witnesses, that the operatives came to turn out as much work in the day after the Ten Hours Act as they had done before it and naturally came to earn as high wages. What happened was exactly what happened in Mr. Allan's works, and Mr. Brunner's and many others; wages were lowered for a time in anticipation of a lowered production and raised again immediately this anticipation was found to be false.

This, again, is precisely what we should be taught to expect to happen by a consideration of the general causes that govern the rate of wages. Temporary or auxiliary causes may occasion fluctuations one way or other in the movement of wages, but the one great cause by which its general level is ruled is the productiveness of labour itself. (Pp. 227-228-229.)

If shorter hours caused shorter production in the great body of the workshops of the country, shorter hours would obviously reduce the rate of wages, because, in the first place, the employers could not afford to pay the same wages for less work, and because, in the second, the demand for labour would necessarily fall greatly off when everybody produced less wealth, and had less means of buying goods and employing labour. (Pp. 230-231.)

The effect of shorter hours on the general wages of labour depends entirely on their effect on production. If they lessen production generally, they will lower wages generally, but they have not, in fact, lowered production generally in the past, and they have consequently not lowered wages. The men have unconsciously or from design worked better in the shorter hours, and the masters have been led to make more effective arrangements, and introduce improved methods of production, and there is no reason to think they will be unable—there is, on the contrary, every reason to think they will be able—to conspire together to produce the same result again. (Pp. 242-243.)

Short Hours and Wages.—Great Britain

Journal of the Royal Statistical Society. Vol. LXV. 1902. Factory Legislation considered with reference to the Wages, etc., of the Operatives protected thereby. GEORGE HENRY WOOD.

In summing up the impressions gathered from the foregoing review, we find that in one or two cases the limitation of hours of labour by Factory Acts has, for the time being, reduced wages, especially of time workers, but that as soon as the industry affected has become settled under the new conditions, wages have risen to a higher point than previous to the passing of the Act, and that this has been ascribed by competent observers to the increased efficiency of the operative and the increased intensity of the work. (Pp. 305-306.)

During the era of Factory Legislation, that is, since the "Ten Hours" Act, and its extension, in a more or less modified form, to other industries than textiles, women's wages have risen by about 66 per cent., while the average increase for the United Kingdom is about 45 per cent. . . . But the chief point to be noticed is that factory legislation has not lowered wages, but has been accompanied by a decided and progressive increase. How far this legislation has *caused* this increase I am not prepared to say, but in so much as by reducing hours of labour, raising the minimum age of entrance to the factory and so insuring a certain amount of education, improving the sanitary and other accommodations of the worker, and regulating dangerous trades it has increased the standard of efficiency and encouraged a higher standard of living; it seems to have been a factor making for the increase. (Pp. 308-309.)

We may now shortly summarize in a few words what we have seen. It is not certain that there is always a direct connection between Factory Legislation and women's wages, but as a rule the effect of each limitation of the hours of labour has been to raise wages, though for a while they may have fallen a little. This usually operates through an increase in the efficiency of labour, which maintains or increases the former output in the lessened hours. While such an increased efficiency is maintained, the expenses of production are not increased, and no damage is done to foreign trade in the product of the industry affected. . . . All these effects have been for the general good,—women have shared in the progress of the past sixty years, and their wages have risen with men's but at a faster rate and more consistently. (P. 313.)

Report of the 72nd Meeting of the British Association for the Advancement of Science. 1902. London, Murray, 1903. Women's Labour. Second Report of the Committee . . . appointed to investigate the Economic Effect of Legislation Regulating Women's Labour.

. . . To the third question (whether legislation restricting women's labour has raised or lowered wages) the answer (from the employers) was in almost every instance that wages had not been affected. Many were agreed that the legislation on the whole had improved health, and consequently efficiency. (P. 290.)

Report of the 73rd Meeting of the British Association for the Advancement of Science. 1903. London, Murray, 1904. Women's Labour. Third Report of the Committee . . . appointed to investigate the Economic Effect of Legislation Regulating Women's Labour.

The experience of a merino factory in Nottinghamshire is very interesting: "The reduction of hours in 1875 did not reduce wages. The men and girls at first asked for a rise of piece prices as compensation for an anticipated loss. The employer promised to consider it in a while, if the loss actually took place and became permanent. In 4 weeks it was found, however, that earnings were equal in 56½ hours to what they had been in the previous 60-hour week. To the employer there was, in the winter, an actual gain, as the same work being done in 3½ hours less, and the hours not worked being taken off the evening when artificial light was needed, less gas was burnt. The same firm reduced to 55½ hours voluntarily in 1900, and again no loss was occasioned to the operatives." (P. 338.)

Industrial Efficiency: A Comparative Study of Industrial Life in England, Germany, and America. ARTHUR SHADWELL, M. A., M. D. *London, New York, and Bombay, Longmans, Green and Co. 1906.*

If reason fails economic pressure will enforce the principle both on employers and employed, just as it is steadily shaping the course of labour conditions in the direction of shorter hours and higher pay. It is economic pressure at the back of organized labour which has forced employers out of the blind way of keeping men at work as long and paying them as little as possible; and the same pressure at the back of employers is forcing men out of the equally blind way of doing as little and trying to get as much as possible. Industrial victory will rest with those who most fully and speedily recognize the situation. . . .

In a Prussian mill which competes successfully with Bradford and Lawrence, and sells its goods in the English and American markets, the weekly hours in 1895 were 64¾, and the average earnings of male workers were 21.42 shillings a week; in 1899 with the same hours the earnings had risen to 23.58 shillings; in 1903 the hours were reduced to 60 without any diminution of earnings; in 1904 the mill was working short time, namely 54 hours, yet the earnings were then precisely the same as they had been with 64¾ hours in 1895. (Pp. 143-144.)

National Conference on the Prevention of Destitution. 1912. Papers and Proceedings. London, P. S. King & Son, 1912. The Reduction of the Hours of Work and the Limitation of Overtime. Discussion.

Mr. H. Barrass (Edmonton Urban District Council) said that he had been working under the eight-hour system ever since 1894 in a Government factory, and he might mention he was one of those who took a great part in the bringing about of that system in the Government factories. After that system had started the manager decided to time the men and find out strictly the hours they made and the money they received. They took six weeks working under the nine-hour system and six weeks under the eight-hours system. After that had been done, the manager stated that the men had made more regular time, that the wages had been greater, and that the expenses for fuel and light had been much reduced under the eight-hours system compared to what they had been under the nine-hour system.

The Chairman: Will you explain how the wages were greater? Do you mean that the men produced more?

Mr. Barrass explained that the greater portion of the men were on piecework, and when they worked under the nine-hours system they very often lost an hour in the morning, but when they only had eight hours in which to do the same amount of work they left off losing an hour and made the full time. That system had been in vogue ever since 1894, and he had asked some few weeks ago what was the percentage of lost time with the men to-day. He was told that it did not amount to ½ per cent. of the workmen employed in the factory, but under the nine-hours system the loss of time had been 5 or 6 per cent. The men were now more contented at being able to do the work in quicker time and to get away for recreation and to take part in municipal affairs. If it acted like that in a Government factory, it would act similarly in private firms. When the system was introduced in the Government factory the whole of the rates of the men were raised so as to bring the amount of the day rate money up to the amount under the nine hours, and it was an understood thing that if any of the pieceworkers found that through working only eight hours they could not earn the same amount of money as under the nine-hours system, it was to be reported to the officials in order to be investigated and the price raised to bring it up to that amount. But although there were 3,000 men at that time at work, not one of the pieceworkers applied for his piecework rate to be raised, so it did not entail any extra amount in price. (P. 463.)

Conditions in British Iron and Steel Works. A Speech delivered to the Special Commission on Hours of Labour, International Association for Labour Legislation, June 11th, 1912. ALDERMAN P. WALLS.

There are, according to the *Labour Gazette,* about twenty-four thousand men employed about blast furnaces in Great Britain, but a large number are what we term day-men. That means that they do not work day and night shifts. There are about eight thousand on the eight-hour shift, and about seven thousand still working on the twelve-hour shift.

The eight-hour shift is general in the North of England. In certain portions of the Midlands, in Scotland, and in South Wales the twelve-hour shift prevails. This is not a matter of competition but of organization. In the districts where the eight-hour shift is worked, wages are from 25 per cent. to 30 per cent. higher than where twelve-hour shifts are worked.

The Case for the National Minimum. With Preface by MRS. SIDNEY WEBB. *London. National Committee for the Prevention of Destitution, 1913.*

Wages Under Reduced Hours.—It is necessary to insist that reductions of hours shall not be accompanied by reduction of wages. It will be no gain to the worker to purchase increased leisure at the cost of diminished wages. Moreover, it has been seen that the only method of maintaining production at its old level after a reduction of hours, is to pay wages sufficient to call for the requisite skill and energy. Several examples to this effect have already been given. A further one is given by Mr. Alderman P. Walls, J. P. (Blastfurnacemen), in the following words:

"In the districts where the eight hours shift is worked wages are from 25 per cent. to 30 per cent. higher than where the twelve hours shifts are worked."

Australian experience points to the same conclusion. In the four industries where the Wages Boards introduced the forty-eight hours' week in Victoria, wages were simultaneously advanced as follows:

Average Enhancement of Weekly Wages.

Trade	Men.		Women.	
	From	To	From	To
	s. d.	s. d.	s. d.	s. d.
Boot	27 7	33 8	12 7	14 7
Clothing	35 8	39 6	15 8	18 3
Aerated Water	26 8	28 6	....	....
Saddlery	27 8	34 5	14 5	17 2

Similarly in New Zealand where the awards are more localized than in Australia, in the long list of awards there are numerous instances of reductions of hours accompanied by stationary or by rising wages. Thus over a wide range of experience it can be demonstrated that reductions of hours are possible without any necessity for reduction of wages. (Pp. 21-22.)

Bulletin de l'Office du Travail. Ministere du Commerce, de l'Industrie, des Postes et des Telegraphes. Tome XII. Mars, 1905. [Bulletin of the French Labor Office. Vol. XII. March, 1905.] L'Application de la Loi de Dix Heures et les Salaires. [Wages and the Application of the Ten Hour Law.]

The rise in piece-work prices is very variable and in most cases difficult to estimate; . . . at Troyes, in certain cotton-spinning mills, the rise in price was combined with an increase of speed so as to enable the workers to earn the same daily wage. . . .

The maintenance of the old piece-work prices does not always result in diminished wages. According to the inspectors, the piece-worker in hosiery factories may in large part make up for reduction of hours by increased activity: employers and operatives are said to agree in this: "exact experiments have proved that the working day of the male or female operative may even be reduced below ten hours without diminishing production or in consequence the wages that vary with; moreover, under certain conditions of methodical organization, it has been possible to maintain the wages of needle-workers with a day of 8½ to 9 hours." In the dye-works at Aube also, it is said that the piece-workers can make up for the loss of working time; the employers moreover require a minimum output for piece-workers as well as day-workers . . . and this minimum output has remained the same for 10 hours as for 10½. . . .

Of the 5,982 workers paid by the hour, the day, the month, or the week, in regard to whom we can secure definite information as to whether their wages were affected or not by the 10 hour day, 75.6 per cent. continued to receive their former wages. (Pp. 204-205.)

Ibid. May, 1905.

Building Trades.

In no case has the ten hour day resulted in a decrease of the previous daily wage. As the great majority of workers in the building trades were paid by the hour, wages were maintained by an increase in the price per hour; sometimes this increase was exactly proportioned to the reduction of working time; it was often larger, so that the 10 hour workman found himself with a larger daily wage than he had received for 10 and ½ hours, 11 hours, 11 and ½ hours, and even 12 hours. (P. 430.)

Summary.

. . . The substitution of piece work or pay by the hour for payment by the day has been very rare in the introduction of the 10 hour day; in general, we might almost say always, where workmen were paid by the day, their previous wage was maintained.

As for those paid by the hour, we may consider those whose hourly wage was raised as having had their previous day's wage maintained, the increase in hourly wage being in general calculated to make up exactly for the reduction of working hours. The maintenance of the daily wage by the raise of hourly wages is not nearly so general as the maintenance of wages paid by the day; more than ⅔ of the workers by the hour have nevertheless benefitted by it. . . .

To sum up, if we put aside the 47,769 piece-workers, for whom we cannot exactly determine the effect of reduction of hours on daily wages, it is evident from the two tables given that for the 95,570 other workers the 10 hour day has not resulted in decreased wages except in the case of 8,320 of them, and that for the remainder of 87,250 who form 91.3 per cent. of the total, the former daily wage has been maintained if not increased. (P. 434.)

Gesammelte Abhandlungen. Bd. III. 1906. (*Complete Works. Vol. III.*) *Die Volkswirthschaftliche Bedeutung der Verkürzung des industriellen Arbeitstages.* [*The Economic Significance of a Shorter Working Day.*] Ernst Abbé. *Two Lectures read before the Economic Society at Jena, November 6 and December 5, 1901.*

Comparison of Hourly Earnings of 233 Piece-Workers in the Zeiss Optical Works.

In the last year of the Nine-Hour System (April 1, 1899-April 1, 1900) and in the first year of the Eight-Hour System (April 1, 1900-April 1, 1901).

Year	Total Number Piece-work Hours	Earnings (in Marks)	Earnings. per Hr. (in Pf.)	Ratio of Increase
	559,169			
1899-1900	Average per man 2400	345,899	61.9	
	509,599			100:116.2
1900-1901	Average per man 2187	366,484	71.9	

(P. 158.)

The last column shows, then, that the pay per hour rose in the ratio of 100:116.2; but the ratio of 8:9 is 100:112.5. If the wages per hour had risen in the ratio of 100:112.5, the men would have earned exactly the same in 8 hours as before in 9, and would also have done just the same amount of work, since with piece-work prices remaining the same the wages are the measure of production. Now if the ratio is not 100:112.5, but 100:116.2, that is, 3 3/10% more, the day's output has risen by 3 3/10%, that is, by 1/30 of the former day's output. In the second year, then, every 30 of these 233 operatives did as much as 31 did the year before, or each man in the second year did ten extra days' work. That is no insignificant difference. (P. 211.)

What interpretation can be put upon the fact that the last column shows an increase of 3 3/10% in the day's output ? . . . I have thought over very carefully what possible causes might have been at work. One thing must be dismissed in advance, the idea of any change in business conditions: there was no difference in the two years in the demands made upon the shops. . . . At last it occurred to me that there might have been differences of the weather in the two years, . . . for extremes of temperature cripple work greatly. But the meteorological tables show that the years were alike with respect to the weather also.

I have no course left but to say that the cause of this variation in the day's output of 1/30% is precisely the change in working-time and what is involved in it. In our case I think we can say with decisiveness what was merely assumed in earlier instances, that the reduction of working-hours may bring about not only no decrease but even an increase, paradoxical as it may sound, of the resultant work. (Pp. 213-214.)

C. RELATION TO REGULARITY OF EMPLOYMENT.

Wherever the hours of labor have been shortened employment tends to become more regular. In place of alternating periods of intense overwork and periods of idleness, employers have found it possible to distribute work more evenly throughout the year. No incident of industrial life is more disastrous to the worker than the irregularity which characterizes most industries. The "rush" season of long hours often strains health and vitality beyond the power of recovery during the slack season.

Work and Wealth: A Human Valuation. J. A. HOBSON. *New York, The Macmillan Company, 1914.*

If all unemployment could be spread evenly over the working year, taken out in a shortening of the ordinary workingday, and in the provision of periodic and sufficient holidays, an immense addition would be made to the sum of industrial welfare. Thus, without any reduction in the aggregate of labor-time, a sensible reduction in the human cost of labor might be achieved, if law, custom, or organized labor policy made it impossible for employers to vary violently or suddenly the volume of employment and to sandwich periods of overtime with periods of short-time. These baneful irregularities of employment appear inevitable so long as they remain permissible, as do sweating wages and other bad conditions of labor. When they are no longer permissible, the organized intelligence of the trade will adjust itself to the new conditions, generally with little or no loss, often with positive gain. (P. 229-230.)

The human wastes or excessive costs, entailed by conditions of employment which impose unequal burdens upon workers with equal capacity to bear them, or which distribute the burden unequally in time over the same set of workers, alternating slack periods with periods of excessive over-time, are obvious. Unfortunately the operation of our industrial system has not hitherto taken these into sufficient account. Though the physical, moral and social injuries, due to alternating periods of over and under work, are generally admitted, the full costs of such irregularity, human and even economic, are far from being adequately realized. While some attempts at "decasualisation" are being made, the larger and more wasteful irregularities of seasonal and cyclical fluctuations are still regarded as irremediable. By the workers themselves and even by social reformers, the injury inflicted upon wages and the standard of living by irregularity of employment is appreciated far more adequately than the related injury inflicted on the physique and morale of the worker by sandwiching periods of over-exertion between intervals of idleness. . . .

Over a large number of the fields of industry the excesses and defects of such irregularity prevail to an extent which adds greatly to the total human cost of the products. (Pp. 79-80.)

Principles of Labor Legislation. John R. Commons, *University of Wisconsin, and* John B. Andrews, *Secretary American Association for Labor Legislation. New York, Harpers, 1916.*

Shorter hours likewise tend to steady employment. When no restrictions are placed on hours of work in a seasonal industry, the tendency is to concentrate the work in a brief, busy season with long hours of overtime. Hour regulation except in the case of perishable products and those subject to change in fashion, forces a more even distribution of the work over a longer period. When the woman's eight-hour law was in force in Illinois factories inspectors noted "a greater uniformity of work and rest" as one of its results. (Pp. 203-204.)

Massachusetts House Document, No. 153, 1850. Minority Report of the Special Committee Re Limitation of Hours of Work.

Taking all the factories in the State into consideration, they probably do not keep their machinery in operation, on an average through a series of years, more than sufficient time to make ten hours a day for the whole time. They run a portion of the time from eleven to fourteen hours a day, and at other times, in consequence of over-stocked markets, many of them are obliged to stop entirely. The operatives are thus subjected at times, to the evils of excessive labor, and at other times, to the no less evil of being altogether unemployed. If the hours of labor were restricted, both evils would in a great measure be avoided, and the advantages of greater regularity and safety be secured to both employers and employed. (P. 30.)

Report of the Illinois Factory Inspectors. 1893.

A valuable result of the new law already to some extent obtained, is the greater uniformity of work and rest. . . . Formerly the custom prevailed of working overtime in many trades during a part of the year and then closing the factory outright, or working three or four very long days a week. This irregularity is one of the most cruelly demoralizing experiences . . . injurious alike to health and to every habit of thrift and persevering effort. (Pp. 18-19.)

Some Ethical Gains Through Legislation. FLORENCE KELLEY, *General Secretary of the National Consumers League. New York and London. Macmillan, 1905.*

In the needle-trades, the effectual establishment of the legal working day and the working week serves, wherever this has been accomplished, as for instance, in Massachusetts, to mitigate both the enforced overwork and the enforced idleness which characterize those trades when left to the free play of industrial forces. Where the working time is effectively limited, preparations are made systematically, in advance of the height of the season, for meeting the coming pressure. Space and machinery are provided, and extra hands are trained, by preparing stockwork, for the finer work to be demanded of them later. Thus some of the unemployed are temporarily absorbed into the regular industrial army, and the contrast between the extremes of the seasons is mitigated. (Pp. 120-121.)

Report of the Wisconsin Bureau of Labor and Industrial Statistics. 1907-1908. Part VII. Women Workers in Milwaukee Tanneries. IRENE OSGOOD, *Special Agent.*

These illustrations are sufficient to indicate the importance of considering irregularity of employment, overtime and undertime, in any study of wages. It affects the wages, habits and morals of employees more than any other factor in the industry. Certainty of an occupation, and regularity of work are practically essential to the welfare and happiness of those who earn their living day by day. (P. 1060.)

Bulletin of the United States Bureau of Labor. No. 80. January, 1909. Woman and Child Wage-Earners in Great Britain. VICTOR S. CLARK, Ph. D.

Though in many factories the later laws have not reduced hours of work, they have exercised an important influence in making these hours more regular. Irregularity is due principally to two causes, both of which are in great part remediable. The first is the bad working habits of the operatives themselves. In the old days workmen would lay off the first part of the week and then try to make up wages by excessive hours just before pay day. This is still an evil where manufacturing is carried on in the homes. The second cause is the seasonal demand for goods in some industries, which presses manufacturers for heavy deliveries in certain times of the year.

They used to meet this by putting on extra employees, sending work to outworkers, and by overtime. These were uneconomic expedients, and under the influence of the factory regulations a better distribution of work throughout the year has in many trades already been accomplished. . . . Factory accommodations are more adequate than formerly, so that extra hands can be taken on when needed. This causes some irregularity of employment for these temporary employees; or rather it might be said that they are given an opportunity for employment that would not exist if the regular hands worked longer hours. (P. 52.)

The great effect of this act (1867) stipulating a normal day was to lessen irregularity rather than to lessen hours worked per week, for even before 1867 the hours of work in a week often would not exceed 60. The need for alteration was not so much due to the number of hours as to the irregularity of work. At times of pressure employers worked their employees any number of hours they pleased, and the irregular habits of the work people themselves often compelled employers to work long hours to make up for lost time. (P. 53.)

. . . There are some material and moral benefits to be traced directly to the factory laws. They have made the hours of work more regular, relieving workers of the tyranny of their own bad habits and of inefficient industrial administration, whereby formerly they experienced alternations of idleness and excessive labor, injurious alike to their health and morals. (P. 72.)

United States Congress. Senate Document, No. 110. Report on Conditions of Employment in the Iron and Steel Industry in the United States. Vol. III. Working Conditions and the Relations of Employers and Employees. Sixty-second Congress, 1st Session, 1911. Washington, 1913.

It might be expected that in an industry where there was so much pressure for Sunday and overtime work there would be constant employment throughout the year. As a matter of fact, however, the iron and steel industry is more irregular in its operation and shows greater fluctuations in its labor force during the course of the year than any of the larger manufacturing industries whose demand is not seasonal. This high degree of irregularity of employment was the subject of more frequent complaint on the part of the workmen interviewed than any other condition connected with the industry. Some of the managers and superintendents also consider it one of the greatest obstacles to securing a highly efficient working force.

Both the overtime work and the irregularity of operation are in large part results of the same cause, which is one of the fundamental policies in the present day management of the industry. This policy consists in running a department at top speed and under the heaviest pressure while there is an active demand for its particular products and then shutting it down as soon as the market becomes weak. During these periods of heavy pressure the production is large and the immediate costs frequently are far below normal, presenting a fine showing for the mill when only a single month's cost sheets are considered. When the mill is shut down, however, not only do the heavy fixed charges continue and the machines depreciate, but the workmen lose their skill and efficiency rapidly and the working organization is frequently injured by the loss of the best workmen who leave to seek places elsewhere. Some of the best managers assert that the losses from these causes more than counterbalance the gains secured during the months of rush work, and they are confident that they could make a better showing in economy of production for the year as a whole if the mills were operated regularly at a moderate pace.

The irregularity of employment constitutes a ground of complaint on the part of the employees not only because it considerably reduces their annual income, but because it makes it impossible for them to make or carry out any plans extending at all into the future. . . .

The reports of the Immigration Commission show how during the long periods of depression in the steel industry the families of steel workers are supported by the work of the women and children in cigar factories and other so-called "complementary" industries. These industries locate in the steel towns to take advantage of the large supply of woman and child labor which can not be utilized in the steel mills. (Pp. 21-22.)

English Factory Legislation. ERNST VON PLENER. *London, Chapman and Hall, 1873.*

By establishing a uniform and restricted working day, the Legislature exerted a most beneficial influence over the whole working class; the compulsory fixed time for commencing and leaving off work acted as a salutary check upon idleness as well as against excessive zeal, both of which are alike injurious to morals and health. Fortunately both working men and masters alike are generally beginning to appreciate the advantages which regularity in the working system and in the mode of living, resulting from a judicious adjustment of the working hours, confers on all concerned, and thus it has come to pass that factory legislation, which on its first introduction was ridiculed as a monstrosity and prima facie, an abortive experiment, and which, moreover, was attacked and set at nought as an infringement on personal and industrial liberty, is today recognized in England as one of the soundest foundations of social reform and one of the most beneficial institutions of the State. (Pp. 114-115.)

British Sessional Papers, Vols. XXIX-XXX. 1876. Factory and Workshops Acts Commission. Vol. XXIX. Report. Appendix E. Report of Conference of Members of Women's Trade Unions on the Factory and Workshops Acts, 1875.

. . . The permission granted to season trades for the extension of the hours to fourteen per day, during certain periods of the year, should be withdrawn, with the view of equalizing the work throughout the year. . . .

Bookbinders complained that the trade was most unnecessarily considered by the law a season trade, . . . The existence of the modification made employers careless of due economy in time. (P. 193.)

British Sessional Papers. Vol. XXIX-XXX. 1876. Factory and Workshops Acts Commission. Vol. XXIX. Report.

A very large number of the orders of customers, which it has been usual to keep back till the last minute, and then throw upon the already fully burdened workers, not merely can be quite as easily given so as to have plenty of time for their completion, but also will be so given, and are in fact so given, when and as often as the customer is made to recognize that he otherwise runs the risk of not having his orders completed in time to suit his own convenience. It is from their feelings that this is so that the workers in some of the most overworked of trades, and a few of the sub-inspectors, have represented to us that what is needed from a reform of the Factory Acts is not a further restriction of hours, but the total abolition of all modifications whatever. We so far concur in this that we believe it is not necessary to retain in all the Acts any provisions by way of relaxation which it is unadvisable to grant once and for all to the whole trade. (Pp. XLI-XLII.)

The Eight Hours Day. Sidney Webb *and* Harold Cox, B. A. *London, Walter Scott, 1891.*

If it were known beforehand that excessive hours of work were absolutely forbidden, then the general public and the shopkeepers would make their arrangements accordingly. If, for example, Jones knows that, owing to the operation of an Eight Hours' Act, a pair of trousers cannot possibly be made in less than three days, he will take care to give three clear days' notice to his tailor. Or to take a still more homely illustration, the housewife who knows that she cannot buy bread on Sunday will take care to order a double supply on Saturday. In the same way, if the biscuit trade, the fancy box trade, and the artificial flower trade were subject to the same rigid law as the cotton trade, every one would soon accommodate himself or herself to the necessities of the case. Orders would be given longer in advance, and the work would be spread more equally over the whole year, to the great advantage of the workers.

In support of this contention we cannot do better than quote the opinion of Mr. Lakeman. This most energetic of factory inspectors has frequently stated, as the result of his long experience in watching almost every industry in the kingdom, that overtime is in most trades an utterly unnecessary evil. For a particular illustration we may further appeal to the opinion of the head of a large firm of tobacco manufacturers in Southwark. This gentleman informed one of the present writers in the course of conversation that he always refused to allow overtime. "Possibly," he said, "we lose a few orders in consequence, but we get a more regular and steady business, and we prefer it." Nor would even the few orders be lost if the rule applied to all competing firms. (Pp. 161-163.)

British Sessional Papers. Vol. XXXIX. Part I. 1893. Royal Commission on Labour. Minutes of Evidence.

Testimony of Mr. William Allan, Allan & Co., Marine Engine Builders.

. . . Irregularity of employment is the first and obvious effect of the system. . . . Until all the men in a trade are in steady employment, overtime is clearly uncalled-for in practice as it is wrong in principle, that is systematic overtime; occasional or incidental overtime to meet emergencies will always be unavoidable, and does no harm. The real cause of overtime will be found in the cupidity of employers. In busy times an employer is tempted to take on more work than he can hope to accomplish within the legitimate hours of labour. Hence his resort to systematic overtime. No employer, once aware of the capabilities of his establishment, has a right to do this unless he is prepared to employ extra shifts of men. But, in any case, overtime would not be possible unless the men themselves were amenable to the prospect of increase of gains. The system is thus demoralising as well as pernicious economically. The universal limitation of the hours of labour to that term during which the human machine can do its work without fatigue or weariness is only a question of time. The principle is being recognized more and more; its economic value is attested alike by analogy and experience. Therefore, the absurdity of permitting overtime whilst agitating for shorter hours is apparent. No man can work systematic overtime without physical degeneration. (P. 465.)

Eight Hours for Work. John Rae. *London and New York, Macmillan & Co., 1894.*

Even in trades where the irregularities of the work-hours have come from the dilatoriness of customers in sending orders or from the exigencies of the seasons, greater regularity has generally resulted from a shortening of the day. Orders arrived in better time, and the work was better distributed through the year. (P. 118.)

Getting a Living: The Problem of Wealth and Poverty —of Profits, Wages, and Trade Unionism. George L. Bolen. *New York and London, The Macmillan Company. 1903.*

The weariness of the workmen next day brings loss to the employer also, especially when they are paid by time. And unless the hurried job is one that must be done quickly or not at all, it is not an addition to the business of the trade. It would otherwise be done later in regular hours, and would postpone a little further the dull season of partial employment. Wise employers know overtime is bad. (P. 409.)

A Handbook of Political Questions of the Day and the Arguments on Either Side. Sidney Buxton, M. P. *11th Edition. London, John Murray, 1903. Legal Limitation of Hours.*

The legal limitation of hours is supported on the grounds: . . . 37. (a) That the limitation of hours would lead to a more uniform output year by year, and thus tend to diminish the great fluctuations in trade: Inflations and depressions so injurious to all classes. (b) That the limitation of hours, and especially the prohibition of "overtime," would lead to a more steady and equal production over the year; and thus tend to diminish over-pressure at one period of the year, and the under-pressure at another.

38. That the abolition of systematic "overtime" would tend to make work and wages more regular and less spasmodic. The existence of "overtime" is largely due to the irregularity and uncertainty of employment. (P. 169.)

British Association for the Advancement of Science. 73rd Meeting. 1903. Women's Labour: Third Report of the Committee . . . appointed to investigate the Economic Effect of Legislation Regulating Women's Labour. London, Murray, 1904.

Employees, so far as their opinions have been gathered, are unanimous in approving the restriction to the maximum allowed. . . . The Acts have had considerable effect in spreading work more uniformly through the week, month, or year, where there is occasional pressure. . . . (Pp. 340-341.)

British Sessional Papers. Vol. X. 1905. Report of Chief Inspector of Factories and Workshops.

I am glad to be able to report, however, that many employers are beginning to aim at better economic conditions for those they employ. They recognize, and rightly, that it is better if possible to spread their orders over a longer period for execution and to induce their clients to fall in with this idea, than to have a tremendous rush for a short time and then be forced to turn away many of their better trained and more highly skilled workers at short notice. (P. 232.)

A History of Factory Legislation. B. L. HUTCHINS *and* A. HARRISON. *Second Edition. London, King, 1911.*

. . . The "Manchester School" had taken it as self-evident that the output of industry must be reduced in proportion to the reduction of hours. The inspectors went about making friends with the manufacturers and studying the relation of hours and wages in concrete instances, and discovered, with a surprise that now-a-days strikes us as naive, that the output of eleven hours' work might be greater than that of twelve.* Evidence accumulated that the long hours customary in other trades, far from being productive, positively tended to irregularity of trade, periodical slackness alternating with seasons of excessive hurry and work, an amount of labour being put into a few months that might with better organization, have occupied a year. (Pp. 122-123.)

Seasonal Trades. Edited by SIDNEY WEBB *and* ARNOLD FREEMAN. *London, Constable & Co., 1912.*

Introduction.

Considering the paramount importance of regularity of employment in preserving the standard of life, an importance even transcending that of the wage, it seems extraordinary that no Trade Union regulations have been devised to insure continuity of employment. . . .

The main point of attack on the part of Trade Unions at the present time seems to be overtime. . . .

The Lancashire cotton operatives resist overtime on principle and thereby greatly diminish the tendency to seasonal fluctuation in the trade which emanates from the dealings on the Stock Exchange. The recent introduction of heavier locomotives on the railways and the consequent reorganisation of traffic might have meant wholesale discharges had not the Railway Servants' Association made arrangements to minimise the effects of the transition from busy to slack seasons by shorten-

* See Factory Inspectors' Report, May, 1845, p. 20.

ing hours, paying out-of-work benefit and acting as labour exchanges in the trade. . . .

The unions have found a vulnerable point of seasonal irregularity in overtime, for from it arise some of the worst evils of irregularity. But the trades in which overtime is found to the greatest extent are often those where the workers are least organised to resist it, and the law, if there is any, is often evaded. Without doubt seasonal unemployment and under-employment could be much diminished by distributing the work more evenly throughout the year by means of restriction of overtime, general shortening of the working day, and short time rather than dismissal during slackness. (Pp. 61-63.)

Short of extending to the men the protection of the Factory and Workshop Act in regard to the limitation of hours, there seems to be no effective means of checking the excessive overtime worked at present in the trade. The whole paraphernalia of men, women, flaring gas, machines, iron, and garments cannot be smuggled away as the one or two offending women; and an 8 a. m. to 8 p. m. time limit, or other limit on the basis of a fixed period for all alike would be checked at once by the Factory Inspector. Nor would the regulation affect employment in the West End trade to any great extent. Except in so far as the bespoke garment can be interchanged for the high-class "readymade" or "wholesale bespoke" garment, trade cannot leave the district; and here, as we have seen, it is already passing to the factory. The West End customer will be compelled to wait, if the West End firm is compelled to withstand his call for undue haste; and the effect will be for the customer to exercise a greater forethought in orders for bespoke garments, with the result to eliminate the "special," to prolong the busy season, and to confine hours within normal limits throughout the year. (P. 89.)

National Conference on the Prevention of Destitution. 1912. Papers and Proceedings, London, P. S. King & Sons, 1912. The Limitation of Overtime. ALEX GOSSIP, *General Secretary, National Amalgamated Furnishing Trades' Association.*

In addition to the extra hours of work, with all this means in an unhealthy atmosphere such as usually obtains in workshops and factories, the invariable accompaniment of overtime is a feverish unrest and unhealthy excitement due to the pressure which the foreman nearly always brings to bear upon the workmen. In too many instances this means a resort to alcoholic stimulants, with all their evil effects upon the tired and weary worker. (P. 452.)

About fourteen years ago, owing to the excessive and systematic overtime which was being worked in several of the cabinet-making districts in Scotland, the Trade Union determined to place further restrictions upon its working, and were successful in reducing it to a maximum of five hours per man per week, irrespective of the number of hours he might have put in during the regular recognized working hours of the day. This was found to be very successful, and many of the employers told the writer afterwards that it had been a good thing for them, as they had been forced to adopt better methods and look a little more ahead than they had previously been in the habit of doing, thereby admitting that the previous systematic overtime had not been necessary at all. (P. 454.)

(Mr. A. A. Watts, a compositor, spoke as follows:) . . . He also could not see how any keen employer could be in favor of overtime, as the productivity of the worker certainly decreased as the overtime went on. He always got the best work out of the men in the first four or five hours in the morning, and he considered that from 7 in the morning to mid-day would be as good a working day as they could have. The overtime system was also expensive, and he did not see why any employer should keep it up. (P. 464.)

Mr. Fred Hughes (Birmingham N. C. P. D.) spoke

as follows: . . . Cycle accessories was a seasonal trade, and although they had got a working week of a certain specified number of hours, the men were not actually working those hours because there was a great amount of short time, and it did seem that if the hours were limited to a greater extent than they were there would be a great deal less short time. Instead of waiting for the rush of the season's trade, the firm would so organize its work as to prepare for that rush in advance; and even in the case of contract work he did not think there was a necessity for the constant spells of "rush" which meant that more men had always to be kept on hand than were actually wanted at other times. He thought that the limitation of hours might avoid that. With regard to office staffs, they were subject in an extraordinary degree to systematic overtime, and when it occurred for eight months out of the twelve, it was clearly due to understaffing, and he thought that if the staffs were increased it would simplify the unemployment problem. Slovenly management was no doubt often the cause. A friend of his, after some years in one office, ultimately reached the position of managing clerk, and one of the first things he did was to prohibit overtime entirely. He made it a rule that at 5:30 every evening every book was to be closed, and that any work unfinished was to be taken on the next morning by the clerk in charge of that particular work. The result was that in six months' time the same amount of work was done by the same staff without the necessity for any overtime at all, and there was a saving in gas and, in the winter, in coal. All that happened to the staff was that instead of working late at night and slacking in the morning, they came fresh in the morning and got through more work than they could possibly do in the hours of the evening. There was a distinct gain in health and increased leisure and opportunities for the workers concerned, and there was also a gain to the firm. (Pp. 465-466.)

Short Hours and Regularity of Employment.—New Zealand

Report of the New Zealand Department of Labour. 1895.

That the Inspector should have full power over permits for overtime is essentially necessary, for the physique and strength which would enable one person or set of persons to work very long hours with impunity may be absent in the case of others. Few trades are entirely healthy; almost every industrial employment has its own particular disease and its own particular drawback. Even shop-assistants suffer from too long standing. Overtime-work at all is a thing to be deprecated. It is generally unnecessary and preventable, and I look forward to a time when the general public will be educated highly enough to desist (except under absolute necessity) from rushing to their trades-people with sudden orders for clothing, etc., when a little forethought for the health and comfort of those employed would dispense with undue haste caused by obedience to some whim of fashion. Overtime-work engenders habits of irregularity, and the small extra money earned is often dearly gained by the draft upon future strength, and by the slackness of employment which results in the relaxation from full tension. (P. 3.)

Jahresberichte der Gewerbe-Aufsichtsbeamten im Königreich Württemberg für das Jahr 1902. [Reports of the Factory Inspectors in the Kingdom of Württemberg for 1903]. Stuttgart, Lindemann, 1904.

But it is urgently necessary that the abuses (of overtime) which have become common should be prevented and that the habit of some employers of working overtime to the utmost legal limits, should be stopped by the gradual restriction and ultimate prohibition of all overtime. . . . . These abuses are repeatedly spoken of in the reports, . . . employers compelling their women to work at times, with feverish intensity for 13 hours, while perhaps a little later there is no work or scarcely any. (P. 194.)

Handwörterbuch der Staatswissenschaft. Bd. I. [*Compendium of Political Science. Vol. I.*] *Edited by* Drs. J. Conrad, *Professor of Political Science in Halle;* L. Elster, *Ober Reg. Rath in Berlin;* W. Lexis, *Professor of Political Science in Göttingen and* Edg. Loening, *Professor of Law in Halle. Arbeitszeit.* [*Hours of Work.*] Dr. H. Herkner, *Berlin. Jena, Fischer, 1909.*

A rigid limitation of the daily hours of work is often advocated, to be only relaxed under circumstances of extraordinary urgency, with the idea that thus the extremes in the lives of workers, the evil alternation between forced production and crises might be obviated. (P. 1204.)

VII. UNIFORMITY ESSENTIAL TO JUSTICE TO EMPLOYERS.

Few employers are able to grant their employes reduction of hours, even if they are convinced of its advantages, while their competitors are under no such obligation. The uniform requirement of limited working hours, therefore, not only checks the unscrupulous employer, but makes it possible for the enlightened and humane employer to shorten the working day without fear of underbidding competitors.

Massachusetts House Documents. No. 80. 1855. Report on Ten-Hour Petition.

If the large manufacturing companies reduce their hours of labor, all the smaller corporations immediately follow their example. The reason for this is found in the fact that the most intelligent portion of the operatives invariably seek employment at such places as run their machinery the least number of hours; and as the intelligent operative is the most profitable to the company, hence the fact, if the smaller corporations wish to retain their good help, they *must* conform to the same rules adopted by the larger ones. (P. 4.)

Report of the Massachusetts Bureau of Statistics of Labor. 1881.

As a further result, we have found that a large majority of the manufacturers would prefer ten hours to any greater number, "if only all would agree to it." Repeatedly has it occurred, when our agents have made known their errand, that almost the first words of the manufacturer would be, "It (ten hours) would be better for manufacturer and operative, if it could only be made universal"; and these words, always spoken so spontaneously as to show that they were the expression of a settled conviction, may be fairly taken to express the united wisdom of the manufacturers of textile fabrics in New York and New England. (P. 458.)

As one reason for this it was constantly said, that, if all worked but ten hours, then it would be the same for all, and so everybody would have just as fair a chance for success under ten as now under more hours. (P. 459.)

Report of the United States Industrial Commission on the Relations and Conditions of Capital and Labor Employed in Manufactures and General Business. Vol. XIV. 1901.

Testimony of Mr. Thomas O'Donnell, Secretary of the Fall River Mule Spinners' Association, and of the National Spinners' Association:

It is what I might term sometimes the selfishness probably of some of our manufacturers that would keep the mills open at night. I do not think it is the press of orders, for this reason: In enlarging their plants, sometimes we have had an instance of it in this city where a manufacturer made an addition to his plant, and instead of supplying it with machinery for the various departments, he only supplied it with machinery for one department. The result was that, in order to get the necessary product to run that department, he had to run the other department nights. Now, when he built the addition, if he had equipped it with the requisite machinery, he would not have had to do that. This was one instance, but during all the progress and history of the cotton industry in this city our manufacturers always have got along without working overtime to fill their orders up to 2 or 3 years ago, and the innovation in this matter by this man was the cause mostly. He was the cause of the other manufacturers wanting to do the same. If he had never done it, there would not have been any other manufacturer in the city of Fall River attempting it, and they said: "Stop him from doing it, and we will stop doing it." That shows that they were doing it for their own protection. (Pp. 570-571.)

Need of Uniformity.—United States

Bulletin of the United States Bureau of Labor, No. 80. January, 1909. Woman and Child Wage-earners in Great Britain. VICTOR S. CLARK, Ph. D.

Two distinctions need to be made at the outset—between the average and the abnormal day in all establishments, and between the average and the abnormal establishment. For instance, in a clothing factory, the average working hours throughout the year may be 54 a week; but during the spring and autumn these hours, unless regulated, may rise to 66 or 72 a week. Likewise, of several boot and shoe factories a majority, and those generally the largest and best establishments, may have a 54-hour week, while a number of small shops, ranking as factories under the law, may work their hands 60 hours a week. Furthermore, of a number of clothing factories, several may be able to keep very near the 54-hour weekly average throughout the year, while supplying the same trade and competing successfully with factories that work short hours some months in the year and excessively long hours the remaining months.

These time variations, as well as the wage variations described later, found in competing industries in the same vicinity, indicate a margin within which the condition of workers might be improved without increasing the maximum labor cost of production, so as to raise the market price of the articles manufactured. For it is not reasonable to suppose that mills which regularly work fewer hours at higher wages than establishments which compete with them are working at a loss. Indeed, they are generally making a satisfactory profit. If so, it follows that the other establishments are either making an excessive profit out of their employees or that they are operating under uneconomic conditions. If the entire production of the articles in question could be centered in the best-organized mills, the articles could be sold at the same price, and the workers enjoy the advantage of shorter hours and higher wages. So far as legislation is able to hasten the uniform application of these superior conditions of production in any industry, by requiring the conditions observed in the best mills to be enforced in all, it is serving the workers without taxing the rest of the community, unless it be a few incompetent, over-grasping, or it may be merely unfortunate employers. English factory legislation—at least the modern acts—has followed the principle of bringing average conditions of employment up to the best conditions of employment in each industry. (P. 48.)

British Sessional Papers. Vol. XXVI. 1847-1848. Reports of Inspectors of Factories for the half-year ending April 30, 1848.

Justice requires that, when the law interferes with the productive power of capital, all who are in the restricted trade should be kept to one rule as to time; and it was upon the urgent representation of mill-owners that such was notoriously not the case, that in the amended Bill of 1844, restrictions were proposed to check such fraudulent over-working . . . (P. 7.)

British Sessional Papers. Vol. XXII. 1849. Reports of Inspectors of Factories. Appendix. Evidence of the Opinions of Persons employed in Factories, respecting the Ten Hours' Act, collected in September, October and November, 1848.

R. J. Saunders, Inspector:

Former reports from some of my colleagues and from myself, declare clearly the opinion, that nothing but one uniform set of hours for all the persons employed in the same mill, in each of the protected classes, can effectually guard such operatives from overwork. (P. 107.)

British Sessional Papers. Vol. XVI. 1867. Reports of Inspectors of Factories.

With respect to overtime, competition in commerce is successful often by decimal profits. If a man has 50,000 spindles, and each spindle revolves 4,000 times a minute, and at each revolution wraps round the bobbin three and a half inches of thread, it is easy to see how valuable minutes become, and what moral energy it must sometimes require on the part of the manufacturer to resist the winding on of a few more yards. Thus the power given in the Bleaching and Dyeing Works Act to make up time said to be lost, from any cause whatever, offers an equally irresistible temptation to a bleacher with not a very susceptible conscience, to add to the profit of his day against the conscientious labor of a neighboring bleacher, who would deem it a degradation to be suspected of overwork. It also places the conscientious bleacher at a very great disadvantage with his neighbor in the same market, besides exciting acrimonious feelings between them, weakening also the law, and the power of its administrators. (Pp. 56-57.)

British Sessional Papers. Vol. XIV. 1868-1869. Reports of Inspectors of Factories for half-year ending October 31, 1868.

Every manufacturer ought to feel perfectly satisfied that the restrictions upon the labor of his "hands" should be neither more nor less than those upon his competitors, and he ought to be recognizant of what his competitors are able to do and are doing. (Pp. 15-16.)

Feeling that uniformity of working is essential to a just administration of the law, I have endeavored to obtain this uniformity for all establishments in which the occupations are precisely the same in establishments whether under the Factory Acts or under the Workshops Acts. (P. 19.)

Report of the Birmingham and District Trades Council upon the Factories Act and the Workshops Bill.

We are of opinion—2nd. That any measure for the regulation of the labor in factories should apply to all equally irrespective of the number employed therein, whether it be a detached building, or part or parts of a dwelling house so occupied. 3rd. That all should be subject to the same system of inspection and penalties for non-compliance. (P. 313.)

British Sessional Papers. Vol. XXIX-XXX. 1876. Factories and Workshops Acts Commission.

Vol. XXIX. Report.

Mr. Redgrave states: "I believe that the difficulty in making (The Acts) uniform arises from the fact that the circumstances of the different trades vary very much,—but then all the main features of the restrictions could be made very fairly uniform without injury to the employers at all."

Similarly Mr. Baker urges, in reference to the present unequal condition of the law, that "we should, as far as we possibly can, equalize it all," and again to a question as to the reason for including all trades under the latest of the Factory Acts, he says, "the one great evil is that they work different hours." (P. 14.)

A Shorter Working Day. R. A. HADFIELD, *of Hadfield's Steel Foundry Co., Sheffield, and* H. DE B. GIBBINS, *M. A. London, Methuen, 1892.*

Again the writer is inclined to think that shorter hours would eventually tend to more uniform output, and to some extent, assist in modifying the serious fluctuations of business which are baneful alike to master and man. There is nothing that an employer peruses with more interest than his order sheets. Now, under the present system, too often there is extremely high pressure at one time, followed by a reversal which is exceedingly disastrous to all concerned. Trade suddenly expands, machinery is wanted in haste, telegrams fly to and fro, promises are made which often cannot be performed. If an order of importance is given probably penalties are specified. The manufacturer is in a state of feverish anxiety until the matter is cleared off his books. Overtime must be worked, and there is high pressure all round. If a uniform day existed, and overtime were made more difficult all employers in each particular branch being on the same footing would alike work under the same conditions, and would not have the same temptations as at present to outbid one another and work at such high pressure. (Pp. 116-117.)

British Sessional Papers. Vol. XXXIX. Part I. 1893. Royal Commission on Labour. Minutes of Evidence.

Testimony of Mr. Tom Mann.

4390. . . . In some of the earlier Factory Acts almost every enactment was guarded by permission to work overtime in various circumstances. For various reasons those exceptions have been very largely diminished in amount, and in, I believe, all cases, it is held with advantageous results upon the regularity of employment. I think that irregularity comes very largely from the freedom which the employer has to pile up the labor at any time that he pleases, and that if he were prevented, and all his rivals were prevented from doing that, there would be no necessity on the part of any of them to do it. At the present time an employer very often puts on overtime, or, in the case of East London, says that work must be done by tomorrow, when he knows that it will take all night to do it, merely because he is afraid that if he is not as compliant as all that, some other rival will be more compliant, and he will lose the order. But if he were prevented from exercising that option, as I believe, to the detriment of the workers, he would find that his rivals would be equally prevented, and that there would be no need at all for that overtime. (P. 293.)

British Sessional Papers. Vol. XXI. 1894. Report of the Chief Inspector of Factories and Workshops.

I believe, therefore, that although a withdrawal of the overtime exception would meet with protest from employers who have developed its use from an exception into a principle, there are some who would welcome, and many who would be indifferent to such an amendment; that the large class of employers engaged in the textile and allied trades from whom permission to work overtime has been rigidly withheld, would greet as a measure of justice its withdrawal now from trades, logically no more entitled to the exception than their own; and that by the workers its abolition would be welcomed with feelings of the warmest gratitude. (P. 11.)

Need of Uniformity.—Great Britain

The Case for the Factory Acts. Edited by MRS. SIDNEY WEBB. *London, Richard, 1901.*

Now and again an employer complains of some hard experience, and forgets that a departure from rigid rule would destroy the certainty which he feels that the law is treating him exactly as it is his competitors. Such a feeling of security is essential to business enterprise. (P. 93.)

British Sessional Papers. Vol. X. 1901. Report of the Chief Inspector of Factories and Workshops.

. . . A lack of loyal adherence to reasonable hours of employment by many laundry occupiers [illegible]es the difficulty for those who make the attempt in real earnestness. Many employers gladly welcome further regulation as a means of organizing and controlling the workers. "What is the use of my making the effort to so organize my work that the laundry shall close at 8 p. m. like other reasonable work-places do," said a disheartened employer; "all the neighboring laundries are open until nine, ten, or even eleven o'clock. If we all had to keep the same rules and close at the same time, the law would work fairly; as it is I must just scramble on with the others in the stupid expensive old way." (P. 385.)

British Sessional Papers. Vol. XII. 1903. Report of the Chief Inspector of Factories and Workshops.

After six years' experience of the effect of the present regulations, it is impossible not to feel greatly depressed by the result; the elasticity of the law has tended to encourage rather than check these unsettled hours. (P. 174.)

The innumerable loopholes and subterfuges which it affords to a sharp and unscrupulous employer places his more stupid or more scrupulous competitor at an unfair disadvantage, which is preventable, and therefore should be prevented. The broad, clear limitations, easily understood and capable of being exactly and thoroughly enforced, which apply to other industries under the Act, impose the same obligations and provide the same protection for all alike. This is impossible where regulations cannot be properly enforced and can be continually evaded with success. (P. 174.)

Handwörterbuch der Staatswissenschaften. Bd. I. [*Compendium of Political Science. Vol. I.*] *Edited by* DRS. J. CONRAD, *Professor of Political Science in Halle;* L. ELSTER, *Ober Reg. Rath in Berlin;* W. LEXIS, *Professor of Law in Halle. Arbeitszeit.* [*Hours of Work*]. DR. H. HERKNER, *Berlin. Jena, Fischer, 1909.*

As reduction of hours, under some circumstances, is entirely in the interests of intelligently managed enterprises, it has not been uncommon for employers to establish a shorter day of their own accord.

It is doubtful whether the State would have arrived at the restriction of hours so soon, had it not been for the experiments of such enlightened men. Nevertheless, it would not do to leave the whole domain of hours entirely to the growing insight and good intentions of employers. They are not always enlightened, and furthermore there are many cases which need reduced hours, but where it is not to be expected that the employers would think so. (P. 1217.)

VII. PROGRESS OF THE SHORTER DAY.

A. STATISTICAL EVIDENCE.

Statistics show that in certain important manufacturing industries, a trend towards shorter hours of labor is manifest. In these industries the relative full time hours (irrespective of unemployment and irregularity) have tended slowly but steadily to decrease.

Bulletin of the United States Bureau of Labor, No. 77. Washington, 1908. Wages and Hours of Labor in Manufacturing Industries, 1890 to 1907.

As compared in each case with the average for the years from 1890 to 1899, the average wages per hour in 1907 were 28.8 per cent. higher, the number of employees in the establishments investigated was 44.4 per cent. greater, and the average hours of labor per week were 5.0 per cent. lower. (Pp. 1-2.)

Relative Employees, Hours Per Week, Wages Per Hour, Full-time Weekly Earnings Per Employee, 1890 to 1907.

(Relative numbers computed on basis of average for 1890-1899=100.0.)

Year	Employees	Hours per week	Wages per hour	Full-time weekly earnings per employee
1890	94.8	100.7	100.3	101.0
1891	97.3	100.5	100.3	100.8
1892	99.2	100.5	100.8	101.3
1893	99.4	100.3	100.9	101.2
1894	94.1	99.8	97.9	97.7
1895	96.4	100.1	98.3	98.4
1896	98.6	99.8	99.7	99.5
1897	100.9	99.6	99.6	99.2
1898	106.4	99.7	100.2	99.9
1899	112.1	99.2	102.0	101.2
1900	115.6	98.7	105.5	104.1
1901	119.1	98.1	108.0	105.9
1902	123.6	97.3	112.2	109.2

Year	Employees	Hours per week	Wages per hour	Full-time weekly earnings per employee
1903	126.5	96.6	116.3	112.3
1904	125.7	95.9	117.0	112.2
1905	133.6	95.9	118.9	114.0
1906	142.9	95.4	124.2	118.5
1907	144.4	95.0	128.8	122.4

(P. 7.)

While wages per hour were higher in the manufacturing and mechanical industries in 1907 than in any other year covered by this report, the regular hours of labor per week were lower in 1907 than in any other year of the period. The table shows that in 1890 the relative hours of labor per week were 100.7, which means that they were 100.7 per cent. of the average hours of labor per week for the ten years from 1890 to 1899, or 0.7 per cent. more than the average for that period. From 1890 the weekly hours decreased until 1894, when the relative number was 99.8. In 1895 there was a slight increase, after which there was a gradual decrease to the minimum in 1907, the relative number for that year being 95.0, or 5 per cent. less than the average hours worked during the base period, 1890 to 1899. It is seen from the table . . . that during the period covered the changes have not been so marked in hours of labor as in wages per hour, but the general course has been toward a reduction. The table on page 4 shows that the hours of labor in 1907 were 5.7 per cent. lower than in 1890, while wages per hour were 28.4 per cent. higher in 1907 than in 1890. (P. 8.)

Bulletin of the United States Bureau of Labor Statistics, No. 128. Washington, 1913. Wages and Hours of Labor in the Cotton, Woolen and Silk Industries, 1890 to 1912.

Cotton Goods Manufacturing and Finishing.

General Summary.

This study shows, for cotton-goods manufacturing, rates of wages per hour, and nominal full-time hours per week for the years 1907 to 1912, inclusive, and in addition it summarizes data published in previous reports of the Bureau of Labor Statistics, and thus furnishes a comparison for the 23-year period, 1890 to 1912, inclusive. This study also shows wages and hours of labor in cotton-goods finishing for 1911 and 1912.

This present report and also previous reports show wages and hours of labor for each of the most important productive occupations in cotton-goods manufacturing, but do not show data for all the occupations in the industry. The occupations for which data are shown in this report . . . include a very large proportion of the total employees on productive work and more than two-fifths of the total employes engaged in both productive and nonproductive work. (P. 5.)

Relative Nominal* Full-time Hours per Week and Relative Rates of Wages Per Hour in Cotton-Goods Manufacturing, 1890 to 1912. (Data are included from 26 establishments, 1890-1903; 23 establishments, 1903, 1904; 30 establishments, 1904, 1905; 30 establishments, 1905, 1906; 38 establishments, 1906, 1907; 36 establishments, 1907-1910; 59 establishments, 1910, 1911; and 88 establishments, 1911, 1912.)

* For definition see p. 919.

Year	Relative nominal full-time hours per week	Relative rate of wages per hour
Average, 1890-1899	100.0	100.0
1890	100.5	101.6
1891	101.2	99.4
1892	101.6	99.2
1893	100.0	105.0
1894	97.5	98.9
1895	99.8	98.2
1896	99.5	104.1
1897	99.1	100.4
1898	100.3	96.7
1899	100.3	95.8

Progress of the Shorter Day.—United States

Year	Relative nominal full-time hours per week	Relative rate of wages per hour
1900	100.1	108.4
1901	99.9	108.8
1902	99.5	113.3
1903	99.3	117.5
1904	99.2	117.1
1905	99.2	118.7
1906	98.7	131.3
1907	97.5	149.8
1908	96.3	148.4
1909	96.4	143.0
1910	94.1	147.7
1911	94.1	149.1
1912	92.4	164.1

(P. 8.)

Woolen and Worsted Goods Manufacturing.

This present report and also previous reports show wages and hours of labor for each of the most important productive occupations in woolen and worsted goods manufacturing, but do not show data for all the occupations in the industry. The occupations . . . include a very large proportion of the total employees on productive work and more than two-fifths of the total employees both in productive and non-productive work. (P. 110.)

Relative Nominal Full-time Hours Per Week and Relative Rates of Wages Per Hour in the Principal Occupations in Woolen and Worsted Goods Manufacturing, 1890 to 1912. (Data are included from 16 establishments, 1890-1903; 17 establishments, 1903, 1904; 27 establishments, 1904, 1905; 26 establishments, 1905, 1906; 29 establishments, 1906, 1907; 19 establishments 1907-1910; 27 establishments, 1910, 1911; and 46 establishments, 1911, 1912.)

Year	Relative nominal full-time hours per week	Relative rate of wages per hour
Average, 1890-1899	100.0	100.0
1890	101.0	99.6
1891	101.0	99.3
1892	101.0	100.7
1893	99.5	105.7
1894	99.0	94.9
1895	100.1	95.3
1896	100.1	98.1
1897	98.4	100.4
1898	99.9	103.3
1899	100.0	102.3
1900	99.8	111.3
1901	99.9	111.9
1902	98.8	114.9
1903	98.7	118.7
1904	97.9	115.4
1905	98.5	119.3
1906	98.4	127.1
1907	97.9	135.3
1908	97.7	128.1
1909	97.8	129.0
1910	96.1	132.5
1911	96.2	133.3
1912	94.6	149.1

(P. 112.)

Total Number of Employees in Woolen and Worsted Goods Manufacturing and Number of Employees in Establishments From Which Data Were Secured in 1912.

Number of employees reported by United States Census Office.		Establishments furnishing information to the Bureau of Labor Statistics in 1912.		
			Number of employees	
1910.	1905.	Number of establishments.	On pay roll	For whom data were secured.
163,192	141,998	46	43,504	17,505

According to the census of 1905 and to the census of 1910, more than 90 per cent. of the total number of employees in the industry are found in the States in which the establishments furnishing information to the Bureau of Labor Statistics are located.

The number of employees in the establishments from which the Bureau secured 1912 data was equal to 26.7 per cent. of the total in the industry in 1910. (P. 120.)

Silk Goods Manufacturing.

This study of wages and hours of labor in silk-goods manufacturing shows rates of wages per hour and nominal full-time hours per week for the years 1907 to 1912, inclusive. . . .

This present report and also previous reports show wages and hours of labor for each of the most important productive occupations in silk-goods manufacturing, but do not show data for all occupations in the industry. The occupations include a very large proportion of the total . . . employees on productive work and approximately two-thirds of the total employees both in productive and non-productive work. (P. 171.)

Silk Goods Manufacturing.

Relative Nominal Full-time Hours Per Week and Relative Rates of Wages Per Hour in Silk-Goods Manufacturing, 1890 to 1912. (Data are included from 12 establishments, 1890-1903; 12 establishments, 1903, 1904; 18 establishments, 1904, 1905; 19 establishments, 1905, 1906; 19 establishments, 1906, 1907; 10 establishments, 1907-1910; 42 establishments, 1910, 1911; and 42 establishments, 1911, 1912.)

Year	Relative nominal full-time hours per week	Relative rate of wages per hour
Average, 1890-1899	100.0	100.0
1890	102.6	98.6
1891	102.9	93.2
1892	101.9	98.6
1893	98.8	102.0
1894	98.6	102.9
1895	98.5	101.5
1896	99.0	106.5
1897	99.1	99.1
1898	99.3	98.4
1899	99.5	97.4
1900	99.6	98.4
1901	99.2	98.1
1902	98.7	101.4
1903	98.8	102.6
1904	97.2	101.8
1905	98.2	102.5
1906	98.4	106.1
1907	98.0	112.1
1908	97.6	109.2
1909	97.5	110.5
1910	97.4	112.5
1911	97.4	113.3
1912	96.6	117.1

(P. 174).

Total Number of Employees in Silk-Goods Manufacturing and Number of Employees in Establishments From Which Data Were Secured in 1912.

Number of employees reported by United States Census Office.		Establishments furnishing information to the Bureau of Labor Statistics in 1912.		
			Number of employees	
1910.	1905.	Number of establishments.	On pay roll.	For whom data were secured.
99,037	79,601	42	17,579	11,534

According to both the census of 1905 and the census of 1910, more than 95 per cent. of the total number of employees in the industry are found in the states in which the establishments furnishing information to the Bureau of Labor Statistics are located.

The number of employees in the establishments from which the Bureau secured 1912 data was equal to 17.7 per cent. of the total in the industry in 1910. (P. 183.)

Bulletin of the United States Bureau of Labor Statistics, No. 129. Washington, 1913. Wages and Hours of Labor in the Lumber, Millwork and Furniture Industries. 1890 to 1912.

Lumber Manufacturing.

The occupations for which data are shown in this report . . . include more than three-fifths of the total employees. (P. 6.)

Relative Nominal Full-time Hours Per Week and Relative Rates of Wages Per Hour in Lumber Manufacturing, 1890 to 1912. (Data are included from 56 establishments, 1890-1903; 49 establishments, 1903, 1904; 69 establishments, 1904, 1905; 68 establishments, 1905, 1906; 75 establishments, 1906, 1907; 40

establishments, 1907-1910; 245 establishments, 1910, 1911; and 301 establishments, 1911-1912.)

Year	Relative nominal full-time hours per week	Relative rate of wages per hour
Average, 1890-1899	100.0	100.0
1890	100.4	101.9
1891	100.2	101.4
1892	100.2	101.5
1893	100.0	99.9
1894	100.0	96.7
1895	99.9	97.0
1896	100.1	97.4
1897	99.9	97.7
1898	99.6	101.5
1899	99.8	104.5
1900	99.5	105.4
1901	99.3	108.6
1902	98.7	112.1
1903	98.3	114.2
1904	97.8	112.3
1905	97.6	116.3
1906	96.6	124.4
1907	96.4	129.6
1908	96.6	118.7
1909	96.5	121.6
1910	96.5	130.0
1911	96.5	129.9
1912	96.6	131.5

(P. 8.)

Total Number of Employees in Lumber Manufacturing and Number of Employees in Establishments From Which Data Were Secured in 1912.

Number of employees reported by United States Census Office.		Establishments furnishing information to the Bureau of Labor Statistics in 1912.		
			Number of employees	
1910.	1905.	Number of establishments.	On pay roll.	For whom data were secured.
547,178	404,626	301	49,822	30,189

According to both the census of 1905 and the census of 1910 more than 80 per cent. of the total number of employees in the industry are found in the 20 states in which the establishments furnishing information to the Bureau of Labor Statistics are located.

The number of employees in the establishments from which the Bureau secured 1912 data was equal to 9.1 per cent. of the total in the industry in 1910, and the number for which the Bureau secured detailed information in 1912 was equal to 5.6 per cent. of the total in the industry in 1910. (P. 14.)

Millwork.

The occupations for which data are shown in this report . . . include more than five-eighths of the total employes. (P. 86.)

Relative Nominal Full-time Hours Per Week and Relative Rates of Wages Per Hour in the Millwork Industry, 1890 to 1912. (Data are included from 94 establishments, 1890-1903; 112 establishments, 1903, 1904; 113 establishments, 1904, 1905; 116 establishments, 1905, 1906; 120 establishments, 1906, 1907; 62

establishments, 1907-1910; 232 establishments, 1910, 1911; and 269 establishments, 1911, 1912.)

Year	Relative nominal full-time hours per week	Relative rate of wages per hour
Average, 1890-1899	100.0	100.0
1890	101.3	99.2
1891	100.6	100.4
1892	100.7	100.1
1893	100.1	100.0
1894	100.3	97.0
1895	99.7	98.1
1896	99.0	99.3
1897	99.6	100.0
1898	99.4	101.7
1899	99.2	104.1
1900	98.9	105.9
1901	98.7	108.6
1902	97.7	112.5
1903	97.2	116.5
1904	97.9	115.7
1905	98.1	116.7
1906	96.9	120.6
1907	96.7	124.5
1908	96.7	123.4
1909	96.7	124.9
1910	96.9	127.8
1911	96.8	129.0
1912	96.2	132.3

(P. 88.)

Total Number of Employees in the Millwork Industry and Number of Employees in Establishments From Which Data Were Secured in 1912.

Number of employees reported by United States Census Office.*		Establishments furnishing information to the Bureau of Labor Statistics in 1912.		
			Number of employees	
1910.	1905.	Number of establishments.	On pay roll.	For whom data were secured.
112,392	97,674	269	20,972	13,323

* The designation used by the United States census is "Lumber, Planing, Mill Products," including Sash, Doors and Blinds.

According to both the census of 1905 and the census of 1910 more than 60 per cent. of the total number of employees in the industry are found in 11 States in which the establishments furnishing information to the Bureau of Labor Statistics are located.

The number of employees in the establishments from which the Bureau secured 1912 data was equal to 18.7 per cent. of the total in the industry in 1910, and the number for which the Bureau secured detailed information in 1912 was equal to 11.9 per cent. of the total in the industry in 1910. (Pp. 93-94.)

Furniture Manufacturing.

The occupations for which data are shown in this report . . . include almost three-fifths of the total employees. (P. 123.)

Relative Nominal Full-time Hours Per Week and Relative Rates of Wages Per Hour in Furniture Manufacturing, 1890 to 1912. (Data are included from 58 establishments, 1890-1903; 61 establishments, 1903, 1904; 63 establishments, 1904, 1905; 63 establishments, 1905, 1906; 67 establishments, 1906, 1907; 52 establishments, 1907-1910; 128 establishments, 1910, 1911; and 199 establishments, 1911, 1912.)

Progress of the Shorter Day.—United States

Year	Relative nominal full-time hours per week	Relative rate of wages per hour
Average, 1890-1899	100.0	100.0
1890	101.3	100.5
1891	100.7	101.5
1892	99.8	102.5
1893	99.9	101.1
1894	98.2	99.4
1895	99.8	97.9
1896	100.0	97.7
1897	99.6	100.2
1898	100.4	98.0
1899	100.3	102.0
1900	100.2	102.4
1901	99.3	107.3
1902	98.3	114.1
1903	98.1	115.2
1904	97.3	117.5
1905	96.6	121.0
1906	95.8	125.7
1907	95.7	127.3
1908	95.9	127.5
1909	95.5	126.7
1910	95.1	130.5
1911	94.5	132.1
1912	93.9	135.1

(P. 125.)

Total Number of Employees in Furniture Manufacturing and Number of Employees in Establishments From Which Data Were Secured in 1912.

Number of employees reported by United States Census Office.		Establishments furnishing information to the Bureau of Labor Statistics in 1912.		
			Number of employees	
1910.	1905.	Number of establishments.	On pay roll.	For whom data were secured.
123,426	110,133	199	23,259	13,111

According to both the census of 1905 and the census of 1910, more than 88 per cent. of the total number of employees in the industry are found in the 13 States in which the establishments furnishing information to the Bureau of Labor Statistics are located.

The number of employees in the establishments from which the Bureau secured 1912 data was equal to 18.8 per cent. of the total in the industry in 1910, and the number for which the Bureau secured detailed information in 1912 was equal to 10.6 per cent. of the total in the industry in 1910. (P. 133.)

Bulletin of the United States Bureau of Labor Statistics, No. 153. Washington, 1914. Wages and Hours of Labor in the Lumber, Millwork and Furniture Industries. 1907 to 1913.

Lumber Manufacturing.

It will be observed that the general tendency of the several occupations is toward a reduction of working hours and an increase in rates of wages per hour and of earnings per full week. No data are available to show the amount of work afforded employees each year or the variation from year to year. The relative full-time hours per week indicate the change in the hours of labor of employees working full time, but do not reflect in any way the greater or less amount of full-time work afforded. (P. 9.)

Relative Full-time Hours Per Week, Rates of Wages Per Hour and Full Time Weekly Earnings in Lumber Manufacturing, 1910 to 1913.

(1913=100.0)

Year	Relative full-time hours per week	Relative rate of wages per hour	Relative full-time weekly earnings
1910	100.5	94.6	94.9
1911	100.5	94.9	95.3
1912	100.7	96.2	96.7
1913	100.0	100.0	100.0

(P. 10.)

The full-time hours of labor per week shown in the tables of the report are the regular full-time hours of work of the occupation under normal conditions in the establishment. The working time is the hours on duty including intervals of waiting for work. The full-time hours per week and the relatives based thereon do not in any way indicate the extent of unemployment. Employees may work overtime, or broken time, or be laid off, or a temporary reduction may be made in working hours, without such change affecting the full-time hours per week, as presented in this Bulletin. (P. 15.)

Total Number of Employees in Lumber Manufacturing and Number of Employees in Establishments for which Data are Shown for 1913.

Number of employees reported by United States census of 1910.	Establishments for which data are shown by the Bureau of Labor Statistics for 1913.		
		Number of employees	
	Number of establishments.	On pay roll.	For whom data are shown.
547,178	361	67,092	34,328

The number of employees in the establishments from which the Bureau obtained 1913 data was equal to 12.3 per cent. of the total in the industry in 1910, and the number of such employees for which the Bureau presents detailed information for 1913 was equal to 6.3 per cent. of the total in the industry in 1910. (P. 15.)

Mill Work.

Relative Full-time Hours Per Week, Rates of Wages Per Hour, and Full-time Weekly Earnings in the Mill-work Industry, 1910 to 1913.

(1913=100.0)

Year	Relative full-time hours per week	Relative rate of wages per hour	Relative full-time weekly earnings
1910	100.9	94.2	94.9
1911	100.9	95.3	96.2
1912	100.4	97.7	98.0
1913	100.0	100.0	100.0

(P. 83.)

This report on millwork includes establishments engaged in the manufacture of sash, doors, blinds, frames, fixtures, and building trim. . . . (P. 86.)

Total Number of Employees in the Millwork Industry and Number of Employees in Establishments for which Data are Shown for 1913.

Number of employees reported by United States census of 1910.*	Establishments for which data are shown by the Bureau of Labor Statistics for 1913.		
		Number of employees	
	Number of establishments.	On pay roll.	For whom data are shown.
112,392	344	24,616	16,251

According to the census of 1910, more than 64 per cent. of the total number of employees in the industry are found in the States in which the establishments furnishing information to the Bureau of Labor Statistics are located. The number of employees in the establishments

* The designation used by the United States census is "Lumber, planing mill products," including sash, doors and blinds.

from which the Bureau secured 1913 data was equal to 21.9 per cent. of the total in the industry in 1910, and the number for which the Bureau presents detailed information for 1913 was equal to 14.5 per cent. of the total in the industry in 1910. . . . (P. 87.)

Furniture.

Relative Full-time Hours Per Week, Rates of Wages Per Hour, and Full-time Weekly Earnings in Furniture Manufacturing, 1910 to 1913.

(1913=100.0.)

Year	Relative full-time hours per week	Relative rate of wages per hour	Relative full-time weekly earnings
1910	102.8	92.7	96.1
1911	102.1	94.5	97.3
1912	101.6	96.5	98.2
1913	100.0	100.0	100.0

(P. 109.)

Total Number of Employees in Furniture Manufacturing and Number of Employees in Establishments for which Data are Shown for 1913.

Number of employees reported by United States census of 1910.	Establishments for which data are shown by the Bureau of Labor Statistics for 1913.		
		Number of employees	
	Number of establishments.	On pay roll.	For whom data are shown.
123,426	231	31,245	17,378

(P. 112.)

According to the census of 1910, more than 87 per cent. of the total number of employees in the industry are found in the States in which the establishments furnishing information to the Bureau of Labor Statistics are located. The number of employees in the establishments from which the Bureau secured 1913 data was equal to 25.3 per cent. of the total in the industry in 1910, and the number for which the Bureau presents detailed information for 1913 was equal to 14.1 per cent. of the total in the industry in 1910. . . . (P. 113.)

Bulletin of the United States Bureau of Labor Statistics, No. 137. Washington, 1913. Wages and Hours of Labor in the Building and Repairing of Steam Railroad Cars. 1890 to 1912.

By nominal full-time hours per week is meant the usual full working time, such as prevails when there is no industrial depression, overtime rush, or other unusual factor affecting the industry.* (P. 5.)

Bulletin of the United States Bureau of Labor Statistics, No. 163. Washington, 1914. Wages and Hours of Labor in the Building and Repairing of Steam Railroad Cars. 1907 to 1913.

Car Building.

Year	Relative full-time hours per week	Relative rate of wages per hour	Relative full-time weekly earnings
1910	101.1	91.0	91.8
1911	100.4	94.0	94.3
1912	100.7	94.1	94.8
1913	100.0	100.0	100.0

(P. 11.)

* For tables showing increase or decrease in full-time hours per week see Bulletin No. 137, pp. 8-11.

This report includes information obtained from establishments engaged in building and repairing steam railroad cars, both passenger and freight, and both wood and steel. (P. 15.)

Total Number of Employees in Car Building and Repairing and Number of Employees in Establishments for which Data are shown for 1913.

Number of employees reported by United States census of 1910.	Establishments for which data are shown by the Bureau of Labor Statistics for 1913.		
		Number of employees	
	Number of establishments.	On pay roll.	For whom data are shown.
325,260	73	71,341	42,281

According to the census of 1910 more than [illegible].7 per cent. of the total number of employees in the industry are found in the States in which the establishments furnishing information to the Bureau of Labor Statistics are located. The number of employees in the establishments from which the Bureau obtained 1913 data was equal to 21.9 per cent. of the total in the industry in 1910. (P. 17.)

Bulletin of the United States Bureau of Labor Statistics, No. 161. Washington, 1914. Wages and Hours of Labor in the Clothing and Cigar Industries. 1911 to 1913.

Men's Clothing.

Year	Relative full-time hours per week	Relative rate of wages per hour	Relative full-time weekly earnings
1911	105.6	86.0	90.3
1912	105.4	88.1	92.3
1913	100.0	100.0	100.0

From the table above it is seen that the relative (or index) numbers for full-time hours per week in the manufacture of men's ready-made clothing decreased from 105.6 in 1911 to 100.0 in 1913; or, in other words, full-time hours per week were 105.6 per cent. in 1911 of what they were in 1913, and in 1912, 105.4 per cent. of what they were in 1913. The relative number for rates of wages per hour increased from 86.0 in 1911 to 88.1 in 1912 and 100.0 in 1913. The increase in full-time weekly earnings was somewhat less than in rates of wages per hour because of the reduction of hours in the industry. Relative full-time weekly earnings increased from 90.3 in 1911 to 92.3 in 1912, and to 100.0 in 1913. (P. 11.)

The material for this report was obtained from establishments making men's outer garments—coats, pants, vests, and overcoats—for the trade; or in other words, what is commonly known as men's ready-made clothing.

The number of establishments and shops for which comparable data are presented are as follows:

For 19[illegible] and 1912, from 80 identical establishments and 15[illegible] identical shops.

For 1912 and 1913, from 117 identical establishments and 221 identical shops. (P. 14.)

Total Number of Employees in Men's Clothing Manufacturing and Number of Employees in Establishments for which Data are Shown for 1913.

Number of employees reported by United States Census Office, 1910.	Establishments for which data are shown by the Bureau of Labor Statistics for 1913.			
	Number of establishments.	Number of separate shops.	No. of employees—On pay roll.	No. of employees—For whom data are given.
191,183	117	221	22,766	18,197

Men's factory-made clothing is made almost exclusively in large cities. The table shows 191,183 persons employed in this industry in 1910. Of this number 134,281, or 70.2 per cent., were employed in the 7 cities in which data were collected. . . . Data are presented in this bulletin for 18,197 employees in 1913, or 9.5 per cent. of the total number of employees in the industry in the United States in 1910. (P. 15.)

Bulletin of the United States Bureau of Labor Statistics, No. 154. Washington, 1914. Wages and Hours of Labor in the Boot and Shoe and Hosiery and Underwear Industries. 1907 to 1913.

In order that the summary figures in regard to rates of wages and hours of labor in the two industries covered in this Bulletin, heretofore published for the years 1890 to 1912, may be available for reference, the tables following are reproduced from Bulletin No. 134.

Progress of the Shorter Day.—United States

Relative Full-time Hours Per Week and Relative Rates of Wages Per Hour in Boot and Shoe Manufacturing, 1890 to 1912. (Data are included from 46 establishments, 1890-1903; 50 establishments, 1903, 1904; 52 establishments, 1904, 1905; 52 establishments, 1905, 1906; 54 establishments, 1906, 1907; 26 establishments, 1907-1910; 60 establishments, 1910, 1911; and 81 establishments, 1911-1912.)

Year	Relative full-time hours per week	Relative rate of wages per hour
Average, 1890-1899	100.0	100.0
1890	100.3	98.5
1891	100.6	97.5
1892	100.2	99.3
1893	100.0	100.6
1894	100.0	99.8
1895	100.0	101.4
1896	100.0	100.5
1897	99.8	100.7
1898	99.7	100.5
1899	99.6	101.8
1900	99.3	104.1
1901	99.6	104.1
1902	98.4	108.0
1903	97.0	113.2
1904	97.1	116.9
1905	96.8	119.9
1906	96.3	121.8
1907	96.0	128.0
1908	95.9	125.5
1909	95.7	130.4
1910	95.5	129.6
1911	95.3	131.7
1912	93.9	132.8

(P. 119.)

Relative Full-time Hours Per Week and Relative Rates of Wages Per Hour in Hosiery and Underwear Manufacturing, 1890 to 1912. (Data are included from 8 establishments, 1890-1903; 9 establishments, 1903, 1904; 22 establishments, 1904, 1905; 25 establishments, 1905, 1906; 30 establishments, 1906, 1907; 15 establishments, 1907-1910; 62 establishments, 1910, 1911; 62 establishments, 1911, 1912.)

Year	Relative full-time hours per week	Relative rate of wages per hour
Average, 1890-1899	100.0	100.0
1890	101.1	105.6
1891	101.1	106.9
1892	101.2	100.3
1893	100.5	100.1
1894	94.8	96.7
1895	100.4	102.8
1896	100.3	99.3
1897	100.3	96.1
1898	100.3	96.4
1899	100.2	93.2
1900	98.9	95.4
1901	98.8	102.0
1902	98.9	111.0
1903	97.9	117.6
1904	97.8	114.8
1905	97.7	119.9
1906	97.2	126.9
1907	96.8	133.4
1908	96.5	133.7
1909	96.6	134.1
1910	94.8	135.5
1911	94.7	135.8
1912	93.1	143.7

(P. 127.)

Bulletin of the United States Bureau of Labor Statistics, No. 177. Washington, 1915. Wages and Hours of Labor in the Hosiery and Underwear Industry 1907 to 1914.

Relative Full-time Hours Per Week, Rates of Wages Per Hour, and Full-time Weekly Earnings, 1910 to 1914, Together with Per Cent. of Increase or Decrease in Specified Years, in the Principal Occupations.†

Year	Hours per week.			Wages per week.			Weekly earnings.		
		Per cent. of increase (+) or decrease (−) in.			Per cent. of increase (+) or decrease (−) in.			Per cent. of increase (+) or decrease (−) in.	
	Relative full-time hours per week (1914–100)	1914 as compared with each specified year	Each specified year as compared with year preceding	Relative rate of wages per hour (1914–100)	1914 as compared with each specified year	Each specified year as compared with year preceding	Relative full-time weekly earnings (1914–100)	1914 as compared with each specified year	Each specified year as compared with year preceding
The industry:									
1910..........	105	−5	...	84	+19	...	89	+12	...
1911..........	105	−5	*	85	+18	+1	89	+12	*
1912..........	103	−3	−2	90	+11	+6	93	+ 8	+4
1913..........	101	−1	−2	97	+ 3	+8	98	+ 2	+5
1914..........	100	...	−1	100	...	+3	100	...	+2

In the above table it will be observed that the general tendency is toward a reduction of working hours and an increase in rates of wages per hour and of earnings per full week. This table does not consider the amount of work afforded employees each year or the variation in the volume of employment from year to year. The relative full-time hours per week indicate the change in the hours of labor of employees working full time, but do not reflect in any way the greater or less amount of full-time work afforded. This point is further discussed on page 27. (P. 13.)

The full-time hours of labor per week shown in the general tables of the report are the regular hours of work of the occupations under normal conditions in the

† Summary only given here. * No change.

establishments. The figures given show the average full-time hours per week of the employees in each occupation and the number of employees whose full time came within specified classification limits. The working time is the hours on duty, including intervals of waiting for work. The full-time hours per week and the relatives based thereon do not in any way indicate the extent of unemployment. Employees may work overtime, broken time, or be laid off, or a temporary reduction may be made in working hours without such change affecting the full-time hours per week as presented in this bulletin.

The full-time weekly earnings tabulated are the earnings per week of employees working full time, or the earnings on broken time reduced to equivalent earnings for a full week. In considering changes in full-time earnings per week, notice should also be taken of changes in full-time hours of labor per week. A reduction in the hours of a pieceworker may reduce his earnings in a week and leave his earnings per hour unchanged, while a reduction of hours for a week worker will, if his weekly rate remains the same, increase his rate per hour. (Pp. 27-28.)

Total Number of Employees, Census 1910, and Number of Employees in Establishments for which Data are Shown in this Report for 1914.

Number of employees reported by United States Census, 1910.	Hosiery.		Underwear.		Total.	
	Number of Establishments	Number of Employees.	Number of Establishments.	Number of Employees.	Number of Establishments.	Number of Employees.
129,275	42	17,361	40	15,008	82	32,369

According to the census of 1910, more than 91 per cent. of the total number of employees in the industry are found in the States in which the establishments furnishing information to the Bureau of Statistics are located. The number of employees for which the Bureau secured 1914 data and for which detailed information for 1914 is presented in this report was equal to 25 per cent. of the total in the industry in 1910. (P. 26.)

Bulletin of the United States Bureau of Labor Statistics, No. 178. Washington, 1915. Wages and Hours of Labor in the Boot and Shoe Industry. 1907 to 1914.

Boot and Shoe Manufacturing.

Relative Full-Time Hours Per Week, Rates of Wages Per Hour, and Full-time Weekly Earnings, 1910 to 1914, together with per cent. of Increase or Decrease in Specified Years, in the Principal Occupations. (34 in number.)

Year	Hours per week.			Wages per hour.			Weekly earnings		
		Per cent. of increase (+) or decrease (−) in.			Per cent. of increase (+) or decrease (−) in.			Per cent. of increase (+) or decrease (−) in.	
	Relative full-time hours per week (1914–100)	1914 as compared with each specified year	Each specified year as compared with year preceding	Relative rate of wages per hour (1914–100)	1914 as compared with each specified year	Each specified year as compared with year preceding	Relative full-time weekly earnings (1914–100)	1914 as compared with each specified year	Each specified year as compared with year preceding
The industry:									
1910	103	−3	...	89	+12	...	92	+9	...
1911	103	−3	*	91	+10	+2	94	+6	+2
1912	102	−2	−1	92	+ 9	+1	93	+8	−1
1913	101	−1	−1	99	+ 1	+8	100	*	+8
1914	100	...	−1	100	...	+1	100	...	*

(P.13.)

In the above table it will be observed that the general tendency is towards a reduction of working hours and an increase in rates of wages per hour and of earnings per full week. (P. 13.)

This report includes establishments whose principal

* No change.

or only products are shoes made by the McKay, welt, or turn process. . . .

In addition to the 84 establishments from which data were secured for 1913 and 1914, data were secured from 7 establishments for 1914 only, making a total of 91 establishments from which data for 1914 are presented. (P. 21.)

Total Number of Employees in Boot and Shoe Manufacturing and Number of Employees in Establishments for which Data are Shown for 1914. (This table includes 7 establishments from which data were secured for 1914 only.)

Number of employees reported by United States Census, 1910.	Establishments and employees for which data are shown by the Bureau of Labor Statistics for 1914.	
	Number of establishments.	Number of employees.
198,297	91	53,071

According to the census of 1910, more than 97 per cent. of the total number of employees in the industry are found in the States in which the establishments furnishing information to the Bureau of Labor Statistics are located. The number of employees for which the bureau secured 1914 data and for which detailed information for 1914 is presented in this report was equal to nearly 27 per cent. of the total in the industry in 1910. (P. 22.)

B. THE RECORD OF 1915.

During 1915 shorter hours have been gained by many workers, primarily the machinists and the employees of munition plants and of other establishments filling war orders. From these the movement of shorter hours has spread to many other trades.

United States Bureau of Labor Statistics. Monthly Review. Vol. I. October, 1915. No. 4.

Movement for Reduction of Hours of Labor in the Machine Trades.

A movement for the reduction of hours of labor, notable for its rapid progress, is that which has taken place in the machine trades within the last few months. It has chiefly affected the firms having contracts for the making of war munitions, though not exclusively restricted to such establishments. The demands for reduced hours have usually come from the machinists, although other occupations have joined, and in most establishments all employees have received the benefits which have been granted to the machinists. Reduced hours of labor have in all cases been effected with no reduction in weekly wage and in many cases with increased wages.

A partial list of the firms which have established the 8-hour day within the past two months has been furnished the bureau by the International Association of Machinists. The following firms have established an 8-hour day, these in most cases involving a reduction of 7 hours in the working week. These changes, it should be stated, were made without a strike except in five firms.

Ansonia, Conn.:
- O. K. Tool Holder Co.

Bridgeport, Conn.
- American-British Manufacturing Co.
- Batcheller Corset Co.
- Bridgeport Body Co.
- Bridgeport Brass Co.
- Bridgeport Metal Goods Co.
- Bryant Electric Co.
- Bullard Machine Co.
- Burns & Bassick Co.

Crawford Laundry.
Electric Cable Co.
Grant Manufacturing Co.
Harris Engineering Co.
Harvey Hubble Co.
Hawthorne Co.
International Silver Co.
Locomobile Company of America.
Remington Arms Co.
Remington Union Metallic Cartridge Co.
Sprague Motor Co.
Standard Manufacturing Co.
Warner Corset Co.
Wolverine Motor Co.

Chicago, Ill.:
Automatic Electric Co.

Plainfield, N. J.:
Bosch Magneto Co.
Pond Machine Tool Co.
Potter Press Co.
Sauer Motor Truck Co.
Scott Printing Press Co.
Vitaphone Co.
Hall Printing Press Co.

Raleigh, N. C.:
Raleigh Iron Works.

Springfield, Mass.:
Bosch Magneto Co.
Westinghouse Co.

Taunton, Mass.:
Call & Carr Co.
Mason Machine Co.
Miehle Printing Press Co.

Toledo, Ohio:
Bunting Brass & Bronze Co.
Toledo Machine & Tool Co.
Willys-Overland Car Co.

Du Pont Powder Works of Wilmington, Del., and other points.

The following firms have established a 54-hour week, reducing hours from 55, 58, and in some cases 60 per week:

Springfield Mass.:
Hendee Motorcycle Co.

Taunton, Mass.:
Bell & Dyer Co.
Evans Machine & Stamping Co.
Lincoln & Williams Twist Drill Co.
Vans Machine & Stamping Co.

Toledo, Ohio:
Acklyn Stamping Co.
Advance Machine Co.
Toledo Electro Plating Co.

Derby, Conn.:
Dairy Machine Co.

United States Bureau of Labor Statistics. Monthly Review. Vol. II. February, 1916. No. 2.

Reduction of Hours of Labor in the Machine Trades.

A movement for the reduction of hours of labor, notable for its rapid progress, has taken place in the machine trades since late in the summer of 1915. . . .

A partial list of the firms which had established the 8-hour day or granted a reduction in hours up to the middle of September was published in the October, 1915, issue of the Review. The International Association of

Machinists has furnished the bureau a list supplementing the earlier list of firms which had granted reductions of hours up to the end of 1915. The following firms have established an 8-hour day, with reductions in most cases of 7 hours in a working week.

Bridgeport, Conn.:
- American Graphophone Co.
- Lake Torpedo Boat Co.

Meriden, Conn.:
- New England Westinghouse Co.

New Haven, Conn.:
- Geometric Tool Co.

Sheldon, Conn.:
- The R. N. Basset Shop.

Wilmington, Del.:
- Vogel Machine Co.

Chicago, Ill.:
- Stewart Warner Speedometer Co.
- Western Electric Co.

Baton Rouge, La.:
- Standard Oil Co.

Baltimore, Md.:
- Pool Engineering Co.
- Universal Machine Co.

Lowell, Mass.:
- Heinze Electric Co.
- U. S. Cartridge Co.

Springfield, Mass.:
- Barley Machine Co.
- Barney & Berry (Inc.).
- Bausch Machine Tool Co.
- Bay State Corset Co.
- Blake Machine Co.
- Duckworth Chain Co.
- Gilbert & Barker Co.
- Hendee Motorcycle Co.
- Kibbie Candy Co.
- Knox Automobile Co.
- Knox Motor Co.
- National Equipment Co.
- Package Machinery Co.
- Rider Bagg Co.
- Russell Machine Co.
- Stacy Machine Co.
- United States Saw Co.

Detroit, Mich.:
- Siewek Bros.
- The Studebaker Corporation.

Camden, N. J.:
- Victor Talking Machine Co.

Garwood, N. J.:
- Bell Electric Co.
- Hyatt Roller and Bearing Co.

Perth Amboy, N. J.:
- American Smelting & Refining Co.
- Annes-Potter Brick Co.
- Barber Asphalt Co.
- Lyons-Flynn Co.
- Perth Amboy Dry Dock.
- Raritan Dry Dock Co.
- Raritan Copper Works.
- R. & H. Chemical Co.
- Shantz & Exkert.
- Standard Cable Co.
- Union Lead Co.
- United States Cartridge Co.
- Patrick Whites.

Plainfield, N. J.:
- Manganese Steel Safe Co.

South Plainfield, N. Y.:
- Spicer Manufacturing Co.

Trenton, N. J.:
- J. L. Mott.
- Harry Stahl.
- E. Wilkes.

New York City and vicinity:
- Adriance Machine Co.
- Acme Die Casting Co.
- Auto Press Co.
- Blair Machine Co.
- Bliss Manufacturing Co.
- Cameron Machine Co.
- Carpenter Tool Co.

Hoe Printing Press Co.
Doehler Die Casting Co.
W. W. Kellog Co.
Notham Manufacturing Co. (49 hours).
Rockwell Engineering Co.
Schroeder Machine Co.
Sperry Gyroscope Co.
Wappler's Electric Co.

Cincinnati, Ohio:
United States Printing & Lithograph Co.
United States Playing Card Co.

Cleveland, Ohio:
Cleveland Automatic Co.
F. B. Stearns Auto Mfg. Co.
Sewer & Morgan Co.

Springfield, Ohio:
Springfield Machine Tool Co.

Toledo, Ohio:
American Can Co.
Bock Bearing Co.
City Machine Tool Co.
Consolidated Manufacturing Co.
O'Neill Machine Co.

Youngstown, Ohio:
William Todd Co.

Pittsburgh, Pa.:
Pittsburgh Machine Tool Co.

Providence, R. I.:
Providence Engineering Co.

Milwaukee, Wis.:
Milwaukee Die & Casting Co. (44 hours a week).

The following firms have granted reductions in hours, although the hours are still somewhat in excess of the straight 8-hour day:

Forty-nine and one-half hours per week.

Columbus, Ohio.—Hearne Manufacturing Co., Rudd Manufacturing Co., Shiriner Co., Modern Tool & Die Co.

Fifty hours per week.

Connecticut.—New Departure Roller Bearing Co., Bristol; Birmingham Foundry & Machine Co., Derby. New Jersey.—Wickes Bros., Jersey City; J. A. Roebling Co., Trenton. New York City and vicinity.—Davis Bourville Co.

Fifty-four hours per week.

Connecticut. — Hendee Machine Co., Torrington. Pennsylvania.—Westinghouse Co., East Pittsburgh. (Pp. 37-38.)

The Survey. April 1, 1916. The Sudden Spread of the Eight Hour Day.

Twenty-five years ago in England, the skilled mechanic was building his Utopia out of "eight hours for work, eight hours for play, eight hours for sleep and eight bobs a day." In America this movement has lagged among the machinists. At the outset of the war, the skilled men, though they had their two dollars a day or more, had by no means reduced their working day to eight hours. In the last twenty months, however, they have done more to effect that standard than in the twenty-five years preceding the war.

On January 1, 1915, only 7,000 members of the International Association of Machinists were working the eight-hour day; on January 1, 1916, 60,000 men were working eight hours. . . .

The awakening of the machinists seems to have come first to public notice in March, 1915, when there was a slight stir in Worcester, Mass., and scores of machinists were reported as joining the local union. In August the movement was well on its way. In September, even the corset manufacturers in Bridgeport, Conn., and that neighborhood, beginning to feel the pressure from the demand for labor in the munitions plants, shortened the working day of the girls to eight a day. In the last six months, the movement has swept not only through the munitions plants and the corset factories, but through automobile and motor cycle works, paper mills and skate making establishments, the garment trades, and shops making musical instruments.

Centers where sudden and wholesale changes have occurred, which are easily traceable through the newspaper accounts, are Bridgeport, Conn., where more than fifteen firms reduced hours; Perth Amboy, New Jersey, from which came the nonchalant report that after strikes in twenty-one shops, thirteen shops conceded immediately; Springfield, Mass., Plainfield and Bayonne, New Jersey. In Wilmington, Del., the shorter work day was granted to the employes of the Du Pont Powder factory, and the Gulf Refining Company in Port Arthur, Texas, gave it to 2,125 men. Fourteen or more small firms followed the movement in New York City. In Toledo, Ohio, the three largest firms to fall into line were the Willys-Overland Automobile Co., the Bunting Brass and Bronze Company, and the Toledo Machine and Tool Company.

Aside from a few scattered changes in the south and middle west, the war demand has made itself felt most widely in the sea board states. In these states official returns as to the extent of the movement are obtainable. The Department of Labor of New Jersey reported that 25,395 persons in twenty-four various plants of that state had for the first time benefitted during the past year by the eight-hour day. Out of all these, only one firm, the Victor Talking Machine Company, employing 7,500 men and women, is not "engaged in the production of one or another kind of war material for the European belligerents." The New York Department of Labor reported gains by 850 metal workers and 850 magneto workers in the city of New York. The Connecticut Bureau of Labor estimated that 30,000 machinists in the munitions plants alone were affected. . . .

To interpret the attitude of employers toward this activity letters were sent by The Survey to 125 firms reported in the American Federation of Labor News Letter and by the Federal Bureau of Labor Statistics as having recently adopted the eight hour day. About one-half replied and some of the answers are illuminating.

Only one firm, The Brown and Sharpe Manufacturing Company, of Providence, R. I., was belligerent in its opposition to the eight hour day. . . . Half a dozen other firms expressed themselves against the change on economic grounds. A Massachusetts firm, manufacturing motors, which reduced the daily hours of work of 315 men at the request of a committee of employes contended that "the ultimate effect in our opinion will be increased cost to consumer and a disadvantage in competition with foreign producers for the world market." One or two other companies wrote in similar vein that the ultimate effect they look for is "decreased efficiency, and increased cost to producer and consumer." Two or three plants reported decreased output because of the reduction in the working hours, but accepted it as a permanent condition since "the eight-hour day was shortly coming into general use in this country."

A printing press manufacturing company replied that it thought there might be increased efficiency "by resorting to driving;" that "all shops will run the eight hours" and the "management must wake up to ways and means of increasing production." Another wrote that one effect of the change would be that the "unions will ask for further reductions in hours." On the contrary, a Cleveland maker of automobiles "found that the majority of the men prefer the longer hours—We feel sure that if we were to take a vote in our shop to-day, the men would ask to go back to the fifty-four hour a week basis." "But of course they would expect no cut in pay," he adds. It was in October that this firm granted a reduction of seven hours per week to its employes, with the same pay, and time and one-half for overtime.

These were the negative or near negative replies. They were exceeded in number by the employers who, in answering the question, "What was the result of the change from the longer work day, increased efficiency or decreased output?" and "What in your opinion will be the ultimate effect?" were positively and explicitly favorable to the change. In all these plants, the change is of course too recent for the evidence to be accepted as final either one way or the other; the thing is in progress but the testimony is fresh, and elicited at a time when both managers and men are alert to the contrasts between old and new schedules.

A western manufacturer who gave the eight hour day to 1700 men and women, writes, "while the time that has elapsed has been quite short, we feel that increased effort has resulted, partly due to appreciation on the part of the employes of the fact that they now receive 54 hours pay for 48 hours work, and partly through the fact that the higher rate of wages has improved the quality of workers; that is, numerous high grade mechanics who have been earning less money elsewhere, have come to us. . . . Immediately after the change went into effect, there was naturally a considerable decrease in output, but this has partly been made up since that time through the increased effort mentioned above."

"Less discontent and greater relative efficiency, with practically the same production in forty-eight hours as formerly" was reported by the Sperry Gyroscope Company of Brooklyn which granted the eight hour day last September to 480 employes.

Another Brooklyn corporation wrote that the change has resulted in increasing both the quality and the quantity of the work of the men per hour. The voluntary reduction of the hours of work of its employes to forty-eight per week by the Universal Machine Company in Baltimore has already resulted in increased efficiency according to the management and they believe that in the end, too, there will be "finer work, increased output per hour, on account of the men being happy and contented."

The Vitaphone Company of Plainfield, New Jersey, on September 29, 1915, went on the eight-hour basis. "We had contemplated for some time adopting the eight-hour day as we felt that it would only be a question of time before it would be demanded by the union. Our results were at first decreased output and a slight increase in efficiency, but we feel that it will be only a question of time before we get both increased efficiency as well as increased output." "Satisfactory" results prevail in the Studebaker Company's plant in Detroit where between 6,000 and 7,000 men have recently been given the eight hour day. Of two smaller firms making a change one said, "The men seem very well contented and we seem to be getting the work out just as rapidly as with the ten hour day." The other said, "We believe it possible to get a better class of mechanics and at the same time improve the efficiency of the workmen."

More extended testimony came from the Victor Talking Machine Company, at Camden, New Jersey, and from the Remington Arms and Ammunition Plant in Bridgeport. The former folded the following announcement in the pay envelope of each of its employes on October 1:

Why the Victor Talking Machine Company Changed to the Eight-hour Day!

"The Victor Talking Machine Company has changed from the standard working hours to the eight-hour basis, without reduction in wages, for the reason that, after a thorough investigation into the conditions in our manufacturing departments, the Directors have concluded it was the right thing to do and the right time to do it. A resolution, embodying this change was adopted by a unanimous vote on September 22 to go into effect at the earliest possible date. There had been no demand for such a change on the part of the employees of the Company, who number 7,500.

"The change will reduce the company's profits on the present volume of business about $1,000,000 for the first year. The company expects that it can, by certain adjustments and improvements, gradually restore its profits to normal, but the changes necessary to accomplish this result are expected to consume about three years.

"The equipment of special automatic machinery and the unusual efficiency organization in the Victor plant requires an intensity of application on the part of a certain proportion of skilled operators that cannot be maintained with satisfactory results under the old schedule of hours.

"The company believes that the new schedule of shorter hours will result in the production of goods of a higher grade than was possible under the old schedule. The company believes that the shortening of the hours will greatly reduce the nervous strain which is so evident in modern industrial organizations.

"The company also hopes that the new hours will increase the spirit of co-operation which it is anxious to promote in its organization.

"The company feels certain that it will not fail to achieve the economizing of the new schedule, nor will it fail to secure superior quality of goods, nor will it fail, eventually, to secure even greater reimbursement for its employees than under the old system, unless the company's business is interfered with by the influence of unwise legislation, tending to place the control of the market value of its goods in the hands of cut-price conspirators, or unless the co-operation expected on the part of the employees does not materialize, owing to the influence of a misguided policy based on the theory of limiting individual efficiency.

"The company must receive fair and standard prices for its goods or it cannot pay satisfactory wages for eight hour work. The company must also receive a fair day's work if the eight hour day is to be a success. Nothing but honest co-operation between labor and capital can replace drudgery and dissatisfaction."

The Remington Arms Company adopted the eight hour day on August 1, 1915, and 1,000 men were then affected. On January 15, 1916, 6,500 more men were granted the shorter working hours. To quote: "The company could foresee that the eight hour day would sooner or later be universal. They believed that it was fair in principle and they wished to show their willingness to concede to a popular sentiment which they considered just, and so they instituted the eight hour day at their works. This action, however, was entirely voluntary, as no demand had been made upon them.

"As the output previous to the adoption of the eight-hour day was very small the exact difference is difficult to determine, but experience has since led the company to believe that the output has been increased by the change. . . . They believe that the eight-hour day provides increased efficiency in the quality of the work performed and adds to rather than diminishes the quantity of the out-turn."

Another very large firm, employing 11,500 men and women, felt that they could not yet report on the success or failure of the change to a forty-eight hour week for their employees, but their concession, the company said, was due to the fact that the demand and public discussion of the subject seemed so general.

Running through most of this testimony from these employers is this suggestion that they were but anticipating the inevitable adoption of the shorter working day. "Sooner or later," they forecast, despite the fact that the issue, as they faced it, was an emergency one, "the eight-hour day will be universal." . . .

In the last ten months nearly 100,000 men and women have won the eight hour day. . . . Their gains have given such impetus to the issue that among 175,000 anthracite miners and 350,000 members of the railroad brotherhoods, the employees of two basic industries, it has been the keynote of this spring's demands.

VIII. THE NEED OF LEGISLATION: INSTANCES OF EXCESSIVE HOURS OF LABOR.

The preceding section has shown the trend toward shorter hours in some important lines of industry. But side by side with those who have benefited from the introduction of the shorter day, other workers in various trades are still employed twelve hours a day or more. Thus, for instance:

The investigation of the United States Bureau of Labor showed that in 1910, 62.79% of over 31,000 men employed in blast-furnaces worked 84 hours and over per week, that is 12 hours a day on 7 days in the week. Only one per cent. were customarily employed 60 hours per week. Nearly 43% of the 173,000 employes in the iron and steel industry were employed at least 72 hours per week, or 12 hours per day on 6 days in the week.

While these are examples of extreme hours of employment in the absence of all regulation, such extremes are not confined to the steel industry alone.

In railroading, for instance, during the year 1913, 261,332 men are recorded as exceeding sixteen hours' work. Almost 200,000 of these men worked between 16 and 21 hours on a stretch.

According to the Census of 1910, men were employed *72 hours and over per week* in the following among other industries:

Sugar and Molasses
Factories* .... 95. per cent. of 4,127 employes

* Do not include sugar refineries.

Blast Furnaces	85.9 per cent. of	38,429 employes
Ice	64.4 per cent. of	16,114 employes
Glucose and Starch	57.8 per cent. of	4,773 employes
Gas	57.4 per cent. of	37,215 employes

According to the Census, men were employed *more than 60 hours per week* in the following among other industries:

Blast Furnaces	96.4 per cent. of	38,429 employes
Sugar	95. per cent. of	4,127 employes
Ice	77.6 per cent. of	16,114 employes
Gas	72.9 per cent. of	37,215 employes
Glucose and Starch	71.9 per cent. of	4,773 employes
Sulphuric, Nitric, and Mixed Acids	64.1 per cent. of	2,252 employes
Butter, Cheese and Milk	42. per cent. of	18,431 employes
Paper and Wood Pulp	41.1 per cent. of	75,978 employes
Steel Works and Rolling Mills	34.2 per cent. of	240,076 employes
Flour Mill and Grist Mill	30.7 per cent. of	39,453 employes
Coke	24.5 per cent. of	29,273 employes
Petroleum	23.5 per cent. of	13,929 employes
Salt	23. per cent. of	4,936 employes

The Need of Legislation.—United States

Since Collective Bargaining Has Proved Ineffectual in Checking these Abuses, the Need of Legislation to Limit Such Excessive Hours of Labor is Unmistakable.

Principles of Labor Legislation. John R. Commons, University of Wisconsin, former Member Wisconsin Industrial Commission; John B. Andrews, Secretary, American Association for Labor Legislation. New York and London, Harper, 1916.

In spite of the general tendency in this country towards a shorter workday, the old ideal of "eight hours for work, eight hours for rest, eight hours for what you will" has not yet been realized by the majority of American wage-earners. Out of the 6,615,046 wage-earners enumerated in 1909 by the Census of Manufactures, only 7.9 per cent. were employed in establishments where the eight-hour day prevailed. "Prevailing hours" for three-quarters of them were from fifty-four to sixty weekly. But no fewer than 344,011 or 5.2 per cent. of the whole number worked where prevailing hours were between sixty and seventy-two weekly; 116,083 worked in establishments where the seventy-two-hour week prevailed, and 114,118 where the prevailing hours were more than seventy-two. Out of the eighty-six principal manufacturing industries employing more than 10,000 wage-earners in 1909, twenty employed over 10 per cent. of their workers more than sixty hours a week. Among those exacting more than seventy-two hours weekly from several thousand employees were beet-sugar, cement, chemical, glucose, and sugar and molasses factories, coke-works, gas-plants, the manufacture of ice and lime, petroleum refineries, blast-furnaces, and rolling-mills. Among railroad employees, also, continuous service for long periods is very common. Records of the Interstate Commerce Commission show that during the year ending June 30, 1913, 261,332 railroad men were reported as on duty for periods exceeding the legal limit of sixteen hours, and that over 33,000 of them worked more than twenty-one hours continuously. . . .

Then, too, many employees are working seven days a week. Investigations show that much of the present-day continuous operation of industries involves work seven days a week. For instance, in Minnesota in 1909, 98,558 men, or approximately 14 per cent. of the gainfully employed males in that State, were working seven days a week. In New York in 1910, out of 179,000 union members in a number of specified industries, almost 20 per cent. were engaged in seven-day labor.

Worst of all, many establishments which operate continuously, such as iron and steel plants, paper-mills, and glass and chemical works, combine the twelve-hour day with the seven-day week, and in not a few cases require their employees to alternate weekly or fortnightly between day and night shifts, working twenty-four hours without rest when the change is made. (Pp. 200-201.)

Aside from voluntary reductions by individual employers there are two methods by which the desirable goal of shorter daily and weekly hours has been reached, by labor organization and by labor legislation. Many workers, prominent among whom in this country are printers, granite-cutters, cigar-makers, and building-trades workmen, have gained the nine- or eight-hour day by organization. But the present prevalence of longer hours of labor in the United States shows that the unions alone have not been everywhere adequate to the task. It has so far proved difficult to form stable labor organizations among women and among some classes of unskilled men workers. In some cases, too, as in the Pittsburgh steel plants, large scale business has used its power to stamp out labor organization. After a century of effort probably four-fifths of those employed in trade, transportation, and manufacturing are still unorganized, and in recent years there has been a growing demand for the protection of unorganized workers by legislation. (P. 204.)

The Need of Legislation.—United States

The Survey. Vol. 31. New York, January 3, 1914. Editorial.

The twelve-hour day hangs like a dead weight on the workers in the continuous industries of America. It means bad citizenship, broken home life, limp workmanship. . . .

Twelve-hour shifts rule more or less completely not only in steel and paper mills, but in the manufacture of cement, beet sugar and artificial ice, in heat, light and power plants, water works, railroad shops, bakeries, hotels and restaurants. In most of these establishments work must keep up for twenty-four hours without a break; but there is no reason why the men should work twelve hours on end The choice lies between two shifts of twelve hours or three shifts of eight. There is no other choice. The [illegible]acking of the twelve-hour day would mean four hours' leisure for every day, 1,200 hours a year for every man, to put into fatherhood, citizenship, recreation—into the ampler life. (Pp. 41[illegible])

United States Congress. Senate Document, No. 110. Report on Conditions of Employment in the Iron and Steel Industry in the United States. Vol. I. Wages and Hours of Labor. 62nd Congress. 1st Session, 1911. Washington, 1911.

A brief summary of the conditions as regards earnings, hours, and days worked per week in the industry is given in the table which follows.

SUMMARY OF EARNINGS AND HOURS OF LABOR, BY BRANCHES OF THE INDUSTRY.

Branches of Industry	No. of plants	No. of employees	Earnings per hour: Per cent. of employees earning			Hours per week: % of employees customarily working			% of employees customarily working 7 days per week
			Under 16 cents	Under 18 cents	25 [illegible]	84 hrs. and over	72 hrs. and over	60 hrs. and under	
Blast furnaces	156	31,354	31.70	65.96	[illegible]	*62.79	*68.55	*10.71	*87.88
Steel works and rolling mills:									
Bessemer converters	24	5,018	13.88	47.00	20.00	10.00	65.61	17.84	94.07
Open-hearth furnaces	80	14,318	20.04	48.80	23.75	23.65	76.29	8.07	30.20
Puddling mills and crucible furnaces	58	7,489	1[illegible].53	27.89	51.46	.65	3.85	72.47	1.42
Rolling mills	212	43,631	15.88	[illegible]0.25	32.45	†8.28	†40.68	31.23	†10.00
Tube mills	12	4,252	8.77	47.81	11.71	1.55	3.71	65.85	1.93
Total, steel works and rolling mills	212	75,608	16.30	41.61	31.03	†10.85	†43.69	†31.79	†13.65
Power, mechanical and yard force	168	65,744	18.45	51.22	22.64	11.70	28.94	55.56	19.34
Grand total	‡338	172,706	19.92	49.69	23.60	§20.59	§42.58	§37.02	§29.28

*Not including 31 employees who worked 2 days only, and 2 employees who worked three days only.

†Not including 2 employees who worked 1 day only.

‡Actual number of plants. The total number of plants can not be obtained by simple addition of the number of plants having the specified departments, as many plants have two or more departments. For example, many plants with blast furnaces have also steel works and rolling mills.

§Not including 2 employees who worked 1 day only, 31 employees who worked 2 days only, and 2 employees who worked 3 days only. (Page xvii.)

The fact that stands out most strikingly in any study of the labor conditions in the iron and steel industry in the United States is the unusually long schedule of working hours to which the larger number of the employees in this industry are subject.

During May, 1910, the period covered by this investigation, 50,000, or 29 per cent., of the 173,000 employees of blast furnaces and steel works and rolling mills covered by this report customarily worked 7 days per week, and 20 per cent. of them worked 84 hours or more per week, which, in effect, means a 12-hour working day every day in the week, including Sunday. The evil of 7-day work was particularly accentuated by the fact developed in the investigation, that the 7-day working week was not confined to the blast furnace department where there is a metallurgical necessity for continuous operation, and in which department 88 per cent. of the employees worked 7 days a week; but it was also found that, to a considerable extent in other departments where no such metallurgical necessity can be claimed, productive work was carried on on Sunday just as on other days of the week. For example, in some establishments the Bessemer converters, the open-hearth furnaces, and blooming rail, and structural mills were found operating 7 days a week for commercial reasons only.

The hardship of a 12-hour day and a 7-day week is still further increased by the fact that every week or two weeks, as the case may be, when the employees on the day shift are transferred to the night shift, and vice versa, employees remain on duty without relief either 18 or 24 consecutive hours, according to the practice adopted for the change of shift. The most common plan to effect this change of shift is to work one shift of employees on the day of change through the entire 24 hours, the succeeding shift working the regular 12 hours when it comes on duty. In some instances the change is effected by having one shift remain on duty 18 hours and the succeeding shift work 18 hours. During the time that one shift is on duty, of course, the employees on the other shift have the same number of hours of relief from duty. (P. XIV.)

Since the beginning of the present investigation, however, this matter of abolishing 7-day work for the individual employees in the blast furnaces, as well as in other departments of the industry, has received the attention of the American Iron and Steel Institute, and through a committee of that organization a plan has been proposed which gives each employee one day of rest each week. A number of the plants throughout the country have, at the instance of the Institute, adopted this plan or some modification of it, and have successfully operated it for several months. . . .

Nothing has been done by the manufacturers nor have any proposals been made to lessen the proportion of men working 72 hours or more per week. It was found in this investigation that nearly 43 per cent. of the 173,000 employees in the iron and steel industry were working at least 72 hours per week, or 12 hours per day for 6 days a week. This proportion remains unchanged, being unaffected by the plan to give the men who were working 84 hours per week one day of rest in seven. (P. XV.)

Hours of Labor.

Customary working hours per full week were reported for 24,689 employees in special occupations in 156 blast-furnace plants. For 67.11 per cent. of the 24,689 employees the customary working time was 84 hours or more per week. This means at least a 12-hour day for every day in the week, including Sunday. It will be shown later, however, that a far larger proportion work 7 days per week than would be suggested by this table.

It may be noted that 93.35 per cent. of these employees fall in two groups—60 and under 72 hours and 84 hours and over per week. The customary working hours for only 1 per cent. of the 24,689 employees were less than 60 per week.

The following table shows the classified customary working hours per week for each district and for the total of all districts:

Per Cent. of Employees Customarily Working Each Classified Number of Hours Per Week, by Districts—Blast Furnaces.

Districts	Normal number of employees	Average customary working hours per week	Per cent of employees whose customary working hours per week were: Under 60	60 and over	72 and over	84 and over
New England	328	76.9	4.27	36.59	1.22	57.93
Eastern	4,232	78.4	1.89	26.47	7.11	64.53
Pittsburgh	*9,555	78.7	.87	26.21	8.38	64.54
Gt. Lakes & Middle West	6,290	79.4	.68	24.99	3.12	71.21
Southern	4.284	79.4	.65	27.12	2.15	70.07
Total, all districts	*24,689	78.9	1.00	26.24	5.65	67.11

* Not including 31 employees who worked 2 days only and 2 employees who worked 3 days only.

The proportion of employees whose customary working time per week was 84 hours and over is approximately the same in the Great Lakes and Middle West district and in the Southern district, the percentages being 71.21 and 70.07, respectively. The proportion is somewhat lower in the Pittsburgh district and in the Eastern district, the percentages in those two districts being 64.54 and 64.53, respectively, and considerably lower in the New England district, where the percentage is 57.93. Only 328 employes are included, however, in the New England district.

A further combination shows that the customary working time is 72 hours per week or over for 74.33 per cent. of the 6,290 employees in the Great Lakes and Middle West district, for 72.92 per cent. of the 9,555 employees in the Pittsburgh district, for 72.22 per cent. of the 4,284 employees in the Southern district, 71.64 per cent. of the 4,232 employees in the Eastern district, and for 59.15 per cent. of the 328 employees in the New England district.

Days Per Week.

Seven days or turns per week was the customary working time for 22,531, or 91.26 per cent. of the 24,689 employees in the special occupations in the 156 blast-furnace plants. Six days per week was the customary working time for 2,136 employees, or 8.65 per cent. of the total. In the case of the 15 employees reported as working 5 days per week, this probably represents the time which they were employed at the specific occupation in which they were reported, they being employed at other work for the remainder of the week.

The proportion of employees whose customary working time per week was 7 days in each of the 5 districts was as follows:

Per Cent. of Employees Whose Customary Working Time Was 7 Days Per Week, By Districts—Blast Furnaces.

Districts.	Normal number of employees.	Per cent. of employees whose customary working time was 7 days per week.
New England	328	96.65
Eastern	4,232	87.36
Pittsburgh	*9,555	89.95
Gt. Lakes and Middle West	6,290	93.28
Southern	4,284	94.65

* Not including 31 employees who worked 2 days only and 2 employees who worked 3 days only.

In general it may be said that in May, 1910, all the employees directly connected with the operation of blast furnaces were working 7 days or turns per week, the small number working 6 days being employed in such occupations as yard laborers or stockers, whose services can be dispensed with on 1 day without interfering with the operation of the furnaces. (Pp. 11, 12 & 13.)

Ibid. Vol. III. Working Conditions and the Relations of Employers and Employees. 62nd Congress, 1st Session, 1911. Washington, 1913.

Working Hours in 1912.

For the greater part of the workmen in the iron and steel industry the condition as regards working time may be briefly stated as the combination of a schedule of unusually long hours of labor with an alternation of day and night work and with frequent extended periods of overtime. Approximately one-half of the employees in the iron and steel industry have a regular working-day of 12 hours, usually from 6 a. m. to 6 p. m. when on the day shift and from 6 p. m. to 6 a. m. when on the night shift. Every week or two weeks practically all of these 12-hour workmen change from the day shift to the night shift, or vice versa, and must consequently accustom themselves to the changed conditions of eating and sleeping. Apart from the difficulty of making this periodic readjustment of habits, to which all of the workmen interviewed testified, there is in the case of the married employees the added hardship of almost complete separation from their wives and children. Furthermore, at the end of the 12-hour day, whether on the day shift or the night shift, the workmen are, as is shown elsewhere, liable to be called upon to work 12 hours more in place of absent workmen, or to work for several hours until some repair job is completed. Many cases were encountered in the investigation where workmen were on duty continuously for 36 hours, often without an hour's sleep or rest and sometimes without even hot food. Moreover, a large number of the employees work every day in the week, including Sunday, and, at the time the shifts are changed from day to night, these workmen are on duty continuously for either 18 or 24 hours. In May, 1910, 30 per cent. of the employees worked 7 days a week, but during the past year (1911-12) a number of companies have made such arrangements that none of their employees is permitted to work more than 6 days per week. Between 40 and 50 per cent. of the employees formerly working 7 days per week have been affected by these arrangements for 6-

day work, but this still (August, 1912) leaves more than 15 per cent. of the employees in the industry generally and more than 50 per cent. of the blast-furnace workmen on a regular schedule of 7 days a week with a long turn of 18 or 24 hours at the change of shift.

Such a schedule of working hours is now recognized by the leading steel manufacturers and the public, as well as by the workmen, to be undesirable socially and productive of industrial inefficiency. The 7-day week has been particularly condemned and certain steps for its elimination have already been taken. The 12-hour day has likewise come to be regarded as undesirable and certain definite recommendations for its abolition have been made. (Pp. 159 and 160.)

Hours of Labor in the Steel Industry. A Communication to 15,000 Stockholders of the United States Steel Corporation. Written, after full investigation by JOHN A. FITCH, *for Charles M. Cabot, 95 Milk Street, Boston, a stockholder of the Steel Corporation. Boston, 1912.*

In Pittsburgh in 1907, I talked with men who had worked in repairing break-downs in steel mills thirty-six and forty-eight hours continuously, without rest or sleep, and who expected to have to do it again. Such periods of overwork were not regular. They did not come every week or every month. Yet, most of the ten-hour machinists that I met had at different times worked anywhere from twenty-four to forty-eight hours at a stretch. In McKeesport I accidentally met a man on the street one day and walked a block with him, and he told me that he had worked thirty-six consecutive hours at the steel mill the week before. Since 1907, I have met steel workers in all parts of the United States who have at times been obliged to put in just such terrific periods of overtime.

A twelve-hour man, you would naturally think, would be relieved by a man on the other shift at the end of his twelve hours. He generally is. But I have talked in the last year with twelve-hour steel workers who have been obliged to work thirty-six hours at a stretch because the other man did not relieve them. Such cases occurred not in any emergency, not because of a breakdown, but in the regular routine of events in the running of the mill. It is all very simple. Jones goes to work in the morning and works until night—twelve hours. Smith should take his place at that time, but Smith's wife is sick and he doesn't come out. The mill doesn't stop when Smith's wife is sick. It needs a man in a certain position, and what are the odds whether his name be Smith or Jones? Jones stays and works the night shift. Next morning his own day shift begins again; so he works that, too, before he goes home, making a total of thirty-six hours on duty.

Let me be more specific. It was a man in Lackawanna, N. Y., an employe of the Lackawanna Steel Company, who had had several times exactly the experience described here, who told me about his working schedule just the week before I saw him. On Saturday, October 9, 1910, this man went to work at six in the morning and worked continuously until two o'clock Sunday afternoon, thirty-two hours. Monday should regularly have been his day off, but the man on the other shift for some reason could not work that day, so he went out again at six in the morning and did the other man's regular work. Monday night he worked his own shift again, finishing his twenty-four hour stretch Tuesday morning. From Saturday morning to Tuesday morning there is a total of seventy-two hours. This man worked fifty-six of the seventy-two—a period out of which a brick-layer, a plumber, or a compositor would have worked twelve hours, four of them on Saturday and eight on Monday.

If these statements seem incredible, turn to the decision of the Supreme Court of the State of Indiana in the case of Republic Iron and Steel Company *vs.* Ohler.* The facts of the case are reviewed in the opinion of the Court. Ohler got hurt at four o'clock in the morning of December 20, 1899, while working in a rolling mill at Frankton, Ind., a plant that has since been abandoned.

* 161 Indiana—393.

He had begun the shift that ended so disastrously in the morning of December 18, forty-eight hours before. And he had worked, repairing a break-down, all of these forty-eight hours. At the end of the thirty-sixth hour, he had told the foreman that he didn't believe that he could stand it any longer. The foreman told him that he must stay until the job was finished, as he wanted to start the mill the next morning at six o'clock. Ohler remembered that when, a few months previously he had refused to work on a Sunday, he had been discharged by this same foreman; so he stayed on and worked twelve hours longer and then he got hurt. (Pp. 5-6.)

Half the steel workers in America have a regular twelve-hour day. A third of those actually engaged in manufacturing processes, the United States Bureau of Labor says, worked in 1910 not only twelve hours a day but seven days a week; thousands of ten-hour men also worked a seven-day week. Fifty thousand or more throughout the country faced at intervals varying from two weeks to a month a solid stretch of work eighteen or twenty-four hours long. Ten-hour men may at any time be called upon to work twelve hours as a regular thing, while before all of the workers, whether listed in the ten- or the twelve-hour class, there looms the ever imminent possibility of the stretching of a six-day week to seven days, of seven days to eight, and the drawing out of a single shift to lengths that approach and occasionally even reach the limit of a whole weeks' work in other and more favored crafts. (P. 9.)

Republic Iron & Steel Co. v. *Ohler, 68 N. E. Reporter, 901 (1903)*:

At the time the plaintiff sustained the injury alleged, he had been working continuously, at the instance and request of the defendant, in the said factory, for a period of forty-eight hours, without any sleep; and when he was ordered by said foreman to hold the rod, by reason of his continuous work, without sleep, he did not realize or appreciate the danger to which he was being subjected. . . . It is disclosed that after he had worked continuously some thirty-six hours in turning the rod, he informed Kelley, the foreman, that he did not believe he could endure the labor any longer; but the latter informed him that he must continue at work until the rod was finished. It is not reasonable to assert that a man who has labored continuously for a period of forty-eight hours without sleep, or for even a much shorter time, is in his normal condition, or that he, under the circumstances, can properly exercise all of the faculties or senses with which he is endowed. . . . A human being deprived of sleep for the period which appellee was, becomes dull in intellect and apprehension, and necessarily must be more or less unmindful of his surroundings. . . . The jury had the right at least to consider this feature of the case, as bearing upon the question whether, under all of the circumstances, appellee apprehended and appreciated the danger to which he was subjected.

The Steel Workers. John A. Fitch. *The Pittsburgh Survey. Russell Sage Foundation Publication. New York. Charities Publication Committee. 1910.*

A comparison with European practice is illuminating. A recent writer on the subject of American industrial conditions reports more overtime and Sunday work in America than in either Germany or England, and fewer holidays. The working day is longer in America than in England, and less time is allowed for meals. The eight-hour day has been developed much farther in England than in America, and it has, he states, been very successful. America has not a single blast furnace with an eight-hour work day, but furnaces in the north of England have the eight-hour day in successful operation.

The open-hearth furnaces are operated on the twelve-hour basis in Allegheny County, and as far as I have been able to learn, on this basis everywhere else in the United States. With a few exceptions they have always been operated on that basis. In Wales, on the contrary, there are a number of open-hearth plants where an eight-hour day is established. John Hodge, M. P., secretary of the British Steel Smelters, Mill and Tin Plate Workers, is authority for the statement that there are seven establishments in Wales and two in England where the three-shift system is in operation. . . .

In England the system is reported by Mr. Hodge as satisfactory, and the eight-hour work day is growing in popularity. (Pp. 177-178.)

American Labor Legislation Review. March, 1914. Working Hours in Continuous Industries. Long Hours in Railroading. Austin B. Garretson, *President, Order of Railway Conductors.*

If we go back before there was any effort to regulate hours of labor in this service, before there were organizations in existence strong enough to voice the determination of the men that they would have amelioration of their conditions, twenty-four, thirty-six, fifty, seventy or even 100 hours were not uncommon in continuous service with no opportunity for rest, and slight opportunity for food. More than twenty times in my own career as a freight conductor I have been on duty for seventy-two hours. (P. 122.)

It would probably excite doubt if I told you what was the limit of service I have ever known performed by men continuously, but I am not making a statement that is not capable of absolute demonstration. I have known one case in which a train crew put in only two time slips in one calendar month, and were continuously on duty except for one interval of a day and a half between the two trips, and the end of the month did not finish the second trip. The general manager of the railway upon which it happened, when I produced the time slips forty days after that, in a collective deal where ten general managers were representing forty-nine railways, identified the slips without my giving the name of the road, and added, "By heaven, I don't know whether they are in yet!" (Pp. 124-5.)

For the fiscal year ending June 30, 1913. a total of

261,332 men are recorded as exceeding sixteen hours. But that does not tell you much unless you get the subdivisions of that 261,000. Seventy-one thousand of these cases were between sixteen and seventeen hours; 70,000 more between seventeen and eighteen hours; 40,000 above eighteen hours and less than nineteen hours; 15,000 above twenty and less than twenty-one hours. Then they run in the thousands until there were 1,095 cases above twenty-seven hours and less than twenty-eight hours. Then they run in hundreds until, when we get up to over forty hours and less than sixty-five hours, there were less than twenty-five instances in the year. And from sixty-five hours and upwards—they took the limit off—there were 213 instances. And they call this a civilized country! . . . Probably one-third of the men engaged in train and engine service work in excess of ten or twelve hours. (P. 126.)

Constitutional Amendments Relating to Labor Legislation and Brief in Their Defense. Submitted to the Constitutional Convention of New York State by a Committee organized by the American Association for Labor Legislation. June 9, 1915.

Need of Regulation of Hours of Labor for Adult Males.
Existing Conditions.

Unregulated hours of labor mean overwork. There is a general belief that the tendency in this country is everywhere toward shorter hours of labor. A study of the situation demonstrates that this belief is not justified by the facts. While there is a marked tendency in certain industries and in certain localities toward an eight-hour day, that tendency is not universal and there are large and important industries, some of the most important of them being largely represented in New York, in which there is no movement whatever toward a shorter work day but instead the standards of fifty years ago are maintained.

Extent of the Evil.

The two tables reproduced as Appendix II of this Brief are compiled from Volume X of the 1910 Census

Reports. Table I shows the industries where a considerable proportion of the employees are working respectively 60 hours, 60 to 72 hours, and 72 hours and over per week. (P. 14.)

TABLE I.

NUMBER OF U. S. WAGE-EARNERS, AND PER CENT. OF TOTAL, WORKING SPECIFIED NUMBER OF HOURS PER WEEK, BY INDUSTRIES.

Industry.	Total Wage Earners Employed 1909	Hours per week.						
		60 hrs.	Per Cent.	Bet. 60 & 72	Per Cent.	72 hrs. and over	Per Cent.	Per Cent. 60 hrs. and over
Cotton	378,880	119,226	31.4	64,687	17.0	215	...	48.6
Hosiery and Knit Goods	129,275	49,934	38.6	...	...	4,927	3.8	42.4
Woolen Goods	168,722	45,300	26.8	1,075	.6	...	...	27.4
Silk	99,037	12,881	13.0	...	...	...	...	13.0
Cordage and Twine, Jute and Linen	25,820	6,023	23.3	667	2.5	...	...	25.9
Dyeing and Twisting Textiles	44,046	12,639	28.6	1,628	3.6	...	...	32.2
Oilcloth and Linoleum	5,201	2,727	52.4	...	...	...	...	52.4
Blast Furnaces	38,429	1,149	2.9	4,057	10.5	33,033	85.9	99.5
Steel Works and Rolling Mills	240,076	82,130	34.2	30,267	12.5	52,318	21.7	68.6
Wire	18,084	10,232	56.5	...	...	...	...	56.5
Electrical Machinery, Apparatus and Supplies	87,256	5,874	6.7	...	...	40	...	6.7
Shipbuilding, including Boat Building	40,506	14,038	34.6	1	...	...	...	34.6
Agricultural Implements	50,551	16,307	32.2	131	...	1	...	32.3
Slaughtering	89,728	64,776	72.1	638	...	494	...	73.4
Butter, Cheese and Milk	18,431	6,379	34.6	6,825	37.0	932	...	76.6
Flour Mill and Grist Mill	39,453	19,060	48.3	4,660	11.8	7,470	18.9	79.0
Ice	16,114	2,007	12.4	1,975	12.2	10,549	65.4	90.1
Glucose and Starch	4,773	1,251	26.2	672	14.1	2,760	57.8	98.1
Salt	4,936	2,991	60.5	550	11.1	587	11.9	83.9
Sugar	4,127	...	...	...	...	3,920	95.0	95.0
Canning and Preserving	59,968	42,908	71.5	2,904	4.8	2,495	4.1	80.5
Lumber	695,019	469,292	67.5	90,983	13.0	2,312	.3	80.9
Musical Instruments	38,020	10,789	28.2	...	...	...	...	28.2
Chemicals	23,714	6,581	27.7	2,050	8.6	4,707	15.6	56.2
Explosives	6,274	5,344	85.2	136	2.2	...	...	87.4
Fertilizer	18,310	14,502	79.2	1,408	7.6	1,189	6.4	93.4
Essential Oils	290	172	59.3	15	5.2	28	9.6	74.1
Paint and Varnish	14,240	3,440	24.1	67	...	463	...	27.8
Sulphuric, Nitric and Mixed Acids	2,252	555	24.6	446	19.8	997	44.3	88.7
Coke	29,273	11,629	39.7	3,904	13.3	3,280	11.2	64.2
Petroleum	13,929	1,894	13.5	673	...	2,588	18.5	37.0
Soap	12,999	4,706	36.2	23	...	2	...	36.2
Gas	37,215	5,806	15.6	5,786	15.5	21,363	57.4	88.5
Steam Laundries	109,484	36,884	33.6	598	.5	147	...	34.3
Turpentine and Rosin	39,511	19,607	49.8	997	...	172	...	52.6
Boots and Shoes	198,297	29,339	14.7	221	...	12	...	14.7
Leather	62,202	30,981	49.8	2	...	7	...	49.8
Gloves and Mittens	11,354	1,122	9.8	...	...	...	...	9.8
Paper and Wood Pulp	75,978	22,941	30.1	14,882	19.5	16,457	21.6	71.4
Printing and Publishing	258,434	10,911	4.2	488	...	231	...	4.5
Automobiles	75,721	22,280	29.4	48	...	1,407	1.9	31.3
Carriages and Wagons	69,928	27,771	39.7	406	.5	59	...	40.3
Glass	68,911	10,764	15.6	3,423	4.9	4,133	5.9	26.5
Brick and Tile	76,528	50,613	66.1	1,979	2.5	493	.6	69.3
Pottery, Terra Cotta and Fire Clay	56,168	21,909	39.1	967	...	434	...	41.5
Carpets and Rugs	33,307	12,084	36.2	...	...	...	...	36.2

It appears from these figures that 85 per cent. of all employees in blast furnaces in 1909 worked 72 hours or more per week. The same schedule of hours was followed by 21 per cent. of the steel workers, 18 per cent. of the workers in flour mills, 65 per cent. of those engaged in ice manufacturing, 57 per cent. of those in glucose and starch factories, 95 per cent. of the workers in sugar refineries, 15 per cent. of those in chemical plants, 44 per cent. of the workers in acid factories, 18 per cent. of the petroleum workers, 57 per cent. of the gas workers and 21 per cent. of the paper workers.

These are but a fraction of those working 60 hours or more per week. Taking only those industries where the hours of labor ran 60 hours or more for at least 50 per cent. of the working force, we have oilcloth and linoleum 52 per cent., blast-furnaces 99 per cent., steel works and rolling mills 68 per cent., wire 56 per cent., slaughtering 73 per cent., butter, cheese and milk 76 per cent., flour mills 79 per cent., ice 90 per cent., glucose and starch 98 per cent., salt 83 per cent., sugar 95 per cent., canning and preserving 80 per cent., lumber 80 per cent., chemicals 56 per cent., explosives 87 per cent., fertilizer 93 per cent., essential oils 74 per cent., acids 88 per cent., coke 64 per cent., gas 88 per cent., turpentine 52 per cent., paper 71 per cent., brick and tile 69 per cent.

These figures, limited to manufacturing plants alone, indicate that there is a vast amount of employment involving 10 hours a day and over. The column "72 hours and over" leaves room for speculation as to the maximum limits of the working day. A 60-hour week of course means 10 hours a day and a 72-hour week means a 12-hour working day.

In this list the transportation industries are not included. Sixteen hours a day is the maximum that a railroad employee engaged in the operation of trains can legally be employed. The record of actions brought by the Interstate Commerce Commission against railroads for exceeding this 16-hour limit indicates the extent of inhuman hours of labor in that field. Hours of labor on street car lines extend to enormous periods of overtime by the swing run system which employs a man for a few hours during the rush hour in the morning and then lays him off to wait until the rush hour in the evening, when he is to complete his working day. There is nothing that he can do in the interim. He must be on call. Usually he cannot go home. His actual working day extends from the time he starts work in the morning until he is through with his last trip at night. (Pp. 14-15.)

The tables quoted are inadequate because they stop at 72 hours a week. There is no intimation given of the 84-hour week which marks the continuous industries. Eighty-four hours means 12 hours a day, 7 days a week. Industries where the 7-day week prevails to a greater or less extent are blast furnaces and steel mills, ice factories, sugar refineries, chemical factories, coke ovens, paper and pulp mills and gas plants. (P. 17.)

Most of the work done in steel works and rolling mills has no technical requirements necessitating seven-day labor. Nevertheless, such labor is often required. A report made to the Senate by the United States Bureau of Labor on *Conditions in the Bethlehem Steel Works* in 1910 (Senate Document No. 521, 61st Congress, Second Session) showed that out of 9,184 men on the pay roll in January, 1910, 4,041, or 43 per cent. of the entire pay roll, worked 7 days a week. A majority of these men were in departments which were thus operating for commercial reasons alone, that is, to facilitate the production of steel. (P. 17.)

APPENDIX

HOURS OF LABOR AND REALISM IN CONSTITUTIONAL LAW

BY

FELIX FRANKFURTER

[REPRINTED FROM THE HARVARD LAW REVIEW, VOL. XXIX., No. 4]

HOURS OF LABOR AND REALISM IN CONSTITUTIONAL LAW*

THE Massachusetts Supreme Court was called upon recently to consider the constitutionality of the following statute:

"Employees in and about steam railroad stations in this Commonwealth designated as baggage men, laborers, crossing tenders and the like, shall not be employed for more than nine working hours in ten hours' time; the additional hour to be allowed as a lay off."

The increasing demand for shorter hours of labor throughout the industrial world, the likelihood that such demand will receive legislative recognition, the nation-wide importance of the attitude of the judiciary toward such legislation; conversely, the attitude of public opinion upon the continued exercise by the courts of their traditional power under the American constitutional system—all these considerations, and more, justify a constant critique within the profession of the point of view, no less than the explicit factors, which control judicial decisions upon social and industrial legislation.[1]

The question before the Massachusetts Supreme Court was not a new question. Necessarily, therefore, the court had to consider the applicable precedents, and the legal thinking which was embodied therein.[2] What

---

* For laborious help in the preparation of this article I am indebted to one of my students, Mr. Howard F. Burns.

[1] Valuable contributions have been made in recent years which will be referred to later, particularly the admirable papers of Professor Ernst Freund, "Limitation of Hours of Labor and the Federal Supreme Court," 17 GREEN BAG 411; Judge Learned Hand, "Due Process of Law and the Eight Hour Day," 21 HARV. L. REV. 495; and Professor Roscoe Pound, "Liberty of Contract," 18 YALE L. J. 454.

[2] This paper will concern itself wholly with the validity of the regulation of hours of labor as a problem in what Mr. Justice Holmes calls the "apologetics of the police power." Therefore, objections to the specific statute under consideration because (1) it fails to make provision for emergencies. (2) it is a denial of the equal protection of the laws by reason of arbitrary classification, and (3) it interferes with a field taken over by Congress in the Hours of Service Act of March 4, 1907, or special arguments in its favor, based (*a*) on the power to amend corporate charters, and (*b*) on the fact that a special obligation may be imposed on public-service companies, are all put on one side.

then was the legal background? It will be serviceable perhaps briefly to summarize the state of the authorities dealing with regulation of the hours of labor. Such a summary will tell a useful tale of legal history; it will do more—it may guide us not a little in the solution of present-day constitutional problems.

For the purpose of legal analysis, these cases fall into three groups:[3] (*a*) regulation of the labor of women and children; (*b*) regulation of labor in dangerous or peculiarly unhealthful employments; and (*c*) regulation of labor in industry generally.

(*a*)—Regulation of Labor of Women and Children

1876 Commonwealth v. *Hamilton Mfg. Co.*, 120 Mass. 383, sustained a law prohibiting the labor of women and children for more than sixty hours per week in manufacturing establishments. The statute was sustained as a matter of course. No reference whatever was made to the Fourteenth Amendment and counsel was apparently unable to "refer to any particular clause of the [Massachusetts] Constitution to which this provision is repugnant" (p. 384).

1895 Ritchie v. *People,* 155 Ill. 98,[4] invalidated an eight-hour law for women as "a purely arbitrary restriction r'pon the fundamental right of the citizen to control his r her own time and faculties" (p. 108).

02 Wenham v. *State,* 65 Neb. 394,[5] sustained a sixty-hour per week law for women on the ground that "women and children have always, to a certain extent, been wards of the state"; and that while "the employer and the laborer are practically on an equal footing . . . these observations do not apply to women and children" (p. 405).

---

[3] Cases involving the validity of legislation as to hours of labor upon public works or work done for the public are not considered. All recent important authorities now sustain such legislation, not as an exercise of the police power, but as an assertion by the state of its right to regulate the conditions under which public work shall be done. Atkin *v.* United States, 191 U. S. 207 (1903); People *v.* Crane, 214 N. Y. 154, 108 N. E. 427 (1915), affirmed, 239 U. S. 195 (1915); Heim *v.* McCall, 214 N. Y. 629, 108 N. E. 1095 (1915), affirmed, 239 U. S. 175 (1915).

[4] 40 N. E. 454.

[5] 91 N. W. 421.

1902 State v. *Buchanan,* 29 Wash. 602,[6] sustained a ten-hour law for women in mechanical and mercantile establishments.

"It is a matter of universal knowledge with all reasonably intelligent people of the present age that continuous standing on the feet by women for a great many consecutive hours is deleterious to their health. . . . While the principles of justice are immutable, changing conditions of society and the evolution of employment make a change in the application of principles absolutely necessary to an intelligent administration of government. In the early history of the law, when employments were few and simple, the relative conditions of the citizen and the state were different, and many employments and uses which were then considered inalienable rights have since, from the very necessity of changed conditions, been subjected to legislative control, restriction, and restraint" (p. 610).

1907 People v. *Williams,* 189 N. Y. 131,[7] declared invalid a statute prohibiting night work of women because "it is, certainly, discriminative against female citizens, in denying to them equal rights with men in the same pursuit" (p. 135).

1907 Burcher v. *People,* 41 Colo. 495,[8] nullified an eight-hour law for women and children because (1) under the Colorado Constitution the legislature must specifically designate what pursuits are unhealthful; and (2) even if the court had power to pass on the issue "the laundry business must be considered healthful; for counsel themselves, in their stipulation of facts, on which the record shows the cause was decided, are in accord that such occupation is healthful" (p. 504).

1908 Muller v. *Oregon,* 208 U. S. 412, sustained the constitutionality of a ten-hour law for women in any mechanical establishment or factory or laundry.

"The legislation and opinions referred to . . . may not be, technically speaking, authorities, and in them is

[6] 70 Pac. 52.
[7] 81 N. E. 778.
[8] 93 Pac. 14.

little or no discussion of the constitutional question presented to us for determination, yet they are significant of a widespread belief that woman's physical structure, and the functions she performs in consequence thereof, justify special legislation restricting or qualifying the conditions under which she should be permitted to toil'' (p. 420).

''The limitations which this statute places upon her contractual powers, upon her right to agree with her employer as to the time she shall labor, are not imposed solely for her benefit, but also largely for the benefit of all'' (p. 422).

1910 Ritchie & Co. v. *Wayman,* 244 Ill. 509,[9] sustained a ten-hour law for women in any mechanical establishment, factory or laundry. A heroic effort is made to distinguish the first Ritchie case from the second Ritchie case. It is true that one was an eight-hour law and the other was a ten-hour law, but the two cases are, in fact, irreconcilable in their underlying point of view.

1914 Sturges v. *Beauchamp,* 231 U. S. 320, sustained the Illinois Child Labor Law as an exercise ''of the protective power of government.''

1914 Riley v. *Massachusetts,* 232 U. S. 671, sustained a Massachusetts fifty-four-hour per week statute.

1914 Hawley v. *Walker,* 232 U. S. 718, sustained an Ohio nine-hour statute.

1915 Miller v. *Wilson,* 236 U. S. 373; *Bosley* v. *McLaughlin,* 236 U. S. 385. In these two able opinions by Mr. Justice Hughes the United States Supreme Court sustained the extremest regulation of hours of labor to date—California statutes limiting the labor of women in certain pursuits to forty-eight hours per week.

''It is manifestly impossible to say that the mere fact that the statute of California provides for an eight-hour day, or a maximum of forty-eight hours a week, instead of ten hours a day or fifty-four hours a week, takes the case out of the domain of legislative discretion. This is not to imply that a limitation of the hours of labor

[9] 91 N. E. 695.

of women might not be pushed to a wholly indefensible extreme, but there is no ground for the conclusion here that the limit of the reasonable exertion of protective authority has been overstepped'' (p. 382).

1915 People v. *Schweinler Press,* 214 N. Y. 395.[10] The Court of Appeals sustained a statute prohibiting night work for women and with courageous frankness expressly overruled *People* v. *Williams, supra.*

''Impairment caused by exhaustion or even ordinary weariness must be repaired by normal and refreshing sleep and rest if health and efficiency are to be preserved'' (p. 401).

'' . . . surely it is a matter of vital importance to the state that the health of thousands of women working in factories should be protected and safeguarded from any drain which can reasonably be avoided. This is not only for their own sakes but, as is and ought to be constantly and legitimately emphasized, for the sake of the children whom a great majority of them will be called on to bear and who will almost inevitably display in their deficiencies the unfortunate inheritance conferred upon them by physically broken down mothers'' (pp. 405-406).

(*b*)—Regulation of Labor in Dangerous Employments

1898 Holden v. *Hardy,* 169 U. S. 366,[11] sustained a Utah statute limiting to eight the hours of labor in underground mines. Familiar as this case is, a few sentences from the powerful opinion of Justice Brown will bear re-quoting:

''The enactment does not profess to limit the hours of all workmen, but merely those who are employed in underground mines, or in the smelting, reduction or refining of ores or metals. These employments, when too long pursued, the legislature has judged to be detrimental to the health of the employés, and, so long as

[10] 108 N. E. 639.
[11] It is worth while to note that Mr. Justice Brewer and Mr. Justice Peckham dissented.

there are reasonable grounds for believing that this is so, its decision upon this subject cannot be reviewed by the Federal courts'' (p. 395).

''The legislature has also recognized the fact, which the experience of legislators in many States has corroborated, that the proprietors of these establishments and their operatives do not stand upon an equality, and that their interests are, to a certain extent, conflicting. The former naturally desire to obtain as much labor as possible from their employés, while the latter are often induced by fear of discharge to conform to regulations which their judgment, fairly exercised, would pronounce to be detrimental to their health or strength. In other words, the proprietors lay down the rules and the laborers are practically constrained to obey them. In such cases self-interest is often an unsafe guide, and the legislature may properly interpose its authority'' (p. 397).

''The question in each case is whether the legislature has adopted the statute in exercise of a reasonable discretion, or whether its action be a mere excuse for an unjust discrimination, or the oppression, or spoliation of a particular class'' (p. 398).

1899 In re Morgan, 26 Colo. 415.[12] The opinion of the United States Supreme Court in *Holden* v. *Hardy, supra*, was not convincing to the Supreme Court of Colorado and with sturdy independence that court nullified a similar eight-hour law as to underground mines.[13]

''The result of our deliberation, therefore, is that this act is an unwarrantable interference with, and infringes, the right of both the employer and employé in making contracts relating to a purely private business, in which no possible injury to the public can result'' (p. 450).

---

[12] 58 Pac. 1071.

[13] To avoid the grotesque clash between state courts and the Supreme Court as to the scope of constitutional protection of the same fundamental rights, a recommendation to leave the protection of such rights entirely to the Fourteenth Amendment, and therefore omit the corresponding provisions of the Bill of Rights in our state constitutions, has received the support of distinguished members of the profession and of statesmen like ex-President Taft and ex-Attorney-General Wickersham.

1902 Re Ten Hour Law for Street Railway Corporations, 24 R. I. 603,[14] in an advisory opinion declared constitutional a ten-hour statute for employees operating street railways.

1904 Ex parte Boyce, 27 Nev. 299;[15] followed in *Ex parte Kair,* 28 Nev. 127: *ibid.,* 425 (1905);[16] and

1904 State v. *Cantwell,* 179 Mo. 245,[17] sustained an eight-hour law for underground mining work.

1911 Baltimore & Ohio R. R. v. *Interstate Commerce Commission,* 221 U. S. 612, sustained the constitutionality of the Hours of Service Act of March 4, 1907.

"The fundamental question here is whether a restriction upon the hours of labor of employés who are connected with the movement of trains in interstate transportation is comprehended within this sphere of authorized legislation. This question admits of but one answer. The length of hours of service has direct relation to the efficiency of the human agencies upon which protection to life and property necessarily depends. This has been repeatedly emphasized in official reports of the Interstate Commerce Commission, and is a matter so plain as to require no elaboration. In its power suitably to provide for the safety of employés and travelers, Congress was not limited to the enactment of laws relating to mechanical appliances, but it was also competent to consider, and to endeavor to reduce, the dangers incident to the strain of excessive hours of duty on the part of engineers, conductors, train dispatchers, telegraphers, and other persons embraced within the class defined by the act. And in imposing restrictions having reasonable relation to this end there is no interference with liberty of contract as guaranteed by the Constitution" (pp. 618-619).

---

[14] 54 Atl. 602.

[15] 75 Pac. 1.

[16] 80 Pac. 463; 82 *id.,* 453.

[17] 78 S. W. 569.

(*c*)—REGULATION OF HOURS OF LABOR IN GENERAL

1894 Low v. *Rees Printing Co.,* 41 Neb. 127,[18] declared unconstitutional an eight-hour day for mechanics and laborers, both because it was class legislation and violative of liberty of contract. After naively regarding it as irrelevant to consider the impulse back of such legislation,[19] the court nullified the statute as an attempt by the legislature to "prohibit harmless acts which do not concern the health, safety, and welfare of society" (p. 147).

1905 Lochner v. *New York,* 198 U. S. 45. In this well-known case the Supreme Court invalidated a ten-hour law for bakers. Speaking for the five majority judges, Mr. Justice Peckham declared that "to common understanding the trade of a baker has never been regarded as an unhealthy one" (p. 59), and therefore

"the act is not, within any fair meaning of the term, a health law, but is an illegal interference with the rights of individuals, both employers and employés, to make contracts regarding labor upon such terms as they may think best, or which they may agree upon with the other parties to such contracts. Statutes of the nature of that under review, limiting the hours in which grown and intelligent men may labor to earn their living, are mere meddlesome interferences with the rights of the individual . . ." (p. 61).

The vigorous dissenting opinions of Harlan, White, Day, and Holmes, *JJ.*, are familiar. But the following from the opinion of Mr. Justice Holmes pithily and completely puts the other point of view in the clash of ideas then before the Court:

"I think that the word liberty in the Fourteenth Amendment is perverted when it is held to prevent the natural outcome of a dominant opinion, unless it can be

[18] 59 N. W. 362.

[19] "For some reason, *not necessary to consider,* there has in modern times arisen a sentiment favorable to paternalism in matters of legislation" (p. 135, italics ours).

said that a rational and fair man necessarily would admit that the statute proposed would infringe fundamental principles as they have been understood by the traditions of our people and our law. It does not need research to show that no such sweeping condemnation can be passed upon the statute before us. A reasonable man might think it a proper measure on the score of health. Men whom I certainly could not pronounce unreasonable would uphold it as a first instalment of a general regulation of the hours of work'' (p. 76).[20]

1909 State v. *Miksicek,* 225 Mo. 561,[21] invalidated a six-days act—rest one day in seven—for bakers as an arbitrary infringement of liberty of contract.

1912 State v. *Lumber Co.,* 102 Miss. 802,[22] [illegible]ined a ten-hour law for labor employed in manufa[illegible]ing. The court decided that the Lochner case did not [illegible]ontrol on the facts, and, significantly, relied on the dissenting opinions in that case for the statement of the governing principles.

''It would not be unreasonable for the legis[illegible]e to decide that it would promote the health, peace[illegible]rals, and general welfare of all laborers engaged in [illegible] work of manufacturing or repairing if they were not permitted to extend their labor over ten hours a day, and the legislature could also decide that the best interests of the people in the state would be promoted by limiting the time of work of this numerous class of its citizenry to the time mentioned. In fact, when we consider the present manner of laboring, the use of machinery, the appliances, requiring intelligence and skill, and the general present day manner of life, which tends to nervousness, it seems to us quite reasonable, and in no way improper, to pass such law so limiting a day's labor'' (p. 834).

On rehearing the decision was affirmed,[23] the court taking occasion to comment upon

---

[20] See the elaboration and application of this last thought in Mr. Justice Holmes's dissenting opinions in Adair *v.* United States, 208 U. S. 161, 190 (1908), and Coppage *v.* Kansas, 236 U. S. 1, 26-27 (1915).

[21] 125 S. W. 507.

[22] 59 So. 923.

[23] State *v.* Lumber Co., 103 Miss. 263, 60 So. 215 (1913).

"the notable fact that it is rare for the seller of labor to appeal to the courts for the preservation of his inalienable rights to labor. This inestimable privilege is generally the object of the buyer's disinterested solicitude. Some day, perhaps, the inalienable right to rest will be the subject of litigation . . ."[24] (103 Miss. 267-268).

1913 State v. *Barba,* 132 La. 768,[25] held unconstitutional an eight-hour law for stationary firemen, both because it constituted an arbitrary classification and impaired the liberty of contract.

1914 State v. *Bunting,* 71 Ore. 259,[26] sustained a ten-hour law for labor in factories. In this case the court again found the dissenting opinions of the Lochner case rather than the decision on the facts of that case the relevant authority.

"A certain minimum of physical well-being is necessary in order that social life may exist, the usefulness and intelligence of the citizens be increased, and the progress of civilization accelerated: Freund, Police Power, secs. 8, 10. . . . The required minimum of well-being varies in different periods, but rises with advancing civilization until it includes a certain standard of comfort. . . . It is an undeniable fact that prolonged and excessive physical labor is performed at the expense of the mental powers, and it requires no argument to show that a man who day in and day out labors more than 10 hours must not only deteriorate physically, but mentally. . . . In view of the well-known fact that the custom in our industries does not sanction a longer service than 10 hours per day, it cannot be held, as a matter

---

[24] See a similar observation in Holden *v.* Hardy, 169 U. S. 369, 397, *supra:* "It may not be improper to suggest in this connection that although the prosecution in this case was against the employer of labor, . . . his defence is not so much that his right to contract has been infringed upon, but that the act works a peculiar hardship to his employees, whose right to labor as long as they please is alleged to be thereby violated. The argument would certainly come with better grace and greater cogency from the latter class."

[25] 61 So. 784.

[26] Appeal now pending before the Supreme Court of the United States.

of law, that the legislative requirement is unreasonable or arbitrary as to hours of labor. . . . It is urged. . . . that if it is possible for the legislature to make the declaration that to work in a factory more than 10 hours in one day is injurious to the health, then that body can make four hours a day's work, and require two hours of the work to be performed before 8 o'clock A. M. It is sufficient to say that the question of four hours constituting a day's labor, or when any part of it shall be done, is not now before this court" (pp. 267, 272, 273).

1915 People v. *Klinck Packing Co.,* 214 N. Y. 121.[27] "The right to rest"—or rather the need for leisure—to which the Supreme Court of Mississippi adverted in 1912, quickly received authoritative recognition from the New York Court of Appeals. In this case there was sustained a statute requiring one day of rest in seven. The proper sphere of legislative discretion and a correspondingly limited scope of judicial review are put most excellently by Judge Hiscock:

"Our only inquiry must be . . . whether it can fairly be believed that its [the statute's] natural consequences will be in the direction of betterment of public health and welfare, and, therefore, that it is one which the state for its protection and advantage may enact and enforce. It seems to me very clear that we may answer that it is such an one. . . . A constantly increasing study of industrial conditions I believe leads to the conviction that the health, happiness, intelligence and efficiency even of an adult man laboring in such employments [factory and mercantile] as those mentioned in this statute will be increased by a reasonable opportunity for rest, for outdoor life and recreation, for attention to his own affairs, and, if he will, study and education.

"Then we come to the question what is a reasonable opportunity, and within wide limits that problem is for the legislature. Anybody would probably say that one day in thirty or sixty would be too little and one day in each two days extravagant. Between these extremes

[27] 108 N. E. 278.

none can safely assert that the mean adopted by the legislature of one day in seven is unreasonable" (p. 127-128).[28]

A study of these opinions indicates a change not only in the decisions but in the groundwork of the decisions. We find a shift in the point of emphasis, a modification of the factors that seem relevant, a different statement of the issues involved, and a difference in the technique by which they are to be solved. The turning point comes in 1908 with *Muller* v. *Oregon*.[29] While lone voices of wisdom had been heard for almost two decades,[30] and the tendency was clearly in its direction, yet this case marks the culmination.

Prior to 1908 the decisions disclose certain marked common characteristics:

(1) Despite disavowal that the policy of legislation is not the courts' concern, there is an unmistakable dread of the class of legislation under discussion.[31] Intense feeling against the policy of the legislation must inevitably have influenced the result in the decisions. In truth this presents the point of greatest stress in our constitutional system, for it requires minds of unusual intellectual disinterestedness, detachment, and imagination to escape from the too easy tendency to find lack of power where one is convinced of lack of wisdom.

---

[28] Since the decision of the Massachusetts case under discussion the Supreme Court of Louisiana has again declared unconstitutional an eight-hour law for stationary firemen partly as unfair classification (because applying only to cities over 50,000) and partly as an impairment of liberty of contract. 77 So. (La.) 70 (1915).

[29] 208 U. S. 412, *supra.*

[30] See the dissenting opinion of Mr. Justice Holmes in Commonwealth *v.* Perry, 155 Mass. 117, 123 (1891); THAYER, LEGAL ESSAYS, 1; 26 GREEN BAG 511, 514.

[31] "The tendency of legislatures, in the form of regulatory measures, to interfere with the lawful pursuits of citizens, is becoming a marked one in this country, and it behooves the courts, firmly and fearlessly, to interpose the barriers of their judgments, when invoked to protest against legislative acts plainly transcending the powers conferred by the Constitution upon the legislative body." People *v.* Williams, 189 N. Y. 131, 135, 81 N. E. 778, 780 (1907).

"This interference on the part of the legislatures of the several states with the ordinary trades and occupations of the people seems to be on the increase." Lochner *v.* New York, 198 U. S. 45, 63 (1905).

(2) Legislation is sustained as part of the prevailing philosophy of individualism, as an exceptional protection to certain individuals as such, and not as a recognition of a general social interest. Thus legislation is supported either because women and children are wards of the state, are not *sui juris*, or to relieve certain needy individuals in the community from coercion.[32] The underlying assumption was, of course, that industry presented only contract relations between individuals. That industry is part of society, the relation of business to the community, was naturally enough lost sight of in the days of pioneer development and free land.[33]

(3) The courts here deal with statutes seeking to affect in a very concrete fashion the sternest actualities of modern life: the conduct of industry and the labor of human beings therein engaged. Yet the cases are decided, in the main, on abstract issues, on tenacious theories of economic and political philosophy. There is lack of scientific method either in sustaining or attacking legislation. Legislation is sustained or attacked on vague humanitarianism, on pressure of immediate suffering, or "common understanding." This is not the fault of the courts. It was characteristic of our legislative processes, as well as of the judicial proceedings which called them into question. It was true, substantially, of the social legislation of the nineteenth century.[34]

The courts decided these issues on *a priori* theories, on abstract assumptions, because scientific data were not available or at least had not been made available for the use of courts. But all this time scientific data had been accumulating. Organized observation, investigation, and experimentation produced facts, and science could at last speak with rational if tentative authority. There was a growing body of the world's experience and the validated opinions of those competent to have

---

[32] Holden *v.* Hardy, 169 U. S. 366, 397, *supra.*

[33] See the stimulating paper, "Labor, Capital and Business at Common Law," by Edward A. Adler, 29 HARV. L. REV. 241, particularly 262-274.

[34] The earliest Factory Act was the "work of benevolent Tories." DICEY, LAW AND OPINION IN ENGLAND, 2 ed., p. 110, and Lecture VII, particularly pp. 220 *et seq.*, 228, 229; GOLDMARK, FATIGUE AND EFFICIENCY, ch. I.

opinions. Instead of depending on *a priori* controversies raging around jejune catchwords like "individualism" and "collectivism," it became increasingly demonstrable what the effect of modern industry on human beings was and what the reasonable likelihood to society of the effects of fixing certain minimum standards of life.

The Muller case, in 1908, was the first case presented to our courts on the basis of authoritative data. For the first time the arguments and briefs breathed the air of reality. The response of the court on this method of presenting the case is significant.

"In patent cases counsel are apt to open the argument with a discussion of the state of the art. It may not be amiss, in the present case, before examining the constitutional question, to notice the course of legislation as well as expressions of opinion from other than judicial sources. In the brief filed by Mr. Louis D. Brandeis, for the defendant in error, is a very copious collection of all these matters. . . .[35]

"The legislation and opinions referred to in the margin may not be, technically speaking, authorities, and in them is little or no discussion of the constitutional question presented to us for determination, yet they are significant of a widespread belief that woman's physical

---

[35] Muller *v.* Oregon, 208 U. S. 412, 419 (1907). The great mass of data contained in the brief is epitomized in the margin of the court's opinion. Miss Josephine Goldmark, Publication Secretary of National Consumers' League, collaborated with Mr. Brandeis in the preparation of this and subsequent briefs, which are now available in part II of Miss Goldmark's book, FATIGUE AND EFFICIENCY.

The present-day demand for scientific ascertainment of facts for legislation and administration is strikingly illustrated by Miss Lathrop in her Third Annual Report as Chief of the United States Children's Bureau (1915). "The whole field of child labor is thus far singularly barren of scientific study. . . . Full and intelligent protection of the physique and mental powers of the youthful workers in this country requires costly and laborious studies in laboratory and in workshop. . . . The Children's Bureau now desires to call attention to these studies and to submit the reasonableness of spending money to make them. It proposes a later presentation of carefully considered plans for which certain preparatory studies are now going forward. The more rapidly the restrictive child labor legislation becomes uniform, the more evident must be the need of studying the welfare of the young worker within the occupation, so that we may secure just standards for the use of labor, as new standards for material are being developed" (pp. 23, 24).

structure, and the functions she performs in consequence thereof, justify special legislation restricting or qualifying the conditions under which she should be permitted to toil. Constitutional questions, it is true, are not settled by even a consensus of present public opinion, for it is the peculiar value of a written constitution that it places in unchanging form limitations upon legislative action, and thus gives a permanence and stability to popular government which otherwise would be lacking. At the same time, *when a question of fact is debated and debatable, and the extent to which a special constitutional limitation goes is affected by the truth in respect to that fact,* a widespread and long continued belief concerning it is worthy of consideration.''[36] (Italics ours.)

That upon such showing the Supreme Court should sustain the contested statute was inevitable. But the Muller case is ''epoch making,'' not because of its decision, but because of the authoritative recognition by the Supreme Court that the way in which Mr. Brandeis presented the case—the support of legislation by an array of facts which established the *reasonableness* of the legislative action, however it may be with its wisdom—laid down a new technique for counsel charged with the responsibility of arguing such constitutional questions, and an obligation upon courts to insist upon such method of argument before deciding the issue, surely, at least, before deciding the issue adversely to the legislature. For there can be no denial that the technique of the brief in the Muller case has established itself through a series of decisions within the last few years, which have caused not only change in decisions, but the much more vital change of method of approach to constitutional questions.[37]

The most striking illustration is the attitude of the New York Court of Appeals in *People* v. *Schweinler*

[36] Muller *v.* Oregon, 208 U. S. 420-421.

[37] See briefs in Ritchie & Co. *v.* Wayman, 244 Ill. 509, 91 N. E. 695 (1910); Hawley *v.* Walker, 232 U. S. 718 (1914); Miller *v.* Wilson, 236 U. S. 373 (1915); Bosley *v.* McLaughlin, 236 U. S. 385 (1915); Stettler *v.* O'Hara, 69 Ore. 519, 139 Pac. 743 (1914) (and brief in the same case now pending before the Supreme Court of the United States); People *v.* Schweinler Press, 214 N. Y. 395, 108 N. E. 639 (1915).

Press.[38] In that case, it will be recalled, the court courageously overruled *People* v. *Williams, supra*,[39] and sustained a statute prohibiting night work for women. We find a careful ascertainment of facts by the legislature as the basis of its action, and thereafter a careful presentation of facts before the court to support the legislative reason. Not only was there a presentation of facts in 1915 such as counsel failed to make in 1907, but there was a presentation of new facts acquired since 1907. If the point of view laid down in this case be sedulously observed in the argument and disposition of constitutional cases, it is safe to say that no statute which has any claim to life will be stricken down by the courts.

"While theoretically we may have been able to take judicial notice of some of the facts and of some of the legislation now called to our attention as sustaining the belief and opinion that night work in factories is widely and substantially injurious to the health of women, actually very few of these facts were called to our attention, and the argument to uphold the law on that ground was brief and inconsequential.[40]

"There is no reason why we should be reluctant to give effect to new and additional knowledge upon such a subject as this even if it did lead us to take a different view of such a vastly important question as that of public health or disease than formerly prevailed. Particularly do I feel that we should give serious consideration and great weight to the fact that the present legislation is based upon and sustained by an investigation by the legislature deliberately and carefully made through an agency of its own creation, the present factory investigating commission."[41]

These recent cases, dealing with regulation of the hours of labor, do not stand apart but illustrate two dominant tendencies in current constitutional decisions:

(1) Courts, with increasing measure, deal with legis-

---

[38] 214 N. Y. 395, 108 N. E. 639 (1915).

[39] 189 N. Y. 131, 81 N. E. 778 (1907).

[40] People *v.* Schweinler Press, 214 N. Y. 395, 411, 108 N. E. 639, 643 (1915).

[41] *Ibid.*, 214 N. Y. 395, 412-413, 108 N. E. 639, 644 (1915).

lation affecting industry in the light of a realistic study of the industrial conditions affected.[42]

(2) The emphasis is shifted to community interests, the affirmative enhancement of the human values of the whole community—not merely society conceived of as independent individuals dealing at arms' length with one another, in which legislation may only seek to protect individuals under disabilities, or prevent individual aggression in the interest of a countervailing individual freedom.[43]

As a result we find that recent decisions have modified the basis on which legislation limiting the hours of labor is supported. As science has demonstrated that there is no sharp difference in kind as to the effect of labor on men and women, courts recently have followed the guidance of science and refused to be controlled by outworn ignorance. And so we find the Supreme Court of Oregon, in sustaining the ten-hour law for men, observing that "legislative regulation of the hours of labor of men and that of women differ only in the degree of necessity therefor."[44] True enough, we are not out of the woods of difficulty by saying the question is a matter of difference of degree. But once that is recognized, once we cease to look upon the regulation of women in industry as exceptional, as the law's graciousness to a disabled class, and shift the emphasis from the fact that they are *women* to the fact that it is *industry* and the relation of industry to the community which is regulated, the whole problem is seen from a totally different aspect. Once admit it is a question of degree, there follows the recognition—and the conscious recognition is important—that we are balancing interests, that we are exercising judgment, and that the exercise of this judgment, unless so clear as to be undebatable, is solely for the legislature.[45]

---

[42] McLean *v.* Arkansas, 211 U. S. 539, 549-550 (1908) (it is significant that Mr. Justice Brewer and Mr. Justice Peckham dissented); Baltimore & Ohio R. R. *v.* Interstate Commerce Commission, 221 U. S. 612, 619 (1911).

[43] People *v.* Klinck Packing Co., 214 N. Y. 121, 128, 108 N. E. 278, 280 (1915).

[44] State *v.* Bunting, 71 Ore. 259, 271, 139 Pac. 731, 735 (1914).

[45] Price *v.* Illinois, 238 U. S. 446, 452 (1915).

What, then, are the common factors in the labor of men and women that would make a limitation of the hours of labor, in employments not dangerous or inherently unhealthy, to ten hours or nine hours an exercise of legislative discretion not beyond the pale of reasonable argument, and therefore to be respected by the courts? They are:

(1) "The common physiological phenomenon, fatigue," and the need of rest to repair the waste of the toxin.[46] Can the point where the line is to be drawn possibly be drawn *a priori?* Or, at the least, in the light of modern physiology is any layman entitled to say that a limitation of routine manual labor of masses of men to nine hours is a capricious and wilful oppression, without sustaining reason?[47]

(2) An enlarged conception of leisure and the tendency to regard not only its relation to the immediate effects upon animal health but also its bearing on the industrial output and the demands of citizenship.[48]

(3) Experience, based upon adequate trial, with the gradual reduction of labor and the slow increase of hours of leisure encouragingly demonstrates that such limitation of labor and increase of leisure have been put to fruitful uses. The tried measures of curtailing manual labor have added to the sum total of that by which we measure the civilized aspects of life.[49]

This then was the "state of the art" which confronted the Massachusetts Supreme Court in passing upon the constitutionality of the nine-hour law in question. One would suppose that in the light of all this it would be an easy matter for the court to hold that a nine-hour day is not "so extravagant and unreasonable, so disconnected with the probable promotion of health

[46] See GOLDMARK, FATIGUE AND EFFICIENCY, ch. 2. The scientific views set forth in Miss Goldmark's book recently formed the basis of an arbitration judgment, in Australia, by Mr. Justice Higgins, in the Waterside Workers' case (not yet reported).

[47] Price *v.* Illinois, 238 U. S. 446, 452 (1915), *supra.*

[48] See *e. g.* HOBSON, WORK AND WEALTH, particularly chapters XIV and XV; TAUSSIG, INVENTORS AND MONEY MAKERS, pp. 63, 65 *et seq.*, 71 *et seq.;* U. S. Commissioner of Labor Statistics Royal Meeker, 63 Annals Amer. Acad. of Pol. and Soc. Sci., 262, 267.

[49] See GOLDMARK, FATIGUE AND EFFICIENCY, p. 279.

and welfare that its enactment is beyond the jurisdiction of the legislature,"[50] or, at the very least, that, since the subject is "debatable, the legislature is entitled to its own judgment."[51]

Quite the contrary. The court held that the statute "is an unwarrantable interference with individual liberty and an interference with property rights, and therefore contrary to constitutions which secure these fundamental rights."[52]

How could such a result have been reached?

(1) The case was inadequately presented. The court was not called upon to pass on the validity of the statute as such, but upon an agreed statement of facts under the statute to the effect that there is nothing inherently unhealthy about the work which the employee did, as it was half performed in the open air and was not arduous.[53] The assumption back of such a statement is that where work is not inherently unhealthy it is immaterial how long such work is pursued. Thus a wholly unscientific concession of fact was made, and therefore a wholly unscientific issue was presented to the court. But even such an issue was not supported by the available body of scientific facts. No attempt was made to bring to the attention of the court a detailed, painstaking, thoroughly marshaled array of facts to explain and to fortify the experience and theory back of labor legislation. In other words, the case was not argued in the way in which the decisions in the Muller case, the second Ritchie case, the Hawley case, the Miller case, the Bosley case, and the Schweinler case demanded that it should be argued.

(2) One can therefore understand why the court found the case "governed" by the Lochner case, *supra.*[54] Nevertheless, one is compelled to conclude that the illumination that has been cast upon the Lochner case during the past decade does not leave to that case any principle which *ipso facto* controls the validity of specific meas-

---

[50] People *v.* Klinck Packing Co., 214 N. Y. 121, 127, 108 N. E. 278, 280 (1915).

[51] Price *v.* Illinois, 238 U. S. 446, 452 (1915).

[52] Commonwealth *v.* Boston & M. R. R., 110 N. E. (Mass.) 264 (1915).

[53] Commonwealth *v.* Boston & M. R. R., 110 N. E. (Mass.) 264 (1915).

[54] Lochner *v.* New York, 198 U. S. 45 (1905).

ures regulating hours of labor. The principle of the Lochner case is simple enough: that arbitrary restriction of men's activities, unrelated in reason to the "public welfare," offends the Fourteenth Amendment. As to the principle, there is no dispute. But the principle is the beginning and not the end of the inquiry. The field of contention is in its application. The Lochner case, judged by its history and by more recent decisions of the Supreme Court, does not in itself furnish the yardstick for its application.

(*a*) It is now clearly enough recognized that each case presents a distinct issue; that each case must be determined by the facts relevant to it; that we are dealing, in truth, not with a question of law but the application of an undisputed formula to a constantly changing and growing variety of economic and social facts.[55] Each case, therefore, calls for a new and distinct consideration, not only of the general facts of industry but the specific facts in regard to the employment in question and the specific exigencies which called for the specific statute.

(*b*) The groundwork of the Lochner case has by this time been cut from under. The majority opinion was based upon "a common understanding" as to the effect of work in bakeshops upon the public and upon those engaged in it. "Common understanding" has ceased to be the reliance in matters calling for essentially scientific determination. "Has not the progress of sanitary science shown," Professor Freund pertinently inquires, "that common understanding is often equivalent to popular ignorance and fallacy?"[56] On the particular issue involved in the Lochner case "study of the facts has shown that the legislature was right and the court was wrong."[57] Either because matters as to which the court of its own knowledge cannot know, or, because not know-

[55] See People *v.* Schweinler Press, 214 N. Y. 395, 411-412, 108 N. E. 639, 643 (1915); Bosley *v.* McLaughlin, 236 U. S. 385, 392 *et seq.* (1915); Miller *v.* Wilson, 236 U. S. 373, 382 (1915); McLean *v.* Arkansas, 211 U. S. 539, 549-550 (1908).

[56] 17 GREEN BAG 411, 416.

[57] Professor Roscoe Pound, "Liberty of Contract," 18 YALE L. J. 454, 480, and n. 123.

ing, it cannot assume the non-existence of facts, contested legislative action should be resolved in favor of rationality rather than capricious oppression. Happily the fundamental constitutional doctrine of the assumption of rightness of legislative conduct, where the court is uninformed, is again rigorously being enforced by the United States Supreme Court.[58]

(*c*) So far as the general flavor of the Lochner opinion goes, it surely is no longer "controlling." If the body of professional opinion counts for anything in the appraisal of authority of a decision (itself decided by a divided court, and since departed from in effect in an important series of cases), it has been impressively arrayed against this decision. If ever an opinion has been subjected to the weightiest professional criticism it is the opinion in the Lochner case. Judge Andrew Bruce, Professor Ernst Freund, Judge Learned Hand, Professor Roscoe Pound—to mention no others—surely speak with high competence upon this subject. Nevertheless, the body of persuasive authority which their writings present was not brought to the court's attention and failed to be considered in the disposition of the case.[59]

The circumstances which resulted in this decision reveal anew a situation of far-reaching importance. For it affects the very bases on which constitutional decisions are reached and, therefore, affects vitally the most sensitive point of contact between the courts and the people.

---

[58] Thus, in one of its latest opinions, the Supreme Court refused to upset a "police measure" with the following language:

"Petitioner makes his contention depend upon disputable considerations of classification and upon a comparison of conditions of which there is no means of judicial determination and upon which nevertheless we are expected to reverse legislative action. . . . " Hadachek *v.* Sebastian, 239 U. S. 394, 413 (Dec. 20, 1915).

Here, as elsewhere in the law, Mr. Justice Holmes long ago put the matter with acute finality: "I cannot pronounce the legislation [prohibiting fines against weavers for defective workmanship] void, as based on a false assumption, since I know nothing about the matter one way or the other." Commonwealth *v.* Perry, 155 Mass. 117, 124-125, 28 N. E. 1126, 1127 (1891). As to the reasonableness of the legislature's belief that a system of fines affords dangerous temptations for oppressive use see R. H. TAWNEY, MINIMUM RATES IN THE TAILORING INDUSTRY, pp. 60 and 95.

[59] A. A. BRUCE, "The Illinois Ten Hour Labor Law for Women," 8 MICH. L. REV. 1; G. S. Corwin, "The Supreme Court and the Fourteenth Amendment," 7 MICH. L. REV. 643; Ernst Freund, "Limitation of Hours

The statute under discussion may well have been of no particular social import. The decision which nullified it, one may be sure, offers no intrinsic obstruction to needed legislation, and in itself has merely ephemeral vitality. But, unfortunately, the evil that decisions do lives after them. Such a decision deeply impairs that public confidence upon which the healthy exercise of judicial power must rest.

Under the present-day stress of judicial work it is inevitable that courts, on the whole, can only decide specific cases as presented to them.[60] In other words, the substantial dependence upon the facts and briefs presented by counsel throws the decision of the courts largely upon those chances which determine the selection of counsel. These are, of course, necessary human drawbacks, and the practice works out well enough in controversies where purely individual interests are represented by counsel. This is not the situation in cases such as the one before the Massachusetts court. The issue submitted to the court in fact was the issue as determined by the District Attorney of Worcester and counsel for the Boston and Maine Railroad. In truth, the issue was between the Court and the Legislature. In such a case either the legislative judgment should be sustained if there is "no means of judicial determination" that the legislature is indisputably wrong,[61] or the court should demand that the legislative judgment be supported by

---

of Labor and the Federal Supreme Court," 17 GREEN BAG 411, "Constitutional Limitations and Labor Legislation," 4 ILL. L. REV. 609; L. N. Greeley, "The Changing Attitude of the Courts toward Social Legislation," 5 ILL. L. REV. 222; Learned Hand, "Due Process of Law and the Eight Hour Day," 21 HARV. L. REV. 495; Sir Frederick Pollock, "The New York Labor Law and the Fourteenth Amendment," 21 L. QUART. REV. 211; Roscoe Pound, "Liberty of Contract," 18 YALE L. J. 480. *Cf.* Mr. Wigmore's comment on "The Qualities of Current Judicial Decisions," 9 ILL. L. REV. 529, 530-1.

But see Atkins *v.* Grey Eagle Coal Co., 84 S. E. 906 (1915), where the Court of Appeals of West Virginia sustained a truck act, in effect overruling the decision in State *v.* Goodwill, 33 W. Va. 179 (1889), and cited among its authorities Professor Pound's article, "Liberty of Contract," 18 YALE, L. J. 480.

[60] See Mr. Justice Swayze in "The Growing Law," 20 YALE, L. J. 1, 18-19. People *v.* Schweinler Press, 214 N. Y. 395, 411, 108 N. E. 639, 643 (1915).

[61] Hadacheck *v.* Sebastian, 239 U. S. 394, 413 (1915). Price *v.* Illinois, 238 U. S. 446, 452 (1915).

available proof.[62] It would seem clear that courts have inherent power to accomplish this by indicating the kind of argument needed to reach a just result; or even by calling for argument from members of the bar—officers of the court—of particular equipment to assist in a given problem.[63] If legislation be necessary New York furnishes an example in its recent enactment authorizing the courts to request the attendance of the attorney general in support of an act of the legislature when its constitutionality is brought into question.[64]

These, after all, are only expedients. Fundamental is the need that the profession realize the true nature of the issues involved in these constitutional questions and the limited scope of the reviewing power of the courts.[65] With the recognition that these questions raise, substantially, disputed questions of fact must come the invention of some machinery by which knowledge of the facts, which are the foundation of the legal judgment, may be at the service of the courts as a regular form of the judicial process. This need has been voiced alike by jurists and judges.[66] Once the need shall be felt as the common longing of the profession the inventive powers of our law will find the means for its satisfaction.

Felix Frankfurter.

HARVARD LAW SCHOOL.

---

[62] Professor Ernst Freund, "Constitutional Limitations and Labor Legislation," 4 ILL. L. Rev. 609, 622.

[63] It is interesting to note that the chief arguments in the series of cases beginning with the Muller case were made by an *amicus curiae,* Mr. Louis D. Brandeis, in behalf of the National Consumers' League.

[64] NEW YORK LAWS, 1913, ch. 442, p. 919.

[65] See 28 HARV. L. REV. 790.

[66] Professor Roscoe Pound, in "Legislation as a Social Function," 7 Pub. Am. Soc. Soc'y, 148, 161: "In the immediate past the social facts required for the exercise of the judicial function of law-making have been arrived at by means which may fairly be called mechanical. It is not one of the least problems of the sociological jurist to discover a rational mode of advising the court of facts of which it is supposed to take judicial notice." So (in dealing with a somewhat similar problem) Judge Learned Hand, in Parke Davis & Co. *v.* Mulford & Co., 189 Fed. 95, 115: "How long we shall continue to blunder along without the aid of unpartisan and authoritative scientific assistance in the administration of justice, no one knows; but all fair persons not conventionalized by provincial legal habits of mind ought, I should think, unite to effect some such advance." *Cf.* also, Steenerson *v.* Great Northern Ry., 69 Minn. 353, 377, 72 N. W. 713, 716 (1897).

APPENDIX II

LIST OF SOURCES QUOTED

I. PUBLIC DOCUMENTS

United States

Federal

BUREAU OF THE CENSUS — PAGE

Principal Causes of Death. Summary of the Statistics for the Registration Area in 1914. Jan. 16, 1916 ... 14

BUREAU OF LABOR

11th Special Report of the Commissioner. 1904. Regulation and Restriction of Output ... 728

Bulletins

No. 75. March, 1908. Industrial Hygiene. George M. Kober, M. D., LL. D. ... 65

No. 77. July, 1908. Wages and Hours of Labor in Manufacturing Industries, 1890 to 1907 ... 902

No. 79. November, 1908. The Mortality from Consumption in Dusty Trades. Frederick L. Hoffman ... 255, 435

No. 80. January, 1909. Woman and Child Wage-earners in Great Britain. Victor S. Clark, Ph. D. ... 854, 879, 895

No. 95. July, 1911. Industrial Lead Poisoning in Europe. Sir Thomas Oliver, M. D., F. R. C. P. ... 261

BUREAU OF LABOR STATISTICS

Bulletins

No. 118. April, 1913. Ten Hour Maximum Working-Day for Women and Young Persons ... 822, 856

No. 127. August 12, 1913. Industrial Accidents and Hygiene Series: No. 3. Dangers to Workers from Dusts and Fumes and Methods of Protection 242

No. 128. 1913. Wages and Hours of Labor in the Cotton, Woolen and Silk Industries, 1890 to 1912 ... 909

No. 129. 1913. Wages and Hours of Labor in the Lumber, Millwork and Furniture Industries. 1890 to 1912 ... 909

No. 137. 1913. Wages and Hours of Labor in the Building and Repairing of Steam Railroad Cars. 1890 to 1912 919
No. 153. 1914. Wages and Hours of Labor in the Lumber, Millwork and Furniture Industries. 1907 to 1913 915
No. 154. 1914. Wages and Hours of Labor in the Boot and Shoe and Hosiery and Underwear Industries. 1907 to 1913 922
No. 161. 1914. Wages and Hours of Labor in the Clothing and Cigar Industries. 1911 to 1913 920
No. 163. 1914. Wages and Hours of Labor in the Building and Repairing of Steam Railroad Cars. 1907 to 1913 919
No. 177. 1915. Wages and Hours of Labor in the Hosiery and Underwear Industry. 1907 to 1914 925
No. 178. 1915. Wages and Hours of Labor in the Boot and Shoe Industry. 1907 to 1914 927

Monthly Reviews

Vol. I, No. 4. October, 1915 929
Vol. II, No. 2. February, 1916 ..... 847, 930
Vol. II, No. 3. March, 1916 569

Children's Bureau

Third Annual Report. 1915. Julia C. Lathrop 975

Industrial Commission. 1900.

On the Relations and Conditions of Capital and Labor Employed in Manufactures and General Business.

Vol. VII. 1900 503
Vol. XIV. 1901 ..... 677, 894
Vol. XIX. 1902. Final Report 196, 222, 457, 487, 614, 633, 684, 727, 746, 784, 854

Interstate Commerce Commission

18th Annual Report. 1904-1905 378
19th Annual Report. 1905-1906 379

Public Health Service

Weekly Public Health Reports. May 29, 1914. Industrial Conditions. Their Relation to the Public Health. B. S. Warren, Surgeon, U. S. Public Health Service 70, 248, 478

Supplement No. 24. May 7, 1915. Exercise and Health. Frederick Charles Smith, Passed Assistant Surgeon, U. S. Public Health Service 38

Bulletin No. 71. May, 1915. Studies in Vocational Diseases. I. The Health of Garment Workers. J. W. Schereschewsky, Surgeon, U. S. Public Health Service 90

Weekly Reports. Oct. 1, 1915. Industrial Hygiene. A Plan for Education in the Avoidance of Occupational Diseases and Injuries. J. W. Schereschewsky, Surgeon, U. S. Public Health Service ... 36

Senate Reports and Documents

Document No. 141. Eight hours for Laborers on Government Work. 57th Congress, 1st Session. 1901-1902 486

Report No. 2321. The Eight-Hour Law. 57th Congress. 2nd Session. 1902-1903 505

Document No. 521. Report on Strike at Bethlehem Steel Works. 61st Congress. 2nd Session. 1909-1910 200

Document No. 110. Report on Conditions of Employment in the Iron and Steel Industry in the United States. 62nd Congress. 1st Session. 1911.

Vol. I. Wages and Hours of Labor 605, 945

Vol. III. Working Conditions and the Relations of Employers and Employees. 62nd Congress, 1st Session, 1911 ... 461, 750, 801, 880, 950

Document No. 645. Report on Condition of Woman and Child Wage-Earners in the United States. Vol. XI. Employment of Women in the Metal Trades. 61st Congress. 2nd Session, 1911 372

Report No. 601. Hours of Daily Service of Laborers and Mechanics upon Government Contracts. 62nd Congress, 2nd Session, 1912 .... 489, 543

Document No. 1124. The Eight-Hour Day. Various Articles, Arguments, and Bills relating to the Eight Hour Law. 62nd Congress. 3rd Session. 1913. (Letter from William J. Crawford, President, William J. Crawford & Co., Inc., to Mr. James Duncan, International President Granite Cutters' International Association. December 19, 1912) 690

HOUSE OF REPRESENTATIVES

Report No. 1793. Hours of Laborers on Public Works of the United States. 57th Congress, 1st Session. 1901-1902 ..... 196, 472, 505, 746, 853

CONGRESSIONAL RECORD

Vol. XXI. Part X. Pages 9,300-9,301, August 28, 1890. Remarks of Mr. McKinley upon the Eight-hour Bill 484

California

Commission of Immigration and Housing. 1st Annual Report. January 2, 1915 560

Connecticut

Bureau of Labor Statistics. Report, 1886 631

Georgia

Hennington *v.* The State, 90 Ga., 396 (1892) 508

Illinois

Factory Inspectors. Report, 1893 ..... 606, 878

Commission on Occupational Diseases. Report, January, 1911 ..... 51, 247

Ibid. Drs. George E. Shambaugh and G. W. Boot. Report on Occupational Deafness 247

Indiana

Republic Iron and Steel Co. *v.* Ohler, 161 Ind. 393, 68 N. E. Reporter, 901. (1903) 953

Maine

Senate Document No. 19. 1848. Report on Petition Praying Passage of Law making 10 Hours Legal Day's Work 742

Bureau of Industrial and Labor Statistics. Report, 1892 ..... 194, 410

List of Sources.—Public Documents.

Massachusetts

HOUSE DOCUMENTS

No. 153. 1850. Minority Report of the Special Committee Re Limitation of Hours of Work. 132, 408, 453, 742, 850, 878

No. 80. 1855. Report on Ten-Hour Petition 893

No. 98. 1866. Report of the Special Commission on the Hours of Labor and the Condition and Prospects of the Industrial Classes 133, 455

No. 44. 1867. Report of Commissioners on the Hours of Labor 409, 532

No. 44. 1867. Report of Commissioners on the Hours of Labor. Minority Report. Edward H. Rogers 480

No. 2300. 1914. Report of the Commission on Immigration on the Problem of Immigration in Massachusetts 554

SENATE DOCUMENTS

No. 1. 1874. Address of Governor William B. Washburn to the two Branches of the Legislature. January 8, 1874 134, 553

No. 33. 1874. Report of the Committee on the Labor Question 416, 665

EVIDENCE Submitted to the Legislature in Favor of the Enactment of a Ten-hour Law. Lawrence, 1870. 410, 415, 500

ARGUMENT of Hon. William Gray on Petitions for Ten-Hour Law Before the Committee on Labor. February 13, 1873 664

BUREAU OF STATISTICS OF LABOR

Reports

1870 410, 482

1871 416, 663, 819, 848

1872 482

1873 664

1881 631, 665, 743, 848, 893

Chief of District Police

Reports

1883 666
1885 820
1886 666
1899 .... 483, 726

State Board of Health

Reports

1873 429
1906. Report on the Sanitary Conditions of Factories, Workshops, and other Establishments 166

Michigan

Bureau of Labor Statistics. Report, 1898 431

Mississippi

Buckeye Cotton Oil Co. *v.* The State, 60 Southern Rep., 775. (Miss., 1913) 606

Nebraska

Bureau of Labor Statistics. Report, 1887-1888 482
Bureau of Labor and Industrial Statistics. Report, 1907-1908 822

New Hampshire

House Journal. June, 1847. Report recommending Shortening Hours of Labor, Regulating Child Labor, and Establishing 10-Hour Day 131

New Jersey

Bureau of Statistics of Labor and Industry

Reports

1886 851
1905. The Eight-hour Movement: How reducing the Hours of Labor has affected the cost of Production 717

Commission of Immigration

Report

1914 557

New York

STATE FACTORY INSPECTOR

Reports

1887 666
1894 .... 632, 725, 852
1899 411
1890 744

DEPARTMENT OF LABOR

Report on Factory Inspection. 1901 727
Bureau of Labor Statistics. Report, 1900.
48, 195, 416, 457, 485, 526, 538, 632, 745, 852
Bureau of Industries and Immigration. Report, 1913 551

STATE FACTORY INVESTIGATING COMMISSION

4th Report, Feb. 15, 1915 .... 316, 797

LEGAL DECISIONS

People *v.* Havnor, 149 N. Y., 195 (1896) 602
People *v.* Klinck Packing Co., 214 N.Y., 121 (1915) .. 507

DEPARTMENT OF HEALTH

Monthly Bulletin, May, 1915.
Controlling the Diseases of Adult Life. C. E. A. Winslow 12
Diseases of Adult Life and Middle Age. Eugene Lyman Fisk, M. D., Director of Hygiene, Life Extension Institute, New York 28

DEPARTMENT OF HEALTH OF THE CITY OF NEW YORK

No. 18. Reprint Series. June, 1914. The Next Step in Preventive Medicine. S. S. Goldwater, M. D., Commissioner of Health 31

DEPARTMENT OF EDUCATION

1916 Citizenship Syllabus. Prepared by Research Department of the Committee for Immigrants in America 568

Pennsylvania

Proceedings of the Government and Citizens of Philadelphia on the Reduction of the Hours of Labor and Increase of Wages. July, 1835 479

List of Sources.—Public Documents.

BUREAU OF INDUSTRIAL STATISTICS

Reports

1880-1881 457

1913-1914. The Henry Ford Plan 857

FACTORY INSPECTOR

Report

1895 725

Wisconsin

BUREAU OF LABOR AND INDUSTRIAL STATISTICS

Reports

1903-1904 .... 458, 488, 785

1907-1908. Part III. Industrial Hygiene and the Police Power. Henry Baird Favill, M. D. 434

Part VII. Women Workers in Milwaukee Tanneries. Irene Osgood, Special Agent 879

Great Britain

British Sessional Papers

Reports

Vol. III. 1816. Report from the Select Committee on the State of the Children Employed in the Manufactories of the United Kingdom. Minutes of Evidence, 25 April, 18 June, 1816. Testimony of Robert Owen 464, 654

Vol. XXI. 1833. 2nd Report of . . . the Commissioners for inquiring into the Employment of Children in Factories and . . . Reports by the Medical Commissioners 420

Vol. X. 1840. 1st Report from Select Committee on the Act for the Regulation of Mills and Factories 858

Vol. XIII. 1843. Children's Employment Commission 823

Reports of Inspectors of Factories

Vol. XXII. 1842. For Half Year Ending 30th June, 1842 405

Vol. XXV. 1845. For Half Year Ending 30th April, 1845. Robert Gardner, Mill-owner 658

Vol. XXVI. 1847-1848. For Half Year Ending April 30, 1848 896
Vol. XXII. 1849. For Half Year Ending 31st October, 1848 510
Vol. XXII. 1849. Appendix. Evidence of the Opinions of Persons Employed in Factories, Respecting the Ten Hours' Act, collected in September, October and November, 1848........511, 869, 896
Vol. XXII. 1849. For Half Year Ending 30th April, 1849 859
Vol. XXIII. 1850. For Half Year Ending 31st October, 1849 511
Vol. XXIII. 1850. For Half Year Ending April 30, 1850 ....622, 761
Vol. XXIII. 1851. For Half year Ending 31st October, 1850 659
Vol. XL. 1852-1853. For Half Year Ending 30th April, 1853 ....623, 660
Vol. XVIII. 1856. For Half Year Ending October 31, 1855 623
Vol. XII. 1859. For Half Year Ending 31st October, 1858 ....624, 785
Vol. XXXIV. 1860. For Half Year Ending 31st October, 1859 ....625, 862
Vol. XXIV. 1866. For Half Year Ending 31st October, 1865 625
Vol. XVI. 1867. For Half Year Ending 31st October, 1866 896
Vol. XIV. 1868-1869. For Half Year Ending 30th April, 1868 ....513, 626
Vol. XIV. 1868-1869. For Half Year Ending October 31, 1868 897
Vol. XV. 1870. For Half Year Ending 30th April, 1870 ....420, 492
Vol. XXIII. 1877. For Half Year Ending April 30, 1877 826

CHIEF INSPECTOR OF FACTORIES AND WORKSHOPS

Reports

Vol. XVII. 1893. For 1892........ 788
Vol. XXI. 1894. For 1893........494, 827, 899

Vol. XIX. 1895. For 1894 792
Vol. X. 1901. For 1900 830, 900
Vol. XII. 1902. For 1901 831
Vol. XII. 1903. For 1902 421, 794, 900
Vol. X. 1905. For 1904 886
Vol. XXV. 1912-1913. For 1911 249
For 1913 622, 722
For 1914 835

Factory and Workshops Acts Commission
Vol. XXIX-XXX. 1876.
Vol. XX[illegible] Report 217, 883, 898
Appe[illegible] [illegible]. Report of Conference of Members of Women's Trade Unions on the Foundry and Workshops Acts. 1875 882
Vol. XXX 660, 826

Royal Commis[illegible] [illegible] Labour
Vol. XXI[illegible] [illegible]92 688, 765, 863
Vol. XXXVI. 1892 808
Testimony of Mr. Patrick Walls, National Association of Blast-Furnacemen 476
Vol. XXXII. 1893 864
Vol. XXXIV. 1893 421, 864
Appendix CXX[illegible]X. Group C. Summary of Evidence of Mr. C. B. Bowling, Inspector of Factories 789
Vol. XXXVI. 1893 688
Vol. XXXIX. 1893 147, 790, 865, 884, 899
Vol. XXXV. 1894. Fifth and Final Report. Part I. General Review of the Evidence 148, 465, 790
Minority Report by Mr. William Abraham, Mr. Michael Austin, Mr. James Mawdsley, and Mr. Tom Mann 148

Select Committee on Shops. Early Closing Bill
Vol. VI, 1901. Report 609

Select Committee of the House of Lords on Early Closing of Shops
Vol. VI. 1901. Report 72, 407, 609

List of Sources.—Public Documents.

INTER-DEPARTMENTAL COMMITTEE ON PHYSICAL DETERIORATION

Vol. I, II, III. 1904.

Vol. I. Report.......422, 589

Appendix I. Original Memorandum Prepared by Surgeon-General Sir William Taylor, K. C. B., Director-General, Army Medical Service....... 584

Vol. II. Minutes of Evidence....... 594

Vol. III. Appendix XIV....... 595

HANSARD'S PARLIAMENTARY DEBATES

Vol. 73. 1844.......420, 824

Vol. 74. 1844.......439, 658, 825

Vol. 92. 1847....... 825

BOARD OF TRADE LABOUR GAZETTE

July, 1915. Eight-Hour Day in Government Workshops....... 815

BRITISH HOME OFFICE

Interim Report on an Investigation of Industrial Fatigue by Physiological Methods, by A. F. Stanley Kent, M. A., D. Sc. (Oxon), Henry Overton Wills Professor of Physiology in University of Bristol, London, 1915.......170, 180, 276, 293

Canada

INSPECTORS OF FACTORIES FOR THE PROVINCE OF ONTARIO

Reports

1894....... 212

1895....... 213

1896....... 213

BRITISH COLUMBIA ROYAL LABOUR COMMISSION

Report

Canada Labour Gazette, August, 1903....... 616

List of Sources.—Public Documents.

Australasia

NEW ZEALAND DEPARTMENT OF LABOR
Reports
1893 527
1895 .... 527, 891
1900 527
1903 528
1904 528
1905 529
1908 529
1911 530
1912 530

NEW SOUTH WALES LEGISLATIVE ASSEMBLY
Report of the Working of the Factories and Shops' Act. 1904 213

Germany

GERMAN FACTORY INSPECTORS: OFFICIAL ABSTRACTS OF REPORTS
Vol. XVIII. 1893 715
Vol. XVIII. 1895 667
Vol. XXII. 1897 .... 105, 156, 617
1898 668

GERMAN FACTORY AND MINE INSPECTORS
Reports
1903. Vol. I. 717
1903. Vol. III 841
1904. Vol. I 692, 716, 817
1904. Vol. II 668
1904. Vol. III 718, 842
1905. Vol. I 683, 723
1906. Vol. III 157, 722
1907. Vol. I 424
1907. Vol. III 610, 718

List of Sources.—Public Documents.

Factory Inspectors of the Kingdom of Württemberg

Reports

1901 .... 157, 731
1902 .... 519, 612, 618, 731
1903 .... 613, 619, 891
1905 .... 732, 842
1911 .... 521, 733

Factory Inspectors of Baden

Reports

1900 715
1901 701
1903 691

German Imperial Office of Statistics, Department of Labor Statistics

1903. On the hours of Shops Assistants and Apprentices 795

State Invalidity and Old Age Insurance Department for Berlin

Report of the Physician in Chief of the Beelitz Sanitarium. (Tuberculosis not included.)
1906 .... 111, 123, 125, 424
1909 112

Imperial Insurance Department

Report 1910. Appendix I. Part I. Statistics of Industrial Accidents for the year 1907 384

German Reichstag, Proceedings

101st Session, April 16th, 1891 611
103rd Session. April 18th, 1891 574
1st Session. 1908. For the Legal Prohibition of Excessive Shifts Ruinous to Health in Mines. Report No. 701, brought in by Representative Sachse 158

Austria

Royal and Imperial Factory Inspectors

Reports

1898 264

List of Sources.—Public Documents.

Switzerland

FACTORY INSPECTORS

Reports

1879 .... 159, 425
1881 160
1884-1885 839
1894-1895 451

FACTORY AND MINE INSPECTORS

Reports

1898-1899 .... 779, 839

SWISS FACTORY INSPECTORS TO THE SWISS DEPARTMENT OF LABOR ON THE REVISION OF THE FACTORY LAWS

Reports

1904 .... 264, 620, 735

France

PARLIAMENTARY DEBATES AND DOCUMENTS

Chamber of Deputies, Mar. 23, 1881. Discussion of the Sections of the Law relating to the Length of Hours of Work in Workshops and Factories 426, 469

Special Sessions, Nov. 5, 1906. Annex 374. Bill for the 8-Hour Day and Minimum Wage for Male and Female Laborers and Employees 60, 357

LABOR OFFICE

Bulletins

March, 1905. Wages and the Application of the Ten Hour Law 872

May, 1905. Wages and the Application of the Ten Hour Law 873

LABOR DEPARTMENT. 1892.

Bulletins

Original Studies by the Inspectors.

1892. The Effect of Shorter Hours on Production. M. Grillet, Inspector at Rennes 843

1906. A Study of Industrial Accidents. M. Le Roy, Division Factory Inspector, Toulouse 387

1907. The Weekly Rest Day. M. Le Las Casas. Paris 86

REPORTS TO THE MINISTER OF COMMERCE, ETC. 1900.

Division Inspectors on the question of nightwork. M. Lagard, Division-Inspector of the Tenth District of Marseilles 577

Belgium.

HIGHER COUNCIL OF LABOR

Sixth Session. 1901-1902. Vol. I, Part II. Legislation. The Weekly Rest Day. Discussion by M. Denis, Member of Council. Brussels, 1902.....331, 355

Ninth Session. 1907. Regulation of Hours for Adults 450, 846

II. MEDICAL AND LABORATORY

United States

ALGER, ELLIS M., New York Postgraduate Medical School. Occupational Eye Diseases. American Labor Legislation Review, June, 1912..... 167

BLAKE, CLARENCE JOHN, M. D., Occupational Injuries and Diseases of the Ear. (Diseases of Occupation and Vocational Hygiene. Edited by Kober and Hansen. 1916)..... 173

BULKLEY, L. DUNCAN, A. M., M. D., New York Skin and Cancer Hospital. Fatigue as an Element of Menace to Health in the Industries. 39th Annual Meeting of the American Academy of Medicine, 1914.....64, 268

CHURCH, ARCHIBALD, M. D., Northwestern University Medical School, and Frederick Peterson, M. D., President State Commission in Lunacy, New York. Nervous and Mental Diseases. 1901 186

COMMITTEE OF EXPERTS ON OCCUPATIONAL DISEASES, American Association for Labor Legislation. Memorial on Occupational Diseases. American Labor Legislation Review, Jan., 1911.....52, 437

COWLES, EDWARD, M. D., Medical Superintendent of the McLean Hospital, Somerville, Mass. The Mental Symptoms of Fatigue. 1893..... 127

List of Sources.—Medical and Laboratory.

CRILE, GEORGE W., M. D., Professor of Surgery, School of Medicine, Western Reserve University. The Relation Between the Physical State of the Brain-Cells and Brain Functions. (The Origin and Nature of the Emotions. 1913.) 328

Phylogenetic Association in Relation to Certain Medical Problems. 1910 329

DANA, CHARLES L., Cornell University Medical College. Occupational Nervous and Mental Diseases. American Labor Legislation Review. June, 1912 89

DUBLIN, LOUIS I., Ph. D., Statistician, Metropolitan Life Insurance Company. Possibilities of Reducing Mortality at the Higher Age Groups. 1913........39, 193, 243

The Trend of American Vitality. The Popular Science Monthly, April, 1915 43

FAVILL, HENRY B., M. D., The Federal Children's Bureau. National Child Labor Committee. Proceedings of the 5th Annual Conference. Chicago, 1909 434

FISHER, IRVING, Yale University. Report on National Vitality. July, 1909 ....66, 436, 712

Life Extension Institute. What It Is: What It Does. New York, 1915........ 27

FISHER, IRVING, AND EUGENE LYMAN FISK. How to Live. 1915 32

GOLDWATER, S. S., M. D., Commissioner of Health. The Next Step in Preventive Medicine. Department of Health of the City of New York. No. 18. Reprint Series. June, 1914 31

HAYHURST, E. R., A. M., M. D., Director, Division of Occupational Diseases, Ohio State Board of Health. Industrial Health-Hazards and Occupational Diseases in Ohio. 1915........12, 141, 165, 234, 253, 269

HODGE, C. F. A Microscopical Study of Changes Due to Functional Activity in Nerve Cells. Journal of Morphology. Vol. VII. 1892........ 324

HOFFMANN, FREDERICK L., Statistician, Prudential Insurance Company of American, Newark, N. J. Physical and Medical Aspects of Labor and Industry. American Academy of Political and Social Science. Vol. XXVII. No. 3. 1916 .... 49, 432

Tuberculosis as an Industrial Disease. Sixth International Congress on Tuberculosis. Washington, 1908 50

American Public Health Problems. 1915 22

Mortality from Pulmonary Tuberculosis in Dusty Occupations. (Diseases of Occupation and Vocational Hygiene. Edited by Kober and Hanson. 1916) 258

HOWELL, WM. H., Ph. D., M. D., LL. D., Professor of Physiology, Johns Hopkins University. Text Book of Physiology, 1915 .... 270, 292, 321, 343

KOBER, GEORGE M., M. D. Etiology and Prophylaxis of Occupational Diseases. (Diseases of Occupation and Vocational Hygiene. Edited by Kober and Hanson. 1916) 95, 143, 185, 205, 245, 259

LANDIS, W. R. M., M. D., Director Clinical and Sociological Departments, Henry Phipps Institute for the Study, Treatment and Prevention of Tuberculosis, and JANICE S. REED, Research Assistant in Sociology. Factors Affecting the Health of Garment Workers. 8th Report, 1915 92

LEE, FREDERIC S., Ph. D., Professor of Physiology, Columbia University. Fatigue. The Harvey Lectures, 1905-1906 .... 127, 292, 298, 317, 340

The Nature of Fatigue. Popular Science Monthly, February, 1910 .... 296, 340

The Effects of Temperature and Humidity on Fatigue. American Journal of Public Health, Vol. 2, No. 11, 1912 236

Fatigue and Occupation. (Diseases of Occupation and Vocational Hygiene. Edited by Kober and Hanson, 1916.) 71, 79, 94, 203, 228, 244, 266, 294, 318, 341, 490

LEE, THOMAS S., Washington. Diseases of the Blood, Circulatory System and Kidneys. (Diseases of Occupation and Vocational Hygiene. Edited by Kober and Hanson. 1916.) 144

MARTIN, WITHINGTON, PUTNAM, M. Ds., Laboratory of Physiology, Harvard Medical School. Variations in the Sensory Threshold for Paradic Stimulation in Normal Human Subjects. The Influence of General Fatigue. American Journal of Physiology, XXXIV, 1914 342

List of Sources.—Medical and Laboratory.

PRICE, GEORGE M., New York State Factory Investigating Commission. Effects of Confined Air Upon the Health of Workers. American Labor Legislation Review. June, 1912 .... 138, 240

Workers' Health Bulletin. Joint Board of Sanitary Control in the Cloak, Suit and Skirt and the Dress and Waist Industries. 1915 169

RITTENHOUSE, E. E., President Life Extension Institute Inc. Protecting the Human Machine. 1915........................ 29

Increasing Organic Diseases. The New Public Health Problem. 1915 .... 34, 602

SCHWAB, SIDNEY I., St. Louis University. Neurasthenia among Garment Workers. American Labor Legislation Review. Jan., 1911........................ 88, 227

SCHWARTZ, NATHAN, M. D., Acting Medical Inspector, Division of Industrial Hygiene, New York State Department of Labor. Occupation as an Etiological Factor in Diseases. New York Medical Journal, September 4, 1915 .... 142, 419

THOMPSON, W. GILMAN, M. D., Professor of Medicine, Cornell University Medical College, New York. The Occupational Diseases, 1914 .... 47, 72

WHITE, WILLIAM A., M. D., Superintendent, Government Hospital for the Insane, Washington, D. C. Some Considerations Regarding the Factor of Fatigue, with Reference to Industrial Conditions. American Journal of the Medical Sciences, 1913. Vol. 145........................ 319

WILE, IRA S., M. D., Surgical Sociology. American Journal of Surgery, July, 1912........................ 203

Chronic Diseases of the Heart, Kidneys, and Arteries, from the Standpoint of Etiology, Prevalence, Mortality, and Prevention. The Medical Record, June 5, 1915........................ 16

WINSLOW, C.-E. A., Associate Professor of Biology, College of the City of New York, and Curator of Public Health, American Museum of Natural History, New York. Temperature and Humidity in Factories. American Labor Legislation Review. June, 1912........................ 240

The Health of the Worker. 1913........................ 53, 232, 256

List of Sources.—Medical and Laboratory.

Great Britain

ARLIDGE, J. T., M. D., Consulting Physician, North Staffordshire Infirmary. The Hygiene, Diseases and Mortality of Occupation. 1892 .... 147, 187, 218, 261

BRITISH MEDICAL JOURNAL, January 16, 1904. The Physiology of Fatigue. (Editorial.) 220, 229

April 24th, 1915. Munition Factories 154

July 3, 1915. Overtime and Efficiency 346

BURRIDGE, W., Physiological Laboratories of Oxford and Bristol. An Inquiry Into Some Chemical Factors of Fatigue. Journal of Physiology. Volume 41. 1910-11 315

FLORENCE, P. SARGANT. The Question of Fatigue from the Economic Standpoint.—Interim Report of the Committee. British Association for the Advancement of Science, Manchester, 1915 .... 360, 643

FOSTER, MICHAEL. Weariness. The Nineteenth Century. Sept., 1893 271

GUY, WILLIAM AUGUSTUS, M. D., Professor of Forensic Medicine, King's College. The Case of the Journeymen Bakers. Evils of Nightwork and Long Hours of Work. 1848 .... 406, 474

THE LANCET. March 4, 1905. Overwork. (Editorial.) 345

OLIVER, SIR THOMAS, University of Durham; late Medical Expert Home Office Committee on Dangerous Trades. Editor, Dangerous Trades, 1902 .... 206, 248, 275, 285, 299, 330

Diseases of Occupation from the Legislative, Social and Medical Points of View. 1908 .... 207, 407, 517

Occupational Fatigue. Journal of State Medicine. October, 1914 .... 209, 249, 832

STIRLING, WILLIAM, M. D., Professor of Physiology, University of Manchester. On Health, Fatigue and Repose. British Medical Journal. December 6, 1913 .... 179, 300, 346, 392

Italy

CELLI, PROF. ANGELO, Director, Institute of Experimental Hygiene at Rome. The Conflict Between Hygiene and Industry. Il Ramazzini. January, 1907 .... 83, 99

CRISAFULLI, PROF. Imbecility and Criminality in Relation to Certain Forms of Labor. 1st International Convention on Industrial Diseases. Milan, 1906 .... 98, 226, 413, 427

List of Sources.—Medical and Laboratory.

DE SANDRO, DOMENICO. The Significance of Physical Fatigue. La Riforma Medica, No. 31, 1910 ... 80

GIGLIOLI, DR. G. Y. New Researches and Acquisitions in the Pathology and Hygiene of Labor. Il Ramazzini. December, 1907 ... 84, 99

MAGGIORA, DR. ARNALDO, University of Turin. The Laws of Fatigue. Archiv für Anatomie und Physiologie, 1890 ... 307, 310, 335

MOSSO, A., Professor of Physiology, University of Turin, Fatigue. 1896 ... 171, 214, 280, 312, 335, 397, 412, 596

NITTI, FRANCESCO S., University of Naples. The Laws of Human Work. Revue Internationale de Sociologie. November, 1895 ... 74, 353, 396, 412, 609, 842

PALMULLI, V. The Value of the Kenotoxins in the Immunity-processes. La Riforma Medica, No. 44, 1914 ... 82

PIERACCINI, PROF. G., AND DR. R. MAFFEI, Head Physicians, Royal Main Hospital of S. M. Nuova, Florence, Italy. Days, Seasons and Hours when Industrial Accidents Occur. Il Ramazzini. October-November, 1907 ... 231, 389

RUGANI, DR. LUIGI, Army Physician, and DR. VINCENZO FRAGOLA, Assistant Army Physician. The Effect of Fatigue on the Auditory Organ. Archivio Italiano di Otologia, Rinologia e Laringologia, July, 1907 ... 181

SCALFATTI, D. Some Phenomena produced by Fatigue, on the Blood, and in Infections. La Riforma Medica, Vol. XXVIII. 1912 ... 80

TREVES, DR. ZACCARIA, University of Turin. Occupational Fatigue. 13th International Congress of Hygiene and Demography. Brussels, 1903.
83, 96, 128, 282, 306, 332, 354, 399

Fatigue as a Result of Occupation. 14th International Congress of Hygiene and Demography. Berlin, 1907 ... 74, 96

Germany

BINSWANGER, DR. OTTO, Professor of Psychiatry, and Director, Psychiatric Hospital, Jena. Pathology and Therapeutics of Neurasthenia. 1896 ... 102, 121, 123, 128, 617

List of Sources.—Medical and Laboratory.

CLAASEN, DR. W. The Decrease of Fitness for Military Service in the German Empire in City and Country from 1902 to 1907. Archiv für Rassen-und Gesellschaftsbiologie. VI, 1, 1909 ... 600

ERB, WILHELM, Professor of Medicine, Heidelberg University. The Increase of Nervousness in our Times. 1894 ... 101, 107

FEHLINGER, H. The Biological Influence of City Life. Die Naturwissenschaften. August 13, 1915 ... 598

EWALD, DR. WALTHER. Causes of Invalidity. Social Medicine. Vol. II. 1914 ... 121

GROTJAHN, DR. ALFRED. Soziale Pathologie. 1915 ... 610

HEFFTER, DR. WERNER. Industrial Hygiene and the Prevention of Accidents. Zeitschrift für Gewerbehygiene, Unfallverhütung, und Arbeiterwohlfahrts Einrichtungen. Vol. XIV. 1907 ... 192

HIRT, DR. LUDWIG. The Diseases of Working People. Vol. 2. 1878 ... 611

HOFFMANN, DR. AUGUST. The Choice of Occupation and Nerve Life. (Borderland Problems of Nervous and Psychic Life. Edited by Loewenfeld and Kurella. 1904.) 124

KOELSCH, DR. Work and Tuberculosis. Archiv für Soziale Hygiene, VI. 1911 ... 78

KOHLBRUGGE, J. H. F. City and Country as biological Environment. Archiv für Rassen-und Gesellschaftsbiologie. Jahrgang VI, 5, 1909 ... 601

LEUBUSCHER, DR. P., and DR. W. BIBROWICZ. Formerly of the Beelitz Sanitarium, State Old Age and Invalidity Department of Berlin. Neurasthenia in the Working Classes. Deutsche Medizinische Wochenschrift. 25. Mai, 1905. 108, 122, 125, 230

LOEWENFELD, DR. L. On Mental Working Power and its Hygiene. (Borderland Problems of Nervous and Psychic Life. Vol. VI. Edited by Loewenfeld and Kurella, 1906.) ... 337, 445

LUEBENAU, DR., Assistant Physician in the Beelitz Sanitarium, State Old Age and Invalidity Insurance Department of Berlin. Heart Diseases among the Working People of Berlin. Zeitschrift für Klinische Medizin. Bd. 60. 1906 ... 113

List of Sources.—Medical and Laboratory.

MANN. Polyneuritis, as an Associated Phenomenon of Nervous Exhaustion, in Warfare. Neurologisches Centralblatt, No. 5, 1915 104

MOLL, ALBERT. The Influence of the Life and Rush of Great Cities on the Nervous System. Zeitschrift für pädagogische Psychologie, Pathologie und Hygiene. 1902 104

OPPENHEIM, H., M. D., University of Berlin. Diseases of the Nervous System. 1900 103

PAREZ, C. C. TH., German Master, Merchiston School. On the Measurement of Mental Fatigue in Germany. 1902 302

RITZMANN, F. Factory Inspector. Karlsruhe. Work, Fatigue, and Recuperation. Concordia: Zeitschrift der Zentralstelle für Volkswohlfahrt. Nov. 1, 1907 348

ROTH, DR. EMIL, General Industrial Hygiene and Factory Legislation. Handbook of Hygiene. Vol. 8[1]. Edited by DR. THEODORE WEYL. 1894 .... 77, 155, 443, 498, 612

The Influence of Working Hours on the Health of Workers in General. 8th International Congress of Hygiene and Demography. Budapest, September, 1894 87

Fatigue resulting from Occupation. 14th International Congress of Hygiene and Demography. Berlin, September, 1907 .... 117, 189, 225, 230, 288, 349, 382

Physiology and Pathology of Work, with Special Reference to the Fatigue Problem. Deutsche Vierteljahrschrift für öffentliche Gesundheitspflege. Vol. 43. 1911. 159, 190, 352, 778

SCHAEFER, DR. Protection of the Workingman's Health. Archiv für Unfallheilkunde, Gewerbehygiene und Gewerbekrankheiten. 1896 .... 444, 617

SCHMIDT, DR. AD. Over-fatigue. Medizinische Klinik. No. 15. 1913 129

SCHOENHALS, PAUL. The Causes of Neurasthenia and Hysteria among Working People. A Study of 200 Cases in the Workingman's Sanitarium at Schönow Zehlendorf. 1906 .... 105, 115, 126, 403

VERWORN, PROF. MAX. Fatigue and Repair. Berliner Klinische Wochenscrift, February 4, 1901 336

VOGT, DR. H. Causes of Alcoholism. 14th International Congress of Hygiene and Demography. Berlin, 1907 425

List of Sources.—Medical and Laboratory.

WEICHARDT, DR. WOLFGANG. Methods of Estimating Fatigue and Overfatigue, Vierteljahreschrift für öffentliche Gesundheitspflege, 1907 290

Fatigue-substances. Zeitschrift für die ges. Neurologie und Psychiatrie Originale. 1914 291

WOLFF-EISNER, DR. ALFRED. The Toxin of Fatigue. Centralblatt für Bakteriologie, 1906 286

Austria

FÉLIX, DR. JULES. The Influence of Working Hours on the Conditions of Health of Working People. 8th International Congress of Hygiene and Demography. Budapest, 1894 359

LINDHEIM, ALFRED R. VON, Vienna. The Morbidity and Mortality of Occupations. 14th International Congress of Hygiene and Demography. Berlin, 1907. 60, 120, 129

Roumania

BABES, DR. V., University of Bucharest. The Attitude of the State to Modern Bacteriological Investigation. Proceedings of the 11th International Congress of Medicine, Rome, 1895 447

France

CARRIEU, DR. M., University of Montpellier. Fatigue and its Pathogenic Influence. 1878 .... 75, 283

CHARRIN and ROGER. Experimental Investigations of Overexertion and its Influence upon Injections. Archives de Physiologie Normale et Pathologie. No. 2, 1890 84

Fatigue and Microbic Diseases. La Semaine Médicale, No. 4. 1890 85

CORNEILLE, DR. P. The Eight-hour Day. Archives Générales de Médicine. Vol. I. 1906 426

FÉRÉ, DR. CHARLES. Work and Enjoyment. 1904 .... 308, 402

IMBERT, PROF., Montpellier. Fatigue as a Result of Occupation. 14th International Congress of Hygiene and Demography. Berlin, 1907 358

RIBOT, TH., Professor of Comparative and Experimental Psychology in the Collège de France. The Psychology of Attention. 1894 400

SACHNINE, ILIA. Study of the Effect of the Length of Working Hours upon the General Health of Adults. 1900 .... 160, 172, 314, 338, 401

TISSIÉ, DR. PHIL. Fatigue and Physical Training. 1897 400

VAILLANT, ÉDOUARD, M. R. C. S. Labor Legislation and Regulation from the Standpoint of Hygiene. 10th International Congress of Hygiene and Demography. Paris, 1900 .... 356, 470

VERHAEGHE, DR. D. Inquiry into the Sanitary Conditions in the Textile Trades in Lille and its Environs. Revue d'Hygiene. T. 26, 1904 161

Belgium

DE MOOR, DR. JEAN, University of Brussels. Occupational Fatigue. 13th International Congress of Hygiene and Demography. Brussels. 1903 402

JOTEYKO, MLLE J. The Laws of the Ergograph—a Physiological and Mathematical Study. Instituts Solvay. Travaux du Laboratoire de Physiologie, Tome VI. 1904 309

III. ECONOMIC AND SOCIAL

United States

ALGER, GEORGE W. Preparedness and Democratic Discipline. Atlantic Monthly, April, 1916 .... 604-a

ANDREWS, JOHN B., Secretary, American Association for Labor Legislation. Legal Protection for Workers in Unhealthful Trades. American Labor Legislation Review, June, 1912 241

ALTGELD, JUDGE P. The Eight-hour Movement. 1890 .... 221, 744

BAKER, HENRY S., Ph. D. The Relation of Fatigue to Social and Educational Progress. 65th Annual Meeting of the American Institute of Instruction. Boston, 1895 .... 268, 411

List of Sources.—Economic and Social.

BALLARD, S. THURSTON. Ballard & Ballard Milling Company, Louisville, Ky. Working Hours in Continuous Industries. Eight-hour Shifts in the Milling Industry. American Labor Legislation Review, June, 1914 ... 720

BIRD, CHARLES SUMMER, President F. W. Bird & Son. Massachusetts. Three Eight-hour Tours in the Paper Mills of America. The Survey. January 3, 1914 ... 452, 800

BOGARDUS, EMORY S., University of Chicago. The Relation of Fatigue to Industrial Accidents. American Journal of Sociology.
Nov. 1911 ... 375
Jan. 1912 ... 376

BOLEN, GEORGE L. Getting a Living: The Problem of Wealth and Poverty. 1903 ... 506, 727, 749, 805, 821, 885

BROOKS, JOHN GRAHAM. The Social Unrest. 1903 ... 539

CAMPBELL, L. R. (Maine). The Restriction of the Hours of Labor in Factories and Workshops. 4th Annual Convention of the International Association of Factory Inspectors of North America, 1890 ... 725

COMMITTEE organized by the American Association for Labor Legislation. Constitutional Amendments Relating to Labor Legislation and Brief in Their Defense. Submitted to the Constitutional Convention of New York State. June 9, 1915 ... 544, 956

COMMONS, JOHN R., University of Wisconsin, Former Member Wisconsin Industrial Commission, and John B. Andrews, Secretary, American Association for Labor Legislation. Principles of Labor Legislation, 1916.
508, 858, 877, 942

COMMONS, JOHN R., ULRICH B. PHILLIPS, EUGENE A. GILMORE, HELEN L. SUMMER and JOHN B. ANDREWS, Editors. A Documentary History of American Industrial Society. 1910 ... 535, 741

DICKSON, WILLIAM B., Former Vice-President United States Steel Corporation. Can American Steel Plants Afford an Eight-hour Turn? The Survey. Jan. 3, 1914 ... 131, 462, 740

EASTMAN, CRYSTAL. Work Accidents and the Law. The Pittsburgh Survey. 1910 ... 371

List of Sources.—Economic and Social.

FITCH, JOHN A. The Steel Workers. Pittsburgh Survey. 1910 .... 136, 201, 414, 436, 458, 489, 681, 954
Old Age at Forty. American Magazine. March, 1911 .... 202, 227
The Human Side of Large Outputs. Steel and Steel Workers in Six American Cities. The Survey, 1911, 1912 .... 460, 544
Hours of Labor in the Steel Industry. A Communication to 15,000 Stockholders of the United States Steel Corporation. Written after full investigation for Charles M. Cabot, 95 Milk Street, Boston, a Stockholder of the Steel Corporation, Boston, 1912. 138, 461, 951, 606

FRANKEL, LEE K. and MILES M. DAWSON. Workingmen's Insurance in Europe. 1910 137

FRANKEL, LEE K. Metropolitan Life Insurance Co. Occupational Fatigue. 1913 54

FURNITURE MANUFACTURERS OF CHICAGO. Letter of Forty-six to the Manufacturers of Furniture of the United States. The Normal Workday of Eight Hours. 1879........ 536

GARRETSON, AUSTIN B., President, Order of Railway Conductors. Working Hours in Continuous Industries. Long Hours in Railroading. American Labor Legislation Review, March, 1914 .... 380, 955

GUNTON, GEORGE. Wealth and Progress. 1887........ 614
The Economic and Social Importance of the Eight-Hour Movement. 1889 .... 471, 483, 501, 536
The Eight Hour Day. Industrial Conference under the Auspices of the National Civic Federation. New York, 1902 .... 417, 538, 615

HAYES, DENIS A., President of the Glass Bottle Blowers Association of America. Length of Trade Life in the Glass Bottle Industry. American Academy of Political and Social Science. Vol. XXVII. No. 3, 1906 200

HOLBROOK, JOHN, Deputy Commissioner of Labor, Michigan. The Shorter Workday in its Effect upon the Personal Character of the Worker. 14th and 15th Annual Conventions of the International Association of Factory Inspectors of America. Indianapolis, 1900. Niagara Falls, 1901 .... 417, 504, 726

List of Sources.—Economic and Social.

HASKIN, FREDERIC J. The Immigrant. An Asset and a Liability. 1913 561

THE IMMIGRANTS IN AMERICA REVIEW. January, 1916.......... 568

INTERNATIONAL ASSOCIATION OF FACTORY INSPECTORS of North America. 7th Annual Convention, Chicago, 1893.......... 195

JENKS, JEREMIAH W. and W. JETT LAUCK. The Immigration Problem. 1913 561

KELLEY, FLORENCE, Former Chief Factory Inspector, Illinois. Some Ethical Gains Through Legislation. 1905 135, 541, 878

Factory Inspection in Pittsburgh. Charities and the Commons, March 6, 1909 607

KELLOR, FRANCES A. The Education of the Immigrant. The Educational Review, June, 1914 562

LOGAN, WALTER S. An argument for the Eight-Hour Law. 1894 430

McVEY, FRANK L., Professor of Political Economy, University of Minnesota. The Economic Effects of the Eight-Hours' Day. National Convention of Employers and Employees, Minneapolis, 1902 487

Social Effects of the Eight-Hour Day. American Journal of Sociology. Jan. 1903 540

MANLY, BASIL M., U. S. Bureau of Labor. Working Hours in Continuous Industries. Work Periods in Continuous Day and Night Occupations. American Labor Legislation Review, March, 1914 ....462, 819

MARKS, MARCUS M., President National Association of Clothing Manufacturers. Speech at 1st Annual meeting of the New England Civic Federation, Boston, 1906. National Civic Federation Review, Jan.-Feb., 1906 .....223, 507

MAXEY, EDWIN, Southern Normal University, Tenn. The Eight-Hour Day by Legislation. The Arena, Vol. XXIV. 1900 .... 502, 853

MAXWELL, GEORGE H. Our National Defense. The Patriotism of Peace. 1915 603

MEEKER, ROYAL, U. S. Commissioner of Labor Statistics. The Work of the Federal Bureau of Labor Statistics in its Relation to the Business of the Country. Annals of the American Academy of Political and Social Science. Vol. LXIII. January, 1916 806

List of Sources.—Economic and Social.

MITCHELL, JOHN. Organized Labor. 1903 .... 472, 748

NATIONAL AMERICANIZATION COMMITTEE and the Committee for Immigrants in America. Americanizing a City. The Campaign for the Detroit Night Schools Conducted in August-September, 1915, by the Detroit Board of Commerce and Board of Education 563

NATIONAL CIVIC FEDERATION REVIEW. Sept., 1904. Will Labor Make Concessions for a Shorter Work Day? Thomas M. Nolan, Editor Union Label Magazine 473
James Duncan, General Secretary Granite Cutters International Union 474

O'CONNELL, JAMES, President, International Association of Machinists. The Manhood Tribute to the Modern Machine. American Academy of Political and Social Science. Vol. XXVII. No. 3, 1906 .... 199, 418

"THE PENNSYLVANIAN." Comments on the Proceedings of the Government and Citizens of Philadelphia on the Reduction of the Hours of Labor and Increase of Wages. July, 1835 535

POUND, ROSCOE. Legislation as a Social Function. American Sociological Society. 7th Publication 984

REDFIELD, WILLIAM C. The New Industrial Day. 1912 ... 428, 754
The Limits of Efficiency. An Address before the Cleveland Chamber of Commerce, November 12, 1912 752
Working Hours in Continuous Industries. Introductory Address. American Labor Legislation Review, March, 1914 .... 739, 806

RUBINOW, L. M., Chief Statistician, Ocean Accident & Guarantee Corporation. Social Insurance. 1913. 67, 140, 377

SCHOENHOF, JACOB. The Industrial Situation and the Question of Wages. 1885 85
The Economy of High Wages. 1892 .... 722, 805, 820

STEWART, ETHELBERT. The Eight Hour Day and Government Construction by Direct Labor. 1905 679

THE SURVEY. Jan. 3, 1914. Editorial. The Twelve Hour Day 944
April 1, 1916. The Sudden Spread of the Eight Hour Day 933

List of Sources.—Economic and Social.

TAUSSIG, F. W., Harvard University. The Shorter Work-Day. National Civic Federation Monthly Review. October, 1904 500

Inventors and Money-Makers. 1915 224

UNITED STATES STEEL CORPORATION. Report of the Committee of Stockholders. April 15, 1912 534

VAN BUREN, PRESIDENT MARTIN. Letter to certain political inquirers. (A Documentary History of American Industrial Society. Edited by John R. Commons. 1910) 850

WADE, RUFUS R., Chief Factory Inspector of Massachusetts. National Convention of Factory Inspectors in the United States. Philadelphia, 1887 430

WALKER, FRANCIS A., Ph. D., LL. D. Discussions in Economics and Statistics. Vol. II. The Eight-hour Law Agitation. 1899 .... 431, 501, 745

WEBER, A. F., Chief Statistician, New York State Department of Labor. Problems of Factory Inspection. The Social Interest of Statistics of Factory Inspection. 14th and 15th Annual Conventions of the International Association of Factory Inspectors of America. Indianapolis, 1900. Niagara Falls, 1901 486

Great Britain

AVES, ERNEST. The Hours of Labour. (Life and Labour of the People in London. Edited by Charles Booth. Vol. IX., 1897) 465, 495, 516, 772, 830

BARNES, GEORGE N., M. D. The Limitation of the Hours of work. National Conference on the Prevention of Destitution. 1912 .... 518, 794

BARRASS, H., Edmonton Urban District Council. The Reduction of the Hours of Work and the Limitation of Overtime. Discussion. National Conference on the Prevention of Destitution. 1912 546

BRASSEY, THOMAS. Lectures on the Labour Question. The Nine Hours Movement. 1878 661

BRITISH ASSOCIATION for the Advancement of Science. Report of the 72nd Meeting. 1902. Women's Labour: 2nd Report of the Committee . . . appointed to investigate the Economic Effect of Legislation Regulating Women's Labour 831, 868

Report of the 73rd Meeting. 1903. Women's Labour. 3rd Report of the Committee 793, 832, 868, 886

BUXTON, SIDNEY, M. P. A Handbook of Political Questions of the Day and the Arguments on Either Side. 1903. Legal Limitation of Hours 220, 467, 687, 773, 885

CHAPMAN, S. J. Hours of Labour. Presidential Address to the Economic Science and Statistics Section of the British Association for the Advancement of Science 221

Work and Wages: In Continuation of Earl Brassey's 'Work and Wages' and 'Foreign Work and English Wages.' 1914 .... 59, 153, 209, 497, 730, 833

CLARKE, ALLEN. The Effects of the Factory System. 1899 220

CROSFIELD, A. H. Rational Hours of Work. I. The Case for Reduction. Shorter Hours and Greater Efficiency 151, 548, 675

II. Eight-Hour Shifts in Iron and Steel Trades. Reprinted from the "Manchester Guardian," June 27 and 30, 1913 152

DENNIS, JOHN. The Pioneer of Progress. 1860 .... 406, 583

ECCARIUS, GEORGE J. Hours of Labour. 1872 145

FABIAN SOCIETY. (Tract No. 23.) The Case for an Eight-Hours' Bill. 1891 .... 439, 464, 514, 626

(Tract No. 48.) Eight Hours by Law. A Practical Solution. 1895 440

FERGUSSON, WILLIAM. The Evils of Protracted Hours of Labour. 1847 .... 57, 405

GOSSIP, ALEX, General Secretary, National Amalgamated Furnishing Trades' Association. The Limitation of Overtime. National Conference on the Prevention of Destitution. 1912 889

HADFIELD, R. A., of Hadfield's Steel Foundry Co., Sheffield, and H. deB. Gibbins. A Shorter Working Day. 523, 475, 494, 627, 669, 765, 787, 808, 826, 863, 898

Ibid. Letter from Messrs. Short Bros., Shipbuilders of Sunderland 811

List of Sources.—Economic and Social.

HOBSON, JOHN A. The Problem of the Unemployed. 1896..... 516
Work and Wealth: A Human Valuation. 1914. 73, 210, 216, 404, 441, 468, 509, 549, 876

HODGE, JOHN, M. P. Conditions in British Iron and Steel Works. Speech delivered to the Special Commission on Hours of Labour, International Association for Labour Legislation, June 11th, 1912 .....517, 672

HUTCHINS, B. L. Gaps in our Factory Legislation. The Economic Journal. June, 1908 207

HUTCHINS, B. L. and A. HARRISON. A History of Factory Legislation. 1911 .....221, 496, 630, 730, 793, 887

HYNDMAN, H. M., and C. BRADLAUGH. Eight-Hour Movement. Verbatim Report of a Debate. 1890 .....146, 583

JEANS, VICTORINE. Factory Act Legislation. 1892.....763, 786

LARKIN, EDMUND R. A Few Words on the Ten Hours Factory Question. 1846 859

LENO, JOHN BEDFORD. An Essay on the Nine Hours Movement. 1861 464

LILWALL, JOHN. The Half-holiday Question. 1856..... 762

MACAULAY, LORD. Speech on the Ten Hours Bill delivered in the House of Commons on the 2nd of May, 1846 491

MANN, TOM. The Eight Hours Movement. 1889.....513, 862

MURRAY, MARR. Drink and the War. 1915..... 423

NATIONAL COMMITTEE for the Prevention of Destitution. The Case for the National Minimum. With Preface by Mrs. Sidney Webb. 1913 .....153, 596, 631, 776, 871

NATIONAL CONFERENCE on the Prevention of Destitution. 1912. The Reduction of the Hours of Work and the Limitation of Overtime. Discussion 58, 548, 869

THE NEW STATESMAN. Sept. 25, 1915. Men as Machines..... 649

OWEN, ROBERT. Address to the Superintendents of Manufactories. London, 1813 759
The Employment of Children in Manufactories. 1818 621

RAE, JOHN. Eight Hours for Work. 1894.....149, 476, 495, 524, 656, 686, 689, 721, 729, 768, 791, 816, 827, 865, 885

ROWNTREE, B. Seebohm. The Way to Industrial Peace and the Problem of Unemployment. 1914 .....408, 422

List of Sources.—Economic and Social.

SANGER, SOPHY. The Limitation of Hours from the International Point of View. National Conference on the Prevention of Destitution 1912 546

SHADWELL, ARTHUR, M. A., M. D. Industrial Efficiency: A Comparative Study of Industrial Life in England, Germany, and America. 1906 .... 774, 869

TAWNEY, R. H. The Establishment of Minimum Rates in the Tailoring Industry under the Trade Boards Act of 1909. 1915 781

WALLS, ALDERMAN P. Conditions in British Iron and Steel Works. A Speech delivered to the Special Commission on Hours of Labour, International Association for Labour Legislation, June 11th, 1912 .... 422, 547, 871

WEBB, SIDNEY, and ARNOLD FREEMAN, Editors. Seasonal Trades. 1912 .... 150, 887

WEBB, SIDNEY, and HAROLD COX. The Eight Hours Day. 1891 .... 218, 407, 493, 514, 544, 608, 615, 627, 661, 676, 687, 693, 786, 807, 883

Ibid. Appendix II. Letters, etc., received from Firms which have already adopted an Eight-Hours' Day. From Burroughs, Wellcome & Co., Importers, Exporters and Manufacturing Chemists, Snow Hill Buildings, London, 16th December, 1890 515

WEBB, MRS. SIDNEY, Editor. The Case for the Factory Acts. 1901 .... 441, 466, 496, 793, 900

WING, CHARLES. Evils of the Factory System. 1837 607

WOOD, GEORGE HENRY. Factory Legislation considered with reference to the Wages, etc., of the Operatives protected thereby. Journal of the Royal Statistical Society. Vol. LXV. 1902 867

New Zealand

SCHOLEFIELD, GUY H. With an Introduction by the Hon. W. Pember Reeves, Director of the London School of Economics. New Zealand in Evolution. 1909 526

Germany

ADLER, DR. GEORGE, University of Freiberg. International Labor Legislation. Annals of the German Empire. Vol. XXI. 1888 .... 155, 442

List of Sources.—Economic and Social.

ASCHER, DR. OTTO. Injuries of Occupation. (Handbook of the General Welfare of the Working Classes. Edited by Dr. Otto Dammer. Vol. I. 1902.)........87, 173, 188, 575

Protection of Working People (*Ibid.* Vol. II.) 261, 423, 520, 613

BERNHARD, ERNST. Intensification of Work in Shorter Working-hours; its personal and technical basis. (Researches in Political and Social Science. Vol. 138. Edited by Gustav Schmoller and Max Sering. 1909)...61, 251, 384, 635

BRENTANO, LUJO. The Relation of Labor to the Law of To-Day. 1891 519

Hours and Wages in Relation to Production. 1894 629, 677, 772, 792, 829

ENGELS, FREDERICK. Condition of the Working Class in England in 1844 219

FUCHS, DR., Factory Inspector, Baden. Reports on the Importance and Legal Regulation of Night Work of Women. Preface by Étienne Bauer 634

HERKNER, DR. HEINRICH, Professor of Political Economy, Karlsruhe. Social Reform as a Condition of Socio-Economic Progress. 1891........ 574

The Labor Question. 1894........ 443, 777

Hours of Work. Compendium of Political Science. Vol. I. Edited by Dr. J. Conrad and others. 1909........225, 263, 279, 305, 315, 350, 383, 425, 446, 520, 576, 619, 892, 901

INTERNATIONAL CONFERENCE IN RELATION TO LABOR LEGISLATION. Berlin, 1890........ 633

KOECHLIN-GEIGY, A. The Eight Hours Day. 1893........ 795

MARTIN, RUDOLF, Referendar in the Statistical Office of the Kingdom of Saxony. The Reduction of Working Hours in the Mechanical Textile Industry. Archiv für Soziale Gesetzgebung und Statistik. Vol. VIII. 1895........ 840

PRINGSHEIM, DR. OTTO. An Experiment with the Eight-hour Day. Archiv für Soziale Gesetzgebung und Statistik. Vol. VI. 1893........ 715

VON PLENER, ERNST. English Factory Legislation. 1873........ 882

WIEBER, FRANZ, Chairman of the Christian Metalworkers Union of Germany. Working Hours in Continuous Processes of the Iron and Steel Industries. Report to the International Association for Labor Legislation........158a

List of Sources.—Economic and Social.

Austria

DONATH, DR. JULIUS, University of Budapest. The Physical Degeneration of the Population in Modern Civilized Countries with Particular Reference to Austria-Hungary. 8th International Congress of Hygiene and Demography, Budapest, 1894......101, 578, 779

KREJCSI, DR. E. R. J., Vice-Secretary of the Chamber of Commerce in Budapest. The Length of the Working Day in its Relation to the Workman's Health and its Influence upon Public Health. 8th International Congress of Hygiene and Demography. Budapest, 1894
161, 263, 381, 448, 616

France

BOURGUIN, M., Professor of Political Economy, Lille. The New Labor Legislation. Revue d'Economie Politique. Vol. XV. 1901...... 449

BUISSON, ÉTIENNE. The Eight Hour Day. La Revue Socialiste. T. XLI. Jan.-Juin., 1905...... 780

CORIOLAN, J. R., and J. MORTAIR. The First of May and the Eight-Hour Day. 1891......498, 734

FAGNOT, F., Investigator of the Bureau of Labor. Regulation of Working Hours in Continuous Industries. National French Association for Labor Legislation. 1913...... 700

IMBERT, PROF. A., University of Montpellier. Industrial Accidents and Insurance. Revue Scientifique. 4e Juin, 1904......358, 385

JAY, RAOUL, Professor of Law, University of Paris. Is Legal Protection for Working People Necessary? Revue d'Economie Politique. T. XVI. 1902...... 449

LEROY, MAXIME. The Eight Hours Day. La Revue de Paris. Sept.-Oct., 1907...... 735

VIARD, VALENTIN. The Reduction of Working Hours for Employees. 1910...... 577

WALDECK-ROUSSEAU, M., President of the Council, Minister of the Interior. Address at the 10th International Congress of Hygiene and Demography. Paris, 1900...... 448

List of Sources.—Economic and Social.

Switzerland

PROPOSAL OF THE COMMISSION OF A MAXIMUM WORKING DAY FOR ADULT WORKMEN. 4th General Convention of the Committee of the International Association for Labor Legislation. Geneva. 1906 446

SCHULER, DR. FRIDOLIN, Factory Inspector, Switzerland. The Over-work of Women and Children in Factories. 58th Congress of German Scientists and Physicians. Strassburg, 1886 573

Factory Hygiene and Legislation. 6th International Congress of Hygiene and Demography. Vienna, 1887 ... 160, 188

INTERNATIONAL ASSOCIATION FOR LABOR LEGISLATION. Proceedings of the 5th Meeting. Lucerne, 1908 611

SCHULER, DR. FRIDOLIN, Swiss Factory Inspector and DR. A. E. BURCKHARDT, Professor of Hygiene, Basle. Investigations into the Conditions of Health of the Swiss Factory Workers. 1889 215

SPECIAL COMMISSION ON HOURS OF LABOR in Continuous Industries. Report to the 7th Delegates' Meeting of the International Association for Labor Legislation. Zurich, 1912 .... 674, 713, 816

Belgium

DENIS, HECTOR. Proposals regarding Limitation of Hours of Work for Adults in Belgium. Publications of the Belgian Section of the International Association for Labor Legislation. 1908 .... 332, 450

Norway

SCHLYTTER, THOMAS, Match Manufacturer. Norwegian Association for Labor Legislation. Hours in the Continuous Industries. The Survey, Jan. 21, 1911 ... 223, 418, 437, 542

*SOME NOTABLE BUSINESS EXPERIMENTS

United States

BULL, R. A. The Twelve-Hour Shift in the Steel Foundry. Results of its Abandonment in the Commonwealth Steel Company's Open-Hearth Department and the Substitution of an Eight-Hour Shift. The Iron Age. New York, October 3, 1912 639

FEISS, RICHARD A. Cleveland, Ohio. Personal Relationship as a Basis of Scientific Management. Bulletin, The Society to Promote the Science of Management. November, 1915 737

HAZARD, FREDERICK R., President Solvay Process Company, Syracuse. Some Practical Experiences in Shortening Hours of Labor. 15th Annual Report, National Consumers' League. 1916 .... 667, 701, 757, 783

Great Britain

ALLAN, WILLIAM. William Allan and Co., Scotia Engine Works, Sunderland. Letter on the Eight Hour Day. (A Shorter Working Day. Hadfield and Gibbins. 1892) 810

GRANT, JOHN W. Work-Weariness and a Three-Shift System. Engineering. October 22, 1915 652

JOHNSON, S. H. & Co., Engineering Works, Stratford. Statement on the 8-Hour Day. (A Shorter Working Day, Hadfield and Gibbins. 1892) 808

MATHER, WILLIAM, M. P. The Eight Hours Day. Report on a Year's Work with a 48 Hours Week in the Salford Iron Works, Manchester. (Mather and Platt, Ltd.) 1894 .... 671, 767, 812

Appendix. Extracts from Reports of Foremen 768

Germany

ABBE, ERNST. The Economic Significance of a Shorter Working Day. Complete Works. Vol. III. 1906 224, 278, 347, 444, 618, 693, 840, 874

Belgium

FROMONT, L. G. An Industrial Experiment in the Reduction of Hours of Labor. 1906 .... 162, 703, 817

**See Public Documents* and earlier part of *Economic and Social* Sections for main body of business testimony.

www.ingramcontent.com/pod-product-compliance
Lightning Source LLC
LaVergne TN
LVHW010522100826
845148LV00001B/69

* 9 7 8 1 4 2 5 5 7 3 7 9 9 *